Here to Stay

Rock and Roll through the '70s

Third Edition

G.W. Sandy Schaefer

with

Donald S. Smith

and

Mike Shellans

Cover/Interior Design: S4Carlisle Publishing Services

Composition/Illustration: S4Carlisle Publishing Services

Printer/Binder: Central Plains Book Manufacturing/Winfield, KS

ISBN-10:   0-9768021-2-0
ISBN-13:   978-0-9768021-2-9

Printed in the United States of America
10   9   8   7   6   5   4   3   2   1

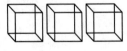

**Dorset
Group**

Contents

Two   **The Transition Years 1946-1954   53**

Nine   Folk Music and Folk Rock   217

Preface

Here To Stay was written to fill the need for a rock history text that fully explores the roots of rock in such a way as to illuminate the natural progression of musical styles. The study of rock often begins with Bill Haley and the Comets and includes only scant information about the blues and rhythm records that he and others used as a model. A musical genre does not simply appear. Rather, it gradually evolves to a point in time when some event—performance, publication, or recording—allows listeners to perceive its unique qualities and apply a label.

Wynonie Harris' 1947 recording of "Good Rocking Tonight" was one of many "rhythm records" made during the late 1940s, however when it was recorded by Elvis Presley in 1954 it seemed like a new and different approach. What made it seem new and different was its context. Without exploring the history of African-American popular music, country and western music, cultural relations, technical developments, and the music business, one could easily be misled to the conclusion that rock and roll was some new and different music, without ancestral sources.

This text begins with the African musical traits brought here beginning in 1619, traces their fusion with the European music brought here by the colonists. The story of this musical interaction is also the story of American popular music and includes the plantation songs of Stephen Foster, the ragtime of Scott Joplin, the blues of Bessie Smith, the jazz of Count Basie, and the jump bands of Louis Jordan. The knowledge of the "stream" of American popular music allows the reader to understand that rock and roll was a natural result of combined influences.

The reader will find the bulk of the text pertains to the beginnings of a rock style, the first bands, and how they developed the new style, rather than an encyclopedic and discographic gathering of facts and dates. There are many fine rock encyclopedias which list a band's/artist's recordings, personnel changes, and dates. Therefore it was not the authors' intent to try to supplant those, but rather to explain the interaction of the facts contained in them.

Within the confines of a text designed for a music appreciation course, *Here To Stay* also offers some insight into the ways business and culture affected the music, and society's perception of the music. The authors are aware that some rock history/popular music courses are taught by faculty whose area of specialization is outside the music discipline and therefore we have attempted to provide "windows of opportunity" through which the discussion can be augmented by other viewpoints and supplementary materials.

One need not be a musician to use this text and the authors have included a series of guided "Listen to the Music" sections at the end of each chapter to help the reader develop a functional vocabulary and ability to appreciate the inner workings of music. The listenings are guided by a time-line based on seconds and minutes outlining the musical form of the recording. By following these, the reader will be able to see and hear the various musical formal sections and hopefully begin to understand how music is "put together." Within each guided listening is a "For Musicians" section written in more specific musical terms than the time-line; those readers with a working knowledge of chords will be able to develop a deeper understanding of musical form.

The authors believe this text fills the stated need for a more comprehensive rock history text and welcome any suggestions or corrections.

About the Authors

G.W. Sandy Schaefer holds a Doctorate in Percussion Performance from Arizona State University and is currently Director of Jazz Studies and Music Business at Chadron State College. He has served on the faculties of the University of Wisconsin, California State University Fresno and the University of Wyoming. Dr. Schaefer has been teaching courses in Jazz and Rock History since 1977 and is active in all areas of percussion including symphony orchestras and contemporary chamber groups as well as jazz combos, big bands, and theater orchestras. He has recorded with Ensemble 21 and the American Serenade Band on Summit Records, Carlos Nakai on Canyon Records, and has released a collection of percussion ensemble compositions on WSMA Records. Dr. Schaefer has performed with Henry Mancini, Milton Berle, the Temptations, Suzanne Somers, Rita Moren, Ben Vareen, the Drifters, the Coasters and others.

Donald S. Smith received his Doctor of Musical Arts degree from Arizona State University. He is currently a faculty member at Glendale Community College where he teaches music history (classical, jazz and rock), brass ensembles and private trumpet instruction. He formerly taught jazz and rock music survey courses at Arizona State University. Dr. Smith freelances in the Phoenix area and performs frequently with the Phoenix Symphony, Arizona Opera and Arizona Broadway Theatre. He has performed with the Smothers Brothers, Wynona Judd, The Dallas Brass, Doc Severinsen, and many others.

Mike Shellans has been a professional performer and music educator in the Phoenix area since 1982. He received his Bachelors in Music from the University of Arizona and his Masters in Music from Arizona State University. Mr. Shellans has played both piano and trombone since the age of nine, joining the American Federation of Musicians at age 17. Mr. Shellans has performed with a wide variety of entertainers, such as Bob Hope, The Moody Blues, Henry Mancini, George Burns, The Temptations, The Four Tops, Gladys Knight, Natalie Cole and others, and has played in orchestras for musicals including *A Chorus Line, Jesus Christ, Superstar, My Fair Lady, Bye Bye Birdie, Annie, Zorba the Greek, and West Side Story.* As a Senior Lecturer at A.S.U., Mr. Shellans has taught over 35,000 students live and online in courses he created such as Popular Music/Rock and Roll, Music of the Beatles, and Elvis Presley. Currently, Mike performs on keyboards and electric bass with the BeTalls, a Beatles and Classic Rock band with each member over six feet tall, and the Big News Band, a seven-piece Jazz/Pop/Gospel horn group.

Chapter One

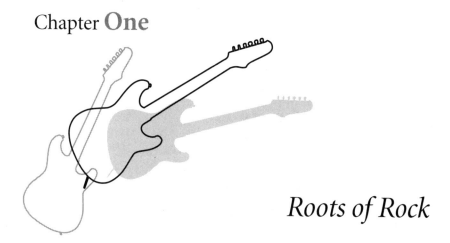

Roots of Rock

Wherever members of an African culture settled in the Western hemisphere, they carried with them musical traits that fused with, and altered, music they encountered. In Brazil, the fusion of African and native Brazilian music resulted in the samba; in the Caribbean Islands, that fusion resulted in the mambo, rumba, meringue, and other dance music now generally categorized as salsa; in America, that fusion produced blues, jazz, and rock.

African musical characteristics have been influencing America's music since the first Africans arrived in Jamestown in 1619—twelve years after the English first landed and one year before the Pilgrims landed in Massachusetts. The music of these Europeans and Africans became part of America's cultural "melting pot," and the by-product of that process became American "popular" music. In the South, African musical characteristics were maintained through work songs and religious music, genres that had subtle but significant influence. In the North, African-American freemen contributed to musical life by supplying music for general entertainment and for the military.

AFRICAN MUSICAL CHARACTERISTICS

It is important to identify prominent African musical characteristics before discussing how those characteristics were preserved. Africa covers 11.7 million square miles and has 250 million inhabitants representing over 2,000 tribal groups speaking between 800 and 2,400 languages. Africans brought to America by traders were from three cultural regions: the tribes of the Yorba, Ashanti, Dohemey, and Ibo from the coastal rain forest of the west, Muslim groups such as the Wolof from the savanna belt, and the Bantu from the Congo/Angolan region. Although many different musical traditions abound, there are certain characteristics that transcend geography:

- Hand-clapping
- The human voice as an important model for instrumental music
- Music as a communal and functional experience
- Call-and-response patterns
- Natural scales and blue notes
- Buzzing or roughening of sound
- Polyrhythms and syncopation
- A percussive approach to sound[1]

Hand-Clapping

Hand-clapping is the single most important instrument used in musical accompaniment. The hands are nature's most basic percussion instrument. Everybody has a pair, and they are used by audience members as a means of participation.

During the nineteenth century, the use of hand-clapping expanded to slapping the thighs and shoulders along with stamping the foot. This technique is called *pattin' juba* and is associated with William Henry Lane, an African American better known as "Master Juba, the greatest of all dancers" during the first half of the nineteenth century. Juba, who accompanied himself on the tambourine, toured with white minstrel shows and, hence, was responsible for helping preserve the African dancing and drumming tradition. Later, *pattin' juba* became known as *hambone* and acquired a particular rhythm that later became known as the "Bo Diddley" rhythm and eventually as the "hand jive" rhythm.

In twentieth- and twenty-first–century America, use of the hands has been one of the most prominent features of gospel music. It is not uncommon for members of a gospel audience to add cross-rhythms to the rhythms being clapped by the choir. These are called *additive rhythms*, another African musical characteristic.

The presence of hand-clapping along with the tambourine was one of the characteristics rock and roll adopted from gospel music. Hand-clapping became such an important sonic element of rock and roll that some of the first synthesized drum sounds were hand-claps.

The Human Voice as a Model for Instrumental Music

The human voice is another significant element of African music. It serves as the basis for the creation of instrumental sound. The voice is capable of making micro-tonal inflections in the shape or color of a note. This aspect of vocal conception greatly influenced the way African-Americans approached European instruments such as the trumpet, saxophone, trombone, and guitar. Another important element is in the way the voice is used in ornamentation, either during a note or on the approach or release of that note. European musicologists use the term *melisma* to describe a series of notes or pitches on a single syllable, and the authors will use *melismatic ornamentation* to refer to this practice.

Remnants of vocal conception appear in the instrumental effects used in jazz and rock. Jazz musicians especially use trumpets, trombones, clarinets, and other instruments in such a way as to imitate the melismatic ornamentation used by singers. An excellent example of this is found in the music of jazz trumpeter and singer Louis Armstrong. Armstrong's singing style was very similar to this instrumental trumpet style, and vice versa, suggesting that a single concept inspired both his singing and his playing. Another good example is B. B. King, whose guitar style is based on vocal models: He initiates micro-tonal inflections by bending the guitar strings with a sideways finger pressure and even moves his mouth while bending the strings, further suggesting the imitation of speech patterns.

Music as a Communal and Functional Experience

The concept that music is purely an aesthetic experience to be thoughtfully comprehended by an attentive audience is foreign to the African tradition, in which listeners are not passive: They sing or clap along. In this way, music is only "part of a greater artistic whole, in which the sound of music is but one element."[2]

Music may function in several ways. It may be ceremonial, as is typical in the European experience, often in connection with religious ceremonies or in praise of an important political figure. Both European and African cultures use music for weddings, birthdays, funerals, and civic celebrations; indeed, music is an indispensable element at these ceremonies. Music may also be functional in that it accompanies everyday occurrences or celebrates life events. All Americans are familiar with the function of the song sung on the occasion of someone's birthday. The use of music to celebrate events is entwined in the fabric of African society to an even greater extent than it is in European cultures. For example, Africans might use songs to celebrate even such events as the arrival of a baby's first tooth.

Another function of music is in keeping the historical record. African cultures were oral cultures, and rather than keeping a written record of history, Africans kept a record in song. There is a class of professional musicians called *griots* who are charged with the responsibility of recording important events and retelling stories in praise of important individuals and families. This history-keeping characteristic helps explain African-American pre-classic blues songs such as "Frankie and Johnnie (Alpert)," "Stagger Lee," (both songs tell stories about crime) and "God Works on the Water" (a song about the sinking of the Titanic). Classic blues continued the tradition with songs like "Backwater Blues" by Bessie Smith, about the 1927 flooding of the Mississippi River.

African music was also functional in assisting physical labor by unifying the action of those working in groups and by making the work time less tedious. *Work songs* were an important element in preserving the vocal model of the African song because they were one of the few African characteristics that remained unchanged during the years of slavery. Slave owners allowed work songs to remain because they were functional in unifying labor and, therefore, increasing productivity. Work songs served an additional purpose by easing the consciences of slave owners because in their European-based culture, people sang when they were happy. Slave owners liked to believe that the sound of singing slaves indicated contentment with their position in life.

Call-and-Response Patterns

The call-and-response form was one of the most useful and adaptable characteristics of African music. In this form there is a leader/soloist who sings a phrase, usually longer and with little repetition, which is answered by the responders/chorus, usually with a short, repetitive phrase. This is an open form because the singer is free to improvise the call, and the responders continue to repeat the phrase until the soloist is finished expressing the desired content or until there is no further need for the song.

The call-and-response form came to America through the work song and from there was applied to Christian hymns used by evangelists in an effort to convert Africans to Christianity. Musicologist Eileen Southern quotes John Watson's "Methodists Error or Friendly Christian Advice to Those Methodists Who Indulge in Extravagant Religious Emotions and Bodily Exercises" (1819), when commenting on the African-Americans' after-hours activities during a revival camp meeting:

> In the Black's quarter, the colored people get together, and sing for hours together, short scraps of disjointed affirmations, pledges or prayers, lengthened out with long repetition choruses. These are all sung in the merry chorus-manner of the southern harvest field, or husking-frolic method, of the slaves blacks . . . .[3]

Some of these from their nature (having very long repetition choruses and short scraps of matter) are actually composed as sung, and are indeed almost endless.[4]

This description of "repetition choruses" and "short scraps of disjointed affirmations" appears to be describing the typical call-and-response format. Identifying the music "composed as sung" indicates that Watson realized that the singers were improvising, or spontaneously composing.

There are many examples of the way in which call-and-response has been adopted in American music.

- In country blues, a singer typically sings a phrase (call) which lasts approximately eight beats (two bars) and is answered by an instrumental response from the guitar or jazz band, also lasting approximately eight beats.

- In a band arrangement during the swing era, a typical method for accompanying a melody or an instrumental soloist was with repeated short phrases known as *riffs*.

By the 1960s, call-and-response patterns had become such an important ingredient of popular music that it is difficult to find a recording made by Motown Records at this time that does not use those ancient African patterns. To give just one example, in the well-known Ray Charles song "What'd I Say" (1959), the vocal lines "Tell me what'd I say" are answered first by the band and later by the background vocalists.

Natural Scales and Blue Notes

The term *blue notes* describes the mournful-sounding lowered notes often occurring in melismatic ornamentation. It is believed that those notes exist because of a collision between the natural scales of Africans and the equal-tempered scales of Europeans. Although there is no single African scale, scholars have identified the use of many different scales: among them, the equidistant, pentatonic, diatonic, tritonic, pentachordal, and heptatonic. European music employed various scale forms based on the laws of physics and mathematics until the early nineteenth century, when Germany, and later France and England, adopted the equal-tempered scale. The notes of this scale are divided into twelve equal parts with no interval being acoustically pure except the octave. By using this scale, Europeans were able to develop a style of music that was more harmonically complex than that of other cultures.

For our purposes, the significance of this information is that the piano, and therefore most European-styled instruments, is constructed to accommodate a system of tuning that is essentially out of tune with the laws of physics and therefore nature. The third note of an equal-tempered scale is fourteen percent higher than the third note of a pure scale. Other notes, such as the fifth and seventh notes, are higher as well.[5] The result is that Africans found the notes of European instruments to be out of tune, and when they sang or played an instrument of adjustable pitch, they tended to lower the third, fifth, and seventh notes of the scale. Today these lowered tones, the so-called *blue notes,* are characteristic of African-American music. However, the term functions only in comparison to European scales. It should be noted that some scholars reserve the identification of blue notes to those pitches that are lowered by increments smaller than a half-step.

Buzzing or Roughening of Sound

The African fondness for *buzzing,* or roughening of the sound, found its way into vocal music where the "beautiful sound" of the voice, in the European sense, is not part of the aesthetic system. There is a great difference between the vocal sound of a European singer and that of the African-American tradition. Today, this roughened vocal character so characteristic of African-American music is an indispensable part of most styles of rock.

This characteristic also found its way into instrumental music. Jazz, blues, and rock artists use a sound that is often criticized as "rough around the edges" by those using a European aesthetic. From Louis Armstrong's trumpet to Jimi Hendrix's distortion-laden guitar, the tone of African-American–based music developed from this basic African characteristic.

Polyrhythms and Syncopation

The use of percussion is fundamental to African music, since the basic approach to most of the music is percussive. Much of the rhythmic activity of African music is layered—meaning, one rhythm is laid upon another until the resulting texture is quite complex. Within the rhythmic framework are repetitive rhythmic voices as well as improvisatory or solo rhythmic voices. Jazz developed in a similar fashion. Very often there are two simultaneous rhythmic planes, one based on two and another based on three. As a rhythmic exercise, try to hear this two-against-three rhythm by counting out loud: 1 2 3 4 5 6. With your right hand, tap your leg on 1, 3, 5, and with your left hand, tap your leg on 1, 4. If you can do this, you are playing two against three, that is, two equally spaced beats in the same space as three equally spaced beats.

Right   1 - 2 - 3 - 4 - 5 - 6 - 1 - 2 - 3 - 4 - 5 - 6

Left   1 - 2 - 3 - 4 - 5 - 6 - 1 - 2 - 3 - 4 - 5 - 6

Many of the rhythms in African music can be described as syncopated. *Syncopation* is traditionally defined as a rhythm that accents the normally unaccented beats, although it is sometimes difficult for contemporary Americans to absorb this definition. We have trouble remembering what the "normally unaccented beats" are since most of our music is syncopated. In traditional music theory, the strong beats are identified as the first and third beats of a group of four. In jazz or rock and roll, the strong beats are usually the second and fourth beats. There can be syncopation within the beat as well. Again, as one divides the beats up into smaller parts, it is the second and fourth parts that will be accented. *Ragtime* in the 1890s used this type of syncopation, which was singled out by European composers as the most interesting aspect of American music, largely because it was a musical characteristic that was not fully developed in European music. Regardless of how the presence of the rhythms are defined or explained, the fact is that there is a great deal of rhythmic vitality in African music.

A Percussive Approach to Sound

Often the voice and instruments are used in a way that is percussive as well as melodic. This characteristic overlaps with the call-and-response patterns because most often the response (riff) is rhythmic enough to function without any change of pitch (melody). In improvised solos, musicians often attack notes in such a way as to call attention to their rhythmic value, and sometimes employ a technique in which one pitch is repeated with various rhythms and tonal shadings. In the rap music of the 1980–90s, both lyrics and accompaniment are essentially rhythmic. Rap performances often included a DJ "record scratcher" who created a complex accompaniment by manipulating the turntable(s) back and forth, using the scratch-like sound of the grooves quickly passing under the needle as a rhythmic sound or by allowing the record to play for short sections and then quickly repeating that section (riffs). Both examples illustrate the way sound can be manipulated to accentuate its rhythmic, rather than melodic, value.

HOW DID AFRICAN MUSICAL CHARACTERISTICS SURVIVE?

An important question to ask is, How did the African and transplanted European musical cultures mix? All too often history focuses on the slavery aspect of African-American music and neglects the music created by freemen in the North and in New Orleans. African-Americans provided much of the music for dances in the colonies, usually with a violin, but later most other European instruments were used as well. Eileen Southern cites the publication of a Negro Jig in a collection of dance music published in Scotland in 1782.[6] It is possible that this was either a transcribed composition or an original composition written to reflect the musical characteristics as witnessed by Europeans.

Military Music

The military was another setting in which African musical characteristics were transmitted. African-Americans frequently enlisted in the military as musicians and provided music for both ceremonial and recreational occasions. The earliest record of an African-American military musician was Nero Benson, trumpeter "for the company of Captain Isaac Clark in 1723."[7] Among the soldiers at the Battle of Bunker Hill in 1775 was Barzillai Lew, an African-American drummer and fifer. In 1778, laws were enacted that offered freedom to slaves who joined the army, further facilitating the mixture of musical culture. In this way, African-Americans absorbed musical characteristics of the European wind band tradition and interpreted them through the filter of their own musical tradition.

Religious Music

Religious worship was a third arena through which the musical lives of European-Americans and African-Americans came into contact. Early Europeans in America felt the need to Christianize all inhabitants. As early as 1693, Cotton Mather organized the Society of Negroes to provide regular religious training for African-Americans. The church setting afforded an opportunity to blend European musical forms, scales, and harmony with African musical characteristics. As African-Americans were engaged in singing hymns, many observers noted that they easily added to the songs by improvising new words or sections.

Singing was one of the most prominent features of interracial tent meetings of the early-nineteenth-century Christian revival movement known as the "Second Awakening" or the "Great Awakening." In these settings, African-Americans made music together with European-Americans. After the participants retired for the evening, the African-Americans returned to their segregated tents and continued singing well into the night. According to Eileen Southern, "Song leaders added choruses and refrains to official hymns ... [,] introduced new songs with repetitive phrases" and "spontaneously" composed songs. Creating spontaneous songs by improvising lyrics and using repetitive call-and-response phrases are typical African musical characteristics.

The type of religious music with the most African qualities in the United States at this time was the *ring shout*, in which participants divided into two groups: shouters (dancers) and singers. The shouters shuffle-stepped around in a circle in such a way that their feet never crossed or left the ground. Doing so would constitute dancing, and religious leaders believed that dancing was sinful. According to witnesses, shouters would circle for as many as four or five hours, with the proceedings taking on the character of a "wild monotonous chant."[8] The tempo of the shout would gradually increase until the trance-like nature of the ceremony would cause members to fall to the ground in a state of religious ecstasy.

African-American religious music was elevated to the position of art music and made famous throughout the United States and Europe by the Fisk University Jubilee Singers. In 1867, George L. White, a European-American teacher at the school, organized the Fisk Jubilee Singers to perform local concerts of standard choral music and "their own music," i.e., harmonized slave songs. Concert selections included "Keep Me From Sinking Down," "O Brothers, Don't Stay Away," and "Go Down Moses," along with popular songs such as "Old Folks At Home" and "Home, Sweet Home." In 1871, White organized a concert tour with the intention of raising money for the university's building fund. The American highlight of the tour was a show-saving performance at Patrick Gilmore's World Peace Jubilee in 1872.[9] After the success of this performance, the Jubilee Singers performed in Germany, Switzerland, and Great Britain, winning acclaim from both audiences and critics. This European tour caused the *Negro spiritual* to become inseparably associated with American culture. Today, when university choral groups tour Europe, they are expected to dedicate a portion of their performance to the spiritual.

Slave celebrations like "Lection Day," "Pinkster Day" and "Sundays at Congo Square" were other forums at which European-Americans could hear and absorb the music of African-Americans. Lection Day, when African-Americans elected their "kings," was celebrated from 1750 to the 1850s. These kings were most likely the same type of "royalty" elected for the Mardi Gras celebrations of New Orleans. Pinkster Day was Pentecost Sunday, originally a Dutch holiday later adopted by other settlements, and was often celebrated with various types of African singing and dancing for as long as a week. Congo Square, or Place Congo in New Orleans, was where slaves gathered every Sunday from around 1786 (if not earlier) until the late 1830s, resuming between 1845 and 1862, to enjoy music and dancing of the "old country." In each case, these festivities were halted by intervention from municipal authorities, who believed the gatherings were a threat to public order. Nevertheless, the celebrations were an important vehicle for the preservation of African musical traditions because young people in attendance were able to experience and absorb its characteristics.

Professional Musicians

In the North and in New Orleans, African-American professional musicians provided much of the musical entertainment enjoyed by European-Americans. The first Unites States census in 1790 revealed that the African-American population was about 750,000, and that 59,000 of those were "freemen," African-Americans who were not bound into slavery. In Philadelphia for example,

Frank Johnson's well-known band provided entertainment for "the fashionable people in cities and resorts along the Atlantic seaboard."[10] Johnson had a reputation as a fiddler, bugler, hornist, and composer. His wind band toured England in 1838 and, as a result of a command performance for Queen Victoria, he was presented with a silver bugle. Johnson was described as having "remarkable taste in distorting a sentimental, simple, and beautiful song, into a reel, jig, or country dance."[11] This "distortion" was most certainly what would be known in the twentieth century as "jazzin' it." In the nineteenth century, this type of musical performance became known by such terms as *syncopated songs, plantation songs,* and finally, by the turn of the century, *ragtime.*

African-American musical characteristics and songs have so permeated the cultural landscape of the United States that the public has forgotten the origins of the material. An example of this type of cultural memory failure is the song "Listen to the Mocking Bird," which was composed by barber-guitarist-whistler Richard Milburn. When published in 1855, the title page gave Milburn composer credit. However, subsequent editions have omitted his name, listing only the name of the transcriber, Alice Hawthorne.

Work Songs

As horrible as it was, slavery served one important musical function already discussed: It helped preserve African vocal music traditions. In fact, work songs were probably the most significant vehicle in the preservation of those traditions. Because works songs served the useful function of increasing productivity, they were allowed to exist; and because the music served the same function in America as it did in Africa, there was no need for the style of the songs to be altered. Work songs functioned for the workers, not an audience; therefore, the musical characteristics did not need alteration to accommodate European-American taste as did the syncopated popular music of the North.

Slaves did, however, occasionally entertain European-Americans, and musically proficient slaves often were loaned out to surrounding plantations to provide entertainment. In fact, on Sundays and holidays when slaves were not working otherwise, they were often free to hire out their musical services to earn extra money.

Once slavery was outlawed, the vocal techniques that were preserved in work songs were applied to music used for entertainment purposes and gradually evolved into what is now known as *the blues.* Later, when these same vocal techniques were applied to European band instruments and used in entertainment music, *jazz* developed.

By the end of the nineteenth century, African-American syncopated music was beginning to typify American music. The taste had been acquired gradually throughout the previous centuries and was being disseminated by the emerging popular music industry, first by minstrel shows, second by the publication of *plantation songs*, and later by *ragtime* songs.

Minstrel Shows

In the early nineteenth century, African-American characters began to appear as comic figures in songs and theatrical performances. These soon expanded into "blackface acts" attempting to depict plantation life. As these acts were assembled into a complete show, they became known as *minstrel* shows, sometimes called *Ethiopian minstrelsy*. Songs emanating from these shows became known as Ethiopian melodies. This was one of the first popular musical forms derived from African-American music. The performances drew directly from religious, dance, and folk music of eighteenth- and nineteenth-century African-Americans, and songs such as "Old Dan Tucker," "Zip Coon," "Jim Along Josey," "Coal-Black Rose," and "Clare de Kitchen" became part of nineteenth-century American musical culture. Minstrel shows were an essential element in the development of *ragtime, blues,* and *country music* because they provided employment for many musicians, including Ma Rainey Blues and Uncle Dave Macon Country.

One of the most famous minstrel characters was Jim Crow, based on a Kentucky stable hand of the same name who happened to walk with an interesting shuffle and occasionally hop-stepped. As the worker shuffle-stepped, he sang a curious song, later immortalized as "Jump Jim Crow." The caricature was created by Thomas Rice in 1828 while appearing on stage in Louisville and became an instant hit, propelling Rice and the character to international stardom. It is interesting to note that the series of laws passed with the intention of imposing racial segregation by requiring separate public accommodations become known collectively as the Jim Crow laws.

These individual black-face acts gradually coalesced into a self-contained entertainment unit, and in 1843 the first minstrel show, the Virginia Minstrels (Daniel Decatur Emmett, Billy Whitlock, Dick Pelham, and Frank Bower) began performing in New York. The group established the essential instrumentation of the minstrel show: fiddle, banjo, bones (twelve-inch horse bones), and tambourine.[12] The Virginia Minstrels were very successful on the East Coast and the next year toured England. Emmett was an important songwriter. Among his compositions were "Bluetail Fly," "Old Dan Tucker," "Turkey in the Straw," and "I Wish I Was in Dixie's Land" (Dixie). Before the 1909 copyright law, being a songwriter often meant notating pre-existing folk songs, so many of Emmett's compositions may have been culled from existing songs.

In 1844, Edwin P. Christy formed the Christy Minstrels and is credited with establishing the minstrel show format: opening jokes and repartee with the performers seated in a semi-circle, Mr. Tambo and Mr. Bones on the ends, and Mr. Interlocutor in the center; the *olio*, a section of songs and skits; and the walk-around featuring the whole case. In the 1850s, there were ten minstrel theaters in New York, but by 1870 the genre began to fade into the next entertainment style, vaudeville.

After emancipation, African-American minstrel troupes that toured the country were organized. By then, the form established by the European-American entertainers was so successful that many black performers found it difficult to break the stereotypes and often gave in to them in order to make a living. When minstrelsy faded, it did not completely disappear. Instead, many of the same characterizations continued in vaudeville, and the syncopated plantation song tradition continued under labels such as *jig* and *coon* songs. Traveling tent shows and medicine shows developed out of the minstrel show tradition and continued to provide employment for blues, jazz, and folk artists well into the twentieth century.

Minstrel shows served two important functions: They helped expose larger audiences to African-American musical characteristics and provided an early place for African-American performers in the entertainment business. The list of entertainers and musicians who worked in this medium would be too large to estimate, but it would include Ma Rainey, "Mother of the Blues," who toured with the Rabbit's Foot minstrels in the first decade of this century, as did Bessie Smith and W. C. Handy, "Father of the Blues," who toured with Mahara's Minstrels.

African-American Musical Theater

Although minstrel shows were the most pervasive form of African-American–based entertainment, they were not the only form. New York City's large African-American population created non-minstrel performance opportunities and gave rise to the African-American Broadway musical. From 1821 to 1828, the African Grove, owned and operated by African-Americans, presented ballets and plays in addition to specialty acts. The Grove was closed by city government because European-Americans began visiting the theater in large numbers and causing "disorder and wanton mischief."[13] In 1898, a musical written by African-Americans appeared on Broadway: *Clorindy, or the Origin of the Cakewalk*, by Paul Laurence Dunbar and Will Marion Cook. The success of this show led to others: *In Dahomey* (1903), *Abyssinia* (1907), *In Bandana Land* (1907), *The Shoo-Fly Regiment* (1906), *The Red Moon* (1908), and *Mr. Lode of Koal* (1910). The most successful of the twentieth-century African-American musicals was *Shuffle Along* (1921) by Noble Sissle and Eubie Blake.

COON SONGS, CAKEWALKS, AND RAGTIME

The musical use of the derogatory racial term *coon* dates to the song "Old Zip Coon" (1834) and was applied to African-American music between 1880 and 1900. *Coon shout* was used to describe the singing style. The post-war reconstruction period saw a rise in the musical use of the term in songs such as "Coonville Guards" (1881), "The Coon Dinner" (1882), "New Coon in Town" (1883), and "The Whistling Coon" (1888). African-American entertainer-pianist Ernest Hogan wrote the most popular of these, "All Coons Look Alike to Me," which was used as the required piece for the semi-final phase of the "Ragtime Championship of the World" held at Tammany Hall in New York City on January 23, 1900.

Some researchers believe that the *cakewalk* was originally an African circle dance to which slaves added those mimicking movements of their masters when they participated in the grand-march parade preceding a minuet. The cakewalk became so popular that competitions were held, and America danced the cakewalk to the strains of "ragged" music; the First Cakewalk Jubilee, a three-day dance contest, was held at Madison Square Garden in 1892.

These two competitions help give an indication of the immense popularity of African-American-inspired dance and music. The *coon song* and *cakewalk* were undoubtedly present in Chicago at the World's Columbian Exposition in 1893, either on the midway or in the surrounding entertainment areas. In the days before the instant media of today, events like a world's fair were a means of exposing the general population, especially those in rural areas, to the latest inventions, trends, and music. It was here that the midwestern population discovered *coon songs, jig piano,* and *cakewalks.*

The term *ragtime* replaced *jig piano* and *coon song* in describing the African-American syncopated song in 1897. The first composition to be published using the identifying term *rag* was "Mississippi Rag" (1897) by European-American bandleader William H. Krell, soon followed by "Ragtime March" by Warren Beebe and "Ragtime Patrol" by R.J. Hamilton., The first African-American published ragtime song, "Harlem Rag" by Tom Turpin, appeared in December 1897. Also that year, pianist-entertainer Ben Harney performed at Tony Pastor's Music Hall billed as "Inventor of Ragtime," and he published a ragtime method book, *Rag Time Instructor.* Harney's earlier compositions, "Mister Johnson, Turn Me Loose" and "You Been a Good Old Wagon But You Done Broke Down," were incredible hits that inspired a glut of over six hundred African-American–styled *coon songs.* It was during this flurry of publication that the term *ragtime* was applied to the syncopated instrumental songs.

Many historians have tried to explain the genesis of the term. The most common explanation is that "ragged-time" described the ragged rhythmic effect of the syncopation. The music was not new and was, in fact, a continuation of the tradition of *minstrel songs, cakewalks,* and *coon songs.* What was new was the ragtime composer's intention to elevate the genre's status by bringing it to the concert stage. Some composers of concert music had already begun to perform African-American pieces.

Louis Moreau Gottschalk, born in New Orleans, was an internationally acclaimed pianist during the middle of the nineteenth century and was billed as "the greatest pianist now before the public."[14] Gottschalk was also a composer of piano pieces that had their roots in African-American street songs, African rhythms, and Latin American music. "La Bamboula-Danse des Negres" (1814) and "Le Banjo" (1855) are two of his compositions.

The term *classic ragtime* has been used to distinguish the compositions of composers such as Scott Joplin from the syncopated songs issued by Tin Pan Alley composers. Classic ragtime was modeled after standard dances and marches, and included European harmony, scales, and musical form. The one element that separates ragtime from other styles is its incessant syncopation. One theory is that the difference between true ragtime and syncopated popular songs is the use of melodic rhythmic groupings of 123-123-12. Simply defined, ragtime has the following characteristics:

- It is a syncopated piano music.

- It is in rondo form, meaning there are four melodies.

- It is counted with two beats to the bar.

- Each melody usually fills sixteen bars.

- It has a syncopated melody played in the right hand.

- It often has rhythmic groupings of the melody of 123-123-12-123-123-12, over an even bass line.

- It has a melodic rhythm that moves at twice the speed of the accompaniment.

- It has a somewhat repetitive rhythmic pattern, bass-chord- bass-chord, played with the left hand.

The rondo form used in ragtime usually employed several different melodies, some returning at regular intervals. When discussing the musical form, each melody is assigned a letter (A, B, C, or D) for purposes of identification. For example, the form of Scott Joplin's "Maple Leaf Rag" is A-A-B-B-A-C-C-D-D; there are four distinct melodies, with the first one returning in the middle.

Scott Joplin

Scott Joplin, born in November 24, 1868, in Texarkana, Texas, was not the first ragtime composer but is considered the foremost composer of the *classic ragtime* style. At a young age, his ability on the piano enabled him to study piano and music theory. As a young man, Joplin earned a living as a traveling musician in the Mississippi Valley, and in 1885 he settled in St. Louis and began a career as a professional musician and teacher. In 1893, Joplin was one of the many African-American musicians who traveled to Chicago to entertain during the World's Columbian Exposition. Joplin eventually settled in Sedalia, Missouri, in 1896 to continue as a musician and teacher, and also studied advanced theory and composition at George Smith College for Negroes. During this period he experienced some success as a composer, first publishing three piano pieces and two songs, none in a ragtime style. In Sedalia, Joplin joined up with John Stark, a publisher who issued many of Joplin's ragtime compositions; however, Joplin's first published ragtime composition, "Original Rags," was published in 1899 by another Kansas City publisher. That same year, Stark published what was to become Joplin's most famous composition, "Maple Leaf Rag," named after the Maple Leaf Club where Joplin was performing.

Joplin, like Gottschalk before him, was educated in the European art music tradition and intended to develop African-American music beyond the bounds of common entertainment into serious concert music. In 1899, he produced a folk-ballet, *The Ragtime Dance,* at Sedalia's Woods Opera House, and in 1903, he staged a ragtime opera called *A Guest of Honor.* Stark copyrighted the work but never published it, and the score has not been found. Joplin followed Stark when he moved his publishing house to New York and continued to publish rags until the ragtime craze was replaced by the next popular music style, the *blues.* Joplin continued to attempt longer forms and composed another ragtime opera titled *Treemonisha.* Unable to get Stark to publish it, Joplin published it himself in 1911 and organized a performance for potential backers in a Harlem hall in 1915. The preview performance failed to attract any backers, and that disappointment, combined with worsening bouts with syphilis he contracted while a traveling musician, put him in a deep state of depression. Joplin's last year was spent at the Manhattan State Hospital where he died April 1, 1917.

Joplin's compositions experienced a resurgence and newfound respectability in the 1970s. In 1971, the New York Public Library published the *Collected Works of Scott Joplin* and Joshua Rifkin's recording of Joplin's "Piano Rag" reached the *Billboard* classical music charts. *Treemonisha* was finally produced in 1972 at the Memorial Arts Center in Atlanta and later, in 1975, on Broadway by the Houston Opera Company. In 1974, Joplin's music was used on the soundtrack for *The Sting,* a movie set in the 1920s. It is interesting to note that jazz would have been the more appropriate period music for the movie, but by that time, Joplin's music was public domain (without copyright protection), and the movie's producer was able to use the music without paying a royalty.

THE BLUES

In the 1920s, recorded *blues* fell into two main categories: country blues (rural blues) and classic blues (city blues). Country blues was, undoubtedly, the first incarnation of this musical form, although city blues was the first to be recorded. Early blues was found in several regions of the United States, but the Mississippi Delta is the primary region where blues is thought to have developed its characteristic form and traditional lyric content. Country blues can be divided into several subcategories based on location, such as Mississippi Delta blues, Texas blues, Piedmont blues. Early performances were usually by men and were either unaccompanied or self-accompanied with a banjo, guitar, or harmonica (instruments that were inexpensive, unamplified, and portable). Pianos were not uncommon but were found mostly in cities and *juke joints*, rural party places known for moonshine, fish fries, and blues. Group performances did occur, especially at juke joints, although formal groups were rare.

Blues musicians were performers who entertained in towns and labor camps and on plantations. In larger cities, pianists performed in a more urban style, which sometimes blurred the boundaries between country and city blues. Country blues musicians were mobile, often floating from one community to another, as their spirits moved them. Some were farmers who entertained on weekends, as were both Muddy Waters and B.B. King.

City (or *classic*) blues is a phrase loosely applied to the songs of the urban singers, most often women. These singers were professional entertainers who featured blues in their repertoire and usually were accompanied by jazz musicians. The blues songs they performed were often written by professional songwriters or musicians who felt, because of their training, that the AAB twelve-bar structure lacked contrast, so they added other sections, usually sixteen-bar forms, to make the twelve-bar blues more structurally complex. Consequently, many of the recordings by classic city blues singers are in an adapted blues form.

Blues Form

The classic twelve-bar blues form can be illustrated as follows:

- twelve bars of music (three groups of four bars)

- three basic chords

- a repetition of the first vocal line

vocal line - - - - - - - - - -]   instrumental answer - - -]
    (chord 1)
‖   / / / /   ‖   / / / /   ‖   / / / /   ‖   / / / /   ‖

repeat vocal line - - - - - - -]   instrumental answer - - -]
    (chord 2)   (chord 1)
‖   / / / /   ‖   / / / /   ‖   / / / /   ‖   / / / /   ‖

vocal line #2 - - - - - - - -]   instrumental answer - - -]
    (chord 3)   (chord 1)
‖   / / / /   ‖   / / / /   ‖   / / / /   ‖   / / / /   ‖

This illustrated definition describes the blues form that was used in the earliest rock recordings. To the form shown above, add the phrase "You ain't nothin' but a hound dog cryin' all the time" for the first line and, "You never caught a rabbit and you ain't no friend of mine" for the second. The results are the first chorus from Elvis Presley's "Hound Dog." Notice that each vocal line has an instrumental answer that is an application of the call-and-response African musical characteristic. The relationship between the time occupied (number of musical beats) by the call-and-response elements is the cause of most of the variation found in early country blues recordings.

ORIGIN OF THE BLUES

No one is certain about the origin of the blues, but most researchers seem to agree that it developed from work songs and possibly religious music. The curious element is that African-American professional and semi-professional musicians had been entertaining since colonial times and typically had developed a repertoire that included many styles, enabling them to perform for a wide variety of audiences of both races. When professional performers became aware of the blues, it was a very simple, even archaic form that fell into the category of folk music. Both Ma Rainey and W. C. Handy commented on how this simple music was received by audiences and how profoundly it affected them. The blues came into contact with the outside world after it was added to the acts of professional entertainers and developed a more regular musical form.

Although the course of development followed by the blues will be forever masked by conjecture, the path it took to reach mainstream America is known. The first real documentation of this course is found in the exploitation of the music by the entertainment industry, as illustrated by the following timeline, which is amplified below:

1902   Blues added to Ma Rainey's minstrel act

1903   Blues first heard by W. C. Handy

1909   "Memphis Blues" written by W. C. Handy

1912   First published blues: "Baby Seals Blues" (August 1912), "Dallas Blues" (September 1912), and "Memphis Blues" (date?)

1916   First recorded blues, "N——- Blues" (Columbia A-2064) by George O'Connor (a European-American performer and lawyer, no less)

1917   First recording of blues by a jazz band, "Livery Stable Blues," by the Original Dixieland Jass Band. (The original spelling of "jazz" was "jass.")

1920   First African-American recording of blues, "Crazy Blues," by Mamie Smith.

Ma Rainey Adds the Blues

Ma Rainey, often called the "Mother of the Blues," was born Gertrude Pridgett on April 26, 1886, in Columbus, Georgia. In an interview with John Work and Sterling Brown published in *American Negro Songs*, Rainey says

Ma Rainey

that she first encountered the blues in Missouri in 1902, when she heard a girl singing a strange and poignant song about a man who had left her. Rainey learned the song and began to use it as an encore for her act. Soon afterward, the favorable audience reaction made the song the highlight of the act.

The First Published Blues

"Memphis Blues (Mr. Crump)" by William C. Handy (1873–1958), is usually credited as the first published blues; however, two other blues compositions actually appeared first: "Baby Seals Blues" (August 1912) by African-American pianist Artie Matthews and "Dallas Blues" (September 1912) by European-American songwriter Hart A. Wand. Handy's song was written in 1909 but was not released commercially until 1912. Born in 1873, W.C. Handy was not a blues singer but rather a professional band leader and cornetist. Handy toured as a musician for a while, eventually becoming the bandleader for Mahara's Minstrels. He later taught at the Teacher's Agricultural and Mechanical College for Negroes in Huntsville, Alabama. When he returned to Memphis, he became a well-known and sought-after musician, so much so that when mayoral candidate Edward H. Crump needed a campaign song to attract African-American voters, he asked Handy to write the song.

Speaking about the roots of the blues, Handy cited an experience when he was a traveling musician waiting for a train in 1903 in Tutwiler, Mississippi, the heart of the Delta. He had fallen asleep on a bench at the train station and was awakened by the sounds of another traveler singing, "I'm goin' down where the Southern crosses the Dog." The singer repeated the line three times while he accompanied himself on a guitar using a knife blade pressed against the strings. Handy asked him what those lyrics meant and the singer told him that he was going to Moorhead. At Moorhead, the eastbound and westbound tracks of the Yazoo Delta Line crossed the northbound and southbound tracks; Yazoo Delta was abbreviated on the cars as "Y.D." and had come to be known as the "Yaller Dawg" by local residents. Handy's story, along with Rainey's, helps establish a date when non-participants began to notice this haunting personal music.[15]

Another story Handy told helps illustrate the way professional musicians adapt their performance styles in order to make themselves more employable by giving the audience what it wants. While performing for a gathering with the Knights of Pithias Band in Clarksville, Mississippi, Handy got what he thought was a strange request: Would the band play some of their "native music"? Not quite understanding, the band played an "old-time Southern melody." The next request was to let a local band sit in for a few songs, which implied that the first request had not been satisfactorily filled. The local band was described by Handy in the following way:

> . . . three pieces, a battered guitar, a mandolin, and a worn-out bass. The music they made was pretty well in keeping with their looks. They stuck up one of those over-and-over strains that seemed to have no very clear beginning and certainly no ending at all. The strumming attained a disturbing monotony, but on and on it went, a kind of stuff that has long been associated with cane rows and levee camps. Thump-thump-thump went their feet on the floor, Their eyes rolled. Their shoulders swayed.[16]

The band Handy described was a string band, a type of ensemble that would be identified today as a bluegrass or country band. This description should help impress upon the reader the fact that African-American music can be found in the roots of most of our popular music, including country and western. Handy went on to describe how the audience showered the local musicians with "dollars, quarters, halves," and soon the string band had "more money than my nine musicians were being paid for the entire engagement." At another point, he writes that his "idea of what constitutes music was changed by the sight of that silver money." . . . I had come to the conclusion . . . that the American people wanted movement and rhythm for their money." He soon began to arrange songs such as "The Last Shot Got Him," "Your Clock Ain't Right," and "Make Me a Pallet on Your Floor," for his band. This lesson in the business of music caused Handy to begin to direct his material to a new audience and would eventually lead to the campaign song commission and its publication as "Memphis Blues."

First Recorded Blues

"N- Blues" (Columbia A-2064) was recorded on July 18, 1916, by George O'Connor.[17] The song was written in 1912 by Leroy "Lasses" White, a blackface minstrel, in Dallas, Texas. This composition follows the standard twelve-bar format, indicating that the form may have been somewhat standardized by the time Handy published "Memphis Blues."

First Jazz Band Records the Blues

New Orleans is often cited as the birthplace of jazz, and the accuracy of this statement depends on how one distinguishes jazz from other styles of African-American syncopated music. The New Orleans style certainly differed from the New York style, and the first important jazz recordings were made by New Orleans musicians. However, those recordings were not made in New Orleans. Older New Orleans musicians claim that the blues and ragtime were fused sometime around 1895 by Buddy Bolden's band and that jazz was the resulting music.

The jazz band that first recorded the blues, or any jazz for that matter, was the Original Dixieland Jass Band (ODJB), a group of European-American musicians. In 1917, they were performing at Reisenweber's and were asked by RCA to record. One of the selections they chose was the "Livery Stable Blues."

First Recorded African-American Blues Singer

Mamie Smith (1883-1946), recorded the first African-American blues, "Crazy Blues" (OKeh No. 4169), on August 10, 1920. Smith was a New York cabaret and theater entertainer. At the time, she had a part in the show *Made in Harlem* at the Lincoln Theater, where she sang "Harlem Blues" by Perry Bradford. Bradford convinced OKeh to record the song but changed the name to "Crazy Blues" at the suggestion of OKeh's president, Otto Heineman. Smith had previously recorded some non-blues selections for OKeh: "That Thing Called Love" and "You Can't Keep a Good Man Down" (February 14, 1920). OKeh was reluctant to record any blues because he had received threats of a boycott if the company had "any truck with colored girls in the recording field."[18]

"Crazy Blues" was in an adapted blues form: Three verses were in the twelve-bar form, and the remaining three verses were in a sixteen-bar form. The recording sold well enough to cause the industry to begin recording blues: 75,000 copies in Harlem during the first month. Immediately after the success of "Crazy Blues," recordings were issued by Ethel Waters, Alberta Hunter, Edith Wilson, Lucille Hegamin, Mary Stafford, Lillyn Brown, Lavinia Turner, Esther Bigeau, Lulu Whidby, and Kate Crippen. Of these early blues singers, only Alberta Hunter, Ethel Waters, and Edith Wilson had substantial careers.

BLUES: 1920-1935
Country (Rural) Blues

Although *city blues* was recorded first, the *country blues* artists who recorded in the late 1920s undoubtedly used the form as it existed before the blues was adapted by the music business. When record companies began looking beyond the female classic city blues singers, they sent field recording units into the South to focus on certain areas: Atlanta, Dallas, Memphis, the Mississippi Delta, and New Orleans. The companies also relied on talent scouts in these locations. Henry C. Speir, a music store owner in Jackson, Mississippi, scouted many important country blues singers, including Charlie Patton, Willie Lee Brown, Son House, Nehemiah Skip James, and Robert Johnson. Through an arrangement with Ralph Peer (assistant producer of "Crazy Blues"), Mississippi store owner Ralph Lumbo (or Limbo) found Bukka White (Booker T. Washington White). The first blues recordings made outside New York were arranged through Ralph Peer by Polk Brockman (1923), OKeh's distributor in Atlanta, who scouted blues singers Barbeque Bob, Lucille Bogan, and Fannie Goosby, as well as country music's Fiddlin' John Carson.[19]

The methods by which these blues musicians were selected and recorded may have led to faulty perceptions about the repertoire of country blues singers. Because the record companies were looking for blues to record, blues is what performers sang for them, regardless of the total content of their repertoire. For example, in the early 1940s, Brownie McGhee asked his record company if he could record some of the hillbilly songs he had in his repertoire but was told it was not "his kind of music." As evidenced by this example, the business of recording probably has tainted the perception of the origin of the blues, blues styles, and the repertoire of country musicians beyond repair.

Country Blues Styles

Early country blues styles between 1926 and 1930 vary from player to player, but some general characteristics are notable.

Form: The "classic" bar structure of the blues contains twelve bars of music arranged in three couplets: AAB. Typically, each vocal line occupies two bars and is followed by a two-bar instrumental answer (call-and-response). This form is approximated in most of the early blues recordings except those that fall into the category of ballads or story-telling songs, such as "John Henry," "Stagger Lee," and "Frankie and Alpert" (later known as "Frankie and Johnnie"). The approximation of the twelve-bar form relates to the manner in which the vocal line and instrumental answer were delivered. Blind Lemon Jefferson, for example, tended to be unconcerned about fitting the lyric into two bars. Sometimes he added an extra two beats or even suspended the time (rhythm) for a long note, as in "Black Snake Moan." Generally his guitar response fit into the two-bar answer style; however, this was often followed by a bass/chord accompaniment pattern that occupies space before the next vocal line, thereby extending the response by a few beats. On Leadbelly's 1935 recordings, the lyric fits into the two-bar space, but like in the music of Blind Lemon Jefferson, the guitar answer often fills more than two bars.

Harmony: Typically, blues songs consist of three basic chords that are also common to European harmony. The changes in the harmony (chord changes) may have been the result of W. C. Handy's publication of "Memphis Blues." It is not uncommon for a blues singer to use a complicated one-chord vamp, like Blind Willie Johnson did. John Lee Hooker often used a one-chord vamp but would imply the second chord with his voice or a change of one note in the guitar part. The most famous one-chord song is probably "I'm a Man (Mannish Boy)" by Muddy Waters, which was remade by the

British Invasion group the Yardbirds in the 1960s. Blues singers tended to use very simple chord changes; however, jazz musicians in the 1940s increased the complexity of the chord changes by sometimes using as many as two different chords per bar.

Guitar Styles: Mississippi Delta guitarists often used a bottleneck, knife blade, or other smooth object to slide over the guitar strings. The bottleneck, after the rough edges were smoothed, was placed over the little finger and used to slide from note to note. This is the origin of the terms *bottleneck guitar* and *slide guitar*. Some believe that this was an attempt to copy the sound of the Hawaiian steel guitar that was popular in the early twentieth century. However, other researchers have found evidence of the bottleneck guitar style being used before the first Hawaiian guitar recordings reached America.

Country Blues Singers

As mentioned earlier, blues styles are usually identified by their geographic location, which gives the impression that there are distinct stylistic characteristics associated with each locale. While there are some distinctions, any attempt to discuss those here would be confusing. The difficulty in identifying any individual characteristics is compounded by these facts:

- City blues recordings were in circulation before any country blues was recorded. This makes it difficult to determine whether the country blues artists were influenced by commercial recordings.

- Blues musicians often traveled between locations, and their styles were most likely an amalgam. For example, Robert Johnson was considered a Mississippi Delta bluesman, but all his recordings were made in Texas.

- Blues artists recorded the songs selected from their repertoire by the producer, so these documents are tainted by the expectations of the music business professionals who paid for the recordings.

Blind Lemon Jefferson (1897–1928): Lemon Jefferson was born in 1897 outside Couchman, Texas, and it appears that he began singing for money in 1911 or 1912, then settled in Dallas by 1917. Evidently, he traveled beyond Texas because there are reports of him singing in Jackson, Mississippi, and Memphis, Tennessee, in 1923-24.[20] Blind Lemon Jefferson's 1926 recordings were the first to sell well enough to encourage record companies to continue recording and to begin searching the South for more "genuine" blues singers. (The first country blues singers—Sylvester Weaver, Daddy Stovepipe, and

Papa Charlie Jackson—were recorded in 1923–24, but their sales did not warrant further recording.) The records Jefferson made for Paramount in Chicago were very popular and served as a model for the next generation of singers.

Jefferson's guitar playing is excellent, and his recordings give the impression that he is trying to imitate the sound of several instruments, jumping back and forth between soprano single-line melodies, bass solos, and bass/chord accompaniment patterns. Jefferson's use of the *boogie woogie* rhythmic pattern in "Match Box Blues" and a recording titled "Booger Rooger Blues" (containing no boogie woogie patterns), has given rise to the speculation that boogie woogie was originally a Texas style.

Charlie Patton (1887–1934): The lineage of the Delta blues began in Drew, Mississippi, around 1910 with Charlie Patton, often considered the king of the Delta blues. Born in 1891, Patton began playing guitar at a young age even though his father believed, as many did, that guitar playing and the blues were sinful acts. Most of his recordings were made between 1929 and 1934, which places him well after Blind Lemon Jefferson and the city blues singers. Patton was most admired by other blues singers, such as Son House and Howlin' Wolf, for his large, raspy voice, even though this quality makes it difficult to understand all of his lyrics. Many of the themes of his lyrics were autobiographical, commenting on sexual relationships ("It Won't Be Long"), trouble with the law ("Tom Rushin Blues"), and community happenings ("High Water Everywhere").

Robert Johnson (1912–1938): While Charlie Patton may be considered the founder of Delta blues, Robert Johnson is reputed to be the greatest country blues singer. The attention given him by such guitar artists as Keith Richards and Eric Clapton caused Columbia Records to issue a set of his complete recordings as their first boxed set in the Roots n' Blues series. Johnson's influence on rock and blues guitarists cannot be overemphasized.

In the early 1930s, Johnson left his hometown of Robinsonville, Mississippi, and traveled around the Delta region for over a year. When he returned, he stunned everyone, including Son House, with his high degree of proficiency on the guitar. Everyone claimed he had gotten his superior technique through black magic, and Johnson did not try to convince them otherwise. Stories connecting blues to the devil were common, and by that time there was already a story about Tommy Johnson (no relation) acquiring his technique through occult means. According to legend, Tommy Johnson took his guitar to the crossroads out in the deserted countryside. Arriving just before midnight, he began playing a song when a large man walked up to him, took his guitar, tuned it, and then played a song on it. After handing it back to him, Johnson could play anything. The price for this wonderful gift was his soul. After Robert Johnson returned to Robinsonville, the same story was used to explain his greatly improved guitar technique.

Robert Johnson's career was typical for an itinerant blues singer: He did not stay in one place very long, constantly hitched rides on trains and played on street corners, in front of barber shops, in restaurants, and at town squares and house parties just for tips. His repertoire consisted of whatever the people wanted to hear: songs by Duke Ellington, Bing Crosby and other pop and jazz tunes, ragtime, waltzes, polkas, and, if the audience was right, blues.

In 1936, Johnson auditioned for H. C. Speir, a music store owner who served as a talent scout for ARC Records.[21] With ARC, Johnson recorded sixteen sides (usually two takes per tune) at the end of 1936. The recording sessions took place in a hotel room in San Antonio that had to have the shades pulled down in order to keep the traffic noise from being recorded. In June 1937, he recorded thirteen more songs in a Dallas warehouse. These two recording sessions comprise all of Robert Johnson's known recordings. Many of his lyrics are of a desperate and gloomy nature that reflect his supposed pact with the devil: "Stones in My Passway,"" Me and the Devil Blues," "Hellhound on My Trail." Musically, Johnson's guitar technique extended that of Blind Lemon Jefferson in that he played both bass and lead on one instrument. His walking bass rhythm was adapted from the *boogie woogie* rhythm that was just becoming popular in the cities.

In 1938, Robert was playing a dance in Three Forks, Mississippi, when he was given some poisoned whiskey. It seems Johnson had been sexually involved with the wife of one of the men in the bar. He continued to play that night although he was sick, and lived for several more days. John Hammond, unaware of Johnson's death, tried to locate him for the famous December 1938 "From Spirituals to Swing" concert at Carnegie Hall, a concert which would have exposed his skills to a wider audience. But Johnson died on August 16, 1938, at the age of twenty-seven.

Johnson was in the last generation of old-style country blues singers, and while he was recording in Texas, other Texas bluesmen such as T-Bone Walker, were beginning to add elements of jazz to their music and soon would be using electric guitars. Johnson probably would have been forgotten had it not been for the British blues movement of Alexis Korner and John Mayall, which helped focus attention on his music, guitar style, and reputed pact with the devil.

Leadbelly (1889–1949): In 1933, John and Alan Lomax traveled the Deep South in search of authentic folk music. Working for the Library of Congress, their mission was to record as much music as possible. They believed that the

musicians in the South were more at ease when they were recorded in their natural environment (fields, homes, churches, schools) than in a sterile recording
studio.

In July 1933, they visited the Angola Penitentiary in Louisiana to record
Huddie Ledbetter (Leadbelly), who was incarcerated there for attempted murder. Leadbelly had been a singer and leadman for Blind Lemon Jefferson and
knew hundreds of folk songs, work songs, and blues.

Eventually, Lomax arranged performances for Leadbelly. Among the
New York radicals, he was an immediate success and became an important
role model for the future Greenwich Village folk scene. Before his death from
Lou Gehrig's Disease in 1949, he was known as the "King of the Twelve-String
Guitar." In 1950, the Weavers, a folk group with Pete Seeger, reached the
number one position on the Billboard popular music chart with a recording
of one of Leadbelly's songs, "Good Night Irene." *

Country Blues Singers

Texas Alexander	Peg Leg Howell	Furry Lewis
Blind Blake	Mississippi John Hurt	Tommy McClennan
Barbecue Bob	Jim Jackson	Brownie McGhee
Sleepy John Estes	Skip James	Memphis Minnie
Blind Boy Fuller	Blind Lemon Jefferson	Charlie Patton
John Lee Hooker	Robert Johnson	Sonny Terry
Lightning Hopkins	Tommy Johnson	Bukka White
Son House	Leadbelly	Big Joe Williams

City (Classic) Blues

City blues or *classic blues* is used to identify the type of blues first recorded
in the early 1920s. These recordings usually were made by professional female
entertainers, either in theaters, cabarets, nightclubs, tent shows, medicine
shows, or minstrel shows, and were accompanied by pianists or jazz bands.
Because these recordings were by professional musicians, the musical form
rigidly adhered to the twelve-bar blues structure, except for those eight- or
sixteen-bar structures that were added to the basic blues form by songwriters.

Ma Rainey (1896–1939): Ma Rainey is often called the "Mother of the
Blues" because she was one of the women, if not the first, to add the blues to
her act. Rainey began her career with a traveling tent show just after the turn
of the century and added the blues to her repertoire in 1902. In 1904, she married Will "Pa" Rainey, and later the two performed as Rainey and Rainey. By
1914, they were billed as Rainey and Rainey, Assassinators of the Blues. In
1924, Rainey began recording for Paramount, and during her career she

recorded ninety-two sides. Most of her blues are in the twelve-bar, AAB form, and her subjects include abandonment, prostitution, lesbianism, sado-masochism, drunkenness, superstition, and murder.

Rainey typically was accompanied by a pianist or jazz band, although she did record with jug bands and string bands. Her performance venues were traveling shows, usually known as minstrel shows and tent shows, and especially theaters on the Theater Owners Booking Association (TOBA.) circuit, a franchise of between thirty and forty-five theaters in the South and the Midwest. Typically, Rainey wore beaded gowns, a headband, feather boas, and gold jewelry designed to capture the attention of the audience.

Bessie Smith (1894–1937): The most famous classic blues singer of this period was Bessie Smith, who began recording before Ma Rainey. Around 1912, Smith joined the Moses Stokes Company, in which Ma Rainey was the headliner. It is impossible to know exactly how Rainey influenced Smith; however, it is certain that every performer in the show would have been well acquainted with the performance style of the show's star. In 1923, Smith signed a one-year contract with Columbia Records, which was renewed yearly until 1931. Her first recording session produced "Down Hearted Blues" and "Gulf Coast Blues," which sold 780,000 copies during the first six months and established her as the leading blues singer. By 1924, she was the highest paid African-American performer in the country and hit the pinnacle of her career in 1925 when she recorded with Louis Armstrong, the jazz trumpet star also widely known for his singing. In 1929, she appeared in the film *St. Louis Blues*, singing the title song. This is the only available film footage of her performing.

The economic depression of the 1930s had a dramatic effect on the country and, although some forms of entertainment managed to stay afloat because of their close association with the upper class, the sale of blues recordings slowed, as did the performance opportunities for blues artists. By 1931, Smith's recordings had stopped selling, and Columbia did not record her again until convinced to do so by John Hammond. In 1933, Hammond found her working as a hostess in a nightclub in Philadelphia and recorded a series of sides with her that later became standards in the Columbia record catalog, including "Gimme a Pigfoot." In 1937, Smith had a successful twelve-week engagement at Connie's Inn in New York, and John Hammond had talked his superiors at Columbia into offering her another contract. On September 26, 1937, while traveling between engagements, Smith's Packard was run off the road, and she died of loss of blood due to a lack of rapid medical attention. Smith's complete recordings have been released on CD and are excellent examples of classic city blues.

Other Classic City Blues Singers

Ida Cox	Sara Martin	Trixie Smith
Bertha "Chippie" Hill	Clara Smith	Victoria Spivey
Alberta Hunter	Mamie Smith	Sippie Wallace

The 1920s blues period ended with the Depression, but not before the fusing of both blues styles by the piano-guitar team of Leroy Carr and Scrapper Blackwell. Of course, recordings in the earlier styles were still released, but their popularity was dwindling. Carr's singing exemplified the city blues approach, blues piano, a stable twelve-bar form, and distinct diction. Blackwell added a touch of the country blues with his single-line guitar playing. Their most popular recording was "How Long, How Long Blues" in 1928. Muddy Waters said he was well aware of the recording and that it may have been the first blues recording he owned; if these recordings reached Waters in his rural community, they certainly reached other small communities and must have influenced many artists.

JAZZ ROOTS OF ROCK

The emergence of blues and its blending with ragtime around 1895 was one of the events that gave birth to the style known as *jazz*. The blues form and its style of melismatic ornamentation were commonly used in jazz. As with blues, the origins of jazz are obscure, but they certainly had to do with the interactions of the newly freed slaves and the New Orleans Creole musicians. The "Creoles of Color" in New Orleans were a distinct social class with both African and European ancestry. The term *Creole* refers to the original settlers of New Orleans and was used by the Spanish when they bought the territory from Napoleon. The Creoles' musical training was primarily European, and typical performance situations were opera companies and symphony orchestras, as well as dancing-style entertainment. In 1896, after the U.S. Supreme Court reaffirmed the "separate but equal" doctrine in its *Plessy v. Ferguson* decision, the status of the Creole class was lowered to that of the newly freed slaves. A musical result of these laws was that African musical characteristics, held in suspension by slavery, once again fused with the European musical characteristics of the Creoles. The fusion resulted in a new method of approaching dance and other functional music. Legend has it that cornetist Buddy Bolden was the first to mix elements of the blues with ragtime and other current music styles. For this reason, Bolden is considered to be the first jazz cornetist and jazz band leader.

The blues has been an important element in jazz but has remained a separate entity that developed along a parallel course; some jazz is blues but not all blues is considered jazz. As mentioned previously, the first recorded blues by a jazz band, the Original Dixieland Jass Band, was "Livery Stable Blues" (1917). Many of the most popular early jazz recordings were also blues: "Dippermouth Blues" by King Oliver, "Deadman Blues" by Jelly Roll Morton, and "West End Blues" by Louis Armstrong.

Although the bands recorded many blues songs, they were still identified as jazz bands rather than blues bands. That designation was generally reserved for ensembles that specialized in blues. In the late 1930s, however, the Kansas City band of Count Basie became associated with a style that relied more heavily on the blues than his swing-era counterparts. Basie began using a singer, Jimmy Rushing, whose method of delivering the blues became known as *blues shouting*. Singers in this style are known as Kansas City Blues Shouters. This is not so much an identifiable style as it is a label identifying the music of a particular time and place. The shouting style was similar to the way most blues singers delivered lyrics in the entertainment industry: A singer was forced to project the voice because the lack of adequate sound amplification made it difficult to be heard over a jazz band.

Joe Turner and Boogie Woogie

The most important link between the blues shouter and rock and roll was Joe Turner (1911–1985). In the 1930s, Joe Turner was a Kansas City bartender who, according to Basie, was "*the* blues singer in that town," and often worked with pianist Pete Johnson. It was with Johnson that Turner appeared in the "From Spirituals to Swing" concert John Hammond staged at Carnegie Hall in 1938. It was this performance, along with others that night, that helped fuel the boogie woogie revival that took place at the end of the 1930s.

In 1951, Joe Turner signed with Atlantic Records and recorded a series of records that were, by that time, identified by *Billboard* magazine as *Rhythm and Blues*. The series included "Chains of Love" (No. 4, 1951), "Hush Honey" (No. 21, 1953), "Shake, Rattle and Roll" (No. 5, 1954), and "Flip, Flop, Fly" (No. 15, 1955). "Shake, Rattle and Roll," a twelve-bar blues, was covered by Bill Haley in the same year and was one of his first national hits, making it one of the first important recordings in rock. This song helps illustrate the link between rock and earlier styles. Turner's vocal style in 1954 was practically identical to his style in 1939, when he and Pete Johnson had recorded "Cherry Red." This being the case, it is possible to defend the statement that a major element (the singing style) of rhythm and blues, and thus rock and roll, can be traced back at least as far as 1939.

Boogie Woogie

Boogie woogie was first used to describe a piano style and then later a vocal and instrumental style. The first use of the term in a song title was "The Boogie Rag" (1917) by Wilbur Sweatman, and in 1927 Jimmy Blythe cut a player-piano roll called "Boogie Woogie Blues," which used some boogie woogie rhythm. Clarence "Pine Top" Smith (1904–1929) recorded "Pine Top's Boogie Woogie" at the end of December 1928, and this became the recording most often cited as the first boogie woogie recording.

Some scholars have suggested the boogie woogie rhythmic pattern arrived in the twentieth century via Texas guitar styles. Evidence cited is Blind Lemon Jefferson's recording of "Match Box Blues" (1927), which used the boogie rhythm on one section; however, Jefferson could have been imitating a piano style that had not yet been recorded. Earlier, Jefferson recorded a song titled "Booger Rooger Blues" (1926), but this recording does not use the boogie woogie rhythm or the phrase. The use of the phrase in the title, without using the characteristic rhythmic pattern, suggests that it may have had other extra-musical social meanings, such as "to dance" or "to party."

Boogie woogie is typified by a repeating bass line that outlines the chord with a skipping rhythm; the form is generally twelve-bar blues. The boogie woogie rhythmic feel can vary from swing eighth-notes to almost straight eighth-notes. It is interesting to note that the rhythmic feel of "Pine Top's Boogie Woogie" used straighter eighth notes than did the boogie woogie of the late 1930s.

After Pine Top's death three weeks after the recording session, not much happened with the style until John Hammond's "From Spirituals to Swing" Carnegie Hall concert, which included several boogie woogie pianists. After the concert, boogie woogie patterns began appearing in many swing band arrangements, the most famous of which is Jimmy Dorsey's "Boogie Woogie," and "Beat Me Daddy, Eight to the Bar." The Andrews Sisters, a popular 1940s vocal group, recorded many songs with a boogie-style arrangement. The style is so infectious that in the early 1970s, Bette Midler reached number eight in the Billboard charts with an interesting remake of the Andrews Sisters' "Boogie Woogie Bugle Boy."

Jump Bands

In the 1940s, while America was engaged in World War II, *big band swing* was the most popular music in the country. However, by the time the war ended, the power of the swing era had faded. Although swing music was used by the government as a means of wartime morale-building, many factors, including rationing, entertainment taxes, the ASCAP strike, and the Musicians Union strike, helped hasten the demise of the style. The most important factor, however, was more likely a generational shift in musical taste.

During the period, musicians began to form smaller bands that used the swing band format and featured songs using boogie woogie rhythms. These groups were known as *jump bands*. The jump band consisted of a rhythm section and a reduced horn section (tenor saxophone and a combination of other saxophones, trumpets, and possibly trombones). The horns functioned to provide riffs to accompany the singer, who had become the focal point of the music. The tenor sax was the principal instrument for solo improvisation, and the jump band was the prototype for one strain of rock and roll.

Louis Jordan (1908–1975): Louis Jordan was one of the earliest and most successful jump bandleaders. He left Chick Webb's swing band in 1938 to form a smaller quintet known as the Tympany Five ("Five" was used in the name of the group regardless of the actual size). Jordan was an extremely vibrant performer who made several films and, according to *Billboard*, almost crossed over to the European-American market. Among his hits were "Five Guys Named Moe" (1943), "G.I. Jive" (1944), "Caledonia Boogie" (1954), "Mop Hop" (1946), "Choo Choo Ch'Boogie" (1946), "Buzz Me" (1946), "Salt Pork, W. VA. (1946)," "Ain't That Just Like a Woman" (1946), "Don't Worry About That Mule" (1946), and "That Chick's Too Young to Fry" (1946). He was so popular that he held nine of the top fifteen positions of the *Billboard* year's end race music charts in 1946, and five of the top ten positions in 1947. It is interesting to note that the producer of Jordan's Decca hits was Milt Gabler, who was still a producer at Decca when Bill Haley was signed. Gabler stated that during recording sessions, he taught Jordan-style riffs to Haley's band, the Comets, which helped give Haley's recordings the same boogie woogie feel as Jordan's.[22]

Wynonie Harris (1915–1969): Wynonie Harris was another popular jump artist whose number-one 1947 hit "Good Rocking Tonight" was one of the songs that early rock artists learned and copied. Elvis Presley's version of that song is a good example. Elvis did his best to copy the energetic delivery of jump performers, but Presley's version sounded different from Harris's. One reason for the difference is that, in the accompaniment, Harris used a jump band and Elvis used "Scotty and Bill," a western swing ensemble. Some observers explain the difference between the two recordings as the difference between rock and roll and rhythm and blues. However, the authors would prefer this explanation: It is the essential difference between the genuine article (Harris) and a copy (Elvis).

Lionel Hampton: Jazz vibraphonist Lionel Hampton (1908-2002) had a very popular jump and boogie band during this period. Hampton's popularity

was such that he did not need to reduce the size of the band to remain prof-
itable and had the most popular rhythm and blues recording of 1946, "Hey-
Ba-Ba-Re Bop." *Scat* syllables like those in this title were used later in *doo-wop*
and in Gene Vincent's "Be Bop A Lula." Although he has not been labeled
rhythm and blues since the late 1940s, Hampton's band was an example of the
close relationship between jazz bands of the 1940s and rhythm and blues of
the same period.

Jump bands were responsible for establishing several of the important
musical characteristics later used by rock groups of the mid-1950s, including
incorporating the words "rock" or "rock and roll" in the titles of their recordings. Some late-1940s jump tunes using "rock" in the title are "Good Rockin'
Tonight" (1947) by Wynonie Harris, "Rockin' at Midnight" (1949) by Roy
Brown, "Rockin' Blues" (1950) by Johnnie Otis, and "Rock the Joint" (1951)
by Jimmy Cavallo.

BLUES OF THE 1940s

Both world wars caused an increase in migration among the African-
American population. During World War II, factories in the North were in
need of labor, so they advertised jobs with attractive wages in Southern newspapers, which lured many African-Americans away from their Southern
homes. Among them were blues performers such as Muddy Waters. After the
war, soldiers, who had experienced life away from home and were reluctant to
return to their old social circumstances, settled in the Northern cities, especially Chicago and Detroit. Between 1940 and 1950, census figures show that
154,000 of these migrants arrived in Chicago from the South, half of those
from Mississippi. Although Chicago was closer, some segments of the population headed west toward California. The type of blues preferred in Chicago
was closely related to the Delta blues; however, the West tended to prefer more
jazz/jump-oriented blues.

This shift in population created new markets for the blues, and in the
1940s, this need was filled by many new independent record companies, often
called *indies*. Chess Records in Chicago became famous for recording musicians from the Delta in an electric setting, whereas the independents in Los
Angeles, such as Modern and Black and White, recorded a smoother type of
urban blues.

The terms used to identify various blues styles are sometimes confusing
and lack concrete definitions. *Urban blues* is often applied to all the blues types
that developed after the Depression, but some use the term just to describe the
blues of the 1940s. Ascribing terms to African-American music has always
been problematic, and record companies and popularity charting agencies
have used terms like *race music, sepia,* and *Harlem Hit Parade* to describe the

music. In 1949, *Billboard* magazine, the most respected of the popularity charting agencies, adopted the phrase *rhythm and blues* to refer to its African-American music charts. This identified two different types of recordings; there were blues and rhythm records. Today we use the phrase *rhythm and blues*, or *R&B*, as if it were only one style of music.

Smooth Urban Blues

The West Coast produced a jazzy relaxed blues tradition that can best be described as "smooth urban piano-playing" blues singers. The authors will refer to *smooth urban blues* to discuss this often overlooked style. These singers delivered the blues in a crooning style with only a tinge of their gospel backgrounds. Many of the artists came from Texas or the Southwest, the same region that produced T-Bone Walker and Charlie Christian. In some cases, there is some crossover between the jump blues and the smooth urban blues.

Nat "King" Cole's inclusion may surprise those who know only of his crooning pop hits, but Cole was the most important model for the smooth urban piano blues style of Charles Brown, Cecil Grant, Ray Charles (the pre-soul Ray Charles), and others. Cole formed the King Cole Trio with guitarist Oscar Moore and bassist Wesley Prince and began recording in 1939. Following their 1942 hit recording "That Ain't Right," they were asked to record for then-new Capitol Records. Cole's first Capitol recording, "Straighten Up and Fly Right," was very successful and reached number nine on the pop charts in 1944. He recorded several other sides for Capitol before becoming a pop ballad crooner. Worthy of mention is "Route 66," not the theme for the television show, but the same song recorded by the Rolling Stones and others. By the 1950s, Cole's ballad style recordings regularly reached the top of the pop charts. The blandness of these records was part of the reason young European-American teens began looking towards rhythm and blues for more energetic music.

Other West Coast transplants playing in this style were Charles Brown (Texas), originally with Johnny Moore's Three Blazers (Johnny was Oscar Moore's older brother); Ivory Joe Hunter (Texas); Cecil Grant (Tennessee); Amos Milburn (Texas); Roy Brown (New Orleans); and Ray Charles (Florida). Guitarists T-Bone Walker and B. B. King could also be included in this style because of the cool emotional tone of their singing and the jazz roots of their instrumental style.

Chicago Blues

Another type of urban blues, the Chicago blues, is essentially electrified Mississippi Delta Blues; the Chicago blues is on the opposite side of the spectrum from the smooth urban blues of the West Coast. Chess Records,

operated by Phil and Leonard Chess, was the most visible company recording the style, although they later recorded other styles of rhythm and blues.
Typically, a Chicago blues band consisted of guitar, bass, drums, harmonica,
piano, and possibly a second guitar. Guitarists would often use the Delta
bottleneck technique, which took on a new dimension when added to the
sustaining power of an amplified guitar; it is a metallic howling sound heavily laden with upper overtones. This was possibly the "king of guitar" sound
that rock guitarists of the late 1960s were trying to duplicate when they
added electronics to purposely distort their sound. The harmonica player
filled a role similar to that of the sax player of the jump band by blowing riffs
behind the singer and intertwining with the melodic line. Many of the
British Invasion bands tried to emulate the sound of these Chess recording
artists, especially the Rolling Stones, who named themselves after a Muddy
Waters song. So important was the lure of Chess studios to the Rolling
Stones that they visited and recorded there during their first tour of the
United States.

Muddy Waters (1915–1980): The most important Chicago blues performer, and possibly the creator of the style, was Muddy Waters (McKinley
Morganfield). When he was three, his mother moved to the Stovall Plantation
in Mississippi, where he worked as a tractor driver, entertainer, and juke-joint
operator until he moved to Chicago. Waters began playing guitar at seventeen
and, like many others, ordered his instrument from the Sears catalog. He
learned to play guitar by imitating the Delta masters, such as Charlie Patton,
Son House, and Tommy Johnson, and from the recordings of Blind Lemon
Jefferson, Robert Johnson, Memphis Minnie, Leroy Carr, Lonnie Johnson, and
Tampa Red.

In 1941, Alan Lomax and John Work were again recording in the South
for the Library of Congress and searching for Robert Johnson (not knowing
that he had been poisoned). In the process they discovered Muddy Waters.
They recorded him singing "Country Blues" and "I Be's Troubled," and a year
later they returned for more. In 1943, Muddy left the Delta for Chicago where,
in addition to factory work, he began entertaining. In 1944, he bought his first
electric guitar and applied it to the Delta blues.

Waters made his first professional recordings as a sideman in 1946 when
agent-promoter Walter Melrose arranged a session with Columbia Records
for Sunnyland Slim. Later, in 1947, Waters recorded for the Aristocrat label
owned by the Chess brothers. At that session Muddy had attempted a more
modern urban sound, but at a second session in 1948, he reverted to the bottleneck style and recorded "I Can't Be Satisfied" and "I Feel Like Going Home."
These were an unexpected success, and the first pressing sold out within

twelve hours. His updated big Delta sound resonated in the transplanted Southern community.

Howlin' Wolf (1910–1976): Howlin' Wolf (Chester Burnett), also from the Delta area, had once been a student of Charlie Patton on the Dockery Plantation and had traveled with Robert Johnson for a while. Wolf earned his living as a farmer until 1948, when he moved to West Memphis to pursue a full-time musical career. In West Memphis, Wolf earned a reputation that landed him a radio show on WKEM, where he came to the attention of Sam Phillips. Phillips recorded Wolf in 1951, before the Memphis Recording Service became Sun Records and before he discovered Elvis. Phillips recorded "How Many More Years" and "Moanin' at Midnight" and then sold Wolf's masters and contract to Chess Records in Chicago. Braced by the success of the records, Wolf moved to Chicago in 1952 or 1953. His next hit, "Smokestack Lightnin'," came in 1956, and in the early 1960s he recorded a series of classics written by Willie Dixon: "Wang Dang Doodle," "Spoonful," "Back Door Man," "The Little Red Rooster," "I Ain't Superstitious," and "Goin' Down Slow." The recordings became important models for British Invasion groups like the Rolling Stones, the Yardbirds, and the Animals.

John Lee Hooker: John Lee Hooker was born in Clarksdale, Mississippi, in 1917 and moved to Detroit in 1943 to work in the auto factories. His style is electrified Mississippi Delta blues. Born Hooker. Hooker claims his style was derived from that of his stepfather, also a blues guitarist, who occasionally worked with Charlie Patton. Hooker's guitar playing is similar to that of other Delta bluesmen, but his method of construction is quite different, perhaps even a reflection of what nineteenth-century blues was like. The guitar style has been described accurately as "incessant one-chord vamps," though he does imply motion to the second chord in the blues harmonic structure (the subdominant) by moving one or two notes and maintaining the common chord tones. Modern Records in Los Angeles released his biggest records between 1948 and 1951: "Boogie Children" (No. 10, 1949), "I'm in the Mood" (No. 14, 1951), "Hobo Blues" (No. 29, 1949), and "Crawling Kingsnake Blues." Later, from 1955 to 1964, he recorded for Chicago's VeeJay Records and reached the charts several times. The most famous recording was "Boom, Boom" (1962), later covered by the Yardbirds, one of the first post-Beatles British Invasion groups. In recent years, Hooker has experienced renewed visibility after appearing in the movie *The Blues Brothers* and recording with Carlos Santana. In 1997 he released a new album, *Don't Look Back*, that paired Hooker with Van Morrison and Los Lobos.

Muddy Waters, Wolf, and Hooker serve as an important link between the origins of the blues and the groups of the British invasion. All the singers have recorded one-chord vamp style blues. "Smokestack Lightnin' " (Wolf), "Mannish Boy" (Muddy Waters), and most of Hooker's songs have been remade by British Invasion groups.

Electric Guitar Urban Blues

The guitar is the most important instrument in the development of the country blues, and without its transition to electric guitar, rhythm and blues would not have been possible. Many of the Delta guitar stylists ended up in Chicago, maintaining the tradition of roughly hewn blues, but others merged their styles with more modern jazz styles. Two blues guitar players who do not fit easily into any categories are Aaron Thibeaux (T-Bone) Walker and Riley B. (B. B.) King. Both artists have strong country blues roots, yet both played a brand of blues that was every bit as urban as Nat King Cole's or Charles Brown's.

T-Bone Walker (1910–1975), is the link between the Texas blues of Blind Lemon Jefferson and the jazz-inspired urban blues of the late 1940s. Walker was the first bluesman to use an electric guitar when he recorded "T-Bone Blues" with Les Hite's Cotton Club Orchestra in 1939, although he had been using the amplified guitar since 1935.

T-Bone Walker

Walker was born on May 28, 1910, in Linden, Texas, and soon traveled with his family to Dallas. Most of his family members, his mother, father, and uncles, played guitar or some sort of stringed instrument and performed together on Sundays. Walker's musical influences were Lonnie Johnson, the nimble-fingered blues guitarist who recorded with both Louis Armstrong and Duke Ellington, and Scrapper Blackwell, who recorded with Leroy Carr. Another important influence was Blind Lemon Jefferson, who had developed a friendship with Walker's family and visited every Sunday for the private family music sessions. Walker served as a lead man for Jefferson and took him to the nightclubs up and down Central Avenue, where he played for tips.

In 1933, while they were still in school, Walker met young Charlie Christian, who would later become the first important jazz electric guitarist. Walker and Christian often performed together as a duo at dances and on the streets. In 1934, T-Bone moved to the Los Angeles area, where he played in various small groups and big bands. There, he also began experimenting with amplified acoustic guitars. By 1939, Walker had switched to electric guitar and developed a style of finger vibrato that influenced other blues greats such as B. B. King. In 1942, he recorded "Mean Old World" on Capitol with the band of Freddie Slack. The record was as successful as possible, given the wartime rationing of shellac, the prime component of 78 RPM records. Walker's most famous recording, "Call It Stormy Monday" (1947), was probably the most influential blues of its time and is in the smooth West Coast *urban blues* style. The band had the size and instrumentation of a jazz combo: trumpet, tenor saxophone, piano, bass, and drums, with Walker singing and playing guitar. His recording of "T-Bone Boogie" (1945) is in the jump style and foreshadows the sound of the 1950s rock guitar style.

B. B. King: B. B. King (born 1925), serves as the link between the Delta blues and the modern urban blues. King, from Indianola, Mississippi, worked as a tenant farmer and a plantation tractor driver. He made thirty dollars a week, but after the war he found he could make more money singing the blues on the streets. He played guitar by age fourteen, and listened to recordings by Charlie Christian, Blind Lemon Jefferson, and Django Reinhardt, which helped him form his concept of guitar playing. In 1946, he moved to Memphis and stayed with his cousin, bluesman Bukka White, for about a year. White always played a bottleneck Delta blues style, and King says he never learned to use the bottleneck well, so instead he learned to "trill" his finger in an effort to mimic the sound. In 1949, he made some guest appearances on Sonny Boy Williamson's KWEM Hadacol Tonic radio show in West Memphis and eventually acquired the sponsorship of Pepticon Tonic for his own show on WDIA in Memphis. King played the latest jump blues records on his show and continued to develop his single-line style by playing along. Certainly T-Bone's recordings were among those played on his show. In about 1950 King began recording for the Baharis (Saul, Joe, and Jules) and in 1952 had a hit on the RPM label with "Three O'Clock Blues." Once his recording and personal appearances increased, he left WDIA and became a full-time musician.

Since then, King has been one of the most popular blues artists, and his guitar style has been the model for many rock musicians. Although he lived and developed musically in the Delta and in Memphis, his style of blues was not typical of the Memphis artists who tended to have a raw edge to their sound. King has the sound and delivery of the West Coast urban blues.

COUNTRY MUSIC ROOTS OF ROCK

Country music, first known by the music industry as *hillbilly*, and later as *country and western*, developed out of the American *folk* music tradition. While folk and country music may appear to be separate and unrelated to rock and roll, there are many indications to the contrary. The country influences of Chuck Berry's "Maybellene," Elvis Presley's "Blue Moon of Kentucky," the protest songs of Bob Dylan and Joan Baez, and the Southern rock of the Allman Brothers Band all draw on the same traditions that came before them and ran concurrently with them. This section of the text is devoted to the roots of country music and the rise in its popularity, culminating with the emergence of Elvis Presley.

The folk music of America was, in the earliest years of this country, virtually the same as British folk music. The Anglo-Celtic traditions of folk songs, ballads, dances, and instrumental pieces were relatively unchanged when they were transplanted in America. The British ballad tradition seems to have made an especially large impression on American folk music. Ballads utilize a story line that reflects current politics, social commentaries, and particularly memorable events and personalities, such as murderers and outlaws. The principal differences between American folk ballads and their British counterparts were in the lyrics. As time passed, each generation lost touch with the lives of their ancestors, so the songs of British society, politics, and history had less relevance in their lives. Popular songs reflecting the American experience, such as "The Titanic," "John Henry," "Casey Jones," and numerous cowboy and railroad songs began to appear and gradually replaced British ballads.

Despite some pockets of isolation such as the Appalachian and Ozark mountains, which aided in preserving traditional British ballad traditions, most folk music in America underwent gradual but significant changes. Folk music doesn't resist change; it embraces it. British folk music aggregated with other folk music brought to America by immigrants to form innumerable variations. Cajun music, Latin music, German polkas, religious music, blues, and many others are all a part of the American folk culture.

One interesting question to ask concerning the different styles that contributed to country music is how these characteristics combined. Radios and phonographs did not proliferate until the 1920s, so exchange of influences had to occur through direct personal contact. Most Southern communities remained relatively isolated from their neighbors, so the opportunity for mass cultural integration was slim. Despite these conditions and the reality of segregation in the South, there were many other opportunities for interaction. Work activities such as railroad crews, religious activities, and traveling tent and medicine shows are a few of the many possibilities. Many of the tent and medicine shows originated in larger urban areas and traveled to the smaller, rural areas of the South. Local musicians were able to hear new music performed at these shows and some even joined the shows en route, thereby adding their local performing style to the mix. Partly because of this traveling, many Southern folk songs were known all over the South despite the isolation of plantations and other communities. During the assimilation process, musical styles, melodies, harmonies, and rhythms were often altered by performers to accommodate local tastes.

Musical Characteristics

Vocal sounds in country music were often nasal and pinched and had a strained quality to them. The vocal harmony of the nineteenth-century country singers was usually not very elaborate and was possibly the result of the *shaped* note or *sacred* harp singing style used in Southern churches.[23] Another possible source for this vocal harmony was the sound of the open strings of the violin when played together or the sound of the bagpipe drone so common in the British Isles.

The earliest country bands consisted of the fiddle (violin), five-stringed banjo, guitar, and some sort of bass. These string bands, as they came to be known, usually did not include vocalists and usually provided music for dancing; string bands like these are still common in *bluegrass* music. The fiddle, probably because of its portability, became the first popular instrument in the United States. The banjo is a modified version of an African instrument, and it could be fabricated without extensive tools: a stick for a neck attached to a gourd (calabash), with a skin stretched over it for resonance. In early colonial America, Thomas Jefferson referred to the banjo as the "banjar," which was then a fretless, four-stringed instrument. A short, fifth string that acts as a sort of drone was added in the 1830s, and was made popular and probably invented by Joel (Joe) Walker Sweeney of Virginia, a popular minstrel performer in the United States and in Britain. The guitar was not used extensively by musicians in the early years of the country music. In the colonial period, the guitar was associated more with the upper classes of the Northeast. Only gradually did guitar use move south, until it became a popular element of the string band. The violin-guitar-banjo combination dates back at least to the 1870s and was important as a model for future string bands.

Later additions to the string band include the mandolin and the Hawaiian steel guitar. By the 1930s, many of the steel guitarists in country bands were either Hawaiian or were taught by Hawaiians. The steel guitar remains an indispensable element of Nashville music, and is often the only sonic clue that a recording is country music.

Country Artists

In the 1920s, through the popularization of radio and recordings, country music began to flourish and become a commercial commodity. Country music gained popularity across the country, although it would always be most popular in the South. By 1930, country music accounted for as much as twenty-five percent of all popular record sales. The repertoire of a country musician typically included tunes based on British folk music, Tin Pan Alley songs written in a country fashion, and some original and anonymous folk tunes.

Alexander Campbell "Eck" Robertson, a Texas fiddler known for his virtuoso displays at fiddle contests all over the South, and Henry Gilliland, an old-time fiddler from Virginia, were probably the first country musicians to record. In 1922, they went to New York and asked for an audition at Victor Records,[24] even though country music had never before been commercially recorded. They were allowed to do some test recordings at Victor. One of those recordings was "Sallie Gooden," a flashy fiddle number that would forever be associated with Robertson. Sales of the recording were reasonably good, but Robertson was not invited to record again until 1930.

Record producer Ralph Peer was responsible for the first on-location recordings of both blues and country musicians. His most important country music discoveries were Jimmy Rodgers and the Carter Family. In 1923, at the suggestion of a local contact, Polk Brockman, Peer went to Atlanta to record Fiddlin' John Carson. While there, he also recorded other rural artists including bluesman Barbecue Bob. Since it was not clear whether there was a national market for this crude country music, the record company released Carson's recording of "The Little Old Log Cabin in the Lane" only in Atlanta. Sales of the recording surpassed the label's initial expectations, and it was soon issued and advertised nationwide. This established a national market for country music.

Ralph Peer was also responsible for first using the word *hillbilly* to describe the genre when he named Al Hopkins's band "The Original Hillbillies."[25]

Hillbilly had always been considered a demeaning word to any Southerner; however, Hopkins had little power to change the recording company's choice. The term was used by the record industry to describe Southern rural music until 1949 when *Billboard* coined the phrase *country and western* for their country music popularity charts. As with rhythm and blues, Country and Western identified two distinct styles: hillbilly music and cowboy songs.

During the late 1920s, two acts–the Carter Family and Jimmie Rodgers – established the style of country vocal music that was the model for the next two decades. Both acts were discovered in 1927 by Ralph Peer at the same location after he advertised for local talent in a Bristol, Tennessee, newspaper.

The recordings of the Carter Family, the most popular group in early country music, often had a religious theme and conveyed the values of many Southern listeners. The family consisted of A. P. Carter, his wife, Sara (on autoharp or second guitar), and his sister-in-law, Maybelle Addington Carter (on lead guitar and occasionally steel guitar). Maybelle used a "thumb-brush," or "clawhammer," technique on the guitar, which is characterized by the plucking of the melody on the bass strings with the thumb while the fingers brush the strings in a downward stroke, creating a steady rhythm. The group remained popular into the 1940s, and other versions of the family, with "Mother" Maybelle and her three daughters, also performed as the Carter Family. (Maybelle's daughter June married Johnny Cash).

Jimmie Rodgers (1897–1933), often referred to as the "Father of Modern Country Music," recorded 111 songs during his short career. Rodgers, like his father, worked on the railroad at the age of fourteen. With this experience, he earned the nickname the Singing Brakeman. The railroad background gave Rodgers a free, "rambling man" image and put him in close contact with African-American musicians and their blues style.

Rodgers, like many others, began his career as a black-faced minstrel singer in a medicine show in 1925 and began his recording career in 1927 when he answered Ralph Peer's newspaper ad. One of the most unique characteristics of Rodgers's singing was his yodeling. Yodeling had been a part of the minstrel tradition since the mid-nineteenth century and had been recorded previously by country singer Riley Puckett in 1924. But Rodgers's yodel—known as the "blue yodel"—was his own creation. In 1927, he made his first of twelve recordings under the title of "Blue Yodel," some of which were in an adapted blues form that differed from African-American blues. When Rodgers accompanied himself, he omitted the instrumental response so essential to the blues form; his recordings with studio bands have instrumental responses supplied by professional musicians who were well aware of the established form.

Despite the fact that Rodgers's peak recording years were during the Depression, his recordings outsold those of most of Victor's other artists. As popular as he was, his professional career was limited by tuberculosis, which sapped his strength and restricted his touring options. Jimmie Rodgers died in 1933 while in New York for his final recording session. At that session, his health was so poor that a cot was placed in the studio for him to rest on between takes.

Radio Shows

Early recording stars achieved an additional level of success with the help of radio broadcasts. The radio was, in fact, the phonograph's main competitor: As radio popularity rapidly grew in the 1920s, record sales plummeted. In 1920, commercial broadcasting began when KDKA in Pittsburgh became the first radio station. In 1923, WBAP in Fort Worth became the first radio station to broadcast a barn dance show; by 1924, there were many imitators.

Two of the most influential shows were WLS's National Barn Dance and WSM's Barn Dance. In 1924, WLS (World's Largest Store, broadcast from Chicago and owned by Sears-Roebuck until the late twenties) featured popular tunes as well as country and folk tunes. In 1925, the National Life and Accident Insurance Company of Nashville started station WSM (We Shield Millions), to help sell its insurance, and hired rival announcer George D. Hay away from WLS in Chicago to host its barn dance program. The WSM Barn Dance debuted in 1925, emphasizing instrumental music, and in 1927 changed the name of the show to the Grand Ole Opry. Roy Acuff took over as host in 1939 and steered the program to its present position. Through the years, the Opry has been broadcast from several venues around Nashville (all being too small) until its final move to Opryland Park in 1974.

The Grand Ole Opry inspired many local shows around the nation and created a demand for local talent. Every area had a barn dance program and the need to fill radio airtime gave many local performers an entry into show business. The tradition of the barn dance continued, obviously with the Grand Ole Opry, but also with the Louisiana Hayride, which debuted in 1948 and was important to the careers of Hank Williams, Elvis Presley, and many others.

Western Music

Another phenomenon of the 1930s was the rise of *cowboy* and *western* music. Cowboy songs date back to the nineteenth century but were not widely known by Americans until they were recorded. Some cowboy singers were recorded in the 1920s, such as Carl Sprague (1895–1978), who recorded "When the Work's All Done This Fall" in 1925. But the popularity of Western singers was greatly influenced by Hollywood cowboy movies in the 1930s. Westerns had always been a popular movie genre, and the addition of sound made the singing cowboy possible. One of the most influential singing cowboys was Gene Autry (1907–1998), who began performing in 1927, copying Jimmie Rodgers's yodeling style. In 1934, he moved to Hollywood and started a very successful film career, eventually appearing in more than ninety films.

Vocal groups were also popular in the Western style, and the Sons of the Pioneers were the most popular of these. The Pioneers included Bob Nolan, who wrote much of their material, Tim Spencer and Leonard Slye. Slye left the group in 1937 to start a movie career and changed his name to Roy Rogers (1911–1998), possibly attempting associate himself with Jimmie Rodgers's memory. Early in his movie career he met and married Dale Evans, and they had a long career in movies and television as "King of the Cowboys and Queen of the West."

The Western theme seemed to spread throughout the nation, and country singers began using names and images of the West, even artists who had no connection to the West. In 1949, the western theme had so enmeshed itself with country music that *Billboard* magazine renamed its hillbilly music charts country and western. By the 1950s, country and western artists were wearing outlandish attire with rhinestones and fringe that no real cowboy would wear.

Western Swing

With the popularity of big band swing and boogie woogie in the 1930s and 1940s, it was natural for country music to adopt some of the characteristics. The combination of swing and cowboy music resulted in a new style called *western swing*. Originally a designation for string bands that came from Texas in the 1920s, western swing was used to describe western bands that incorporated a jazz-band format and used improvisation much like a jazz group. The instrumentation of the western swing band reflects the fusion of the styles: fiddle, guitar, trumpets, saxophones, steel guitar, and rhythm section.

Perhaps the most important western swing group was Bob Wills and the Texas Playboys. Bob Wills (1905–1975), left the Light Crust Doughboys in 1933 to form the Playboys, and moved to Tulsa, Oklahoma, in 1934 for a radio show on KVOO. At times, the band consisted of eighteen members playing saxophones, brass, electric guitar, steel guitar, drums, and Wills on fiddle. Wills was not a very proficient improviser, but he surrounded himself with players who were skilled in blues, jazz, and country. The lead vocalist for the group was Tommy Duncan, but Wills was always contributing falsetto "ahh-haas" and Fats Waller–like interjections during the course of a song. With all the vocalizing that Wills did, the music had a very loose and humorous feel.

Two of the group's most popular recordings were "New San Antonio Rose" (1940), and "Roly Poly" (1946), which was later covered by Bing Crosby. Other popular western swing bands were Milton Brown and his Musical Brownies, and the Prairie Ramblers, featuring Patsy Montana.

Honky Tonk

In Texas during the 1930s and 1940s, another brand of country music was brewing, called *honky tonk*. Honky tonk refers to a style of music as well as the rural bars where this music was performed. The repeal of Prohibition in the 1930s gave rise to honky tonk as well as the jukebox. The themes of honky tonk songs were alcohol, divorce, affairs, and hard times (Webb Pierce's "Back Street Affair" and "There Stands the Glass" are good examples)—a long way from the family values of the Carter Family. Much like the Chicago blues, these songs were also popular in the industrialized North where Southerners who had left family and farm to seek better financial conditions were trapped in an unforgiving urban setting and confronted by many of the societal ills addressed in blues and honky tonk music.

Honky tonk bands often used electric guitar, electric steel guitar, piano, and sometimes even drums. The artists, such as Ernest Tubb (1914–1984), Floyd Tillman (born 1914), and Moon Mullican (1909–1967), were primarily from Texas. Tillman was especially known for the cheating song "Slipping Around" (1949). He followed it with "I'll Never Slip Around Again" (1949). Tillman's voice was one of the smoothest baritones around, and his style of note-bending influenced many performers, including Willie Nelson.

Undeniably, the greatest influence in country music in the late 1940s and early 1950s was Hank Williams (1923–1952). Born in Alabama, Williams sang a variety of tunes from gospel to honky tonk and was influenced by African-American music as well. He made some recordings with the small Sterling record company in 1946, but it was in 1947, when he signed with MGM, that he recorded some of his most popular tunes, such as "Your Cheatin' Heart" (1952), "Hey, Good Lookin'" (1951), "Cold, Cold Heart" (1951), "Jambalaya" (1952), and "Move It On Over." In 1949, after a short stint with the Louisiana Hayride, Williams joined the Grand Ole Opry. With his popularity at an all-time high, he signed a movie contract in 1951, but he had a heart attack in 1953, complicated by drugs and alcohol, and died before he had an opportunity to make any films.

Teenagers growing up in the South during the early 1950s were raised in an environment permeated by the sound of country music. Once radio stations began broadcasting African-American music on a regular basis, they had easy access to the sounds of African-American religious music and rhythm and blues. Early rock artists, such as Elvis Presley, Carl Perkins, Jerry Lee Lewis, and Buddy Holly, were products of this bicultural atmosphere and combined its elements into a unique type of music now known as *rockabilly*.

VOCAL GROUP ROOTS OF ROCK

Vocal groups are also an important link in the development of rock, from the early gospel groups to the smooth big band singers. The first recording of any African-American music is a gospel jubilee called "Down on the Old Camp Ground" (1902), identified by the announcer as a "Coon shout by the Dinwitty Colored Quartet." This recording possesses some of the characteristics, such as call-and-response patterns accompanying a lead singer, that are found later in Motown vocal groups as well as other pop vocal groups.

Two important African-American popular vocal groups were the Mills Brothers and the Ink Spots. The Mills Brothers were a family group consisting of a father and three (later two) brothers who sang in a smooth, close harmony style and, at times, imitated instruments with their voices. They began in the 1930s and were successful well into the 1960s with hits like "Paper Doll" (1949), "Glow Worm" (1952), and "Cab Driver" (1968).

The Ink Spots also began in the 1930s. Their vocal characteristics, a falsetto lead singer and the "talking bass," were staples of early rock vocal groups. Falsetto, meaning false voice, is the artificially high male vocal sound used by doo-wop groups in the 1950s and the Beach Boys in the 1960s. The talking bass is literally the bass singer who, somewhere in the middle of the song, comes forward and speaks directly to the listener with something like, "Baby, I love you, you're my rhapsody in blue." The Ink Spots recorded their first million-seller, "If I Didn't Care," in 1939 and another, "My Prayer," in 1944.

Toward the end of the 1940s, two new vocal groups, the Ravens and the Orioles, bridged the gap between groups like the Ink Spots and doo-wop groups of the fifties. In the late 1940s, the Ravens reached number fourteen in the charts with "Send for Me If You Need Me," and the Orioles got to number nineteen with "It's Too Soon to Know". Naming themselves after birds, these two groups began a trend that continued well into the 1950s. The Ravens, although they followed in the Mills Brothers/Ink Spots tradition, are considered by many to be the first of the R&B vocal groups, and their updated sound helped pave the way for groups like the Dominos and the Clovers in the 1950s. The most important musical characteristic of the Ravens was the lead, although the falsetto was also an important element of their sound. Their most well-known recordings were "Ol' Man River" (1947) and "White Christmas" (1948).

The Orioles, featuring the lead vocals of Earlington Tilghman (Sonny Til), survived into the 1950s and became one of the first of the R&B vocal groups to cross over to the popular music charts. Their country cover song, "Crying in the Chapel" (1953), reached the pop charts; however, another cover by June Valli (No. 24) kept their recording out of the year-end top thirty.

Vocal groups were also an important element in the popularity of big bands during the swing era. Big bands like those led by Glenn Miller and Tommy Dorsey, considered both jazz bands and pop music groups, regularly featured male and female singers as well as vocal groups. Tommy Dorsey's band featured Frank Sinatra and the Pied Pipers, while Glenn Miller's band featured Tex Beneke and the Modernaires. Those groups sang popular songs, slow ballads, and novelty songs, using jazz harmony. As the swing era ended following WW II, the singers and vocal groups remained popular while interest in the bands faded.

Those singers associated with the last years of the swing bands were the first popular music stars of the early 1950s. In the late 1940s and early 1950s, when the complexity of jazz harmony increased, some groups, such as the Four Freshmen and the Hi-Los, continued in the jazz idiom and consequently stayed on the fringes of popular music. Other groups, such as the Ames brothers, Four Aces, Four Lads, and the Crew Cuts, simplified their harmony and specialized in pop music. These vocal groups also reached the pop charts in the early 1950s but were never considered rock groups; the Crew Cuts came closest with their cover of "Sh-Boom." The European-American pop vocal group style survived into the rock era with groups like, Dion and the Belmonts, the Fleetwoods, and the Four Seasons.

LISTENING TO THE MUSIC

♪♪♪ "Match Box Blues"—performed by Blind Lemon Jefferson

Blind Lemon Jefferson's 1927 recording of "Match Box Blues" is an excellent example of the country blues, echoing the sounds of the Texas streets and roadhouses of the late 1920s. "Match Box Blues" was recorded in Atlanta on March 14, 1927, and released on Okeh Records that October. Blind Lemon Jefferson approached his early country blues as a combined singer, guitarist, and composer, influencing other bluesmen such as Leadbelly and T-Bone Walker. This recording helps the listener acquire some insight into the development of the twelve-bar blues. Jefferson maintains the classic blues lyric repetition scheme of A-A-B, but the length of his guitar responses extends the form beyond the twelve bars that was already established in the city blues recordings of Mamie Smith and Bessie Smith.

Analysis of "Match Box Blues"—2:59 in length, released on Okeh 8455

0:00   During the eight-bar instrumental introduction (8 bars x 4 foot taps per bar/measure = 32 foot taps), Jefferson provides a constant pulse by tapping his foot on the floor. His guitar style is more complex than that of most country blues players because he plays a confusing combination of lead, bass, and chords alternately throughout the recording.

0:14   First Blues Chorus: It begins, "I'm sittin' here wonderin' will a matchbox hold my clothes," which fills up two bars (2 x 4 foot taps). This is standard for the blues form; however, his guitar answers throughout occupy slightly more than three bars rather than the standard two. The answer consists of a lead-line played over bass notes and occupies roughly two bars that are followed by a strumming chord pattern that leads into the repeat of the first lyric line (0:24). Note that in the accompaniment pattern under the lyrics, he plays a guitar melody that seems to add a counter-line (layered rhythms) except on the repeat of the first line where, under the words "matchbox hold my clothes," he doubles his vocal rhythm with the guitar. Under the third line, "I ain't got so many matches but I got so far to go," (0:33) he plays a bass line that leads into the guitar answer. The guitar answers throughout end with a strumming chordal pattern that leads into the next chorus.

0:41   Second Chorus: It begins, "I say (father) who may your manager be," and he extends the "say" so that the remaining line fills up the entire four bars without leaving room for an answer. Note that under the held-out words "say" and "who may," he plays a tremolo on the guitar, mimicking the sound of his voice. Under the repeat of the first line (0:49), he once again doubles the vocal rhythm of "may your manager be," and at the end of the line leaves room for an instrumental answer. The third line beginning, "People ask so many questions" (0:55), is also accompanied by a bass line and is followed by an answer similar to previous ones.

1:03   Third Chorus: It begins, "I got a girl called Sal uptown who coochies all the time," and it is accompanied with figures similar to the first chorus. This time the repeat of the first line is accompanied with a riff pattern rather than a rhythm, which doubles the vocal rhythm. The third line is accompanied by a bass line.

1:28   Fourth Chorus: It begins, "I can't count the times," and is accompanied by a boogie woogie bass line of doubled notes in a swing eighth-note rhythm. This is the point in the recording that gives rise to the speculation that boogie woogie derived from Texas guitar styles, because this is the first recorded appearance of such a pattern. The next two lines are accompanied with similar patterns alternating with a single-line jazz-like melody.

1:50   Fifth Chorus: It begins, "If you want your lover, you'd better pin him to your side," and he accompanies the held-out words "your" and "pin him to" with a guitar tremolo similar to the second chorus. However, he uses a riff pattern to accompany the repeat of the first line. Again, the third line is accompanied by a bass line.

2:13   Sixth Chorus: Similar to the fourth chorus, it begins, "I ain't seen much of gal [or Dallas]," and once again uses a boogie woogie pattern alternating with a single-line melody.

2:32   Seventh Chorus: It begins, "Excuse me mama," and its accompaniment pattern is similar to the first chorus. Again, the repeat of the first line is accompanied with a riff, and the third is accompanied by bass notes.

2:56   Coda: The short tag, or coda, is a boogie woogie pattern that ends on the most colorful tone of the era, the flatted seventh.

For Musicians

The blues was in its infancy, and this simple A major song doesn't stray from the I-IV-V chord progression. While the irregular bars cause a constantly shifting form, the one-string arpeggiated notes on A, C#, E, F#, and G helped create a dotted eighth- and sixteenth-note bass-line pattern we have now used for decades. Jefferson's quick thinking is shown through imaginative guitar figures pinned down by lower string bass notes occurring in response to the lyrics. Each blues verse has its own unique odd meters corresponding to melodic or instrumental motion, and the simple, single flatted seventh note of G for the finale is truly effective in conveying the basic blues tonality. It is interesting to note that the tempo of the song increases from 118 beats per minute in the first chorus to 188 beats per minute in the final chorus.

Final Comments

This song became famous for providing a musical vehicle for such artists as Carl Perkins and the Beatles. Perkins transposed the tune to his rockabilly style, and it was released on Sun Records in early 1957 as "Match Box." The Beatles recorded their cover of Perkins's version with him in the control room overseeing the 1964 session. The Beatles placed "Match Box" in the top twenty in late 1964, where it reached number seventeen and stayed on the charts for five weeks.

♪♪ "St. Louis Blues"—performed by Bessie Smith

Composer W.C. Handy first published "St. Louis Blues" in 1914, although the song is not really a "classic" twelve-bar blues. Instead, Handy combines two twelve-bar blues verses, two eight-bar minor-key verses, and a twelve-bar chorus to create this early classic blues composition. This 1925 Columbia recording by Bessie Smith spawned a seventeen-minute 1929 film of the same name, featuring the only extant footage of this "Empress of the Blues" performing the song.

Analysis of "St. Louis Blues"—3:10 in length

This landmark blues recording, featuring Louis Armstrong on cornet and Fred Longshaw on reed pump organ, exhibits Bessie Smith's powerful vocal style and command of the blues language. Her blues melodies are heavy with emotion, vividly painting the lyrical story of a woman wronged by a two-timing man. The unique musical triangle created by Armstrong's jazzy trumpet fills, Longshaw's church pump organ sound, and Smith's blues vocal phrasing capture the sound of urban African-American music during the mid 1920s as both blues and jazz evolved.

The meter is "in four," i.e., each measure of music is four beats (foot taps) long. Notice that each small section of this, and most blues, is eight foot taps (two measures of four beats).

0:00 Introduction: After holding one chord as the introduction, Smith proceeds with the first verse at a slow, deliberate tempo, exaggerating the lyrics in a dramatic fashion as the song progresses. The organ plods along with passing chords while Armstrong plays trumpet answers to the vocal line.

0:04 First Chorus, Line A (2 measures; 2 x 4 foot taps): Smith sings "I hate to see the evening sun go down," while Armstrong improvises in the spaces.

0:12 Armstrong's trumpet answer (2 measures; 2 x 4 foot taps): the instrumental answer evolved from the call-response tradition. Notice how the trumpet answers are separate from the improvising he does around her vocal line.

0:20 Repeat of line A (2 measures) over the second basic chord in the blues progression.

0:27 Armstrong's trumpet answer (2 measures).

0:34 Line B (2 measures): "It makes me . . . " over the third basic chord in the blues progression.

0:42 Armstrong's trumpet answer to line B (2 measures).

0:49 Second Chorus, Line A of the second chorus (2 measures): "Feeling tomorrow like I feel today."

0:58 Armstrong's answer (2 measures).

1:04 Repeat of line A (2 measures).

1:12 Armstrong's answer (2 measures).

1:17   Line B (2 measures): "I'll pack my grip, make my getaway."

1:27   Armstrong's answer (2 measures).

1:33   Third Chorus: The middle two eight-measure sections are not part of the traditional blues progression and are darker sounding because of the minor key. This section is referred to as the *tango* section and was added by Handy to cater to a Spanish dance popular at the time. Line A (2 measures): "St. Louis woman, wears a diamond ring."

1:41   Armstrong's answer (2 measures).

1:47   Line B (2 measures): "Pulls a man around by her apron string."

1:56   Armstrong's answer (2 measures).

2:02   Line C (2 measures): "Clouds of foot powder. . ."

2:09   Armstrong's answer.

2:15   Line D (4 measures): "The man I love couldn't go nowhere . . . nowhere."

2:28   Fourth Chorus: This is a return to the blues progression. Line A (2 measures) "I got them St. Louis Blues just as blue as I can be."

2:36   Armstrong's answer (2 measures).

2:43   Line A (2 measures): this time the line is not a repeat "he's got her heart like a rock cast in the sea."

2:50   Armstrong's answer (2 measures).

2:57   Line B (2 measures): "An empty wooden heart."

3:04   Armstrong's answer ritards in the first bar, slowing down to end on the first beat of the final measure.

For Musicians

Performed in the key of G major, the introduction consists of the V chord (D7) being held. The verse picks up with a classic twelve-bar blues using the I-IV-V chords behind the blues melody, with improvised trumpet fills. The diminished passing chords on the organ move chromatically at times, adding color to the harmonic motion during the two blues verses. The middle sixteen bars move to G melodic minor, using a I-IV-V chord progression with chromatic diminished passing sonorities. The dominant chord (D7) is held at the end of this section as preparation for the chorus. Vocal pick-ups kick off the tempo for the twelve-bar chorus as the song returns to G major, only to frequently alternate between the I and IV chords behind the lyrics. An elongated V-I cadence in G ends the piece.

---

[1] Walter Harris, *African-American Music*, Lecture presented at Arizona State University, September, 1989.

[2] Ibid.

[3] Eileen Southern, *The Music of Black Americans: A History* (New York: Norton, 1971), 97.

[4] Eileen Southern, ed., *Readings in Black American Music* (New York: Norton, 1971), 63-64.

[5] Willi Apel, *Harvard Dictionary of Music* (Cambridge: Harvard University Press, 1956), 735.

[6] Southern, *The Music of Black Americans*, 64.

[7] Ibid., 30.

[8] Ibid., 161.

[9] Russell Sanjek, *American Popular Music and Its Business: The First Four Hundred Years* (New York: Oxford, 1988), 273.

[10] Southern, *The Music of Black Americans*, 113.

[11] Ibid., 113.

[12] Donald Clarke, *The Rise and Fall of Popular Music* (New York: St. Martin's Press, 1995), 23.

[13] Southern, *The Music of Black Americans*, 119.

[14] Sanjek, 290.

[15] W.C. Handy, *Father of the Blues*, ed. Arna Bontemps (New York: Collier, 1970), 78.

[16] Handy, *Father of the Blues: An Autobiography* (New York: Da Capo Press, 1969, p. 81.

[17] Russell Sanjek and David Sanjek, *American Popular Music Business in the 20th Century* (New York: Oxford, 1991), 15.

[18] Perry Bradford, *Born With the Blues* (New York: Oak, 1965), 33.

[19] Robert Dixon and John Godrich, *Recording the Blues* (New York: Stein and Day, 1970), 27.

[20] Samuel Charters, *The Blues Makers* (New York: Da Capo, 1991), 176.

[21] Ibid., 216.

[22] John Swenson, *Bill Haley: The Daddy of Rock and Roll* (New York: Stein and Day, 1982), 53.

[23] Bill Malone, *Country Music U.S.A.: A Fifty-Year History* (Austin, Texas: University of Texas Press, 1975), 16.

[24] Ibid., 39.

[25] Ibid., 43.

Chapter Two

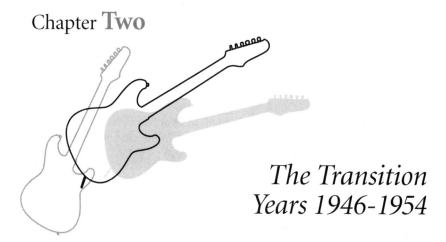

The Transition Years 1946-1954

The post-war era of the late 1940s–50s brought about many changes in American culture. The country was recovering from the war years and veterans were returning home, marrying, attending colleges, and starting families. Many returning African-American soldiers, however, were not about to settle for the society they had left. These veterans had fought for the freedom of the world and now also wanted freedom at home, but treatment of African-Americans did not change so quickly. In 1954, the same year Bill Haley recorded "Rock Around the Clock," a ruling by the Supreme Court, *Brown v. the Board of Education*, ended racially segregated schools. In the past, courts had held that students could be separated by race as long as their facilities and instruction were equal. "Separate but equal" was the euphemism used by those in favor of racism and segregation. African-Americans were segregated and were not treated equally.

The 1954 Supreme Court ruling began the process by which the U.S. government overturned the Jim Crow laws and began to ensure that African-Americans were afforded the same rights as all citizens. But no society changes easily, and the new climate of equality resulted in a great deal of racial tension. That tension was also felt in the music industry. European-Americans had been listening to African-American music for centuries. During the period leading up to the Supreme Court ruling, more and more teenagers were discovering R&B, and this fact was particularly distressing for the segments of the population that favored racial separation.

Those who were against the civil rights movement—and outraged that American youth were attracted to African-American music—worked toward some method of banning the music. Organizations like the Alabama White Citizens' Council worked to ban R&B because the lyrics had topics similar to those of the blues and thus were threatening to those who were accustomed to the pop music of the 1930s and 1940s. If R&B was to continue to prosper, it seemed it would need to be disassociated from the African-American community. Eventually, this music came to be called rock and roll.

Influence of Radio

The radio was the most important method of delivering African-American music to all sections of the country. In the late 1940s, DJs began programming more R&B during normal hours, so teens had more opportunities to hear the music. Teens surfing the airways found a new rhythmic alternative to the bland post-war pop music favored by their parents. Furthermore, they were able to hear the music on the radio in the safety of their homes without having to venture into nightclubs. As a result, they discovered African-American music and liked it. The invention of the transistor by Texas Instruments in 1953 increased the influence of radio by making inexpensive portable radios possible. Between 1953 and 1956, transistor radios were selling at a rate of 3.1 million per year.

Many R&B radio programs were sponsored by record stores who had discovered the power of radio advertising. They found that they could increase their profits by selling records through the mail to people who lived too far away to visit their stores. Since R&B programming was aimed at African-Americans, those recordings were only available in stores in certain neighborhoods. Teens who discovered R&B but lived too far away from an African-American neighborhood found that they could purchase these recordings by mail order. Around 1951, other merchants began to recognize a new audience for R&B and began to keep those recordings in stock.

African-American music had been featured on the radio since the late 1920s. The broadcasts from the Cotton Club of jazz-band leader Duke Ellington helped make his band an international success. In fact, such success probably would not have been possible without the airplay his music received. The African-American music that appeared on the radio during this period used lyrics that were similar to those of most popular music of the time. What changed in the late 1940s was the appearance on the radio of African-American music that had stronger blues roots and topics that were more earthy than the "moon, spoon, June" lyrics of previous popular music.

In the mid- to late-1940s, radio stations serving African-American communities began programming more blues. Most often, these blues shows were hosted by European-American rather than African-American DJs, although in 1947, *Ebony* magazine reported that there were sixteen African-Americans working on the radio in some capacity.[1] Station WLAC in Nashville, Tennessee, was an important early station, featuring European-American DJs Gene Nobles, John Richbourg, and Bill "Hoss" Allen. Gene Nobles began at the station in 1943; Richbourg joined in 1947; and Allen joined in 1949. At some point in the late 1940s, their mixture of music featured all R&B. Adding to the power of WLAC were two mail-order record stores, Randy's Record Shop of Gallatin, Tennessee (the future owner of Dot Records), and Ernie's Record Mart of Memphis. WLAC was a 50,000-watt clear channel station that could be heard from border to border as well as in the Caribbean,[2] and the records heard on the station could be purchased by mail, enabling every listener to purchase R&B from the safety of their own home.

Another DJ, Zenas "Daddy" Sears, programmed R&B for the Atlanta area. During the war, he was a broadcaster for Armed Services radio in India, where eighty-five percent of his audience was African-American. That experience helped him understand the preferences of African-American listeners, and he later used his programming knowledge to build a following in Atlanta. After the war, he returned to Atlanta and began "slipping" R&B recordings into his programs on WATL. However, he was fired in 1948, when the station owner finally heard the music Sears was playing. Sears next went to WGST at Georgia Tech, where he broadcast an R&B show from 10:15 P.M. to 2:00 A.M. He was important enough in the Atlanta market that when RCA was looking for R&B artists in the early 1950s, they called him for recommendations. Sears recommended Little Richard (Richard Penniman), whom he had heard about from band leader Billy Wright. RCA came to Atlanta and recorded "Every Hour," which became a local hit but was not successful enough to warrant further recording. Sears also notified Atlantic Records that Ray Charles (already under contract to them) was breaking away from the smooth, urban blues style and adopting a new gospel-inspired style.[3] Atlantic then recorded Charles's "I Got a Woman," "Greenbacks," "Come Back Baby," and "This Little Girl of Mine" at the WGST studios.

R&B was also popular in areas outside the South. In Los Angeles, Hunter Hancock at KFVD added R&B to his jazz show in 1943, and by the late 1940s, he was playing all R&B. Philadelphia had Joe Niagara on WIBG, who was the highest rated DJ in the market from 1947 to 1957, and Pittsburgh had Porky Chadwick on WAMO.

WDIA in Memphis, the first radio station with all African-American DJs, began broadcasting in June 1947 as a country music station. There were too many other stations broadcasting a country music format and WDIA was losing money, so in an attempt to save the station, they decided to try programming music for African-American listeners. At 4 P.M. on October 25, 1948, WDIA put its first African-American DJ on the air.[4] "Nat D." Williams was a well-known Memphis personality who taught high school, wrote a newspaper column, and hosted talent competitions. Williams was immensely successful, and within a year, WDIA had hired all African-American DJs.

Among WDIA's other DJs were the future recording stars Riley B. King (B. B. King) and Rufus Thomas. WDIA did more than program R&B; it also aired announcements, news, and political issues that were of interest to African-Americans. The station had so much success during the first year that other stations also began trying to attract African-American audiences, although without hiring African-American DJs. For example, in 1949, WHBQ in Memphis hired Dewey Phillips, a European-American who attracted an audience of European-American teenagers (including young Elvis).

Many of these DJs, except those on WDIA, were European- Americans who imitated the vocal patterns of African-Americans. In a sense, this imitation was similar to the earlier minstrel show in which European-Americans presented their perception of African-American behavior and speech. But these were caricatures that perpetuated a flawed racial stereotype that was maintained when African-Americans gained entry into the music business.

The need to sound African-American without actually being African-American was an important business ploy. In the late 1940s, Vernon Winslow, an African-American graduate of the Art Institute of Chicago, taught at Dillard University in New Orleans and also wrote a column in the *Louisiana Weekly* aimed at the African-American community. As an author using the pseudonym "Poppa Stoppa," Winslow created a "jive-talking" character that developed a large audience. The column was so successful that station WJMR in New Orleans began a "Poppa Stoppa" show and had Winslow train one of its European-American DJs to use the African-American dialect better known as "jive." The "Poppa Stoppa" radio show was so successful that the character was syndicated. Soon afterward, Winslow was contacted by the ad agency that handled the Jax Beer account and asked to create a new character to help sell beer to the African-American community. He created "Doctor Dadd-O" for the "Jivin' With Jax" show.[5]

Such radio shows helped spread R&B throughout the nation and created a demand for the records, which further stimulated the market. By 1951, America's European-American teenagers were turning to R&B in large enough numbers that a disk jockey in Cleveland, Ohio, named Alan Freed formatted a whole program for them and would go down in rock and roll history.

ALAN FREED
The Phrase "Rock and Roll"

Alan Freed is often given credit for being the first rock and roll DJ, and this may be, with the proper qualifying statements, a defensible position. In 1951, Leo Mintz, owner of a record store called Record Rendezvous, mentioned to Alan Freed, then a classical music DJ on Cleveland's WJW, that he had noticed unusually large numbers of teenagers coming to his store, bypassing the pop records, and heading straight for the R&B records. Freed investigated and approached his station management about starting an R&B show. According to the radio schedule published in the *Cleveland Plain Dealer*, Freed's first show was July 4, 1951. Freed adopted an on-air persona, "King of the Moon Dogs," and used Todd Rhodes's "Blues for Moon Dog" as his theme song.

Alan Freed was not the first to program R&B recordings. Because the other R&B programs were intended for an African-American audience, Freed may have been the first to aim a show featuring this type of music at primarily European-American audiences. Freed was able to rise to the top of the profession and to become a nationwide symbol for rock and roll. In the process, however, he also became a nationwide target for those hoping to ban the new music.

Alan Freed concert

Freed is given credit for applying the phrase *rock and roll* in place of R&B, but he was not the first to use it. In 1948, Piano Red, an Atlanta DJ who would open his show with the phrase "Let's rock 'n' roll with Red," seems to predate Freed. *Rock and roll* had long been used in blues lyrics as a metaphor for sexual intercourse. As a sexual metaphor, the phrase predates the blues and was used as early as Shakespeare in his sonnet "Venus and Adonis": "My throbbing heart shall rock thee day and night." It also appears in a line from an early nineteenth-century sea chantey, "Oh do, my Johnny Boker, come rock'n'roll me over."

The words "rock and roll" have appeared consistently as sexual metaphors in numerous blues recordings, such as "My Daddy Rocks Me With One Steady Roll" (1922) by Trixie Smith, "I'm a Steady Rollin' Man" (1937) by Robert Johnson, and "Rock Me Daddy" (1937) by Georgia White. Another pertinent example, "Good Rockin' Tonight," recorded by Wynonie Harris, was one of the R&B songs re-recorded by Bill Haley and Elvis Presley in the 1950s. The term "rockin'" in the lyrics of this song also appears to be a metaphor for sex.

Lyrics such as these are often cited as the reason parents of European-American teenagers developed negative attitudes toward R&B. There is a certain irony that the term *rock and roll* became an alternative to *R&B*, because the adults who found R&B offensive did so because of the sexual lyric content, which often included the phrase "rockin' and rollin'."

The Moondog Controversy

The success of Freed's show was most likely responsible for changing the name of the music from R&B to rock and roll. to "Alan Freed's Rock and Roll Party." In 1954, Alan Freed moved his successful radio show—the "Moondog Show"—from Cleveland to WINS in New York City, where he was sued by a street musician, Louis "Moondog" Hardin, for infringement of his name. Having previously used the name "Moondog" on a recording established Hardin's ownership and the ensuing court ruling forced Freed to change the name of his show.

According to Morris Levy, Freed's business partner, the term "rock and roll" was concocted during a luncheon meeting between Juggy Gayles, Jack Hooke, Alan Freed, and Levy at P.J. Moriarty's, a Broadway restaurant. The new name for Freed's radio show that emerged from this meeting was "Alan Freed's Rock and Roll Party."[6] In fact, Freed had used the term "rock and roll" on his show in Cleveland prior to that meeting, so Levy's assertion is correct only in identifying the phrase's origin as the new name for Freed's radio program. This story is further tainted by the fact that Levy and Freed attempted to copyright the phrase.

Many sources provide incorrect information and have caused general confusion with regard to the name of Freed's radio program in Cleveland. Those sources claim that the show was titled "The Moondog Rock and Roll Party." Despite a photograph of a banner hanging over the stage at one of Freed's first rock and roll stage shows, reading "Record Rendezvous Sponsors The Alan Freed's Moon Dog Show WJW 850 On Your Dial," one source claims in a caption under the picture that Freed's radio program was called the "Moondog Rock and Roll Party." An article in the *New York Times* supports the information contained in the photograph: that Alan Freed's show was called the "Moondog Show" until the lawsuit required him to stop using it. However, a radio log in the *Cleveland Plain Dealer* gives the title of the show as "Moon Dog House," presumably a shortened version of "Moon Dog House Party," which adds yet a third title.

Undoubtedly, much of this confusion was caused by Freed, who seemed to refer to his Cleveland show by a variety of titles. In a recording of a portion of a pre-September 1954 program, Freed says:

> This is Alan Freed, king of the Moon Doggers, and it's time again for another of your favorite rock and roll sessions; blues and rhythm records for all the gang in the Moon Dog kingdom. Enjoy Aaron Drew [a brand of beer] as you enjoy the Moon Dog Show.[7]

In the excerpt above, Freed calls his show the "Moon Dog Show" but also appears to refer to it as a "rock and roll session." It is also interesting to note that he uses the words "blues and rhythm records," indicating two different styles—blues records and rhythm records. The reason that R&B now is perceived as one style of music is that in June 1949, *Billboard* magazine renamed two of its popularity charts: "Harlem Hit Parade" became "Rhythm and Blues" and "Hillbilly" became "Country and Western." In reality, the new terms identified four styles: blues, rhythm, country, and western (cowboy) songs.

After 1954, when Freed legally changed the name of his program, European-Americans began to call R&B by its new name, rock and roll, while African-Americans still used the term R&B. Using two names for the same style confounded attempts to create precise definitions of the terms. Within a short time, the European-American public soon forgot how and why the name had originated, and the use of the two terms obscured the origins of the music.

What Is Rock and Roll?

Today, rock listeners continue to segregate the two types of music. They use "rock and roll" when referring to European-American music, and terms like *soul, funk,* and *rap* to identify African-American music. While soul, funk, and rap apply to identifiable sub-styles, those styles still represent the musical preferences of American youth and therefore should be included in any definition of rock and roll. In 1964, *Billboard* magazine, realizing that popular music was African-American music, stopped publishing an R&B chart and instead combined all the music into one chart. The R&B chart was returned in 1965, most likely for reasons that were social, financial, and political.

Alan Freed's use of "rock and roll" occurred at the precise moment in history when society was looking for a word to describe the music, while obscuring its racial implications and origins. In so doing, European-American parents could now say their children were listening to rock and roll and not "Negro" music.

Freed's Rock Concerts

Freed was a visible adult spokesman for the music, who also had a brilliant sense of business and theater. All DJs were required, mostly by their pay structure, to be entrepreneurs and to schedule sponsored public appearances to increase their income. In Cleveland, Freed staged dances called coronation balls, and rock concerts, which disturbed many adults because they were racially integrated events. Many areas of the country still had strict laws governing the way the cultures mixed socially. In the South, ropes were strung down the middle of the dance floor to keep the races apart, even though everyone's presence at the event indicated that their musical preferences were identical. In fact, some say that Freed's television show was canceled abruptly because cameras caught African-American doo-wop star Frankie Lymon dancing with a fan of another race. These anti-integration forces were powerful foes of the music, and soon Freed became a target for their wrath.

Freed's concerts had some typical problems. At the first show on March 21, 1952, in the Cleveland Arena, more tickets were sold than there were available seats, causing some unrest among ticket holders. Critics accused Freed of being a shady businessman who tried to make as much money as possible, while his advocates believed that no one had any idea how popular the concert would be and that he was simply not careful about the manner in which tickets were sold.

When Freed moved to New York's WINS in 1954, he continued to produce rock shows, beginning with a January 14–15, 1955, show at the St. Nicholas Arena. Freed's shows were very successful in exposing a mixed audience to R&B, now called rock and roll. His downfall began as a result of a May 3, 1958, show in Boston, where riots in the streets were reported after an incident inside in which a European-American girl got excited and grabbed the leg of an African-American performer on stage. The police "rushed to her defense" and wanted to turn on the lights. Freed refused, telling the audience, "I guess the police here in Boston don't want you kids to have a good time." According to news sources, the incident sparked roving gangs of juvenile delinquents, and a robbery and stabbing were reported. Although some say the stabbing was unrelated to the rock concert, the blame was leveled directly at Freed. The public was outraged at the reports of violence at the rock concert, and future concerts were canceled in many locations. WINS fired Freed the next day, in spite of the fact that, by contract, WINS received twenty-five percent of the proceeds of all Freed's entrepreneurial efforts, effectively making it a partner in the show. It is suspected that WINS did not stand behind

Freed because it was aware of the upcoming government investigation into the record and radio business and realized that Freed was going to be a problem. From there, Freed went to WABC for a short time, but ultimately a 1960 payola scandal cost him his job there, and he never regained his popularity.

Rock and Roll in the Movies

Freed appeared in several rock movies, *Rock Around the Clock* (1956), *Rock, Rock, Rock* (1956), *Don't Knock the Rock* (1957), and *Go Johnnie Go* (1958). These films were the beginning of a generation of movies dealing with rock and roll. Musicals were not new. In fact, the first important motion picture with sound was a musical, *The Jazz Singer*. Movies of the 1930s and 40s featured performances by jazz and pop stars such as Benny Goodman, Glenn Miller, and Tommy Dorsey. Some films even cast musicians in acting roles, as in the series of movies starring Kay Kaiser and his band. The appearance of rock and roll films at this point, however, indicates that rock and roll had entered the mainstream enough for producers to invest the necessary money.

Freed's movies featured the artists he played on his radio show: Bill Haley and the Comets, the Moonglows, Little Richard, and others. The topics of the films generally revolved around proving to parents that rock was not as bad as they thought. In *Don't Knock the Rock*, for example, kids put on a show with the intent of reminding their parents how their favorite music and dances had been disapproved of by their own parents; everybody ends up happy and dancing at the end.

In the early 1950s, there was a change in the image of teenagers. Previously, teens had been portrayed in innocent film roles such as Mickey Rooney's *Andy Hardy* series (*Love Finds Andy Hardy*) and Judy Garland's movies (*Strike Up the Band, Babes on Broadway*). In the 1950s, juvenile delinquents and rebellious characters appeared as heroes. Teens portrayed in movies of this era were sullen, disaffected youth, searching for the meaning of life. *The Wild One* (1954), starring Marlon Brando, told the story of a real event, in which a motorcycle gang took over the small California town of Hollister. "Johnny" (Brando) was the leader of the BRMC (Black Rebels Motorcycle Club). When asked what he was rebelling against, Johnny replied, "What're ya got?" The movie was produced early enough that it used West Coast jazz as its theme music, not R&B. But *The Wild One* marks the moment when the media began to portray teens in a negative light, and the fear and hysteria parents felt about rebellious teens was projected toward rock and roll and its supporters.

Another film, *The Blackboard Jungle* (1955), was the story of teachers in an inner-city high school and their "troubled teen" students. The movie contains one illuminating scene in which a teacher brings in a phonograph and plays his students some of his favorite jazz recordings. The kids start to riot, and the teacher goes for help. When he returns, the kids are throwing his records around and dancing to rock and roll. The scene ends with the kids "dancing on the grave" of previous pop music. Chuck Berry repeated the sentiment in 1956 when he wrote and sang, "Roll over Beethoven, tell Tchaikovsky the news."

Rock and roll became associated with the kind of teenage rebellion portrayed in *The Blackboard Jungle* partly because "Rock Around the Clock" by Bill Haley and the Comets was used as the movie's theme music. Although the song had met with little commercial success when it was released in 1954, it became an international hit after the film came out, and Haley was catapulted to stardom. The music industry was again reminded of the power of combining the mediums of music and film. So strong was the connection of "Rock Around the Clock" to the 1950s era that much later, when television produced a sitcom about the fifties, *Happy Days*, "Rock Around the Clock" was chosen as its theme song. Interestingly, by the 1970s, "Rock Around the Clock" represented the "good old days," even though it had once symbolized rebellious, disaffected juvenile delinquents.

MUSIC IN 1951
Pop Music

Pop music of the early 1950s was an inoffensive blend of saccharine ballads by "crooners" and up-tempo novelty songs. The pop music charts were dominated by Columbia, RCA, Capitol, Decca, Mercury, and MGM; their output was determined by companies' A&R (artist and repertoire) departments, usually controlled by the musical tastes of one man.

The process by which records were released was typically thus: A music publisher would bring in a song and demonstrate it for the record company's A&R man. If the A&R man liked the song, he would then decide which of the company's artists would record it. The company would schedule studio time, hire backup musicians and an arranger, negotiate production costs, and then record the song. If the A&R man did not like the song, he might have it rewritten or might not record it at all. For the businessmen involved, this was a good system, but it was not very good for the musical consumer. The process was similar at independent record companies: The recorded output was still the result of the musical taste of one man. However, the "indies" did not have the production, distribution, and promotional clout of major record labels and therefore had difficulty getting their records played on mainstream radio. Instead, the indies concentrated on fringe markets like R&B and country and western, which the majors had abandoned in the 1940s. By the mid-1950s, the major labels were in trouble because the markets they had ignored were steadily becoming the dominant force in the marketplace.

Pop Top 10: In 1951, the year of Freed's first rock radio show, the number one song on the *Billboard* charts was "Too Young" by Nat King Cole, who had abandoned R&B and had become a ballad singer. This recording had no beat to speak of and expressed feelings of love in a typical Tin Pan Alley manner. Number two was Tony Bennett's "Because of You," also without a beat, and also a typical love song. The third most popular song was "How High the Moon," a swing-era standard performed by the team Les Paul and Mary Ford. Though not R&B influenced, it was important because of the technology it used. Number four was a little more interesting than number two. "Come On-a My House" by Rosemary Clooney was an up-tempo novelty sung in an exaggerated Italian accent. It was culturally insulting but socially acceptable to portray funny Italian stereotypes. Number five was a pseudo-operatic rendition of "Be My Love" by Mario Lanza, who also held the number nine spot with "Loveliest Night of the Year." Number six was "On Top of Old Smokey," a public domain selection by the Weavers, who were later blacklisted for their left-wing leanings (see Folk Music). Number seven was a cover of Hank Williams's "Cold, Cold Heart" by Tony Bennett, and number ten was "Tennessee Waltz" by Patti Page.

Number three and number ten are technically related: They used the German technology, discovered at the end of the war, of recording sounds on a thin strip of tape (film), which made "over-dubbing" possible and altered the future of the recording industry. Previously, sounds had been recorded, actually etched, directly onto a master disk; once the sounds were fixed on the disk, they could not be altered or changed. Number ten, "Tennessee Waltz," featured Patti Page singing a duet with herself by double-tracking the vocal, over-dubbing a second voice. She sang the first vocal track and then recorded a second track over that while listening to the first. This technique "fattened" the sound of the voice and gave the impression of two voices singing in harmony. The number three song, "How High the Moon," was recorded by the man who helped develop the potential of German tape technology and the over-dubbing process, Les Paul. Les Paul and Mary Ford released a series of recordings in which they overdubbed their guitars and voices until they created a big, wide sound. Although Americans had previously unearthed some German twelve-track tape recorders, Les Paul deserves much of the credit for the development and use of the eight-track tape recorder. Years later, this technology was used by the Beatles to record songs in the studio that could not be duplicated in a live performance.

The selections offered on pop radio in the early 1950s were of little interest to teenagers and were geared more for their parents. Most of the recordings had a weak beat and were not very musically exciting, so teens turned their radio dials and found music that was more interesting to them; they found R&B.

Rhythm and Blues

The point of listing the top ten pop recordings is to demonstrate the lack of anything energetic or interesting to teens at the time. The R&B charts, on the other hand, contained rhythmic vitality and sensual excitement. Within the R&B charts of 1951 are the strains of music that would typify early rock: the jump blues (Joe Turner, Jackie Brenston, Johnny Otis), vocal groups (Dominos, Clovers, Five Keys), smooth blues singers (Charles Brown, Percy Mayfield), and female gospel-influenced singers (Ruth Brown).

R&B Top 10: Number one on the R&B chart, "Sixty Minute Man," was by a vocal group, the Dominos. It tells the story of "lovin' Dan" and his sixty-minute love-making sessions. The recording had an infectious beat, a gospel sound, some elements of humor, and the thing most teenagers think about: sex. It was hardly smutty by today's standards, yet it played into the sexual fears of the mainstream population and caused them to form a negative opinion of R&B as songs containing "leer-ics," with emphasis on the word "leer."

There were other R&B vocal groups in the top ten. The Clovers were at number five with "Don't You Know I Love You," and The Five Keys at number eight with "Glory of Love." The Five Keys were originally a gospel group known as The Sentimental Four, who decided in 1949 to abandon gospel and sing R&B. In 1950, they traveled to New York and won the amateur contest at the Apollo Theater, a victory that landed them a record contract. Like the Dominos, their switch from gospel to R&B helps demonstrate the close relationship between gospel vocal techniques and the techniques used in R&B.

The Clovers were the first of many successful R&B vocal groups signed by Atlantic. They formed in the late forties, were signed by Atlantic in 1950, and had hits until 1959. The Clovers were the link between R&B groups of the forties and doo-wop in the fifties; they encompassed most of the doo-wop traits but are usually omitted from the category because their appearance pre-dates the "official" beginning of rock.

In 1951, "Rocket 88" by Jackie Brenston was a landmark recording for several reasons: (1) It was recorded by Sam Phillips who first discovered Elvis; (2) It was Ike Turner's first success in the recording business (Ike was famous before Tina); (3) Bill Haley's Saddlemen covered it; and (4) It used a distorted guitar sound. Ike Turner, a DJ on Clarksdale's WROX, and his band, the Kings of Rhythm, had worked as a studio band for Sam Phillips on recordings that

The Clovers

later were sold to the RPM label, and this time he recorded under his own name, or so he thought. Although it was Turner's band, Jackie Brenston was the lead singer on the song, so the record company put Brenston's name on the label. Phillips sold the master to Chess Records instead of RPM, and it was a good-sized hit. Since RPM Records had also been doing business with Phillips, RPM's owners, the Bahari brothers, were outraged when he sold the master recording to Chess Records. As a result, the Baharis began using Ike Turner as their Delta talent scout instead of Phillips.[8]

The prominent distorted guitar sound on the recording also has an interesting story attached to it. The amplifier was loaded on top of the car during the band's trip from Clarksdale to Memphis for the recording, and it fell off. Apparently the speaker cone ripped in the fall, and the band stuffed a piece of paper in it to repair it, but it is more than likely that the fall also damaged some of the tubes. Regardless, this session produced the first intentionally recorded fuzz-tone guitar sound; fourteen years later, the Rolling Stones also used fuzz tone on "Satisfaction."

At this time, Bill Haley's Western swing band was working toward a career in country music, but they were aware of the jump blues trend. They were regular entertainers in resort towns along the New Jersey shore and had seen audience reaction to their performances of those songs. Dave Miller of Essex Records in Philadelphia persuaded Haley to cover the song "Rocket 88," which he did. Miller, however, did not like the first version, so he produced and released a second version. Haley's cover of the song wasn't a hit, but it sold well enough to encourage them to record more jump tunes. Nevertheless, "Rocket 88" would have to be included on any list of the very first rock and roll recordings.

Also on the 1951 R&B chart (No. 4) is Joe Turner's "Chains of Love." As previously mentioned, Joe Turner was a "Kansas City blues shouter" and had performed with boogie woogie pianist Pete Johnson at John Hammond's 1938 "Spirituals to Swing Concert" in Carnegie Hall that was in part responsible for the resurgence of boogie woogie. Turner signed with Atlantic records in the 1950s, and "Chains of Love" was his first hit for them. His most influential hit was "Shake Rattle and Roll" (1954) because it was covered by Bill Haley, who reached number twenty-six on the pop charts with it.

Others have commented on the differences between the two versions of "Shake, Rattle, and Roll" and attempted to use those differences to justify the use of both terms ("rock and roll" and "R&B"), and to claim that rock and roll was a new and different style. The only important difference lay in the sanitization of the lyrics. Haley's version has virtually no sexual implications. Decca Records executives understood the nature of mainstream radio and the charges that R&B was lyrically risqué, so they knew they had to alter the lyrics to make the recording suitable for airplay.

Another difference between the recordings was in the instruments and instrumental skills of the bands. Turner's recording used the regular studio musicians hired by Atlantic, and Haley's used his Western swing band. The difference is in the sound of the ensemble and the subtle ways in which jazz musicians alter the placement of the beat to create a swinging eighth-note feel. Haley's group also used the swing eighth-note, but they did not have the same loose feeling that Turner's studio band had.

The similarities in the two recordings are more striking: (1) the twelve-bar blues structure, (2) the "A-A-B" pattern of the vocal line, (3) call-and-response patterns between the soloist and the band, and (4) the "shouter" singing style. It is apparent that Haley attempted to copy Turner's recording the best he could and was willing to change the lyrics to get airplay on the pop stations. The perception that Haley's recording is "rock and roll" and Turner's is "R&B" is likely a result of the racism in the United States at the time. The racist impulses that created the need to find another name for R&B were the same impulses that led some to call Elvis "the King of Rock and Roll."

Although the divisions between the perceived musical tastes of African-Americans and European-Americans in the 1990s are distinct, the music known in the mid-1950s as rock was derived from and was stylistically identical to R&B. Furthermore, any study of rock and roll from any era would be incomplete without first understanding the origins of the music.

Covers

The record *covers* served a useful purpose during the transition period in that they supplied sanitized versions of popular R&B recordings that were attractive to a mainstream European-American audience. The term "cover" was used in the 1950s to indicate the recording by artist B of a song that had been recorded recently by artist A with the intention of replacing it (covering it up) on the charts. People outside the music business often wonder why covers were legal and allowed to exist. The right to perform a song (performance license) belongs to the copyright owner, who usually is not the performer. Because copyright owners get mechanical and performance royalties when their music is recorded and performed, it is to their advantage to have their song recorded by as many artists as possible.

The most often cited example of a successful cover is the Mercury Records cover by the Crew Cuts of "Sh-Boom," which was originally recorded by the Chords on the Cat record label. The Crew Cuts' recording was intended to divert sales from the Chords by replacing it on the pop charts and relegating the original Chords song to the R&B charts. During the transition period between R&B of the late 1940s and rock in the mid-1950s, cover recordings kept African-American performers off pop music radio stations even when there was a demand for their songs. This situation can be viewed from several angles: (1) The airways were segregated places; (2) Cover versions were standard practice during the 1940s; and (3) Performance royalties were maximized by recording a song using several different artists.

Since the beginning of broadcasting, music by African-Americans has been scarce in popular radio. During the period after World War II, only the Ink Spots, Mills Brothers, Billy Eckstine, and Nat King Cole had any success on the popular music charts. In 1951, when European-American teenagers were beginning to discover R&B, several radio stations began to respond to the demand by playing recordings by African-Americans. Some European-Americans felt threatened by the (perceived) change in styles and by the increasing influence of African-American music. To provide an alternative, record producers began to cover recordings by African-Americans with other recordings, often with identical arrangements, by European-Americans (Canadians, in the case of the Crew Cuts). Viewed from this perspective, the cover system was racist; it was an attempt to prevent the R&B artists from being associated with the songs they helped make popular, and thereby prevented them from profiting financially.

This type of cover also obscured the R&B origins of songs and lessened the racial tensions that existed around the music.

The second perspective on covers would consider that covers have always been part of the record business. For example, the *Billboard* top forty records of 1946 contained four recordings of "Symphony" (Freddy Martin, Bing Crosby, Benny Goodman, and Jo Stafford). The music business would maintain that this is the workings of a free market at its best: The public was able to choose versions of the song to suit a variety of musical tastes—a "sweet" version (Martin), a "hot" one (Goodman), a male vocalist (Crosby), and a female vocalist (Stafford). It was also common to have cover records cross genres. Bing Crosby recorded several versions of country songs, such as "San Antonio Rose" (1941), "You Are My Sunshine" (1941), "Pistol Packin' Mama" (1943), and "Sioux City Sue" (1946).

The prevailing attitude in the industry was that it was "the song, not the singer," meaning that the song was more valuable than the artist who performed it, so different versions satisfied the varied tastes of the audience. In the rock era, the aesthetic changed: It became "the singer, not the song." Audiences wanted to hear their favorite singer, regardless of what the song was. These two perspectives on covers conflict only in that all four versions of "Symphony" were given radio airplay to allow the audience to decide which version was their favorite. Pop radio of the 1950s, on the other hand, typically excluded the recording of the Chords' "Sh-Boom" and forced the audience to accept the Crew Cuts' version. Although the cover artists often sold more recordings than the original artists, the original recordings are most remembered today. When "Tutti Fruiti" plays on "oldies" stations, it is usually Little Richard singing and not Pat Boone.

The third view of covers is from the perspective of songwriters and publishers who want to maximize a song's potential profit. The best way to maximize income from mechanical and performance royalties is to have as many versions of the song on the market as possible. It makes little difference to the songwriter or the publisher whose version sells the most, because they receive royalties from all the versions. In the story of "Sh-Boom," Arnold Shaw of Mercury Records noticed the Chords' record doing well on the West Coast and traced the copyright back to Atlantic records. Mercury offered to buy half the rights to the song for six thousand dollars, and Atlantic accepted, apparently unaware of the song's West Coast success. Mercury then had a contract group, the Crew Cuts, record a version that was subsequently played on the pop music stations, relegating the Chords' version to R&B stations and to disk jockeys like Alan Freed, who refused to play covers. Mercury won even if the Crew Cuts' version failed, because they owned half the publishing and would make money from the Chords' version. Everybody won except the artist who sold fewer records.

After the business accepted the premise that it was "the singer, and not the song," the cover trend died out. Since that time, when DJs or critics use the term "cover," they mean remake—that is, a new version of a song recorded some time ago—for example, Carly Simon and James Taylor's 1974 remake of Inez and Charlie Fox's 1963 hit "Mockingbird." The differences between a remake and a cover are the intent and the time period; a cover's intent is to replace the original.

Rhythm and Blues Covers		
__Song__	__Original__	__Cover__
1954		
"Sh-Boom"	Chords	Crew Cuts
"Earth Angel"	Penguins	Crew Cuts
"Earth Angel"	Penguins	Gloria Mann
"Goodnight Sweetheart"	Spaniels	McGuire Sisters
"Heart of Stone"	Charms	Fontaine Sisters
"Shake, Rattle and Roll"	Joe Turner	Bill Haley
"Sincerely"	Moonglows	McGuire Sisters
"Pledging My Love"	Johnny Ace	Teresa Brewer
1955		
"Tweedle Dee"	LaVerne Baker	Georgia Gibbs
"Wallflower," or "Dance with Me Henry"	Etta James	Georgia Gibbs
"Don't Be Angry"	Nappy Brown	Crew Cuts
"Ko-Ko-Mo"	Gene & Eunice	Crew Cuts
"Ko-Ko-Mo"	Gene & Eunice	Perry Como
"Gum Drop"	Otis Williams	Crew Cuts
"Two Hearts"	Charms	Pat Boone
"Ain't That a Shame"	Fats Domino	Pat Boone
"At My Front Door"	El Dorados	Pat Boone
"Tutti Fruiti"	Little Richard	Pat Boone
"I Hear You Knockin'"	Smiley Lewis	Gale Storm

Independent Record Labels

Independent record labels were the first to dominate the rhythm and blues / rock and roll music market. "Independent record label" ("indie") generally refers to a label without its own distribution department. A distribution system is one of the most important branches of the business, in that it delivers copies of recordings into stores and collects money for those recordings. Without distribution, a record label must rely on either an independent distributor or a major label for its distribution and collection.

The major labels in the 1950s—Columbia, RCA, Capitol, Decca, and Mercury—controlled pop music during the transition years when America's teenagers were discovering R&B. The majors were large companies with large overhead that needed to sell a lot of records to break even. The indies, being smaller operations, did not have to sell as many records to break even, so they focused on the fringe markets that major labels had abandoned. These fringe markets included R&B and country and western audiences. After the war, when these two markets began growing, the number of indies increased to meet the demand. When R&B crossed over to the pop charts, the independent labels already had control of the market.

Independent labels were very small operations. Because of their size, they were able to move very quickly and respond to minor trends in the market. Often the output of an indie reflected the tastes of one man, the owner, who was responsible for the success or failure of the records he chose to release. Indies often paid no royalties to their artists and took credit for the song-writing whenever possible. This combination of factors helped indies survive. Indies were successful because

- their size made it easy for them to respond to trends;

- low overhead meant that moderate sales were enough;

- decisions on music often represented the views of one man; and

- they tended to avoid paying royalties by owning both the publishing and song writing.

The most influential indies were Atlantic, King, Chess, Modern, Imperial, Specialty, and Sun. These were responsible for recording some of the most important artists of the late 1940s and early 1950s.

The problem with most indies was that they lacked the capital to produce enough records to satisfy the demand should one of their recordings become a hit. Typically, indies only had small distribution systems (sometimes even distributing records themselves out of the trunk of a car, for example) and only pressed a small number of records. If a record started to sell well, more product would have to be pressed and distributed. As a rule, based on years of experience, pressing plants dealt in cash or at least prompt payment of past accounts. If an indie had a hit record, it would be difficult to supply the demand, since cash flow returning from retailers would not begin for at least thirty to sixty days— that is, if their accounts were paid on time. Typically, distributors and stores were reluctant to pay unless the indie employed some type of leverage over them, such as not distributing the next hit until payment was received for the previous one. If the indie did not have a next hit, then it was very difficult to collect. The nightmare of the independent is a hit record it can't supply.

That is why Sam Phillips of the indie Sun Records had to sell Elvis's contract in order to make any money. Although Phillips could see that Elvis had huge potential, he didn't have the resources to promote and distribute him on a nationwide scale. But when Phillips sold Elvis, he was able to obtain a large infusion of cash that enabled him to search for the next future star.

LISTENING TO THE MUSIC

♪♪♪ "Good Rockin' Tonight"—performed by Wynonie Harris
Whereas early blues consisted of a musician singing out in pain, longing for home and telling personal stories of hard times, R&B became "good time, party music," a celebration of urban life and improving life styles. As the lyrics became more risqué and the performers more flamboyant, the solid beat of twelve-bar "classic" blues led to the strong backbeat and steady bass lines of R&B.

Roy Brown recorded his composition "Good Rockin' Tonight" in the summer of 1947, and Wynonie "Blues" Harris covered it in 1948. Harris, a blues-shouting big band singer, recorded his rhythm and blues hit on King Records.

Analysis of "Good Rockin' Tonight"—2:41 in length
Instrumentation includes Harris, vocals, Hal "Cornbread" Singer on wailing tenor sax, and a band also featuring alto saxophone, trumpet, piano, bass, and drums.

"Good Rockin' Tonight" is a twelve-bar blues (three groups of 4 measures) over a boogie woogie bass line. There are constant hand claps heard on the backbeat (beats 2 & 4), probably by the alto saxophonist and trumpeter who are not heard from after the introduction.

0:00   Introduction: The opening melodic figure by the saxophones is the opening melody of "When the Saints Go Marching In," and is answered by "wa-wa" from the "growling" muted trumpet in a call-and-response riff style.

0:12   Sax Solo: The two-bar stop-time tenor sax break, in which the performer plays unaccompanied, is quite unusual. It moves from the low to high register and back, sounds angular, and seems more composed than improvised.

0:15   First Chorus (12 measures): Harris then proceeds with the first twelve-bar blues chorus in which he sings, "I heard the news, there's good rockin' tonight." He is accompanied by piano and bass playing a boogie woogie bass line. Note: The lyrics of the first line do not repeat in the usual spot, but instead repeat in the third line. At the end of the first line there is no instrumental response, and the lyrics of the second line fill up the whole four bars (16 foot taps).

0:35 Second Chorus: It opens with "Have you heard the news, everybody's gonna rock tonight." Once again the first line is repeated as the third line.

0:54 Third Chorus: This opens with "Oh! Meet me in the alley behind the barn." At the end of the second line (1:04) is a two-bar vocal break with Harris singing, "'Cause tonight I'm gonna rock away all of my blues." The absence of accompaniment here helps emphasize the lyrics and voice.

1:14 Fourth Chorus: This consists of a twelve-bar tenor sax solo built on the basic note of the song. Harris improvises background vocals to add to the party atmosphere. This style of sax playing is sometimes referred to as a "Texas tenor" sound and is heard on many of the rock recordings of the fifties. It was revived by Clarence Clemmons with Bruce Springsteen's Band.

1:33 Fifth Chorus: This opens with "I got the news . . . ." There is another two-bar vocal break at the end of the second line when he sings, "Tonight she'll know I'm a mighty man." Again, the third line is a repeat of the first.

1:52 Sixth Chorus: Harris mentions names of people who will be there and again has a two-bar vocal break at the end of the second line.

2:11 Seventh Chorus: Harris continues to mention names like Sweet Georgia Brown (a famous jazz song) and Caldonia (a famous Louis Jordan jump tune), and includes a break in the second line.

2:31 Final Chorus: The final blues chorus begins with the jive call: "Hoy Hoy Hoy Hoy." Harris improvises and is answered by the tenor saxophone as the song fades out.

For Musicians

The opening horn figure, based on the notes C-E-F-G, combines the alto and tenor sax in octaves. The first six bars of the intro features this lick and the trumpet answering through a wa-wa mute. The chord changes circle around I-vi-IV-V, and the two-bar tenor-sax break stretches across a two-octave V chord arpeggio and is unique in this context. The hand claps on beats two and four are also copied by the drums, and help establish the feel and the tempo. The recurring break at bars seven and eight during verses three, five, six, and seven finds the drums on beat one of the first measure and silent through the end of three and beat four of the second bar. This period of rest effectively sets apart the melodic material while providing "space" for the instrumental sound to resonate. The first three bars of the improvised tenor sax solo during verse four center on the tonic note. The vocal lines and tenor sax response during the final fadeout are also improvised.

Final Comments

"Good Rockin' Tonight," with its driving rhythm, double entendres, and \sexually inclined lyrics, proved the ideal R&B vehicle for both African-American and European-American artists of later decades. Elvis Presley's 1954 version of the song was one of the rhythm and blues songs the young rockabilly artist had in his repertoire. A variety of other artists have also covered the song, including Bill Haley, Pat Boone, and vocalist Jimmy Witherspoon.

♪♪♪ **"Got My Mojo Workin'"—performed by Muddy Waters**

Preston and Foster's classic Chicago blues song "Got My Mojo Workin'" shows Muddy Waters's electrified Delta blues style at its most fiery. Recorded by Waters in Chicago at Chess Records in 1956, this up-tempo recording combines the harmonica, electric guitar, and Waters's deep, powerful voice to create a rough, driving performance that set the standard for future rock and roll artists.

Analysis of "Got My Mojo Workin' "—4:11 in length, recorded December 1, 1956, on Chess 1652

Personnel: Muddy Waters, vocal and guitar; Little Walter, harmonica; Otis Spann, piano; Pete Hare, guitar; an unknown second guitarist; Willie Dixon, bass; and Francis Clay on drums.

0:00   Introduction, First Chorus (12 measures): The song begins two beats before the first bar of this classic twelve-bar blues. The piano starts with three syncopated chords making the opening bar and a half a challenge to count (six foot taps; the first three chords are in between the first three foot taps). The rest of the instruments come in on the second bar. It is clear when the group gets to the IV chord (0:08). The tempo of the song can be interpreted in two ways: as a very fast running tempo or as a very brisk walking tempo that is twice as slow as the first tempo. If the first tempo is chosen, then the blues form is twenty-four bars instead of twelve.

0:23   Second Chorus (12 measures): Waters sings two spirited blues choruses, the first beginning, "Got my mojo [magic] workin'," which is repeated in the traditional blues fashion in the third line, "I want to love you so bad 'till I don't know what to do." Each time, there is a syncopated instrumental response similar to the opening beats of the song featuring piano and harmonica.

0:46   Third Chorus (12 measures): Begins with "I'm goin' down to Louisiana . . . ." Each line is followed with the same syncopated instrumental response as the second chorus.

1:08   Fourth Chorus (12 measures): Still using the twelve-bar blues form, Waters sings a chorus of call-and-response between himself the band, singing the phrase "Got My Mojo Workin'."

1:32   Fifth Chorus (12 measures): A harmonica solo by Little Walter, which follows the blues form.

1:52   Sixth Chorus (12 measures): Walter continues his harmonica solo with coordinated "kicks" established by the piano, guitar, and drums at the beginning of the chorus.

2:15   Seventh Chorus (12 measures): Returns to Waters' vocal: "I got a Gypsy woman. . . ."

2:34   Eighth and Ninth Choruses (12 measures): Call-and-response similar to the fourth chorus, but now adding vocal lip burrs and other sounds so that the song's entire feel loosens up.

3:18   Tenth Chorus (12 measures): One more chorus like the earlier rhythmic instrumental break in the fourth chorus.

3:38   Eleventh Chorus (12 measures): Another call-and-response for the last chorus.

3:57   The abrupt stop in the tempo and music several bars later allows Waters to sing his last lines freely (rubato), and the band returns to finish the song at a slower tempo with an ascending instrumental line and final chord.

For Musicians

This twelve-bar blues in E major uses the standard I-IV-V progression but features a more intricate melodic figure in bars eleven and twelve of every phrase. The line descends in quarter notes (and sometimes eighth notes) on the pitches B, A#, A, and G#, eventually accentuating the note B (the dominant) in an eighth-note pattern. This "turnaround" formula for the final bars of a blues phrase is now a part of the vocabulary of rock and roll. The syncopated rhythm pattern established by the guitars and piano and constant drum accents on all the "ands" of the beat give this tune a "double-time feel," though the actual tempo would most likely be notated as half the implied time. Waters's distinctly rough vocal style and simple blues melodies combine with the repetitive nature of the background rhythms as each section evolves. The band's energy and excitement now shows with more improvisation and a looser approach in general. The raw but effective background vocals during the choruses add authentic charm to the tune, and Waters's exaggerated lip noises here add humor and compel the listener to try it for himself. The highly effective stop-time rubato vocal in bars eleven and twelve of the last chorus lead directly to an implied "half time" ending (really the true-time signature without the implied double-time feel), which ascends chromatically from the dominant chord on a now-traditional blues lick to a fermata on E.

Final Comments

Also recorded by singer Ann Cole in early 1957, "Got My Mojo Workin'" had its greatest influence and impact on the British blues artists of the mid-1960s. A staple in the repertoire of numerous bands, this song become one of the most covered tunes and copied song styles in the history of rock and roll.

---

[1] Nelson George, *The Death of Rhythm & Blues* (New York: Plume, 1988), 41.

[2] Wes Smith, *The Pied Pipers of Rock n' Roll: Radio Deejays of the 50s and 60s* (Marietta, Georgia: Longstreet, 1989), 56.

[3] Ibid., 67.

[4] Ibid., 124.

[5] Ibid., 123.

[6] Fredric Dannen, *Hit Men* (New York: Times Books Random House, 1990), 42.

[7] Alan Freed, *Dedication Vol. 1*, Silhouette SM 10006, 1982.

[8] Colin Escott with Martin Hawkins, *Good Rockin' Tonight: Sun Records and the Birth of Rock n' Roll* (New York: St. Martin's, 1991), 25.

Chapter Three

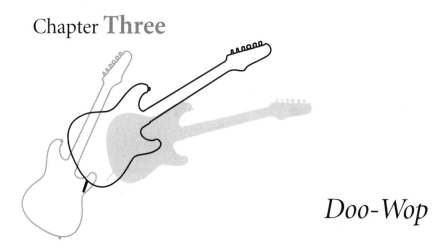

Doo-Wop

Jump blues wasn't the only R&B style to cross over into popular music in the 1950s. It was during this time that harmonizing vocal groups, some of which later became known as *doo-wop*, evolved as a genre. These R&B vocal groups developed out of previous pop models such as the Mills Brothers, the Ink Spots, and gospel groups like the Golden Gate Quartet. As already mentioned, African-American popular music has dual roots in sacred and secular music and, until the 1940s, the prevailing view was that holy music should not be tainted with secular "music of the devil." In the 1940s, gospel vocal techniques were beginning to merge with urban blues and also found their way into the music of the vocal groups. In fact, several early R&B groups, such as the Dominos and the Five Keys, were originally gospel groups.

The term *doo-wop* also conjures up images of amateur vocal groups singing on street corners for the sheer enjoyment of music. Certainly those amateur groups existed; however, many R&B vocal groups were already employed singing in churches and in small clubs. Frequently these groups, both amateur and professional, were "discovered" by a record producer who supplied the money to record, released one or two records, and then faded back into obscurity, often earning no royalties from the recording. This was not always the case, but it happened often enough. A good example is the Chords, who were discovered by a music professional who arranged for them to record "Sh-Boom" in 1954 for Atlantic Records. After the song became popular and was covered by the Crew Cuts, and the Chords faded back into obscurity.

Musical Characteristics

The major characteristics of the doo-wop style include a falsetto lead singer, a prominent bass voice, and, most importantly, backup vocalists singing riff-style accompaniments using *scat* syllables. Falsetto means "false voice"and describes the artificially high male voice used in this style and in Motown (see Chapter 8). Scat singers improvise jazz solos using nonsense syllables instead of words. The musical form of early doo-wop was usually the twelve-bar blues form; however, recordings after 1956 tended to have a thirty-two-bar AABA form with I-vi-IV-V chord changes. In AABA, each letter represents an eight-bar melody and helps identify the repetition scheme: 4 x 8 bars = 32 bars. Musicians use Roman numerals to represent the relationship of the chord to the key (pitch level) of the song. In the key of C, I-vi-IV-V would be C major/A minor/F major/G major.

The most important musical characteristic of this style, the scat syllables, had been used for vocal improvisation since the late 1920s, when Louis Armstrong recorded "Heebie Jeebies." Later in the 1940s, *swing* and *bop* musicians used scat syllables as part of the lyrics to songs. The number one R&B record of 1946 was "Hey! Ba-Ba-Re-Bop" by Lionel Hampton's jump blues band. This use of riff-style scat syllables is an extension of two of the African musical characteristics: call-and-response patterns, and a percussive approach to sound.

Groups, especially amateurs, often sang without instrumental accompaniment. When groups perform without instruments, the musical term *a capella* is applied; this sub-genre is known as *a capella doo-wop*. It is likely that riff-styled scat syllable accompaniments originated because of a lack of instrumental accompaniment; the vocal riffs substituted for instrumental riffs. Most record companies were production-oriented and believed that music needed instrumental accompaniment to sound polished and professional, so they often added a group of studio musicians to acapella doo-wop groups. Typically, the studio musicians had little or no rehearsal time with the singers, so often the arrangements were little more than improvised *head arrangements*: arrangements using no written music.[1] The head arrangements used in doo-wop recordings most often featured a "screaming" saxophone solo derived from musical techniques developed by the late 1940s jump bands.

As doo-wop crossed over to pop stations, the lyric content came under closer scrutiny, became tamer, and tended to focus on innocent love. Although earlier doo-wop had its share of innocent songs, in the late 1940s and early 1950s, many recordings such as "Sixty-Minute Man" and "Work With Me Annie" had sensual themes that offended the sensibilities of mainstream pop audiences. R&B crossover artists such as Chuck Berry and Little Richard, and rockabilly artists such as Jerry Lee Lewis, took a beating from the public for their use of suggestive lyrics. It was no wonder that soon after vocal groups crossed over to the pop charts, they began to appear with clean-cut images and innocent lyrics. With groups such as the Platters ("Only You," "The Great Pretender"), Frankie Lymon and the Teenagers ("Why Do Fools Fall In Love"), and Dion and the Belmonts ("I Wonder Why"), even the harshest critics could not find anything objectionable.

Group Names

During all of rock's style periods, groups chose names that were somewhat similar to each other, and those names can be used to identify the period in which the group was active, just as hair styles can be used to date a photograph. Doo-wop group names are similarly distinctive. A name trend begins because a group achieves success with an unusual name and others somehow want to be connected with that success. The first two important post-war R&B vocal groups were the Ravens and the Orioles; soon other groups used bird names. In 1955, a group called the Cadillacs hit with "Speedo" and began a trend of automobile names. In 1954, that group's manager had changed their name from the Carnations to the Cadillacs because flower names were too common; other name trends developed for similar reasons.

EARLY VOCAL GROUPS

A discussion of only the classic doo-wop would ignore many of the most important vocal groups of the fifties, and a discussion of only the individual groups would ignore the music business professionals who either discovered

---

Doo-Wop Names

Birds:	Ravens, Orioles, Cardinals, Penguins, Robins, Crows, Sparrows, Bluebirds, Larks, Skylarks, Swallows, Blue Jays, Flamingos, Parrots, Swans, Whippoorwills, Buzzards, Eagles, Hawks, Parakeets, Peacocks, Pelicans, Quails, Wrens, Drakes, Ospreys, Doves, Nightingales, Hummingbirds, Pheasants, Warblers, Owls, Whooping Cranes
Jewels:	Diamonds, Crystals, Jewels, Rubies, Emeralds, Gems, Opals, Pearls, Garnets, Jades, Sapphires
Flowers:	Carnations, Asters, Orchids, Daffodils, Marigolds, Gladiolas, Hollyhocks, Roses, Tiger Lilies, Daisies
Cars:	Cadillacs, El Dorados, Imperials, Impalas, Fleetwoods, T-Birds, Rivieras, Corvairs, De Villes, New Yorkers, Galaxies, Packards, Bentleys, Jaguars, Fiats
Numbers:	Five Keys, Five Satins, Jive Five, Five Fashions, Five Discs, Five Sharps, Four Dots, Four Fellows, Four J's, Five Crowns
Musical:	Keynotes, Five Keys, Keys, Delchords, Tones, Harptones, Chords, Blue Notes, Bop Chords, Cleftones, Five Sharps, G-Clefs, Teenchords, Tonettes

or fabricated the groups, wrote or chose songs, and crafted the accompaniments. Behind the groups and recordings is a fixed group of professional recordmen: Ahmet Ertegun, Jerry Wexler, and Jesse Stone of Atlantic Records; Syd Nathan and Ralph Bass of King Records; and George Goldner of Rama and Gee Records.

Groups by Company

Atlantic, Atco & Cat Records:

Clovers, Drifters, Chords, Cardinals, Diamonds, Coasters, Clyde McPhatter, Sensations

King, Federal Records:

Dominos, Hank Ballard and the Midnighters, Checkers, Five Keys, Gum Drops, Hurricanes, Lamplighters, Platters, Strangers, Swallows

Rama, Gee, Gone, and End Records:

Crows, Frankie Lymon and the Teenagers, Valentines, Cleftones, Little Anthony & the Imperials, Chantels, Flamingos, Harptones, Heartbeats, Wrens, Dubs

---

Atlantic Records

Although the Ertegun Brothers intended Atlantic Records to be a jazz label, they experienced early success with R&B recordings. One of their groups, the Drifters, became one of the most influential and longest lasting groups of the decade. The early Drifters are a good example of doo-wop; however, the later version of the Drifters does not easily fall into the category of classic doo-wop, because they did not employ as many doo-wop characteristics as other classic doo-wop groups. They were already evolving out of the older style. The story of the Drifters is a good example of the importance of the professional recordmen to the success of a group.

Their story begins with the Dominos. Originally a gospel group, the Dominos were owned by Billy Ward and featured Clyde McPhatter. Before they met, Billy Ward, a Juilliard graduate, was coaching and managing a gospel group called the Ques, while Clyde McPhatter, just graduated from high school, had formed a gospel group called the Mount Lebanon Singers. Around 1950, McPhatter entered the amateur contest at the Apollo Theater, won, and was approached by Billy Ward, who decided to build a group around him.

The Dominos appeared as a gospel group on Arthur Godfrey's popular *Talent Scouts* program and won. At some point, they came into contact with Ralph Bass, a producer for Syd Nathan's King records and signed with that label.

Ralph Bass, one of the important R&B record producers of the early period, began with Black and White Records, owned several companies, and then worked for Savoy, King, and Chess Records. At King he produced the Dominos, Midnighters, Five Royals, James Brown, Ike Turner, Etta James, and Johnny Otis. When he began working for King, Bass worked out a production deal with Syd Nathan that paid him a one-half-cent royalty, making him the first independent producer. In addition to the royalty arrangement, he was given control of Federal Records, a subsidiary of King.

At some point, the Dominos switched from gospel to R&B, and in 1951 recorded "Sixty-Minute Man," which became the number one R&B recording of the year. Although the topic was sex, the sound of the group was purely gospel, with hand-clapping, singing bass, a falsetto obbligato, and vocal riffs. As mentioned earlier, the record was one of the energetic choices teenagers found on the R&B stations and a cause of great parental concern because of the sexual topic. Their next hit, "Have Mercy Baby," displayed more of their gospel roots than "Sixty-Minute Man" had, and by 1952 they had surpassed the Five Keys and Clovers in popularity.

Billy Ward was a tough band leader and had a system of fines for various infractions of his rules. He paid the Dominos only one hundred dollars a week, from which he deducted fines, taxes, food costs, and hotel bills. In 1953, some members of the group had a fight over Ward's tight control, and they either quit or were fired. The very night that Ahmet Ertegun of Atlantic Records learned of the split, he contacted McPhatter and built the Drifters around him, just as Ward had done.[2] Their first release, "Money Honey," a novelty song, was a big hit. The topic of the song was the importance of money to people like the landlord and his girlfriend. The background singers used the phrase "Bop-bop-uh bop-suh-oop" and there was a screaming saxophone solo by Sam "The Man" Taylor. The group had a string of hits including "Bip Bam," "Honey Love," "Such a Night," and "White Christmas."

After McPhatter was drafted into the Army, he put his career on hold until his discharge in 1956, when he embarked on a successful solo career with hits such as "Treasure of Love," "Without Love (There Is Nothing)," and "A Lover's Question." The Drifters continued with a variety of lead singers. In 1958, the original Drifters quit or were fired, and the group's manager, George Treadwell, who owned the name and wanted to continue, found a new group to be the Drifters. The new group, formerly known as the Five Crowns with lead singer Ben E. King, began their long association with Atlantic, Treadwell, and songwriters/producers Jerry Leiber and Mike Stoller.[3] In 1960, Ben E. King went solo and was replaced by a succession of lead singers. Leiber and Stoller produced songs such as "There Goes My Baby," "This Magic Moment," and "Save the Last Dance for Me," which are probably the best-remembered Drifters hits. King's hits after leaving the Drifters were "Spanish Harlem" (1961), "Stand By Me" (1961), and "I (Who Have Nothing)" (1963). This later incarnation of the Drifters began to evolve out of the doo-wop style and into what would be called *sweet soul music*. Leiber and Stoller's production techniques moved away from the heavy backbeat and screaming sax solos and began to focus on creative orchestrations using strings, Spanish guitar solos, triangle, claves, guiro, and other formerly exotic sounds. During this time, a young Phil Spector was in New York working for Atlantic and watching over the shoulders of Leiber and Stoller. Later Spector used some of these techniques to develop his personal style, which came to be known as the *wall of sound*.

The succession of groups that began in 1950 with Billy Ward and the Dominos and ended in 1966 was manufactured by the record industry. Billy Ward knew the sound he wanted, hired singers to reproduce it, and sold it; however, his lack of people skills caused his group to disintegrate. This downfall opened the door of opportunity for Atlantic Records and Ahmet Ertegun, who seized it and created the Drifters. The Drifters continued to exist in spite of several changes in lead singers because the group was owned and perpetuated by music industry professionals. The artists were merely a spoke in the wheel of the music business. According to Ben E. King, when he was with the Drifters he never made more than one hundred dollars a week. He may have been the star but, like the other group members, he was ultimately only an employee.

Leiber and Stoller

Songwriters Jerry Leiber and Mike Stoller, two of rock's most successful songwriter/producers, were associated with Atlantic Records before starting their own record label, Red Bird Records. From 1957 to 1960, the team crafted a handful of major hit recordings for the Drifters, the Coasters, and Elvis Presley. Leiber and Stoller met and began to write songs while still attending high school in Los Angeles. Their career started to take off one day when they pitched a song to Lester Sill, a salesman for Modern Records, and he invited them to a recording session with a group called the Robins. When Sill quit Modern to become a distributor, he hired Leiber and Stoller as shipping clerks.

Sometime in 1953, an R&B band leader named Johnny Otis ("Willie and the Hand Jive," 1958) called Sill looking for songs for a recording session with Willie Mae "Big Mama" Thornton. Leiber and Stoller instantly began writing on a paper bag and turned out "Hound Dog" (the same one Elvis recorded). At the time, they were seventeen years old.

Sill, Leiber and Stoller eventually decided to go into business together and produce recordings to lease to other record companies. The first song they produced, "Black Denim Trousers," was sold to Capitol and recorded by the Cheers in 1955. The song played on the public's fascination with motorcycle gangs, which had been popularized by the Marlon Brando movie *The Wild One*. Sometime around 1955, they started Spark Records and reached the charts with "I Gotta New Car" by Big Boy Groves. Their first big success, however, came with the Robins.

In 1955, the Robins recorded "Smokey Joe's Cafe," a Leiber and Stoller song, and the recording was purchased and released on Atlantic's subsidiary Atco.[4] At this point Leiber and Stoller began their long and creative association with Atlantic. Soon after the release of the recording, the Robins dissolved and two of them elected to move to New York with Leiber and Stoller and become the core of a new group called the Coasters. Leiber and Stoller's comical mini-drama, "Smokey Joe's Cafe'," set the tone for the future Coasters. The term *playlet* best describes that style because the songs usually told a story in a comedic style of some facet of a teenager's life. The Coasters' most popular recordings were "Searchin'," "Young Blood," "Yakety Yak," "Charlie Brown," "Along Came Jones," and "Poison Ivy." Leiber and Stoller, like Chuck Berry, consciously avoided typical early R&B topics like sex and alcohol, unlike the early Drifters and Clovers. The change in lyric content was unavoidable because record companies needed airplay to make recordings popular and to

---

The Hits of Leiber and Stoller

Black Denim Trousers and Motorcycle Boots (1955)	Poison Ivy (1959)
	Charlie Brown (1959)
Smokey Joe's Cafe (1955)	There Goes My Baby (1959 & 1984)
Down in Mexico (1956)	Save the Last Dance For Me (1960)
Hound Dog (1956)	Little Egypt (1961)
Love Me Tender (1956)	Spanish Harlem (1961)
Ruby Baby (1956 & 1963)	Stand By Me (1961)
Jailhouse Rock (1957)	I (Who Have Nothing) (1963 & 1970)
Loving You (1957)	On Broadway (1963)
Searchin' (1957)	Only in America (1963)
Yakety Yak (1958)	Come a Little Bit Closer (1964)
Along Came Jones (1959)	Is That All There Is (1969)
Kansas City (1959)	I'm a Woman (1974)
Love Potion Number Nine (1959 & 1964)	

collect performance royalties, and radio stations would not play records they deemed offensive.

The Platters

The Platters were another very successful R&B vocal group from the early doo-wop era. Their success came in the 1955–56 period just as classic doo-wop was evolving. The Platters sang in an older Ink Spot style and never quite became a classic doo-wop group. Their biggest hits, "Only You" (No. 29, 1955), "My Prayer" (No. 4, 1956), and "The Great Pretender" (No. 12, 1956), had background singers, used slow, long "ahs" as an accompaniment rather than the rhythmic scat syllables used by the emerging doo-wop style, and did not have a prominent bass voice or extensive use of falsetto. Their three recordings probably did well on the

The Platters

charts precisely because they were more like the older Ink Spots than the newer R&B vocal groups. Regardless, their presence on the charts was helpful in exposing pop audiences to African-American vocal groups.

The success of the Platters was also a result of the work of industry professionals, because they became successful only after lead singer Tony Williams was discovered and placed in the group. Ralph Bass and Hunter Hancock, a Los Angeles DJ, started an amateur show in Los Angeles "specifically to find talent," and it was here that they discovered Tony Williams.[5] They signed Williams to a contract because they perceived him as a modern Bill Kenny

(Ink Spots) and placed him in the Platters because they thought that the group could succeed in that genre. Indeed, the Platters had a successful recording career and today are regulars on the oldies circuit.

Hank Ballard and the Midnighters

Hank Ballard and the Midnighters were an early doo-wop group worthy of mention. They did not rely on falsetto singing or a prominent bass voice, but they used some scat syllables and imparted plenty of gospel feeling. They earned their place in music history with their 1954 series of "Annie" records. The first, "Work With Me Annie," had an infectious groove and was very popular, although it contained some of the sexual inference typical of earlier R&B and was banished from the airways. The word "work" as a metaphor for sex would have gone unnoticed except for the lines "Umm don't cheat, gimme all a my meat," and "Let's get it while the gettin' is good." The record industry had a problem to solve: It was a great song that would sell in large quantities, but it was sexually offensive. The industry's answer was to get another group to cover the song and to change the meaning of the lyrics. "Work with Me Annie" became Georgia Gibb's "Dance With Me Henry" and reached number ten on the year-end chart, just behind two other covers: Fats Domino's "Ain't That a Shame" covered by Pat Boone, and the Moonglow's "Sincerely" covered by the McGuire Sisters. Interestingly, the word "dance" was substituted for the word "work," changing the message in the same way that the phrase "rock and roll" earlier had replaced "R&B" and changed its meaning from a sexual euphemism to music and dancing.

Hank Ballard and the Midnighters recorded two sequels, "Annie Had a Baby" and "Annie's Aunt Fanny." Ballard must not have understood, or cared about, the aversion pop radio had toward sexual innuendo in songs, because his follow-up recordings reinforced the message of the first recording. His new lyrics included "Annie had a baby, can't work no more," and "That's what happens when the gettin' gets good." The songs were humorous and in no way smutty, but they left no doubt that Annie had a sexual history. The title "Work with Me Annie" was contributed by Ralph Bass, who tried to soften the impact of the original title, "Sock It to Me, Mary."[6] It is worth mentioning that Hank Ballard also wrote "The Twist," a song popularized by Chubby Checker in 1960, and a careful listening reveals that the term "twistin'" could easily have a sexual meaning.

CLASSIC DOO-WOP

The doo-wop style crystallized into its classic form around 1955 when many of its defining characteristics—especially falsetto voice, scat syllables, and a prominent bass voice—began appearing together on the same recording.

George Goldner and Frankie Lymon & the Teenagers

For George Goldner, the Teenagers were just one of ninety-three doo-wop groups he recorded. His early experience in the recording industry was in Latin music as the owner of Tico Records. When R&B began to cross over in the early fifties, Goldner created Rama Records and later Gee, Gone, End, Roulette, Mark-X, Cindy, Goldisc, Juanita, and Tee-Gee. Having many different record labels was a common practice among independent companies, because radio disc jockeys tended to avoid playing "too many" recordings from the same label. Atlantic had acts that were noted for their longevity: the Clovers, Drifters, and Coasters. Goldner's acts had shorter careers, but his labels probably released more classic doo-wop than any other company: the Crows, Frankie Lymon and the Teenagers, the Cleftones, the Harptones, the Mello-tones, the Dubs, the Heartbeats, Little Anthony and the Imperials, and the Regents.

The first major R&B group Goldner signed was the Crows, who came to his attention after they won an amateur contest at the Apollo Theater. Their second release in 1954 was "Gee," which reached number five on the charts and put Goldner and his Rama label on the map, so much so that he named his first subsidiary label after the song. This was the label that signed the Teenagers in 1956.

Frankie Lymon's story is a perfect example of the typical path to stardom traveled by young doo-wop singers. In the Washington Heights area of New York, Lymon and some friends formed the Teenagers (originally the Premiers), and with a little luck and a great song they became the best known teenage doo-wop group of the 1950s. The Teenagers were discovered by Richard Barrett, a former singer with the Valentines and a producer for George Goldner's many R&B labels. The Teenagers were rehearsing outside Barrett's home when Barrett heard them through his window. After rehearsing with the group and coaching Frankie Lymon in singing technique, Barrett set up an audition for the Teenagers with Goldner. The song they had rehearsed with Barrett and sang for Goldner was "Why Do Fools Fall In Love?" The song/poem had been written by Lymon when he was in the fifth grade, but not surprisingly, Goldner's name appears as co-writer. It is important to remember that part of the profit structure of indies was to claim ownership and collect mechanical and performance royalties.

Frankie Lymon's voice was high, clear, and pre-adolescent sounding when he recorded the song in 1956 at age thirteen. The Teenagers received a great deal of fame, but unfortunately Lymon experienced the ill effects of becoming famous too fast. After returning from a tour of Great Britain, he left the Teenagers to begin what was to be an unsuccessful solo career. Lymon never made much money from his records because he was under twenty-one; Goldner paid him an allowance of around twenty-five dollars a week and supposedly put

Frankis Lymon and the Teenagers

the remainder in a trust fund. Of course, no trust fund existed—in the record business any money that comes in goes out immediately to finance new records. By 1961, Lymon's voice had changed, his recording career was over, and he had developed an addiction to heroin. His drug use eventually took his life in 1968 at the age of twenty-six.

The Heartbeats

James "Shep" Sheppard and his groups were responsible for two doo-wop classics: "A Thousand Miles Away" as the Heartbeats, and "Daddy's Home" as Shep and the Limelites. They formed in the mid-fifties and appeared on Alan Freed's Academy of Music Stage Show in 1955. Although they specialized in slow ballads, someone at their record company suggested that they alter their style and add up-tempo jump songs; they even hired the Cadillac's choreo-graphers to restyle the group. Their first record in the new style was not successful, but its flip side, "A Thousand Miles Away," was. "A Thousand Miles Away" became a classic in the doo-wop style. It had Shep's high voice, not really falsetto until the final notes, "rat-ta-tat-tat" and "doo-wops" in the accompaniment, a prominent role for the bass singer, and a I-vi-IV-V chord progression. The success of this record was too much for their record company, Hull Records, who did not have the resources to manufacture and distribute enough records to meet the demand. They sold the group, copyrights, and masters to George Goldner's Rama label. The group continued to tour and record, but nothing surpassed their previous success. They disbanded in 1959 after the classic period of doo-wop ended.

In 1960, Sheppard formed Shep and the Limelites, returned to Hull Records, and had a second career in the doo-wop revival. Their first release, "Daddy's Home" (1961), was essentially a remake of "A Thousand Miles Away." It had the same chord changes, used "rat-ta-tat" and "doo-wop" in the accompaniment, and even reprised lyrics from their first hit at the end: "I'm not a thousand miles away." The similarities were recognized by George Goldner, who bought them after their first hit. He sued Hull for copyright infringement and won. This put Hull out of business and ended the career of Shep and the Limelites.

One-Hit Wonders

Doo-wop, unlike other styles, is difficult to discuss because few individual groups stand out as major forces; instead, individual recordings by one-hit groups stand out. For example, "Get a Job" by the Silhouettes (1958) was so popular that the song's scat syllables were used as a name for a comedic doo-wop revival group, Sha-Na-Na, which became immensely popular after their 1969 Woodstock performance. "Get a Job" begins with the bass singing, "dip-dip-dip-dip-dip-dip-dip-wha" and is answered by the group singing, "sha-na-non-na-sha-na-na-na-non-na." Another one-hit group was the Monotones, whose "Book of Love" (1958) had an infectious energy that could not be resisted by record buyers. Although the song's tempo rushes, as much as any recording ever released, the excitement of their delivery more than compensates for their musical deficiencies.

Neo Doo-Wop

After 1958, there was a decline in "classic" doo-wop characteristics until about 1960, when an upturn occurred, creating a revival of sorts. Not only were the characteristics of doo-wop revitalized between the years 1960 and 1963, but the characteristics were often exaggerated, almost parodied. One example is the Marcels' exaggerated use of scat syllables in both their 1961 hits, "Blue Moon" and "Heartaches." Other late doo-wop songs were Maurice Williams and the Zodiacs' "Stay" (1960), the Regents' "Barbara Ann" (1961), the Capris' "There's a Moon Out Tonight" (1961), and the Jive Five's "My True Story" (1961).

After 1963, doo-wop changed considerably to compete with the vocal harmony styles of the Beatles, Byrds, and Beach Boys. Scat syllables were replaced by words, the bass became much less prominent, and falsetto singing was used much less as a lead role. R&B vocal groups continued to produce music, but by 1960, they had new style designations: Smokey Robinson and the Miracles, the Four Tops, and the Temptations were part of the Motown sound; the Spinners and Harold Melvin and the Blue Notes were part of the Philly sound. In the 1990s, the style was reinvented by groups like Take Six and Boyz To Men.

LISTENING TO THE MUSIC ...

♪♪ "Why Do Fools Fall in Love?"—performed by Frankie Lymon and the Teenagers

The form is 32-bar A-A-B-A, and each section (letter) is eight measures (8 measures × 4 sections = 32 measures). The meter is "in two"; you begin tapping your foot to the opening syllables of the bass singer. Personnel: Lymon, lead vocals; Herman Santiago and Jimmy Merchant, tenors; Joe Negroni, baritone; Sherman Garnes, bass; backed by saxophonist Jimmy Wright and his band.

Analysis of "Why Do Fools Fall in Love?"—2:17 in length. Recorded in late 1955 on Gee 1002.

0:00 Introduction (10 measures): The song begins with the bass singer outlining the bass line of the chord progression with the syllables, "Day-dum-what-ta-dum-what-ta-dum-what-ta-dum-what-ta." Two measures later, the group and band enter with the acoustic bass playing the same notes as the bass singer. Lymon and the other voices sing, "ooo-wah, ooo-wah" in choral-style vocal harmony. Lymon's voice, unchanged by adolescence, is high, and he also uses the falsetto voice later.

0:14 A Section (8 measures): The A melody begins with the lyrics, "Why do birds . . . ," and the singers' riff in the background creates a "layered rhythm," with one singer in the falsetto range. The tenor saxophone plays a one-note rhythmic riff (the percussive use of sound is another African musical characteristic).

0:25 A Section (8 measures): A repeat of the "A" melody with different words begins, "Why does the rain . . . ." The way Lymon sings the words "does the rain" is a good example of the subtle syncopation of African-American music. The background parts of this section are unchanged.

0:36 B Section (8 measures): In an AABA form the B section is called the bridge and consists of a contrasting melody. The lyrics begin, "Love is a losing game," and the background singers use long notes rather than the rhythmic background of the A section. The last two measures of this section are in a stop-time style during the lyrics, "For that fool is me."

0:47 A Section (8 measures): The original chords return, but Lymon sings, "Tell me why . . . ," going into the falsetto range on the word "why." The saxophone riff has now expanded and uses several notes in the riff.

0:59 Sax Solo on the A section (8 measures): The rhythm section goes "into four" (4 foot taps per measure), and Jimmy Wright begins a 16-bar saxophone solo based on the chords of the A section. This sax style comes directly from the jump blues style and has been referred to as a "screaming sax solo" and a "Texas tenor sound." Notice how his solo is constructed: a typical riff played three times followed by a closing melody. Notice also that the sax solo is accompanied by a guitar riff.

1:09 A Section (8 measures): The sax solo continues, and the construction should be noted: Instead of three direct repeated riffs, it consists of three similar phrases, each with the same lead-in notes.

1:21 A Section (8 measures): The music of the first section repeats "Why do birds sing," and the background vocal riffs seem more audible, probably because the falsetto singer is no longer in the mix.

1:31 A Section (8 measures): "Why does the rain."

1:42 B Section (8 measures): The bridge, with new lyrics beginning, "Why does my heart."

1:53 A Section (8 measures): The music of the last "A" section is repeated, and Lymon again goes into the falsetto range on the word "why."

2:04 Coda (8 measures): Lymon sings the phrase "Why do fools fall in love," in long notes that occupy the entire eight measures, and the saxophone plays a standard closing formula.

For Musicians

The opening bass vocal line's use of the notes E-C#-F#-B of the "I-vi-ii-V" chord progression is known as "rhythm changes," and is very common in pop songs, as well as dozens of jazz and R&B songs. The eight measure introduction follows this sequence in E major (E-C#m-F#m-B), with two beats per bar for each chord. The vocal break in bars seven and eight prepares the listener for the upcoming verses by stating the title lyric. The verses Lymon eloquently sings consist of two eight-bar phrases harmonically based on the stated chord progression. The bridge moves to the IV chord (A), with two bars following the I-vi-ii-V sequence, this time starting on A (A-F#m-C#m-E6), and two bars of turnaround material moving from A to F#m. to F#7 to B7. The next bars are unique, as Lymon ascends to hold the note B over the earlier chord sequence, once again back in E, creating a wonderful color tone. Lymon smoothly descends melodically to the note G#, and finishes the eight-bar phrase by singing "tell me why" and holding the last word over four descending quarter notes moving down to the tonic. The quick switch to walking bass lines and a swing drum feel initiate the sixteen-bar tenor sax solo, which hovers around an E7 chord and relies heavily on blues riffs. Lymon returns with the opening two verses and bridge once again, treating listeners to the same unusual melodic twist at the end of the phrase. The final section of the piece moves to the IV chord for two measures (A), and the V chord for two more (B), before working its way out over the tonic sonority A band riff in the last bar, silent beat three, and final hold on beat four end the recording.

Final Comments

Released in 1956 by the Teenagers, featuring Frankie Lymon, this single sold two million copies. The pop doo-wop vocal group, the Diamonds, reached number twelve with their cover, and a version by vocalist Gale Storm (star of television's *My Little Margie*) reached number nine in 1957. Decades later, in 1981, Diana Ross's cover reached number seven on the pop charts.

---

[1] Jerry Wexler and David Ritz, *Rhythm and the Blues: A Life in American Music* (New York: Knopf, 19913), 89.

[2] Arnold Shaw, *Honkers and Shouters: The Golden Years of Rhythm & Blues* (New York: Macmillan, 1978), 382.

[3] Ibid., 384.

[4] Ibid., 390.

[5] Ibid., 241.

[6] Ibid., 244.

Chapter Four

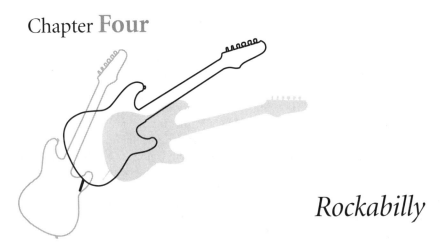

Rockabilly

Rockabilly, more than any other style, is associated with one particular record label, Sun Records, and includes artists such as Elvis Presley, Carl Perkins, Jerry Lee Lewis, and to some extent Roy Orbison and Johnny Cash. A broader definition of the term often includes Buddy Holly, the Everly Brothers, and even Bill Haley. In its most basic definition, rockabilly identifies the first generation of European-American musicians from the Southern states who recorded rhythm and blues or songs in an R&B style. The instruments of a rockabilly band are rhythm guitar, lead guitar, acoustic string bass, drums, and sometimes piano. The instrumentation of the bands most likely evolved from the string-band tradition rather than jazz-based jump bands, which almost always included a saxophone. Acoustic bass players often used a technique called "slap" bass, in which the strings were hit hard enough with the hand so that they hit the fingerboard, making a clicking sound, and then immediately plucked with the fingers of the same hand on the return motion. This technique made the bass more rhythmic and helped substitute for drums, absent in country string bands.

Rockabilly bands often tried to emulate the exuberant showmanship of R&B groups. This usually took the form of dancing and extra-animated stage movements. An example of this is Elvis's hip and knee movements, and exaggerated motions can be seen in Jerry Lee Lewis's piano-playing. Rockabilly clothing styles were often loud and flashy, in an attempt to copy perceptions of African-American clothing styles. Elvis is often described as a "cat," and he purchased his "cat" clothing at Lansky's in Memphis. *Cat* is hipster slang from the bebop era of jazz, and generally means the same thing as "man" or "dude." The rockabilly hair style tended to be a tall pompadour with plenty of hair cream to give it a slick look.

BILL HALEY AND THE COMETS

Bill Haley is a peculiar case because, although he led a western swing band, his musical experiences occurred on the East Coast rather than in the South and, consequently, his approach was more urban than that of the Sun recording artists. Western swing, a hybrid fusion of swing (boogie woogie) and country, provided fertile ground for a further fusion of country and R&B. Haley, one of the first European-American transitional figures, never planned on becoming a rock and roll legend; he started out trying to become America's foremost yodeler. Countless books have discussed Haley as an unlikely candidate for rock stardom because of his pudgy appearance and the funny spit curl dangling on his forehead. What he lacked was the dark, sullen rebel-without-a-cause look of Elvis, James Dean, and Sal Mineo.

Haley, who was from the Philadelphia area, was part of a trend of the postwar period, when country music began to escape the boundaries of the South and infiltrate Northern urban centers. African-American music was experiencing a similar exportation at the same time. Before it became the Comets, Haley's band was called the Four Aces of Western Swing, and their first recording, "Too Many Parties, Too Many Pals" and "Four Leaf Clover Blues," was released in 1948 on Cowboy Records. Around 1949, Haley formed a new group, the Saddlemen, which became the nucleus for the Comets. The instrumentation was typical for a cowboy band, with steel guitar, piano/accordion, acoustic bass, electric guitar, and drums.

It appears that Haley's foray into R&B was accidental, or at least lighthearted. According to biographer Jack Howard, when Haley was performing at the Twin Bars in Gloucester, New Jersey, he started the set off "almost as if he were joking with a blues song called 'Rock the Joint.' The crowd, full of hillbilly fans, went crazy."[1] Haley says he became aware of the song because his country music radio show on WPWA followed an R&B show hosted by Jim Reeves called "Judge Rhythm's Court" that used "Rock the Joint" as its theme song.[2]

In 1951, Dave Miller, a record-pressing plant owner, approached Haley with the idea of covering Jackie Brenston's "Rockett 88." Haley recorded the song, but Miller rejected Haley's first version because it lacked the proper "feel." Miller produced a second version that was released on Holiday Records with "Tear Stains on My Heart" on the flip side.[3] It was not a big hit, but it was the first significant cover of an R&B recording by a country artist. A few years later, Sam Phillips tried the same type of cover with Elvis's recording of "Good Rocking Tonight."

In 1952, Haley and the Saddlemen, after several other recordings, released "Rock the Joint" backed with "Icy Heart" on Dave Miller's new Essex label. "Icy Heart" was intended to be the A-side, but while Haley was in Nashville promoting "Icy Heart," he got a call from Miller informing him that "Rock the

Joint" was getting airplay and he was told to start pushing it. This is most likely the moment Haley became a rock and roll singer. Among the items to be gleaned from this story are (1) Haley became a rock singer because social conditions were right, and (2) producer Dave Miller had instincts that told him European-American teens were looking for R&B in a safe package. These facts do not tarnish Haley's talent as a rock star. They do, however, spread the credit around to include industry professionals.

In 1953, Bill Haley changed the name of his band to the Comets and began to pursue a new sound. When writing songs, he tried to focus on phrases using the word "rock" and other "hipster jive expressions," as he called them. The effort succeeded, and in 1953 he recorded his biggest hit to date, "Crazy, Man, Crazy." After his contract with Essex expired, Haley auditioned for Milt Gabler at Decca Records, who thought the band had potential and signed him. Gabler had years of experience as a jump blues producer because he had produced Louis Jordan's recordings when the artist recorded for Decca during the late forties. Haley's first Decca session (1954) resulted in "(We're Gonna) Rock Around the Clock," which sold 75,000 copies. However, it did not become the emblem of the rock age until after it was used as theme music for the movie *The Blackboard Jungle*. Before that happened, Haley recorded a cover of Joe Turner's "Shake, Rattle, and Roll," which became rock's first million-selling recording. As mentioned earlier, Gabler and Haley cleaned up the lyrics to get the recording past the censors. As producer, Gabler was instrumental in developing Haley's sound and giving him a more authentic jump blues feel by teaching Haley's band members Louis Jordan riffs.[4]

It was Gabler's musical suggestions that helped further the fusion of R&B and country music; thus he was a partner in the formulation of the early rock and roll sound. The credit for helping "Rock Around the Clock" become identified with the growing sense of a teenager rebellion goes to songwriter Jim Meyers, who sent two hundred copies of the recording to Hollywood. Some of them fell into the right hands, as evidenced by the song's selection as the theme music for *The Blackboard Jungle*. It was the first movie to use a rock and roll theme song—a choice that marked the beginning of the acceptance of rock and roll as popular music.

Although Haley became rock's first European-American star, he was destined to be replaced by Elvis Presley and the other stars who presented a more defiant image. By the time Haley returned from his European tour, his style of jump blues had been replaced by newer trends and newer artists. Haley's problems with alcohol thwarted his many attempts to regain his former glory as a recording artist, but he remained popular in England and Mexico until his death in 1981. Haley's true importance was as a transitional figure whose recordings helped demonstrate the approach needed to combine R&B's musical characteristics with those of country and western.

SAM PHILLIPS AND SUN STUDIOS

The first true rockabilly artists were recorded in Memphis by Sam Phillips on Sun Records. Phillips's stable of performers included Carl Perkins, Roy Orbison, Jerry Lee Lewis, Johnny Cash, and Elvis Presley.

Sam Phillips was raised in Florence, Alabama (home of W. C. Handy), where he heard African-American music while quite young and came to appreciate its emotion and intensity. After moving to Memphis in 1944, Phillips became involved in radio as an engineer at station WREC and later, in 1950, he started the Memphis Recording Service. Phillips realized that the city had many talented blues artists, but there was no one willing to record them. By 1951, Phillips was recording blues and selling masters to Chess Records in Chicago and Modern/RPM in Los Angeles. That year, he recorded and sold to Chess Jackie Brenston's recording of "Rockett 88," often considered one of the first rock and roll recordings. The recording was by Ike Turner's band, but because of a mix-up, the label mentioned only Jackie Brenston's name. As a result, Ike became angry with Phillips and began to work as a talent scout for Modern/RPM. After the success of "Rockett 88," Phillips realized that he could start his own record company and, in April of 1952, issued his first recording as Sun Records.

Phillips began recording African-American artists such as Rufus Thomas ("Bear Cat"), Howlin' Wolf, the Prisonaires ("Walking in the Rain"), James Cotton ("Cotton Crop Blues"), Junior Parker ("Mystery Train"), and Little Milton ("If You Love Me"). Once he realized that there was a crossover market for blues-based music, he knew he could make a lot of money if he could find a European-American singer who could capture the emotion and intensity of blues and R&B artists.

Sun Records still did custom work as the Memphis Recording Service, allowing anyone to walk in off the street and make a recording. In the summer of 1953, Elvis Presley wandered into the studio and recorded "My Happiness" and "That's When Your Heartaches Begin," which he said was for his mother's birthday. According to Phillips's secretary (really an office manager), Marion Keisker, Phillips was not in that day so she operated the recording equipment. It was probably Keisker who first recognized Elvis's talent and brought him to Phillips's attention. When Elvis returned to make another recording, Marion took him to see Sam, who also thought he might have some potential.

Elvis became a regional country artist while on the Sun label and, within two years, Phillips sold his contract to RCA. He did this because an independent record label does not have the resources to service a hit record. It does not have the distribution network to get records into stores outside its region or the cash flow to order more recordings from the pressing plant. If Phillips hoped to cash in on Elvis, he had to sell his contract and use the money to search for new stars.

After Elvis, Sam Phillips recorded a string of artists, such as Jerry Lee Lewis, Carl Perkins, Johnny Cash, Roy Orbison, and Charlie Rich. Because Sun was a small record company looking for potential stars and hits, Phillips took as much studio time as he needed to find out what an artist could do. This process led to long, rambling sessions that larger, busier companies would not have had time for. The success of Elvis, Carl Perkins, and Jerry Lee Lewis might not have happened if not for Sun's lengthy discovery and recording process.

THE PHASES OF ELVIS
Phase One: Early Elvis

Elvis's rise to stardom (some would call it royalty) was the result of his being in the right place at the right time. R&B had begun to cross over by 1951, when Bill Haley covered "Rockett 88" and Alan Freed had started his radio show. What few people recognized at that time was that there was an attitude of teenage rebellion becoming associated with the music. American culture had, and has, no clear-cut "rites of passage" from adolescence to adulthood. The main drive is a separation from one's parents. America was still a segregated country, and for a European-American to adopt elements of African-American culture, especially in the South, was a defiant act; it separated teenagers from the culture of their parents. The teen generation of the 1950s was not the first to use African-American culture in this manner, but social conditions of the fifties made that act of defiance more meaningful because the civil rights movement was experiencing resurgence and the polarization of society was becoming more extreme. When "Rock Around the Clock" was used as the theme for *The Blackboard Jungle*, R&B (rock and roll) was identified as the preferred music for the rebellion.

Elvis had physical qualities that helped him represent the non-musical elements of rock's popularity because he looked defiant. He was not really defiant, but he had a look and an attitude that suggested defiance. Other characteristics helped the image: He was a loner; he had dark sullen eyes and a curled-up lip that seemed to snarl; he combed his hair in an extreme style and wore "cat" clothes associated with African-Americans; and when he sang, he drew attention to his pelvic area (a very sensitive issue with puritanical America). These non-musical elements made Elvis a better choice for rock and roll stardom than Bill Haley.

Elvis Presley was born in Tupelo, Mississippi, on January 8, 1935; his twin brother, Jesse Garon Presley, was stillborn seventy-five minutes before Elvis entered the world.[5] Growing up in a poor but religious family, Elvis often heard gospel music sung in both African-American and European-American gospel traditions, and was influenced by the country and blues artists of the region. Elvis's musical talent brought him early recognition at the age of ten, when he won a contest at the state fair singing Red Foley's "Old Shep." In 1948, Elvis and his family moved to Memphis, where Elvis attended Humes High. Memphis had a unique musical culture steeped in the blues. It was the first major city north of the Mississippi Delta, was on the way to Chicago, and it had WDIA, the first radio station with an all African-American DJ roster. In Memphis, Elvis learned blues phrasing and the heartfelt musical style of its artists, and he blended those characteristics with his own musical heritage.

After high school graduation in 1953, Elvis got a job, like that of his father, driving a truck for Crown Electric Company. This same year, Elvis visited Memphis Recording Service, part of Sam Phillips's Sun Records studio. Phillips's and Marion Keisker's versions of events on who first saw promise in Elvis do not agree, but in May or June of 1954, Sam invited Elvis to the studio to try recording a song called "Without You." Although Phillips was not immediately impressed with Elvis's first efforts, he liked him. Reports of their first meeting include Phillips asking Elvis, "What do you sing?" to which Elvis replied, "Anything." Phillips then asked, "Who do you sound like?" and Elvis responded "Nobody." Phillips had been looking for "a white man with the Negro Sound and the Negro feel,"[6] but Elvis's first unreleased recordings show little hint of that.

Phillips asked the two musicians who happened to be in the studio that day, Scotty Moore and Bill Black, to help Elvis work something up.[7] Moore and Black, regular members of Doug Poindexter's Starlite Wranglers, agreed and, although accounts differ, they worked with Elvis for some time, possibly several months. During those sessions, Elvis was singing in a crooning style and working on songs like "Harbor Lights" and "I Love You Because." The recording masters of these crooning attempts have since been released. According to Moore, during a relaxed moment at one of these recording sessions, "All of a sudden Elvis started singing a song ['That's All Right (Mama)'], jumping around, acting a fool, and then Bill picked up his bass and started acting a fool too, and I started playing with 'em." At that point Phillips stuck his head out of the control booth and asked what they were doing, to which they answered, "We don't know."[8] Phillips had them do it again, and the resulting master, backed with "Blue Moon of Kentucky," was released by Sun Records on July 19, 1954.

The events of that recording session demonstrate the importance of the producer in the recording process. Just as Milt Gabler had done with Bill Haley, Phillips had some vision of the sound he wanted, or at least recognized important material when he heard it. Because Elvis was crooning before "That's All Right (Mama)," one must ask whether Elvis saw himself as a crooner or was trying to croon because he thought Phillips wanted a crooner; furthermore, was he just "fooling around" with the song, or did he see himself as a blues shouter and used the occasion to see if anyone responded to it?

Phillips brought a test-pressing to Dewy Phillips, an important local DJ, who liked it and played it on his "Red, Hot, and Blue" show. The response to the radio play was overwhelming, and "That's All Right (Mama)" sold twenty thousand copies and reached number one on the Memphis country charts. Sam also sent a review copy to *Billboard* magazine which, in its August 7, 1954, issue wrote, "Presley is a potent new chanter who can sock over a tune for either country or R&B markets . . . A strong new talent."

To get Elvis more exposure, Phillips booked him into a spot as the opening act for a Slim Whitman show in Memphis on July 30, 1954. During the afternoon performance, Elvis sang mostly ballads—another indication that he saw himself as a crooner—and was not received well. On the evening show, however, Elvis sang his up-tempo R&B selections, wiggling his legs, and the crowd went wild. This must have been the point at which Elvis decided on his performance style. Elvis did not croon again until "Love Me Tender."

Soon after this performance, Scotty Moore signed Elvis to a management contract. Elvis signed a number of other such contracts with different people until eventually settling on Colonel Tom Parker as his manager. During this period, Elvis performed on a country music circuit because there was no other venue for his new style. On October 2, 1954, Elvis did an unsuccessful fifteen-minute act at the Grand Ole Opry but was told by the manager, Jim Denny, "This boy is not bad,"[9] Following that performance, Phillips got Elvis a spot on *Louisiana Hayride,* a popular radio show on KWKH in Shreveport, where he had more success and subsequently was invited back as a regular performer. During a show, the emcee, Frank Page, asked Elvis how he had come up with that R&B style. Elvis replied, "To be honest, we just stumbled upon it." That statement seems to support the position that Elvis was indeed just "fooling around" in the studio the day he recorded "That's All Right (Mama)."

Elvis's style was somewhere between country and R&B. Elvis and his trio helped establish the musical characteristics of rockabilly music using sounds such as slap bass, a stuttering "hiccup," and Sun's slap-back echo. If Sam Phillips had had a different band in the studio the day Elvis showed up, the results might have been quite different. Part of the reason that the recording sounded like country music was that the performance practices of the backup band, Scotty and Bill, were based on their years of experience as country musicians. If, for instance, blues artist Little Milton's band had been in the studio that day, the resulting sound would have been more in the R&B tradition because of their years of experience as blues musicians. If this had been the case, Phillips might have marketed the recording to R&B stations instead of country stations.

Elvis continued to perform as a regional act in the South but traveled as far west as Carlsbad, New Mexico, and as far north as Cleveland, Ohio.

In 1955, Presley began his involvement with Colonel Tom Parker through a booking arrangement and a tour with Parker's partner, country star Hank Snow. On June 3, 1955, he appeared in Lubbock, Texas, where a young and unknown Buddy Holly appeared as an opening act. Holly had originally recorded as a country act and later switched to rock. It is uncertain how much Elvis's performance that day influenced Holly's change in direction, but he was quoted as saying, "We owe it all to Elvis."[10]

As Elvis toured, his stage persona developed into one unlike any other country artist, with his hip-shaking, sexually suggestive (for the fifties) body movements, his "cat"-inspired image, and his blues-shouter delivery: A true rockabilly style emerged. As his popularity spread, Elvis was voted the most promising country and western artist of the year and had his first number one country hit, "Mystery Train."

Colonel Tom Parker. As Colonel Tom Parker took over the management of Elvis, his career started to pick up speed. Parker, a Dutch immigrant born Andreas van Kuijk, entered the United States illegally. His method of illegal entry was unusual and therefore went unnoticed. While in Holland he took a job on a freighter and eventually left the ship and ended up in Mobile, Alabama. From there, he joined the U.S. Army in either 1929 or 1930. Interestingly, the officer who interviewed him when he enlisted was a Captain Thomas Parker who died in an accident at Fort Hood in 1945.[11] It is possible that, at some point, Presley's manager assumed this officer's name as his own. After his service in the U.S. Army, Parker found employment with a carnival, where he learned many of the business practices he used in promoting music.

Parker entered the musical arm of show business in 1939 when he was hired as a booking agent for singer Gene Austin ("My Blues Heaven"). In the mid-forties he became the manager of Eddy Arnold, who was just beginning a solo career. It was around this time that Parker received an honorary commission from Governor Jimmy Davis of Louisiana making him an official colonel. Jimmy Davis had been a country singer back when Parker was in the carnival business and evidently was repaying some previous favor by doing this. While managing Arnold, Parker and the William Morris Agency negotiated a deal for Arnold to make two movies, *Feudin' Rhythm* and *Hoedown*, which did not launch his client to a film career but gave Parker some movie experience with which to build Elvis into an international attraction. Parker also had dealings with Hill and Range, a music publisher owned by Jean and Julian Aberbach, and with Steve Sholes, head A&R man for RCA's country division. Parker used these contacts when he was shopping for a deal for Elvis.

In 1954, Colonel Tom Parker recognized Elvis's true potential and immediately began to insert himself into the situation. On August 15, 1955, Parker negotiated a deal as "special advisor" to Elvis and his then-manager, Bob Neal.

He then began looking for a record company and publisher to set up the same type of deal he had negotiated with Eddy Arnold. Parker's asking price of $50,000 was steep and many companies made counteroffers, but RCA's Steve Sholes came closest, with a $25,000 offer from RCA, combined with a $15,000 publishing deal with Hill and Range Music. The total package was $40,000—$35,000 to Sam Phillips for Elvis's recording contract, $5,000 of it paid to Elvis for Sun's back royalties.[12] Hill and Range set up two publishing companies for Elvis: Presley Music and Gladys Music, with Elvis owning half. This meant that Elvis would get half of the publisher's half of the performance and mechanical royalties of all his recordings, and Colonel Tom Parker would get twenty-five percent of Elvis's share.

Phase Two: Recording Star Elvis

On January 10, 1956, Elvis began recording for RCA in their Nashville studios with "I Got a Woman," "Heartbreak Hotel," "Money Honey," " I'm Counting on You," and "I Was the One." Most of his later sessions took place in Hollywood at Radio Recorders or on the studio lot. Next, Elvis began his television appearances, first with the Dorsey Brothers' *Stage Show,* followed by *The Milton Berle Show, The Steve Allen Show,* and finally *The Ed Sullivan Show.* Initially, Sullivan did not want to book Elvis, saying that Presley was "not his cup of tea," but he succumbed after Steve Allen outscored him in the weekly ratings. Some of the *Steve Allen* shows caused a furor because Elvis's pelvic gyrations were said to be sexually suggestive, so in later productions the cameras moved in for tighter shots to avoid showing Elvis's hips whenever he wiggled. Nevertheless, those performances are worth watching because they show Elvis's polite, honest country charm.

The Colonel's carnival instincts kicked in, and he entered into a merchandising deal with businessman Harry Saperstein to create a giant Elvis souvenir industry. There were Elvis lunch boxes, trading cards, pencil cases, record players, four-string plastic guitars, and stuffed dolls. Parker also developed a promotional device that was later used by the Beatles: A recorded interview with Elvis was issued with the questions edited out so that local DJs could read the questions and make it appear as if they were interviewing Elvis. The idea was a stroke of genius because it increased the status of those DJs and made them more favorably disposed to playing Elvis's latest recording. Movie producer Hal Wallis saw Elvis's Dorsey show appearance and called the Colonel the next day to arrange a film deal. After a screen test on April 1, 1956, Parker negotiated a three-movie deal with Wallace for $100,000, $150,000, and $200,000. Since it was not an exclusive contract, the Colonel also negotiated a two-picture deal with 20th Century Fox. The movies—*Love Me Tender, Loving You, Jailhouse Rock,* and *King Creole*—were made before Elvis was drafted into the U.S. Army.

On March 24, 1958, Elvis entered the Army. Some observers were surprised that Elvis went in as a regular soldier. There were probably several possible alternatives for Elvis. First, he could have gotten a medical deferment as Frank Sinatra had done. Second, Elvis could have been assigned to Special Services to perform for the troops. Third, he could have been a regular enlisted person. The second option presented two problems: First, the Army wanted Elvis to perform for Special Services but at a regular soldier's pay, and Parker demanded Presley's usual fees. Second, because of Parker's illegal immigrant status, he did not have the required paperwork necessary for a passport and therefore would not be able to be travel overseas to control Elvis in his customary fashion.

It was during this period of army service as a regular enlisted man that two life-altering events occurred for Elvis. The first one was an injury to his back that led to an involvement with prescription drugs that eventually killed him. The other event was the death of his mother, Gladys, in 1958. Elvis was extremely close to his mother and was deeply affected by her death.

Elvis was given no special treatment in the army, except for his being able to slip away for occasional recording sessions. Elvis was discharged in 1960. The positive publicity gained from his military service was priceless. His polite, obedient demeanor and personal magnetism won him approval from those who had previously disliked him.

Phase Three: Movie Star Elvis

After his army stint, Elvis focused his career less on recordings and more on movies, and after one television appearance on Frank Sinatra's show, he did not again perform live until 1969. Elvis had several hit records, including "It's Now or Never," and "Stuck on You," but the musical tastes of the next generation had changed and he remained hidden in the safety of the movie studio. During the next eight years, Elvis made movies and spent his time with the so-called "Memphis Mafia," a close-knit group of friends and assistants.

Elvis had hoped for a serious acting career, especially when offered a role opposite Sammy Davis, Jr., in *The Defiant Ones*, but the parts eventually went to Tony Curtis and Sidney Poitier. All of his movies followed a similar format that cast Elvis as a poor boy from the other side of the tracks who faces discrimination because of his roots but who wins the girl in the end because he proves his worth. Most of his movie songs were written by staff songwriters who came up with such titles as "Rock-A-Hula Baby" and "Do the Clam." Elvis eventually earned over $1 million per film plus a percentage, and most of the soundtracks went gold (albums selling 500,000 copies or singles selling one million copies).

Phase Four: Las Vegas Elvis

By the mid-sixties, younger listeners had moved toward British Invasion groups and harder rock sounds, and Elvis's movies were not doing as well. Even so, Elvis was not a has-been because the Colonel's marketing plan had been simple and effective. The Colonel has been quoted as saying, "A sure way to debase your merchandise is to give it away. . . . Elvis is a star because he hasn't appeared too much in person or on television."[13] There is truth in the Colonel's statement; an old show-business adage, "Always leave them wanting more," confirms the wisdom of the Colonel's position. The sixties generation was not very interested in Elvis, but the fifties generation had not seen enough of him because his stardom had been interrupted by the U.S. Army and was amplified by his years as a movie star. Those fans were now older but still eager for more Elvis.

His first live performance in seven years was the *Elvis: NBC-TV Special* in 1968. This comeback concert featured Elvis with guitar, black leather jacket, and a small acoustic band singing his rock and roll favorites in the safe surroundings of a small special audience. This was not a typical rock concert. The performers sat around on chairs, with Elvis standing every now and then while the musicians played acoustic guitars and the drummer played brushes on a chair. The ratings were good, and it proved that Elvis was a viable commodity.

Once Elvis demonstrated that he was still an entertaining live performer, he began a new career in Las Vegas casinos from 1969 to 1975. This time, Elvis's fans were old enough to get into the casinos and appreciate his act. In 1969, Elvis received a million dollars a week for four weeks in Las Vegas. In addition to Las Vegas, Elvis toured the country and averaged 110 live performances a year. *Aloha from Hawaii*, Elvis's television special of 1973, was seen by over a billion people worldwide via satellite, and both Elvis and Colonel Parker continue to accumulate wealth. But the physical and emotional grind of Elvis's life began to affect his health, and by 1973, Elvis had filed for divorce from his wife, the former Priscilla Beaulieu, whom he had first met while stationed in Germany when she was just fourteen years old. His increasing involvement with prescription drugs became apparent by his weight gain and erratic behavior.

Elvis was not a recreational drug user and was highly critical of street drugs and alcohol consumption. He deluded himself by believing the massive amount of drugs he consumed was acceptable because they had been prescribed by a physician. By 1975, Elvis had become grossly overweight, depressed, and reclusive, and his performances suffered greatly. His last live concert was in Indianapolis on June 26, 1977. On August 16, 1977, Elvis was found dead at Graceland. The cause of death was found to be heart failure and related medical problems. A large amount of prescription drugs was found in his system. In 1979, Elvis's doctor was indicted for negligence but was later acquitted.

Priscilla Presley opened Graceland to the public in 1982, and it has since be-come a popular tourist destination and a focus of an annual pilgrimage on the anniversary of Elvis's death. In June 1983, Priscilla and Elvis's daughter Lisa Marie won a court settlement against Colonel Parker, giving them most of Elvis's estate.

Elvis's Sun Records		
That's All Right (Mama)/ Blue Moon of Kentucky	19 July 1954	Sun 209
Good Rockin' Tonight/ I Don't Care If the Sun Don't Shine	22 Sept. 1954	Sun 210
Milk Cow Blues/ You're a Heartbreaker	8 Jan. 1955	Sun 215
I'm Left, You're Right, She's Gone/ Baby Let's Play House	25 Apr. 1955	Sun 217
Mystery Train/ I Forgot to Remember to Forget	1 Aug. 1955	Sun 223

The Music

Elvis's initial recordings were a unique blend of country music and blues, one on each side of the recording. This format tells much about Elvis, his roots, his self-image, and the perceptions of Sam Phillips. The rehearsal tapes made before "That's All Right (Mama)" show a crooning Elvis who spent more time imitating Bing Crosby that did any other R&B singer. After Sam Phillips captured Elvis "acting a fool" on "That's All Right (Mama)," his approach was R&B-inspired. His backup group, Scotty Moore (guitar) and Bill Black (bass), used typical country techniques and rendered performances that were steeped in the country music tradition. Black's slap bass technique was common to both cultures but remained active longer in country music than it did in R&B. The slap bass technique was intended to add a percussive element to the bass, to substitute for drums. Country music was typically drumless and, therefore, so was Elvis's first recording. Scotty's guitar style was characteristic of a good country guitarist; the country roots are obvious, but so are elements of west-ern swing, which has its roots in African-American music.

RCA tried to broaden Elvis's appeal by eliminating the country influence, although Scotty and Bill remained. Record companies are aware that the sound of a recording has as much to do with its success as the performance it embodies, so RCA tried to duplicate the echo that was part of Elvis's earlier

Sun recordings. Sam Phillip's slapback echo technique was the result of faking the echo effect the best he could because he could not afford a real echo unit, but RCA could afford the echo machine. After the one great RCA recording, "Hound Dog," Elvis was back to crooning with ballads such as "Love Me Tender." RCA also added a typical major record company touch: singers (the Jordanaires) to add "bop-shu-wada" in the background.

Much has been written about Elvis's sneering personality, magnetic stage persona, and destructive lifestyle, but it was also his musical talent and versatility that caused fans to give him the title "King of Rock and Roll." Young Elvis sang music of both African-American and European-American cultures with a unique combination of personality and enthusiasm that made the songs hits. He successfully recorded country and western, R&B, rock and roll, gospel, pop, Christmas, and patriotic songs, all of which sold well into the millions. Elvis won three Grammies for his religious recordings and numerous awards for his contribution to contemporary popular music. He was the idol of millions, and his good looks and youthful exuberance came to personify early rock and roll. As the physical embodiment of the spirit of the biracial music embraced by his predecessor Bill Haley, Elvis was the purveyor of this new style to an anxious worldwide audience. Almost twenty years after his death, Elvis Presley recordings still set records for sales longevity and have shown little decline.

OTHER SUN ROCKABILLIES
Carl Perkins

The most important Sun rockabilly other than Elvis was Carl Perkins, whose influence on rock was not fully appreciated until the British invasion. Perkins was a talented singer, songwriter, and guitarist who Phillips believed would be more successful than Elvis Presley. "Blue Suede Shoes," Perkins's 1956 hit, was the first song to reach the top ten on all three charts: pop, R&B, and country.

Perkins spent much of the early 1950s performing with his brothers, Jay and Clayton. In 1955, Perkins heard Elvis's "Blue Moon of Kentucky" on the radio, found out the song was recorded by Sun, went directly to Memphis to audition for Sam Phillips, and was signed to a contract. Although his first release in the fall of 1955 was aimed at a country market, he already had written "Blue Suede Shoes," and it soon became apparent that he had more potential as a hillbilly cat than as a country singer. "Blue Suede Shoes" was released January 1, 1956, and *Billboard* magazine reviewed it later that month. By February, the recording was at the top of the local Memphis charts, and *Billboard* picked it as "Country Best Buy," saying that it would appeal to both pop and R&B listeners. The recording was so successful that Perkins was scheduled to appear on *The Perry Como Show.* Unfortunately, the band was involved in a serious

Carl Perkins

auto accident on the way to New York for the show and had to postpone the appearance. When they later appeared on television, Carl's brother Jay was still wearing a neck brace from the accident.

The appearance on the *Como* show was Perkins's first national television exposure and might have made him a star, but during the period that they were recovering from the accident, Elvis had recorded "Blue Suede Shoes," and that version was outselling the original. Perkins's recording reached number two on the charts, but Elvis's version sold more copies. Perkins's career slowed even more with the arrival of Jerry Lee Lewis, who received much of Sam Phillips's attention. Perkins had some success with other recordings, but none matched the promise of "Blue Suede Shoes." In 1957, he recorded "Matchbox," which was a blues number using lyrics originally recorded by Ma Rainey (1924) and Blind Lemon Jefferson (1927). In 1958, Perkins signed with Columbia Records and moved closer toward country music. His career as a rock star seemed over.

By 1964, his career as a national act was a faded memory when he was booked on a tour of England with Chuck Berry. At his first English show, there were banners in the crowd saying, "Welcome Carl 'Beatle Crusher' Perkins" and "Welcome King of Rock 'n' Roll."[14] Apparently the English had trouble getting American rock recordings, but his album, *Dance Party*, had made it through and had been used as a model by aspiring English guitarists, including George Harrison. This reverence by the British helped enthrone Perkins as a rock legend. The Beatles eventually recorded more of his songs than those of any other writer.

It is hard to say whether Carl Perkins would have been as popular as Elvis had he arrived on time for *The Perry Como Show*. Perkins had the raw musical energy and guitar technique fit for rock stardom, but he lacked Elvis's James Dean looks. But then, Elvis, too, might have faded as a star had it not been for the Colonel's marketing plan and the favorable publicity Elvis received from his army service.

Jerry Lee Lewis

Jerry Lee Lewis also had the potential to be as important as Elvis Presley in the history of rock and roll; however, his behavior, both on and off the stage, scared the music industry away. Born in Louisiana, Lewis's musical background included gospel, country, boogie woogie, and blues. His piano-playing was an energetic blend of Fats Domino and Moon Mullican ("King of the Hillbilly Piano Players"), and his stage movements were borrowed from R&B artists.

Lewis was aware of R&B performance practices because he used to sneak into Haney's Big House bar with his cousin Jimmy Swaggert, in Ferriday, Louisiana, back when they were both under age. Haney's, owned by their uncle Lee Calhoun, was a juke joint that featured R&B acts such as B. B. King. Lewis's piano style was basically boogie woogie, spiced with glissandos (dragging the finger up and down the keyboard) and stage antics reminiscent of Little Richard. His first public appearance was in June 1949 at the Ferriday Ford Dealership. He sang "Drinkin' Wine Spo-Dee-O-Dee" (Sticks McGee), which was Atlantic's first big R&B hit.

In 1954, he unsuccessfully auditioned for the *Louisiana Hayride* show, and while there, he recorded two songs at the KWKH studios. In 1955, he moved to Nashville where he got a job with Roy Hall, a piano player who owned the Musician's Hideaway, an after-hours club. It was there that he picked up the song "Whole Lotta Shakin' Going On," from Hall. Stories vary, and it is possible that Jerry Lee had some part in the compositional process. After reading an article about Elvis in *Country Song Roundup*, he decided Memphis might be the next town to try.

By 1956, Lewis had joined Sun Records' roster of rockabilly performers. His debut song, "Crazy Arms," was a cover of a Ray Price recording, suggesting that Sam Phillips saw him as a performer of country more than of rockabilly. His 1957 recording of "Whole Lotta Shakin' Going On," the song he picked up in Nashville, showed his unique musical approach and earned him a spot on all three music charts. Combining piano glissandos, pounding chords, and clever lyrics, Lewis filled the same market niche as Little Richard had.

On July 27, 1957, Jerry Lee appeared on *The Steve Allen Show* singing "Whole Lotta Shakin'," which helped propel the recording into the number one slot on the R&B and country charts. Lewis's energetic performance style caused an interesting reaction from Steve Allen. During the performance, Lewis stood up so he could play in a standing position, and in doing so, he kicked the piano bench out of the way. Steve Allen, a fine jazz pianist as well as a comedian, tossed the bench back on stage, which sent it flying past Lewis and the television camera. This little moment of ad lib comedy—the piano bench flying across the television screen—is preserved forever in the film clips that continue to surface in various forms. Allen's reaction also helps illustrate prevailing adult attitudes about the new rock performance style.

Soon after appearing on *Steve Allen*, Lewis was given a slot in the 1957 music movie *Jamboree*. This was going to be yet another Alan Freed movie, but Freed was replaced by a selection of DJs from all over the United States and Canada because of a dispute over publishing royalties. Lewis's next hit, "Great Balls of Fire," came from the movie. The producer had cut himself in on some of the copyright, and after Carl Perkins passed on the song, Jerry Lee Lewis inherited it. The movie was released the same month as the recording, which helped propel it to number one by December 1957. His last hit before the infamous English tour was "Breathless," which he performed on "The Dick Clark Saturday Night Show." In a promotion deal in which Lewis agreed to forgo his artist royalties, Clark had kids send in fifty cents and five Beechnut gum wrappers for a free autographed copy of the recording.

The end of Jerry Lee's rockabilly career came in May 1958, when he toured England. In late 1957, Lewis had married Myra Gale Brown, his thirteen-year-old second cousin (twice removed), and when the British press noticed that she was a little too young for marriage, they hounded him until he was forced to leave the tour. In America, his performances were cancelled, and even Dick Clark turned his back on him.[15] His days at the top were over.

Lewis's years of alcohol abuse and his quick temper were personal problems that plagued him during that period. An anecdote about the March 28, 1958, Brooklyn Paramount Theater concert with Chuck Berry sheds some light on his flammable personality. An argument broke out backstage over who was the headliner and would therefore close the show. Lewis lost the argument, but at the end of his performance, he poured lighter fluid over the piano and set it ablaze exclaiming, "Follow that."[16]

Lewis was an exuberant performer whose defiant style set the tone for future rockers, and his talent made him worthy of a longer period of stardom. When the biographical film *Great Balls of Fire!* was released in 1989 (starring Dennis Quaid as Lewis), it gave him and his career the stature it deserved.

Roy Orbison

Characterized by his trademark dark sunglasses and huge pompadour hairstyle, guitarist/songwriter Roy Orbison became one of the most distinctive vocalists of the 1960s. With his operatic tenor, use of falsetto voice, and two-and-a-half-octave range, Orbison flourished as a pop artist, particularly on romantic ballads.

Roy Orbison grew up in Texas, where he began his career at age eight as a western artist playing on the radio. He was determined to make it as a musician. Even the caption in his 1954 high school yearbook stated his goal: "To lead a western band." For a while Orbison attended North Texas State University as a classmate of Pat Boone, who had already begun a career as a pop singer. Around this time, he saw Elvis perform with the Big D Jamboree in Dallas and realized there was a new combination of country and R&B afoot.

Jerry Lee Lewis

The original version of his first song, "Ooby Dooby," was recorded at Norman Petty's studio in Clovis, New Mexico, and released on Je-Wel Records. Soon after that, Sun signed Orbison and rerecorded "Ooby Dooby," which subsequently became a minor hit in 1956. This was his only success with Sam Phillips, who kept trying to squeeze Orbison into the rockabilly mold that he was establishing. While at Sun, Orbison composed prolifically and wrote "So Long, I'm Gone" for Warren Smith, which made the *Billboard Hot 100*, "Down the Line" for the flip side of Jerry Lee Lewis's "Breathless," and "Claudette" for the flip side of the Everly Brothers' "All I Have to Do Is Dream."

Though not as wild as Elvis or Jerry Lee, and less country than Johnny Cash, Orbison's unique vocal crescendos and powerful voice brought him much success from 1960 through 1964. After an unsuccessful stint at RCA, he moved to Monument Records and placed several important hits on the charts: "Only the Lonely" (1960), followed by "Blue Bayou" (1963) and "Oh Pretty Woman" (1964). A 1963 British tour with the Beatles brought him international success, and in 1965, Orbison signed a lucrative recording contract with MGM.

Unfortunately, 1966 through 1968 brought Orbison great personal tragedy when his wife, Claudette, died in a motorcycle accident and his two sons perished in a house fire. Orbison returned to the charts with a 1980 Grammy-winning duet with Emmylou Harris, "That Lovin' You Feelin' Again," from the soundtrack of the movie *The Roadie*.

Orbison returned to touring in the 1980s, and "Oh Pretty Woman," a 1982 hit for Van Halen, became a successful movie theme and Grammy winner in 1987. In the late 1980s, Orbison once again was in the spotlight as a member of the Traveling Wilburys, featuring George Harrison, Jeff Lynne, Tom Petty, and Bob Dylan. Inducted into the Rock 'n' Roll Hall of Fame in 1987, Orbison suffered a fatal heart attack in November of 1988, during his most popular phase since the early 1960s.

THE NON-SUN ROCKABILLIES
The Everly Brothers

Don and Phil Everly were children of the midwestern country stars Ike and Margret Everly, and appeared on family radio shows singing gospel and country as early as 1955. Their sound was more country than that of other rockabillies and featured the type of "country brothers harmony" made popular by the Monroe Brothers and the Delmore Brothers. The solo singing on the Everlys' recordings reveal phrasing and pronunciation almost identical to that of Hank Williams.

Hired as songwriters while still teenagers, the Everly Brothers had several minor country and western hits in Nashville prior to 1957, and in 1955 they recorded "Keep A-Lovin' Me" for Columbia. In 1957, Boudeleaux and Felice Bryant wrote "Bye Bye Love," their first big hit, which helped establish their personal style of combining close, high hillbilly harmony with a pop beat. The furor caused by their next hit, "Wake Up Little Susie," gives an indication of the type of scrutiny rock artists had to contend with. The song tells the story of a teenage couple who fall asleep at the movies and wake up at 4 A.M., and then worry, "What-are-we-gonna tell our maw, what-are-we-gonna tell our paw, what-are-we-gonna tell our friends when they say Oh-la-la, wake up little Susie." Although it is an innocent story, the fact that they had spent the night together was simply too much for some parents.

Musically and visually conservative, the Everly Brothers often played matching acoustic guitars and wore matching suits and haircuts, although fans quickly recognized Don and his darker locks. Other Everly Brothers hits during this time included several originals, such as "All I Have to Do Is Dream" (1958), "Bird Dog" (1958), "When Will I Be Loved" (1960), and "Cathy's Clown" (1960).

After a successful summer television series in 1972, the strain of touring and personal disagreements between Don and Phil led to an on-stage altercation during a performance at Knott's Berry Farm in 1973. In 1985, after ten years of not speaking, the brothers reunited for a successful world tour and were inducted into the Rock 'n' Roll Hall of Fame in 1986. The simple love-story lyrics, close harmonies, and acoustic guitar sound of the Everly Brothers influenced many later pop artists, including the Beatles, the Byrds, the Beach Boys, and Simon and Garfunkel.

Buddy Holly

Buddy Holly, born Charles Hardin Holley, was an important force in shaping the music of the British Invasion, especially that of the Beatles. As was the case for many other rock stars, his premature death elevated him to a status higher than the one he had achieved during his life. Holly's physical appearance—a lanky frame, horn-rimmed glasses, suit and tie—gave hope to future rockers who realized that not everyone had to have the looks of James Dean or Elvis to succeed in rock and roll. In the late 1970s, Elvis Costello's initial image was as the ghost of Buddy Holly. Holly proved the average-looking kid could play rock and roll. Today, he is often thought of as the first rock and roll "nerd."

Holly was an early pioneer as a singer/songwriter and in the use of the band format that includes two guitars, bass, and drums. He composed many of his hits and experimented with studio techniques, including multi-track recording and echo. His unique vocal style included stutters, hiccups, falsetto, and a tongue-in-cheek approach to his lyrics.

Buddy Holly

Playing several instruments as a child, Holly chose guitar for his country and western high school group, developing a country guitar-picking style. In 1949, he teamed up with fellow seventh-grader Bob Montgomery to form the duo Buddy and Bob. By the time they were in high school, they were performing throughout the region and on radio station KDAV. On January 2, 1995, Elvis appeared in Lubbock, Texas, at the Fair Park Coliseum and made a lasting impression. According to Sonny Curtis, Holly's bandmate, "The day Elvis left town, we turned into Elvis clones and we was bookin' out as an Elvis band." Elvis returned to Lubbock that February, and Holly's band served as the opening act.[17]

Buddy Holly's first break came as a result of a performance on a KDAV-sponsored rock show featuring Bill Haley and the Comets. On October 14, 1955, Holly was offered a contract with Decca—without Bob. The Decca sessions in Nashville produced "Blue Days, Black Nights" with a band composed of studio musicians, and "Modern Don Juan," with Holly's new group, the Three Tunes. The recordings received good reviews, but the public did not buy them and Holly was released from his contract and returned to Lubbock. A version of "That'll Be the Day" was recorded at those Nashville sessions, but Decca did not like it. Between record contracts, Holly and Jerry Allison returned to Lubbock and continued performing, opening for one of Elvis Presley's early tours. Holly credited Elvis as his influence for moving into rock and roll, saying, "I owe it all to Elvis."[18]

In 1957, Holly (who had dropped the "e" from his last name a year earlier), and the renamed Crickets recorded a rock and roll version of "That'll Be the Day" in Norman Petty's Clovis, New Mexico, studio. The master was issued by Brunswick, a subsidiary of Decca, and this time the song was a success, reaching number three on the weekly charts (number thirty on the year-end chart) and prompted a national tour followed by a British tour in 1958. His next recordings, "Oh Boy!" and "Peggy Sue," also hit in 1957, and he reached the charts with "Rave On" and "Early in the Morning," in 1958. His new marriage, his move to New York, and problems with his manager led Holly to leave the Crickets in October 1958. A financially strapped Holly, with a young Waylon Jennings as his bass player, joined the "Winter Dance Party Tour" of the Midwest in early 1959, which also featured Ritchie Valens and the Big Bopper (J. P. Richardson). Weary of traveling in a bus with a broken heater, the three chartered a private plane to take them from Clear Lake, Iowa, to Minnesota. In the early morning hours of February 3, 1959, the aircraft crashed, killing all on board. Holly was twenty-two years old.

Holly's posthumous releases did well both in the United States and abroad, and the 1978 film *The Buddy Holly Story* was well received. His influence can be seen in the music of such artists as Paul McCartney and Bob Dylan. Don McLean's 1971 hit "American Pie" was a tribute to Holly.

Eddie Cochran

Eddie Cochran was not a Southerner, but by 1955 he was in Nashville releasing unsuccessful records with songwriter Jerry Capehart. In 1956, he was signed to Liberty Records and sold enough records to earn a spot in the 1957 movie *The Girl Can't Help It*, along with Fats Domino, the Platters, Little Richard, and the Treniers. Cochran was a talented multi-instrumentalist who recorded all his records himself by exploiting the multi-track tape technology that was slowly gaining acceptance in the industry. The most important of those recordings was the 1958 "Summertime Blues," which became a popular seasonal tune for bands after the Who and Blue Cheer covered it. His later hits, "C'mon Everybody" (1958) and "Somethin' Else" (1959), sold better in England than they did in the United States.

Cochran's English popularity led to a tour, the first real American tour since Jerry Lee Lewis's famous English tour disaster. The tour was extremely successful and had been extended when he, along with Gene Vincent, decided to return home for a short visit. On the way to the airport, their speeding car blew a tire and crashed, killing Cochran and injuring Vincent. His talent and the situation made the British public remember him more fondly that do Americans.

Gene Vincent

Gene Vincent and his band, the Blue Caps, had a short run as rockabilly stars with two hits and a movie. Vincent had a much tougher look than Elvis and really did wear black leather and ride a motorcycle. In fact, he acquired a limp and metal leg brace as a result of an accident while in the Navy. After he was discharged from the Navy in 1955, he began singing country music around Norfolk and earned a regular spot on a radio show. Capitol Records became interested in his demo and appearance and signed him to be their answer to Elvis.

The recording he is most remembered for, "Be-Bop-A-Lula," was bathed in echo—Capitol's attempt to duplicate Sun Records' slapback echo sound—and replete with rockabilly hiccups. It is worth mentioning that, although Vincent says he got it from the *Little LuLu* comic character, the title of the song was more likely derived from a set of bebop scat syllables that had fallen into popular usage. Earlier, Basie singer Helen Humes had recorded "Be-Baba-Leba" (1946) as an answer to Lionel Hampton's "Hey Ba-Ba-Re-Bop." Vincent also appeared in the movie *The Girl Can't Help It*. After a smaller hit in 1957, "Lotta Lovin'," he toured Australia, Japan, and finally England, where he was involved in the auto accident that killed Eddie Cochran. His injuries kept him out of circulation, and his career never regained the momentum it once had.

Rockabilly has survived, with a defiant energy that captures the rock and roll spirit. In the 1980s, there was a retro trend started by a band called the Stray Cats (1980–84) that still lives on today. The trend developed several sub-genres such as *psychobilly* (the Cramps, Sharks, Frenzy, and Batmobile) and *trashbilly*. In late 1998, a former Stray Cat, Brian Setzer, added to the popularity of the growing trend of neo-jump blues with a recording of Louis Prima's "Jump, Jive, an' Wail."

LISTENING TO THE MUSIC

♪ ♪ "Rock Around the Clock"—performed by Bill Haley and the Comets

"(We're Gonna) Rock Around the Clock" was composed by Max Freedman and Jimmy DeKnight, and originally recorded by Sunny Dae in 1952. Former country western singer/guitarist Bill Haley and his recently renamed Comets cover this twelve-bar blues/R&B with western swing instrumental techniques and a set of pop lyrics, creating a prime example of R&B as it makes its transition to rock and roll.

Analysis of "Rock Around the Clock"—2:08 in length, recorded on Decca 29124

The Comets personnel: Haley, semisolid-bodied Gibson L7 electric guitar, vocals; Danny Cedrone, electric guitar (lead); Joey D'Ambrose, tenor sax; Billy Williamson, steel guitar; Johnny Grande, piano; Marshall Lytle, acoustic bass; Billy Guesack, drums.

This is a twelve-bar blues form, but the lyrics do not fit the pattern of the classic blues, AAB, in which the second vocal line is a repeat of the first. Instead, the second and third lines serve as a chorus, ABB. The second line is, "We're gonna rock around the clock tonight, we're gonna rock, rock, rock, 'til broad daylight," and the third line is, "We're gonna rock, We're gonna rock around the clock tonight."

0:00   Introduction (8 measures): The introduction has become famous for its lyrics. "One, two, three o'clock, four o'clock rock" count-off is in a stop-time style with the drums marking the beginning of each measure. The drum breaks and solo voice of Bill Haley give impact to the lyrics as he sings on each note of the chord. A heavy backbeat syncopation in the drums and guitars enters just before the first verse to prepare the listener for the blues form to come.

0:11   First Chorus (12 measures): Begins "Well, get your glad rags on" (slang for fancy clothes). This blues uses a shuffle rhythm, a walking bass line played in slap-bass style, while the guitar and sax continue a two-bar (8 foot taps) riff pattern throughout, and the drums play two rim shots at the end of each riff.

0:27   Second Chorus (12 measures): Begins "When the clock strikes two," and the instruments continue the same patterns except that now the drums strike only one rim shot at the end of each two-bar riff.

0:43   Third Chorus (12 measures): An improvised electric guitar solo that relies heavily on technique as Danny Cedrone double-picks each note and outlines a double-time boogie woogie pattern for four bars. In the next four bars he plays a jazzy, riff-based line with swinging eighth notes and returns to the double-time feel of the first part of his solo.

0:59   Fourth Chorus (12 measures): Begins "When the chimes ring five, six, and seven," and the instruments continue the same riff.

1:15   Fifth chorus (12 measures): Begins "When it eight, nine, ten," and the same riff continues. This time, however, the drummer punctuates the end of each two-bar riff with a "splash" cymbal crash that builds up a little more excitement.

1:31   Sixth Chorus (12 measures): A highly rhythmic instrumental chorus with sax and guitars playing a syncopated riff in unison. This is very similar to the shout chorus of a swing band arrangement.

1:46   Seventh Chorus (12 measures): Begins "When the clock strikes twelve." During the last two bars of the form (measures eleven and twelve) the instrumental line descends to the downbeat of the final little section called the coda.

2:02   Coda: It begins with the lowest note and then ascends and ends with the drum fill that features an interplay between the bass drum and the snare drum in a bebop jazz style.

For Musicians

The drum pickups to bar one recur in almost every second bar throughout the piece, unifying the phrases with an "and of three" and beat four syncopated accent. Haley sings each note of the F major arpeggio during the introduction, and the last two bars of this eight-bar phrase have beats two and four emphasized dramatically. The song now follows the traditional twelve-bar blues form, with occasional uses of the ii chord (G minor) before the dominant (C7) in bar ten.

The first six bars of the improvised electric guitar solo feature rapid-fire double-time repeated sixteenth notes centered around the tonic. Bars seven through ten are more melodic along the blues scale, and bars eleven and twelve return to the prior double-time technique of down-and-up stroking with a pick. After two more blues verses, the Comets create an effective twelve-bar rhythmic riff, emphasizing the "and of four" in every first bar, followed by accents on the "ands" of beats one and two, and on four for every second bar. This two-bar riff repeats six times, gaining musical energy through the phrase. On the final blues verse sung by Haley to "wrap up" the story line, bars eleven through fourteen provide the tag, as the instrumentalists descend somewhat chromatically from F, using the rhythm pattern of two eighths and one quarter on each pitch. The notes F-Eb-D-Db-C precede three beats of silence in bar thirteen, followed by an ascending C major scale fragment (starting on C, moving to F). Beat four of bar fourteen, the tonic seventh chord on F, is held until a drum fill ends the piece.

Final Comments

Reissued by MCA Records in May 1974, the tune returned to the pop charts and reached number thirty-nine for one week. "Rock Around the Clock" has now been recorded by over 150 different artists in 35 languages and received a Grammy Hall of Fame award in 1982.

♪♪♪"Hound Dog"—performed by Elvis Presley

Elvis Presley's 1956 version of "Hound Dog"—Jerry Leiber and Mike Stoller's early 1950s R&B hit—has become one of the most commercially successful singles in pop music history. Coupled with its B side, "Don't Be Cruel," the recording sold over five million copies and topped all three charts (pop, country, and R&B). Number one on the pop charts for eleven weeks and on the charts for an additional thirteen weeks, this classic twelve-bar blues became prime early rock and roll as Presley added his own personal touch to the song. This song is one of the most closely identified with Presley, and his live performances of this tune allowed his "hip shakin'" stage persona a chance to emerge to the delight of millions. "Hound Dog" was first recorded in 1952 by Willie Mae "Big Mama" Thornton. Her 1953 Peacock label release reached the number one position on the R&B charts for seven weeks, and should be listened to for both comparison purposes and sheer enjoyment.

Analysis of "Hound Dog"—2:13 in length, recorded 1956, released on RCA single # 47-6604

The recording is in the twelve-bar blues form, and the meter is "in four" (4 foot taps per measure). Personnel: Presley, acoustic guitar and lead vocal; the Jordanaires (vocal quartet led by Gordon Stoker); Scotty Moore, electric guitar; Bill Black, acoustic bass; D.J. Fontana, drums; Gordon Stoker, piano (Floyd Cramer had been credited, but recent discography lists Stoker).

0:00 First Chorus (12 measures): The first chorus begins with the lyrics, "You ain't nothin' but a hound dog," (for those counting measures, the first measure begins on the word "hound") with Elvis singing in the blues shouter style. The second line is a direct repetition, but he varies the rhythm of "ain't nothin but" with a rockabilly-hiccup approach to the words. There is no instrumental answer (response) after the first line, and just a short interjection from the guitar after the second line. The third line, "You ain't never caught a rabbit," is answered by one measure of triplets on the snare drum. Note the syncopated hand claps by the background singers are not used in the traditional manner, outlining the back-beat, and add a rhythmic countermelody.

0:18 Second Chorus (12 measures): Begins with, "You said you were high class," which is repeated as the second line following blues tradition. The third line, "You ain't never caught a rabbit," is also a repeat of the original third line. This is unusual in a blues song where the third line generally adds the final touches to the previous lines of the same chorus. Again, this line is answered by the snare drum.

0:34   Third Chorus (12 measures): This chorus is a direct repeat of the first chorus, including the use of the rockabilly hiccup on the words "ain't nothin' but."

0:49   Fourth Chorus, guitar solo (12 measures): Scotty Moore improvises one chorus in the blues form. As an accompaniment to the guitar solo, the Jordanaires sing long-note "aahs" for the length of each chord in the progression. It is interesting to wonder why the producer did not have them sing rhythmic riffs instead of the rhythmically stagnant long notes.

1:06   Fifth Chorus (12 measures): This is a direct repeat of the second chorus, complete with the guitar interjection after the second line.

1:21   Sixth Chorus, guitar solo (12 measures): Another twelve-bar blues guitar solo, but this is different from the earlier solo, which was primarily a single-line scale-like solo. This time Moore plays riff-like figures on each chord of the progression. In the ninth measure, he plays a very contemporary jazz chord that was common among steel-guitar players of the time.

1:38   Seventh Chorus (12 measures): This is a direct repeat of the second chorus.

1:55   Eighth Chorus (12 measures): This is a direct repeat of the first chorus.

2:08   At the end of this final phrase, the band stops on the word "never," and Presley sings alone until the word "mine," where the persistent drum fill returns for a final blast before the last chord.

For Musicians

Possibly the most famous C blues in history, "Hound Dog" has all the musical elements of early rock and roll. Presley's opening syncopated blues melody occurs solo, and the band enters with a bright tempo on the word "hound."

The bass line uses the notes C-Eb-E-G in a quarter note, eighth rest, eighth note and two-quarter note pattern, a line with which most musicians are now quite familiar. The drums and acoustic guitar emphasize the second and fourth beats of each measure, and the electric guitar often doubles the bass line. The lyrics are hung on a blues scale throughout the two twelve-bar phrases, which Presley repeats over the traditional I-IV-V harmony of the blues. The drum fill in the last two bars of each phrase is built on consecutive eighth-note triplets and may be effective yet overemphasized. Moore's twelve-bar guitar solo is melodic and inventive, not reflecting his true nature as a country performer as much as hinting at the electric guitar riffs of players yet to come. It is unusual that Presley now re-sings one earlier verse and then gives Moore an additional solo section. Moore's guitar chords in the one-bar break before his second solo are so dissonant they must be a mistake, now left for posterity. Presley ends the musical ride re-singing the second and first verses again before the vocal break in bar nine. The final tag consists of the triplet drum pattern at its most frenetic followed by an eighth note chromatic slide down to beat three in the last measure, which is held.

Final Comments

It has been reported that Presley attempted thirty-one takes of this song during the recording session before he was pleased with the results.[19] Little did he know he would have to sing the song dressed in tux and tails to a real hound dog on the *Steve Allen Show* later that year. "Hound Dog" won a Grammy Hall of Fame award in 1988.

---

[1] John Swenson, *Bill Haley: The Daddy of Rock and Roll* (New York: Stein and Day, 1982), 33.

[2] Ibid., 37.

[3] Ibid., 33.

[4] Arnold Shaw, *Honkers and Shouters: The Golden Years of Rhythm & Blues* (New York: Macmillan, 1978), 64.

[5] Peter Guralnick, *Last Train to Memphis: The Rise of Elvis Presley* (New York: Little, Brown, 1994), 13.

[6] Ed Ward, Geoffrey Stokes, and Ken Tucker, *Rock of Ages: The Rolling Stone History of Rock & Roll* (New York: Rolling Stone Press, 1986), 77.

[7] Guralnick, 91.

[8] Ibid., 95.

[9] Ibid., 129, 504.

[10] John Pareles and Patricia Romanowski, eds., *The Rolling Stone Encyclopedia of Rock and Roll* (New York: Rolling Stone Press, 1983), 256.

[11] Dirk Vellenga with Mick Farren, *Elvis and the Colonel* (New York: Delacorte Press, 1988), 35.

[12] Ibid., 88–89.

[13] Ibid., 122.

[14] Colin Escott with Martin Hawkins, *Good Rockin' Tonight* (New York: St. Martin's Press, 1991), 141.

[15] Dick Clark and Richard Robinson, *Rock, Roll & Remember* (New York: Crowell, 1976), 141.

[16] Phillip Norman, *Rave On: The Biography of Buddy Holly* (New York: Fireside, 1997), 193.

[17] Ibid., 59.

[18] Pareles and Romanowski, eds., 256.

[19] Guralnick, 298.

Chapter Five

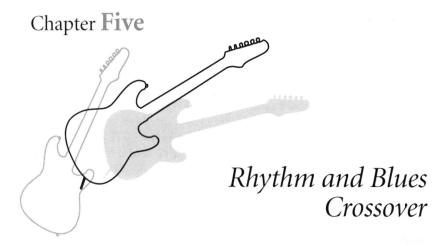

Rhythm and Blues Crossover

In a perfect society, there would not be a need for a chapter called "Rhythm and Blues Crossover." However, many of rock and roll's founding fathers are often excluded from histories because of the way the terms R&B and rock and roll have been employed. During the first half of the 1950s, R&B recordings that had pop chart crossover potential often were covered by pop singers, and those covers received pop radio airplay. Eventually audiences discovered that those cover recordings were not as good as the original recordings, because R&B artists had developed unique performance styles and stage personas which could not be adequately copied by pop singers. The exciting new American music of the 1950s combined the elements of R&B with non-blues song forms, an emphasis on the beat and, in most cases, commercial lyrics that would be acceptable on pop radio.

An established saying in rock and roll is that "it's the singer, not the song," meaning that Little Richard singing any song had more rock appeal than Pat Boone singing the same song. The success of these R&B artists on the pop charts marked the beginning of the eventual crossover success for African-American artists within several different music markets. This chapter includes artists who crossed over from the jump blues and its various forms. Artists who crossed over from the R&B vocal-group style, such as the Orioles, Crows, Moonglows, and Platters, already had started to cross over by this time and are discussed in Chapter Three. It is interesting to note that many of these crossovers from the jump blues were born in the South and many had some connection with New Orleans.

NEW ORLEANS AND THE SOUTH

New Orleans, the unique multicultural city where ragtime and blues combined to create jazz, was an important center for early R&B. Fats Domino and Lloyd Price were raised in New Orleans, and Little Richard recorded his crossover hits there with a New Orleans backup band. Ray Charles spent months at a time living there in the Foster Hotel and performing with Guitar Slim. Many other important R&B artists of the late 1950s, like Huey "Piano" Smith, Clarence "Frogman" Henry, Ernie K-Doe, Chris Kenner, Lee Dorsey, Shirley and Lee, Frankie Ford, Aaron Neville, Barbara George, Bobby Charles, the Dixie Cups, and Smiley Lewis had a connection to the city. Again, not all of these artists were born in New Orleans, but their sound and the production values of their recordings were shaped by New Orleans. The same catalytic musical tradition that allowed ragtime and blues to combine also helped blues, gospel, and pop mix into a unique type of R&B.

Roy Brown

Recording industry professionals were responsible for mining certain areas of the country in an effort to find new talent, usually someplace where talent recently had been discovered. In the late 1980s, it was Seattle and grunge music, and in 1950, it was New Orleans. The first late-forties artist to influence the future of New Orleans was Roy Brown, a native of the city. Brown started his career on the West Coast as a smooth urban blues singer, and he performed throughout the South but ended up back in New Orleans after some "girl trouble" forced him to return suddenly. Back in New Orleans, he began performing at places like the Dew Drop Inn, a famous New Orleans nightspot, and it was there he made an impression on former recording artist Cecil Grant. Grant called Jules Braun of Delux Records in New Jersey and told him about Brown and the song he had written called "Good Rockin' Tonight," and even had Brown sing it over the telephone.[1] Originally Brown had asked Wynonie Harris to record it, but Harris initially refused and instead waited until after Brown had issued a recording in 1947. Brown's version was a hit, but it was overshadowed by Harris's 1948 version; nevertheless, the exposure still helped Brown's career. "Good Rockin' Tonight" was one of the first R&B songs to be noticed by European-American teenagers, and in 1954, Elvis chose it as his second Sun release.

The Delux president took Roy to J&M Recording Studios in New Orleans and eventually produced several hits including "Good Rockin' Tonight," "Boogie at Midnight," and "Hard Luck Blues." Brown's career took off for a while but was plagued by dishonest managers and trouble with the IRS. Between 1948 and 1951, twelve of Brown's recordings made it to the top ten on the R&B charts, but by 1954, his recording career slowed down just at the time that rock and roll was beginning to cross over. Roy Brown's success caused other record companies to begin searching New Orleans for another hit.

In 1950, the focal point of New Orleans' recording scene was Cosimo Matassa's J&M Recording Studio and its local musicians, especially Dave

Bartholomew's band. At first, J&M was just a record shop specializing in R&B, but later Matassa opened a studio in the back room of the record store.[2] Dave Bartholomew was one of the most important bandleaders in the city at that time and therefore was a natural choice as backup band for many recording sessions. Bartholomew's New Orleans roots were firmly grounded in the musical traditions of the city dating back to the beginning of the jazz age: he had taken trumpet lessons from Peter Davis, who was Louis Armstrong's first teacher.

About this same time, radio was beginning to direct its programming toward African-American audiences, and DJs like Vernon Winslow (Dr. Daddy-O) began to exert an influence on the music throughout the South. Winslow's popular "Jivin' With Jax" show often was broadcast live from J&M studios using Bartholomew's band. This broadcast exposure brought further attention to New Orleans' new artistic life. Once R&B record labels realized that there was new life and a new sound in the city, they scrambled to service the new market.

Fats Domino

The first true crossover star was Antoine "Fats" Domino, a round, relaxed piano player whose recordings communicated New Orleans' laid-back, good-time approach to music. Domino came from a musical family and was part of the New Orleans piano lineage from Jelly Roll Morton to Tuts Washington and Professor Longhair. His recordings were without the usual R&B sexual innuendo, and his physical appearance precluded him from being a sexual threat to the mainstream European-American audience.

In 1949, Lew Chudd of Imperial Records was in town scouting for new talent with Dave Bartholomew, who took him to the Hideaway where Domino was performing successfully. Imperial was based in Los Angeles and had previously specialized in music for Mexican-Americans, but Chudd was planning to enter the R&B market. Chudd signed Fats to a contract and recorded him at Matassa's studio with Bartholomew's band.[3] His first recording, a jump blues called "The Fat Man," sold a million copies and made it to number six on the national R&B chart. In 1952, he reached number one with "Goin' Home." Fats also played back-up piano for other artists at Matassa's studio and played on Lloyd Price's recording of "Lawdy Miss Clawdy" (1952).

Domino was touring and building a career during the period when R&B was beginning to cross over and, during that time, discovered a formula that suited him. When he finally crossed over with "Ain't That a Shame" (1955), the song was so infectious and so popular that it was covered immediately by Dot Records' Pat Boone. Dot was building its business by releasing cover recordings of R&B hits, and Pat Boone was one of their artists. Pat Boone usually gets blamed for all the "bleached" (stripped of African-American influence) covers of the period, but it was Dot's owner, Randy Wood, who was responsible for choosing the material Boone recorded. Domino eventually overpowered the cover-record syndrome, but Boone's cover of "Ain't That a Shame" surpassed Domino's and became the number nine pop recording of 1955.

By 1956, Domino's personality and infectious delivery pushed his version of "I'm In Love Again" to the number twenty-five spot on the year-end pop charts. On the business front, Fats' brother-in-law wisely advised him to sign a record contract that paid him royalties rather than a flat payment and allowed him to keep the rights to his songs.[4] Keeping the rights meant that, although Pat Boone was stealing record sales because of the covers, Fats collected mechanical and performance royalties on Boone's sales and airplay.

Domino continued to place recordings on the charts throughout the 1950s, including classics like "Blueberry Hill" (1956), "Blue Monday" (1956), "I'm Walkin'" (1957), and "Walkin' to New Orleans" (1960). He eventually earned eighteen gold records and sold between 30 million and 65 million records. Domino appeared on the *Steve Allen Show* (possibly being the first African-American rock star to appear on national television), the *Perry Como Show*, and was cast in the movie *The Girl Can't Help It*.

Domino's string of hits lasted a decade, but by 1961, when styles began to change, his sales began to dwindle. In 1963, he began switching record companies, going through ABC, Mercury, Warner Brothers, and Atlantic. Domino made a surprise return to the charts in 1968, when he covered the Beatles "Lady Madonna." Fats has been a mainstay on the oldies circuit and is able to perform as much as he would like.

Lloyd Price

Lloyd Price, a gospel-trained New Orleans singer, was in the Army from 1954 to 1956 during the peak crossover years, so it is difficult to project what his impact might have been. Originally, Price had been signed by Art Rupe of Specialty Records, who went to New Orleans for the same reason Lew Chudd of Imperial Records did: Hit recordings were to be made there. Rupe, based in Los Angeles, had been recording African-American gospel music for some time beginning in 1947 with the Pilgrim Travelers, Swan Silvertones, and the Soul Stirrers, whose lead singer was Sam Cooke (later replaced by Johnnie Taylor). Rupe was hooked by the gospel sound he heard in New Orleans music, and that attracted him to Lloyd Price. Their first recording, "Lawdy Miss Clawdy," was a strong hit on the R&B charts in 1952 and was just the type of recording that was beginning to cross over to the pop audience. The recording had the laid-back New Orleans rolling rhythm, because it was produced at J&M Studios with Dave Bartholomew's band and even had Fats Domino playing piano.

Price recorded several other top ten R&B hits, such as "Oooh-Oooh-Oooh" and "Restless Heart" before he was drafted. The Army, like IRS audits, is thought by some to have been used to punish those who made the government uncomfortable, such as African-Americans who were becoming too influential. Historians now know that a program called the Great Lakes Project was used to draft musicians from swing bands and into the army during World War II to improve the quality of the service bands. While these musicians were not selected for purposes of punishment, the fact that the draft was used selectively in this way established a precedent by which the same process could then later be applied for such purposes as "cooling off" the career of an African-American musician who, in the eyes of powerful politicians, was becoming much too popular with young European-American women.

Upon his return from the service, Price settled in Washington, D.C. After starting the Kent Record Company (KRC), he signed with ABC-Paramount and, in 1959, recorded three hits that made the year-end top 100. The biggest was "Personality," which reached number three on the year-end pop chart, probably because it was a very bland, mainstream pop record. "Stagger Lee," which reached the number one spot on the R&B chart and number thirteen on the year-end pop chart, was more interesting. "Stagger Lee" was an old "story-telling" song like "Frankie and Johnnie," and had been recorded by many blues artists under the title "Stagolee." It is the story of a card game gone bad, and ends with Billy the Lion getting shot by Stagger Lee, who was caught cheating at cards; Price's version had the violence removed. This song most likely documents a real event that was kept alive as a song much in the same way African griots enter events into oral history by adding them to songs.

Price did not reach the year-end charts in 1960 (he did make the weekly charts), and it is interesting to speculate about his absence. In 1960, there was a sudden absence of R&B on the pop charts. Some blame this on the effects of the payola hearings in Washington.

Little Richard

Richard Penniman, who was born in Macon, Georgia, but recorded in New Orleans, was one of the most important musicians in the development of early rock and roll. His pounding piano style, falsetto vocalizations, and flamboyant stage persona were unique in the history of contemporary music, and his lyrics were clever, sometimes risqué, but always exciting. Little Richard sent a message to the new teen subculture emphasizing individuality and self-expression with a hint of sexual tension. He was one of twelve children whose father sold bootleg whiskey, and two of his uncles were preachers. The religious contradictions inherent in this situation haunted Richard throughout his life. His openly gay lifestyle was an affront to his family's beliefs and, at age

Little Richard

thirteen, he moved in with a couple who owned Macon's Tick Tock Club and there continued his musical pursuits.

In Atlanta in 1951, Little Richard signed a contract with RCA and recorded two sides in a jump blues style: "Every Hour" and "Get Rich Quick." They did not sell well enough to make him famous but well enough to encourage him to continue in the profession. Next he moved to Houston, where he became associated with Don Robey, owner of the Peacock Club and Peacock Records, and recorded more songs. These recordings were also unsuccessful, but during this time Little Richard traveled the South developing a wild stage persona, which included a pompadour hairstyle, makeup, and an androgynous look—Richard was "glam" before his time.

By 1955, Little Richard must not have been happy with his contract with Peacock, because at the suggestion of Lloyd Price, he sent a demo tape to Specialty Records in Los Angeles. As Richard tells it, he was broke and washing dishes in a bus station. Specialty's gospel producer, Bumps Blackwell, was impressed by the tape and convinced Art Rupe to record Richard, but first they had to get him out of his Peacock contract. They met in New Orleans to record him at J&M studios, and when Richard arrived they were shocked at his outlandish appearance. Though his look was certainly wild, his singing style had been inhibited by the studio, so Chudd had Blackwell take the singer out for lunch at the Dew Drop Inn to loosen him up a little. There Bumps had Richard get up onstage and play one of the numbers he used in his act: "Tutti Frutti," a wild sexual song that had a great groove to it but also had lyrics that would never be acceptable on pop radio.

When they returned to the studio, they had Dorothy La Bostrie, a local songwriter who happened to be there trying to sell some of her own songs, clean up the lyrics.[5] With her edits, the blatantly sexual song with the opening line "Tutti frutti, good booty," became a harmless nonsense song with the change to, "Tutti frutti, aw rooty." "Tutti Frutti" (1956) sold half a million copies, three million by 1968, and reached the number two slot on the R&B charts.

Randy Wood of Dot Records arranged for Pat Boone to cover the song, as he had done earlier with Fats Domino's songs, but Boone could not muster up enough unbridled energy to beat the original. Little Richard's recording of "Tutti Frutti" helped demonstrate to the recording industry that, in rock and roll, it was the "singer not the song." Covers of earlier R&B songs had done better than the originals, at least on mainstream radio, but the wild shouting style of Little Richard did not translate well into bland covers. Soon after this, Pat Boone stopped recording R&B covers, but he continued in his successful recording career with the crooning style for which he was better suited.

Little Richard had chart success for the next two years with "Long Tall Sally" (1956), "Rip It Up" (1956), "Lucille" (1957), "Jenny, Jenny" (1957), "Keep A Knockin'" (1957), and "Good Golly Miss Molly" (1958). The crossover success of "Tutti Frutti" and "Long Tall Sally" was remarkable, because lyrically they were part of the R&B tradition of risqué songs. Lyrics like "I got a gal named Sue, she knows just what to do; She rocks to the East, She rocks to the West" probably got past the censors because the word rock had, by that time, become associated with dancing rather than sexual intercourse. "Long Tall Sally" is a story about an extramarital affair between Sally and Uncle John. Sally is, according to the lyrics, "built for speed, she's got everything that Uncle John need." It is possible that Richard's flamboyant appearance made these lyrics seem harmless and made it possible for them to withstand the scrutiny of the censors.

Richard crossed over into rock and roll far enough to be cast in three early rock movies: *The Girl Can't Help It* (1956), *Mister Rock And Roll* (1957), *Don't Knock the Rock* (1957). However, behind this apparent wild-man image, religious contradictions were brewing, and in 1957, he left show business to become an ordained minister. When Little Richard returned to rock in 1964, he found that he was an important influence on the musicians of the British Invasion, especially the Beatles. By the 1980s, Little Richard was back in the media with talk-show guest shots, movies, television commercials, and recording rock and roll children's songs.

Ray Charles

Ray Charles, born in Albany, Georgia, and raised in Greenville, Florida, contracted glaucoma and was blind by the time he was six. As a piano player in the 1940s, he came under the influence of the smooth West Coast urban blues pianist/singers, especially Nat Cole and Charles Brown; both their "Straighten Up and Fly Right" and "Driftin' Blues" were early staples of his repertoire. After playing around Florida and not being able to break out, he left and went as far away as possible, to Seattle, Washington. Within days of his arrival there, he had organized a trio and found work performing in his Cole/Brown style. Ray's popularity in Seattle led to performances on the radio, live television shows, and a recording contract with Jack Lauderdale, owner of Downbeat Records. His first recording with Swingtime was "Confession Blues" and later, in 1949 or 1950, he recorded his first hit, "Baby, Let Me Hold Your Hand." As a result of that hit recording, he began touring with urban blues man Lowell Fulson.

After splitting with Fulson, Ray landed in New York and, in 1952, began a relationship with Atlantic Records. In 1953, he traveled to New Orleans and began working as a pianist and arranger for Guitar Slim, whose hit recording, "Things I Used to Do" was arranged by Charles.[6] It was during this New Orleans period that he began to break out of the West Coast urban blues sound and to develop a bluesier gospel approach. It may not be possible to credit New Orleans with responsibility for Charles's new gospel approach, but it is safe to assume that the time he spent in the city allowed him the freedom to experiment.

By 1954, Charles was married and living in Houston. While playing a gig in Atlanta, a local DJ named "Daddy Sears" called Jerry Wexler of Atlantic Records to tell him that Charles had developed a new individual style and should be recorded immediately.[7] Wexler went to Atlanta and recorded Charles using the radio station's equipment and produced "I Got a Woman," a secularized version of the gospel song "Jesus Is Alright With Me." The recording reached the number two spot on the R&B charts and marked the beginning of what is now recognized as the Ray Charles style. Charles was one of the first important male singers in the secularized gospel tradition. Although earlier artists like Billy Ward and his Dominos and Ruth Brown had spiced their sound with gospel characteristics, Charles's version had more of the sanctified church feeling.

Ray's next recordings sold well, but it was "Hallelujah, I Love Her So" (1955) that was the first one to sell well outside the African-American community, and, in 1959, he had his first crossover hit recording, "What'd I Say," which reached number two on the pop charts. "What'd I Say," with the call-and-response singing of his backup group, the Raeletts, began as an improvisation at the end of the evening when the band had exhausted its entire repertoire. After the success of "What'd I Say," the Ray Charles style became well known and was referred to as *soul*. In that same year, he signed with ABC Paramount and continued his string of crossover hits with "Georgia on My Mind" (#1, 1960), "Hit the Road Jack" (#1,

1961), and "I Can't Stop Loving You" (#1, 1962). He even recorded an album of country and western standards.

Ray Charles's mixture of R&B and gospel music came to be known as soul music, and he was its most visible artist, although not the only one singing in that style. The most famous singer to emulate his style was Motown Records artist Stevie Wonder, although Charles was also an important model for future British artists, most notably Steve Winwood and Joe Cocker.

James Brown

James Brown, like Ray Charles, did not cross over right away. In fact, he did not become well known by the pop audience until "Papa's Got a Brand New Bag" (1965). From Macon, Georgia, Brown was discovered in 1956 by Ralph Bass of King Records, who recorded the Dominos, Hank Ballard and the Midnighters, and the Platters. Bass brought Brown back to King Records in Cincinnati to record "Please, Please, Please." His boss, Syd Nathan, owner of King Records, hated it and even threatened to fire Bass; however, the recording went on to become Brown's first hit.

James Brown's style of shouting, pleading, gospel-inspired R&B was rawer than the gospel approach of Ray Charles that had been filtered through smooth urban blues techniques. The "James Brown scream" has become part of American culture and is instantly identifiable by most rock fans. Brown's stage act was "dynamite" and featured his own brand of spinning, sliding,

James Brown

high-energy dance steps. In one particularly famous routine, Brown drops down to his knees in an apparent state of complete exhaustion. His manager comes onstage and places a cape over Brown's shoulders and slowly leads him off while the band plays on. Suddenly, Brown throws off the cape and returns to sing just once more, only to fall to his knees once again and repeat this process several more times. These routines and dance steps led to Brown being billed as "the hardest working man in show business," and finally, "Soul Brother Number One."

Brown was well known, practically legendary, with African-American audiences before being discovered by the pop audience in the mid-sixties. First "Out Of Sight" (1964) broke through, reaching number twenty-four on the pop charts. It was soon followed by "Papa's Got a Brand New Bag" (1965) and a string of hits: "I Got You" (1965), "It's a Man's, Man's, Man's World" (1966), "Cold Sweat" (1967), "I Got the Feelin' " (1968), "Say It Loud, I'm Black and I'm Proud" (1968), "Mother Popcorn" (1969), "Get Up I Feel Like Being a Sex Machine" (1970), and "Superbad" (1970).

Along the way, subtle changes in the format of his songs gradually evolved into the foundations of *disco* and *rap*. The band's accompaniment was gradually reduced to a series of short, punchy riffs that were repeated enough times that they could be called a vamp. Over this "funky vamp," Brown sang/talked until he was ready to move on to the next section, when he signaled for the band to switch to the next riff. These arrangements laid the groundwork for the *funk* of the 1970s. In fact, several ex-JB's (his band after the Famous Flames) joined George Clinton's Funkadelic-Parliament organization in 1971. By 1970, Brown's recordings reached the height of simplicity and were beginning to be referred to as "dance grooves." His recordings became a model for the decade's dance music, first known as disco, and his stream-of-consciousness singing/talking laid the foundation for the rapper's art.

James Brown was also an important cultural icon/role model for the African-American community because by the 1970s, he was in control of his music and had created an entrepreneurial empire—he had made it as a black man in a white world. His "Say It Loud, I'm Black and I'm Proud" (the number one R&B recording of 1968) echoed the feelings of the African-American community, which at that time was experiencing another advancement in the civil rights movement. This phase of the civil rights movement was symbolized by two sub-phrases: "Black Power," encouraging people to take charge of the economic life of their communities and operate their own businesses; and "Black Is Beautiful," to encourage people to take pride in their African heritage. James Brown's status in the community was so high that by making a televised appeal to reason, he was able to calm the passions of the African-American community when Dr. Martin Luther King was assassinated. James

Brown's troubles with the IRS and other legal difficulties are viewed by some as a "white" government's attempt to destroy the reputation of a "black" man who had grown too proud.

Sam Cooke

Sam Cooke is usually omitted from rock histories because his recordings are sometimes considered too pop, especially after he was signed by RCA, which surrounded him with syrupy musical arrangements. Cooke, like Ray Charles and James Brown, was responsible for blending gospel musical characteristics with popular music. Cooke's gospel credentials were impeccable. He was lead singer with the Soul Stirrers, one of the most influential gospel groups in the country. Cooke performed with the group for almost six years before leaving to pursue a career in secular music. Cooke's style of gospel music was not the pleading, exhorting style of James Brown, but was a pure, smoother, clearly articulated style that laid the foundation for what later became known as *sweet-soul* music.

Sam Cooke was born in 1931, the son of a Baptist minister, and was singing in his father's church choir by the time he was ten. While in high school, he sang with the Highway QC's who were trained by the baritone singer from the Soul Stirrers, an important gospel group formed in 1934. (They recorded for Aladdin beginning in 1944 and switched to Specialty in 1949). Soon after that, Cooke was hired to replace Rebert Harris, lead singer of the Soul Stirrers, and thus became one of the most important singers in the United States.

It is a shame that gospel audiences of the fifties would not tolerate one of its stars singing popular songs, or so the record company thought. In order to circumvent the stigma of performing the "devil's music," in 1956 Cooke recorded "Lovable" under the pseudonym Dale Cooke, although that still was not good enough for Specialty's owner, Art Rupe. Rupe sold Cooke's contract to his producer, Bumps Blackwell, and Cooke signed with Keen Records and began to release recordings under his own name.[8] A year earlier, Blackwell and Rupe had successfully launched Little Richard's career, which makes it hard to imagine why they did not attempt the same with Cooke; either Rupe had no faith in Cooke's abilities as a pop singer, or possibly his experience with Richard had been too unpleasant.

In 1957, Cooke released his first in a long string of hits, "You Send Me," which reached number one on the R&B charts and number twenty on the year-end pop charts. It remains a mainstay of oldies radio. After signing with RCA, Cooke continued to exploit the gray area between gospel and pop and helped establish vocal techniques that became a standard in the sweet soul style. His most remembered recordings are "Chain Gang" (1960), "Twistin' the

Night Away" (1962), "Bring It On Home to Me"/"Having a Party" (1962), "Somebody Have Some Mercy" (1962), "Another Saturday Night" (1963), and "Shake"/"A Change Is Gonna Come" (1965). Cooke met a violent death in 1964 when he was shot by a Los Angles motel clerk under curious and embarrassing circumstances. Cooke was one of the earliest African-American pop artists to have control over his product by owning a record company, a management firm, and a publishing company.

CHICAGO, CHUCK BERRY, AND CHESS RECORDS

Chess Records, most famous for its Chicago blues artists like Muddy Waters and Howlin' Wolf, was also interested in the new rock market. In 1951, Chess bought "Rockett 88" by Jackie Brenston (a contender for the title of first rock recording) from Sam Phillips, but their biggest crossover artist was Chuck Berry, who produced some of the most memorable recordings in rock and roll history. It is hard to call Chuck Berry a crossover artist because he did not have an R&B recording career to cross over from; his recording life began as a rock artist. Chuck Berry, more than any other performer, established the model of a guitar-playing, song-writing, hot-guitar-soloing rock and roll artist. Many try to give this distinction to Buddy Holly, but Berry was first and most influential. Berry's influence on the next generation of rockers is expressed in John Lennon's comment, "If you tried to give rock 'n' roll another name, you might call it Chuck Berry."

Berry developed musically in St Louis, a city with a long tradition in African-American popular music dating back to Scott Joplin and ragtime. By 1952, Berry was performing with a trio led by pianist Johnnie Johnson, who is heard on most of Berry's early recordings. A careful listening to the early recordings, especially the piano, reveals his music's connection to the long tradition of boogie woogie and jump blues; Berry's guitar solos reveal the influence of T-Bone Walker. While visiting Chicago in 1955, Berry met Muddy Waters, who recommended him to Leonard Chess, who was suitably impressed and signed him to a contract. His first release, "Maybellene" (1955), had a melody based on "Ida Red," an old country song recorded in 1939 by Roy Acuff on Okeh Records. The fact that part of the song is based on a country song has led some to call Berry a country singer. It is true that back in St. Louis, Berry had performed in a club with a racially mixed audience, and he played songs they wanted to hear, including country music, although this in no way makes Berry a country singer. "Maybellene" is quite simple rhythmically and has a very basic country-like bass line. But when Berry begins his guitar solo, it is pure T-Bone Walker jump blues. The irony of the "reverse rockabilly" nature of the situation is not lost on the authors, but it hardly qualifies Berry as an R&B hillbilly.

Legal payola was responsible for "Maybellene" becoming a hit: DJs Alan Freed and Russ Fratto were listed as co-writers along with Berry. The co-writer status meant that those DJs received performance royalties from BMI when they played the recording on the radio, and it also means that if Berry had refused the deal with the DJs, they might have ignored his recording.[9]

While Little Richard's songs emanated from the R&B lyric tradition of alcohol, women, and party songs, Chuck Berry wrote songs that told of teenage life in America in the fifties, and they were written with the teenage market in mind. "Maybellene" was about cars and girls—the stuff teenage boys think about—and was a natural hit. The song tells of a boy who sees his girl with someone else in a Cadillac Coupe DeVille, and he chases her in his V8 Ford singing, "Maybellene, why can't you be true, you done started back doing the things you used to do." In "Carol" (1958), he sings, "Oh Carol, don't let him steal your heart away, I'm gonna learn to dance if it takes me all night and day," and tells of the importance of dancing in the dating game. In "Johnny B. Goode" (1958), he sings of a country boy "who never, ever learned to read or write so well, but he could play the guitar just like a ringing a bell," and reminds his listeners of the boy in their high school who ignored his studies to pursue music. In "Roll Over Beethoven" (1956), he sings of writing a letter to his local DJ because "there's a jumping little record I want my jockey to play." Berry proceeds to sing about rock and roll and tells Beethoven to roll over and play dead. Chuck Berry was singing about his audience, and they responded.

Chuck Berry's 1950s career was ended in 1959 by a charge that he had violated the Mann Act, which involved taking a minor across state lines for immoral purposes. He was charged with bringing a fourteen year-old girl, some say a prostitute, from Texas to work as a hat-check girl in his St. Louis nightclub. They had a falling out and she was fired, causing her to go to the authorities. There were two trials. The first was tainted by racism, and its verdict was overturned. The second trial resulted in a conviction and two years in the Terre Haute Federal Penitentiary. It is hard to believe that racial/social conditions in America were not responsible for the authorities deciding to press charges against an African-American who had become very popular; it is also hard to believe that Chuck Berry was the only rock star guilty of violating the Mann Act. While Berry was out of commission, the Beach Boys used his style to lay the groundwork for surf music; the melody from "Sweet Little Sixteen" was appropriated, some say stolen, for use in "Surfin' USA" (1963).

After Berry was released from prison, he recorded a few more hits like "Nadine" (1964), and "No Particular Place to Go" (1964), but by that time the British Invasion and Motown were beginning to change musical tastes in America. After 1965, Berry did little recording, although he made it to the charts with a remake of an old bawdy nightclub song, "My Ding-a-Ling," in 1972. Chuck Berry's music was very influential in shaping the music of the English groups, especially the Beatles and the Rolling Stones, who included his

Chuck Berry

songs on their early albums. Even in America, Chuck Berry songs were an important part of the repertoire of teenage garage bands of the mid-sixties.

Berry's present status gives insight about the psyche of the American public: Berry did not die at the peak of his popularity like Buddy Holly, Jim Morrison, Jimi Hendrix, and Janis Joplin. If he had, he would have been canonized as a saint; instead he has had to endure the changes in musical taste and life on the oldies circuit, and has been subjected to recurring charges of tax evasion. Nevertheless, Chuck Berry remains one of the most influential figures in the history of rock and roll.

Chuck Berry Hits

Maybellene (1955)	Carol (1958)
Roll Over Beethoven (1956)	Sweet Little Sixteen(1958)
No Money Down (1956)	Johnny B. Goode(1958)
Too Much Monkey Business/	Back in the U.S.A. (1959)
Brown-Eyed Handsome Man (1956)	Nadine (1964)
Rock and Roll Music(1957)	No Particular Place to Go
School Day (1957)	(1964)

Bo Diddley

Chess Records' other contribution to rock was Ellas Bates, although his last name was changed to McDaniel after he was adopted. His family moved to Chicago when he was young, and there he began study of the violin and later the guitar. He developed his style by performing on street corners, including Chicago's famous Maxwell Street, and by 1951, was performing in local Chicago clubs. It appears that he first began using the name Bo Diddley as an amateur boxer, and it is possible that he got the unusual nickname from the African stringed instrument called the "diddley bow." This Mississippi-born vocalist/guitarist/songwriter introduced the "hambone" rhythm (shave and a haircut ... two bits) into rock with his 1955 hit called "Bo Diddley." The rhythm was originally produced by tapping the hands on the body, known as "Pattin' Juba" in the nineteenth century, and subsequently the rhythm has been used in songs like Johnnie Otis's "Willie and the Hand Jive" (1958), the Who's "Magic Bus" and Bruce Springsteen's "She's the One." In 1955, Diddley signed with Chess Records and worked with Chuck Berry on several recordings. He had several minor hits through 1962, including "Say, Man" (1959).

His large build, horn-rimmed glasses, and red, rectangular electric guitar have been trademarks during his long career. His use of an unusually shaped guitar probably inspired the later trend, but his guitar-playing was his most important contribution to rock. Diddley is the bridge between the styles of T-Bone Walker and Jimi Hendrix: He treated the electric guitar as more than just a loud guitar and realized that the amplifier was also part of the instrument. His guitar sound on "Bo Diddley" is unlike anything previously recorded: a big, thick sound, bathed in reverb and vibrato—the only special effects available on 1950s amplifiers. The next advancements in guitar sound had to wait for Jimi Hendrix. Diddley's percussive, chordal-strumming style instantly influenced rock artists like Buddy Holly and the Everly Brothers, who acknowledge using it in the introduction to "Bye, Bye Love," and laid the foundation for heavy metal guitarists.

When the British Invasion swept America in the mid 1960s, Diddley's songs were widely covered by groups such as the Yardbirds and the Rolling Stones. Diddley continued to tour, even recording surf music and traditional blues as the 1970s approached. His wide and lasting appeal could be seen in his 1979 appearance with the Clash, George Thorogood's hit cover of "Who Do You Love," and a small role in the movie *Trading Places* with Eddie Murphy in 1982.

LISTENING TO THE MUSIC

♪♪♪ "Maybellene"—performed by Chuck Berry

Chuck Berry's May 1955 reworking of the old country fiddle tune "Ida Red" into his first hit, "Maybellene," was one of many versions of the traditional song. Bob Wills and his Texas Playboys, Cowboy Copas, and jump blues artist Louis Jordan all recorded this witty, up-tempo melody. This recording reached number one on the R&B charts and number five on the pop charts, where it remained for eleven weeks.

Analysis of "Maybellene"—2:21 in length, recorded in Chicago on Chess 1604

"Maybellene" can be described as a "verse-chorus" (AB) structure, although this song begins with a chorus. Additionally, it is an adapted blues form, meaning that one of the parts is related to the twelve-bar blues. The verse (A), tells the story over one chord (stagnant harmony) and does not repeat any lyrics; the chorus (B) repeats unchanged and uses the chords and lyric repeat scheme of classic blues. Often the verse-chorus form begins with the chorus, which acts like a "hook," i.e., the part of the recording that hooks the listener's interest.

The meter of this recording is "in two" and is counted with two foot taps per bar/measure (tap your foot along with the bass notes of the guitar player). Personnel: Berry, vocals and electric guitar; Johnnie Johnson, piano; Willie Dixon, bass; Jasper Thomas, drums; and Jerome Green, maracas.

0:00 Introduction (3 measures): The song opens with a three-bar (3 x 2 foot taps) solo guitar introduction. Notice the distorted sound of the guitar, which may have been caused by turning the volume of the amplifier up beyond the ability of the speaker, or by a broken tube. Later, electronic devices were invented to duplicate this sound ("fuzz-tone") and it has since become a standard part of the guitar sound. The bass, second guitar, drums, and maracas join in (0:05), alternating back and forth between two chords for two bars.

0:05 First Chorus: Begins "Maybellene, why can't. . . ," and repeats the first vocal line, as in classic blues. Johnny Johnson's piano can be heard distantly in the background playing riffs and instrumental answers. The third line is, "You done started back doing the things you used to do." Note: Chuck Berry, or a second guitar, is playing the simple country bass line, while the acoustic bass player is playing "in four." The acoustic bass is low in the mix and therefore is very hard to hear, so the listener only hears the guitar player giving the feel of "two."

0:16 First Verse: This is not in the classic blues form but is twelve bars long and begins, "As I was motorvatin' over the hill," and Berry begins telling the story of the motor showdown between Maybellene's Cadillac and the singer's V8 Ford.

0:29 Second Chorus: It is an exact repeat of the opening chorus (twelve-bar blues), except that the piano is more audible.

0:41 Second Verse (Part B): It begins, "The Cadillac pulled up to 104," and Berry continues the story of the chase.

0:53   Third Chorus.

1:05   Chorus, guitar solo (12 measures): Berry's guitar solo is two choruses of the twelve-bar blues. The recording mix changes: The volume of the acoustic bass and maracas is turned up while the guitar player stops his simple country bass line, which gives the impression that the music has doubled in tempo. Berry plays a riff pattern that occupies eight bars, then leaves the riff and plays a line that brings the twelve-bar chorus to closure. Notice that Willie Dixon's slap bass technique is audible in this section because the acoustic bass volume is turned up.

1:17   Chorus, guitar solo (12 measures): Begins with a riff pattern similar to that of a big band trumpet section, but this time it occupies only four bars before Berry moves on to another pattern. Notice that during both twelve-bar blues choruses, Johnny Johnson accompanies Berry with complex riff patterns on the piano. The guitar and piano combine to create a complex "layered rhythm," which is one of the African musical characteristics.

1:29   Chorus: The recording engineer does not reset the volume, and the acoustic bass is still heard until the fifth measure when the original recording mix resumes.

1:42   Third Verse: It begins "The motor cooled down, the heat went down," and ends with the V8 catching Maybellene at the top of the hill.

1:54   Chorus

2:06   Coda: Berry plays an ending grouped in four-bar phrases. The second phrase is almost like an answer to the first phrase. The sound fades in the middle of the third phrase.

For Musicians

Berry's bar F7 blues guitar introduction sets the stage for the next two bars, when the rhythm section enters. Alternating between the tonic seventh chord (Bb7) for two beats and the dominant seventh chord (F7) for two beats, the drums and maracas help establish the tempo and feel. Even after the twelve-bar blues vocal chorus starts, the I-V chord alternation gives this blues tune an unusual quality and a back-and-forth motion. Berry relieves this by going to the IV chord (Eb7) in bars nine and ten before returning to the previous pattern. Johnson's upper-register rhythmic piano chords add just the right color to this riff-heavy, backbeat-oriented tune. The insistent use of the flat third (Db) and dominant seventh (Ab) as melody notes highlights the verses, creating tension between the vocal line and accompanying sonorities. The consistent return to the chorus section after every verse gives a rounded binary form to the whole song, with the twenty-four-bar guitar solo helping to break up the pattern to some degree. The final eight-bar fadeout after the last verse rehashes some of the intro material, with improvised electric guitar over alternating tonic/dominant chords.

Final Comments

"Maybellene" was also covered in 1955 by vocalist Jim Lowe, whose Dot Records recording version was a number one R&B hit, and by singer/guitarist Marty Robbins, whose Columbia recording went to number nine on the country charts. Johnny Rivers's version of the tune hit number twelve in 1964, and "Maybellene" won a Grammy Hall of Fame award in 1988.

♩♪♪ "Tutti Frutti"—performed by Little Richard

Little Richard turned an otherwise sedate September 1955 recording session into the birth of rock and roll with this off-the-cuff dirty ditty. The recording brought Little Richard to national prominence, establishing his piano-pounding style and trademark falsetto "woos." A popular song with both African-American and European-American teen audiences, "Tutti Frutti" sold three million copies by 1968 and was Little Richard's first million seller. This song set a musical formula for subsequent releases such as "Long Tall Sally" and "Good Golly, Miss Molly."

Analysis of "Tutti Frutti"—2:06 in length, released on Specialty 561

This song spent five weeks on the charts in early 1956. The form of this recording is twelve-bar blues with the "Tutti Frutti" lines functioning as a refrain ("chorus" in the Tin Pan Alley sense of the term); the meter is in four foot-taps per measure. Personnel: Richard Penniman (Little Richard), vocals, piano, and composer; Crescent City Rhythm section as backup (Fats Domino's group), including Earl Palmer, drums; Alvin "Red" Tyler, baritone sax; Lee Allen, tenor sax; Frank Fields, bass; and manager Robert "Bumps" Blackwell on guitar.

0:00   Introduction (2 measures): Little Richard opens with his famous lyrics, "awop-bop-a-loo-mop-a-lop-bump-bum," sung solo.

0:02   First Chorus (12 measures): Begins with the "Tutti frutti" lyrics, which repeat every two measures. There is a vocal break at measures 11 and 12, where he delivers the "a-wop-bop-a-loo-mop-a-lop-bump-bum" lyrics. The piano accompaniment is a standard boogie woogie pattern, and the saxes contribute background riffs.

0:18   Second Chorus (12 measures): Begins with the lyric "I got a gal," which fills the entire four-bar line and is repeated as the second line, just like classic vocal blues. The accompaniment riffs are the same as the previous chorus. The last four bars of the chorus (0:28) are an instrumental "stop time" where the band hits only the first beat of each measure. The lyrics here, ". . . rocks to the East . . . rocks to the West," imply the sexual usage of the word "rock," although the audience likely assumed the "dance" definition of the term.

0:33   Third Chorus (12 measures): This is a repeat of the refrain "Tutti frutti," with Little Richard's signature "Woooh" scream in the fourth measure.

0:49   Fourth Chorus (12 measures): Also begins "I got a gal," but this time her name is Daisy. The accompaniment is unchanged and there is a similar stop time beginning in measure nine.

1:05   Fifth Chorus (12 measures): This is a repeat of the refrain chorus with a scream at the end, leading into a saxophone solo.

1:19   Sixth Chorus (12 measures): A tenor sax solo is featured, accompanied by the rhythm section and Little Richard's highly rhythmic upper-register piano chords.

1:35   Seventh Chorus (12 measures): A repeat of the refrain chorus.

1:51   Eighth Chorus (12 measures): A repeat of the "Daisy" lyrics.

2:06   Ninth Chorus (12 measures): A repeat of the refrain chorus, but (if your version of the recording does not fade out) Little Richard alters the last two nonsense syllables to "bam-boom."

For Musicians

After Little Richard's scat-style opening two bars, "Tutti Frutti" follows a classic twelve-bar blues form with some clever vocal and rhythm breaks. Over the walking bass line, backbeat drums, and rhythmic piano of early rhythm and blues, Little Richard sings blues melodies in a frenzied style and narrates his encounters with several women. The improvised, octave-leaping "woos" have influenced vocalists from Paul McCartney to Steven Tyler, and gives the sense of wild abandon to this blues melody. The two-bar break occurring at the ends of verses one, three, five, and seven reiterates the opening nonsense words as an interlude in a most simple and effective manner, giving the song an internal continuity. Choruses two, four, and eight use a stop time technique on the down beats of the last four bars of the phrases (over the V chord) for vocal emphasis. The solo section follows the traditional twelve-bar blues, with the melodic sax overshadowed by Little Richard's highly percussive upper-register block piano chords. His technique here falls in line with Chuck Berry's pianist Johnnie Johnson, and draws from boogie woogie artist Pete Johnson as well, setting a standard for rock and roll pianists to follow. Little Richard never fails to keep the drive and energy of "Tutti Frutti" at a high level, and his flamboyant stage performance during the song likely helped contribute to the musical excitement.

Final Comments

Crooner Pat Boone immediately covered this tune in early 1956 with his "parent approved" version, which spent ten weeks on the charts, opening the door for many other professional white singers to cover rhythm and blues material for profit. This classic early rock and roll tune was reworked by AC/DC as "Rockin'" in the eighties.

---

[1] Arnold Shaw, *Honkers and Shouters: The Golden Years of Rhythm & Blues* (New York: Macmillan, 1978), 103.

[2] Grace Lichtenstein and Laura Danker, *Musical Gumbo: The Music of New Orleans* (New York: Norton, 1993), 77–78.

[3] Ibid., 91–92.

[4] Ibid., 92.

[5] Shaw, 189–90.

[6] Ray Charles and David Ritz, *Brother Ray: Ray Charles' Own Story* (New York: Dial Press), 124.

[7] Wes Smith, *The Pied Pipers of Rock n' Roll: Radio Deejays of the 50s and 60s* (Marietta, Georgia: Longstreet, 1989), 68.

[8] Shaw., 270.

[9] John A. Jackson, *The Big Beat: Alan Freed and the Early Years of Rock & Roll* (New York: Schirmer Books, 1991), 106.

Chapter Six

The Style Change
Dick Clark,
Teen Idols, Girl Groups, and
Payola

The period between 1958 and 1963 has been treated in several different ways by rock historians and critics, all accurate, but none creating a complete image of this lull in the evolution of Pop music. One important aspect of it is that by end of the 1950s, most of the original stars of rock and roll were out of commission: Elvis was in the Army, although recordings were still being released; Chuck Berry was in prison for a violation of the Mann Act; Jerry Lee Lewis was, in effect, blackballed because of public response to his marriage; Little Richard had left show business for a religious calling; Buddy Holly had been killed in a plane crash; and Eddie Cochran had been killed in an auto accident in England.

The recounting of these events is accurate, but they do not fully explain the change in music. Furthermore, to explain the "demise" of rock and roll as being due to these events presupposes that the artists would have continued to be an ever-flowing font of creativity. In reality, Elvis had been turned into a crooner by RCA and Hollywood and probably would have disappeared naturally had it not been for his premature removal from audiences by the Army and his later being sequestered in Hollywood by Colonel Tom Parker. Chuck Berry's songs about teenage life were certainly an important element of early rock and roll, but his audience was already looking for something different from him. The same could be said of Little Richard. Buddy Holly had already begun the transformation into a syrupy crooner, if his posthumous hit "It Doesn't Matter Anymore" is any indication. It is likely that these early stars would have faded were it not for their disappearance at the height of their popularity.

An explanation for the change in rock and roll at the end of the fifties to a more commercial, Pop sound is that big business was beginning to take over and professional song-writing factories were dominating the music. The music business had always been a "business," and recordings always passed through the hands of professional record men; the only real change at the end of the fifties was that the faces of those record men were changing. The faces in the early fifties were those of the R&B record men of the late forties: Ralph Bass and Syd Nathan of King, Lew Chudd of Imperial, Art Rupe of Specialty, the Bahari Brothers of Modern and RPM, the Chess Brothers of Chess, and Sam Phillips of Sun. Atlantic would have been mentioned in this group, but they diversified, adding R&B to their original jazz lineup, and were able to remain a vital force in the next phase of the industry. Newer, younger faces like Dick Clark, Leiber and Stoller, Phil Spector, and the Brill Building writers were beginning to take over, feeding the demand for recordings aimed at teenagers. These newer faces were still attached to independent record companies; however, the importance of the major labels increased as a result of the payola scandal.

The payola hearings also had a noticeable effect on the composition of the top ten. In 1960, Percy Faith's "Theme From a Summer Place" was the number one recording of the year. However, except for Elvis in 1956 and 1957, number one recordings had always been of a commercial Pop nature rather than rough-edged Rock'n' Roll. In 1956, directly below Elvis's two hits "Heartbreak Hotel" and "Don't Be Cruel" was "Lisbon Antigua" by Nelson Riddle. In 1957, just below "All Shook Up," was Pat Boone's "Love Letters in the Sand." The strongest evidence for the influence of the payola hearings is that in 1959, six of the top ten recordings were released by independent labels, and in 1960, only two of the top ten were released by indies. This evidence pales slightly when the top 100 is examined: In 1959, sixty-seven of the top 100 were released by indies, and in 1960, fifty-three of the top 100 were by the independents. The evidence would seem to indicate that the payola scandal made it more difficult for independents to compete with the majors for airplay, which in turn affected their ability to get a recording into the top ten.

Many historians neglect the one subtle change in the radio industry, also a result of the payola scandal, that had the most lasting effect: the advent of the music director. To avoid future charges that DJs were accepting money to give records airplay, stations took the responsibility of choosing records away from DJs and put it into the hands of a music director or program director. In the fifties, DJs generally were able to choose records that they thought were either good music or suited to the taste of their listeners. DJs such as Alan Freed, who refused to play cover records, were responsible for allowing R&B to be heard by European-American teens who would have otherwise heard only the pop versions. This DJ-based system was replaced by a system in which only one set of ears, that of the music director, dictated the recordings that would be heard on that station.

The effect of the move away from DJ selection encouraged the rise of the Top 40 radio format. Robert "Todd" Stortz, "father" of the Top 40 format, once noticed that patrons of juke boxes continually spent money playing the same few songs over and over again. From this he deduced that listeners enjoyed hearing their favorite songs often and, therefore, would probably listen to a radio station that programmed music in such a manner. In 1949, Stortz bought KOWH in Omaha, and in 1951 he began programming twenty-four hours of music based on the placement of the recordings on the charts. This was the birth of Top 40 radio. He kept DJ ad-libbing to a minimum, increased the amount of recorded commercial jingles and musical station breaks, and devised methods of attracting telephone response from listeners.[1] This system is still intact, except that the number of recordings being played has been reduced to about thirty.

The final and possibly most important reason for the change in the music of the late fifties was the homogenizing effect of the television show *American Bandstand*. Beginning as *Philadelphia Bandstand* in 1952 under the leadership of Bob Horn, *American Bandstand* went national in 1957 under the leadership of Dick Clark. Within two years the daily ninety-minute show was broadcast on 101 stations with an audience of twenty million. The show emphasized a clean-cut version of rock and roll and increased the importance of a telegenic appearance in the popularization of rock stars. The result was a marked increase in handsome/beautiful recording artists such as Frankie Avalon, Fabian, Paul Anka, Ricky Nelson, Annette Funicello, and Connie Francis.

These factors, plus a new generation of fans, all worked together to change the sound of rock and roll. The prevailing impression, at least according to critics and historians, is that the change was for the worse.

PAYOLA

The payola scandal is the name given to the findings of the Special Subcommittee on Legislative Oversight chaired by Representative Oren Harris, which investigated, among other things, commercial bribery in the record industry. The term "payola" was first used by *Variety* in 1916 to describe the practice of singers making private deals with publishers to sing certain songs in their acts.[2] In 1959, the issue was that DJs accepted gifts and cash from record companies, and it was assumed to be a form of bribery to induce them to play certain recordings, thus spurring record sales and performance royalties. Payola is a very complex issue because, as with all politics, there are several important undercurrents swirling beneath the surface discussions.

The practice of giving artists some financial interest in a composition with the intention of inducing them to publicly perform a song was not particular to rock and roll. Song-pluggers, whose job it was to launch new songs by getting established entertainers to perform them, often made under-the-table deals with stars and producers to add songs to a show. In 1863, Walter Kittredge, composer of "Tenting Tonight on the Old Camp Ground," gave Asa Hutchinson a share of the royalties in an effort to encourage performances of the song by the Hutchinson Family.[3] "After the Ball," written and published by Charles K. Harris in 1892, was one of the biggest hits of the last century. Its success was partly due to the writer/publisher sharing the royalties with J. Aldrich Libby, an important performer. The song was added to a Broadway show, *A Trip to Chinatown*, and within a year the song was earning $25,000 a month.[4] The song would not have earned all that money if it have not been added to the show. In a similar spirit, Al Jolson, one of the most popular musical entertainers of the 1920s, reportedly would agree to perform a song only in exchange for co-writer credits. Frank Sinatra, who owned one-third of Barton Music Publishers, offered similar deals to young songwriters. This arrangement had long been commonplace in the music industry, so its not surprising that it occurs again in rock and roll.

An example of this type of arrangement in rock and roll is what occurred between Chuck Berry and Alan Freed. When Chuck Berry recorded "Maybellene," Freed was one of the most important DJs in the country, and it was important to have him "push" the recording on his show. To encourage this, Chess Records had Berry split the song-writing credits with Freed and Russ Fratto, thus cutting them in on the mechanical and performance royalties. The royalty split of this arrangement gives fifty percent to the publisher, a wing of Chess Records, and fifty percent to the writers, which is split into thirds, one-third each for Berry, Freed, and Fratto. When Freed played the recording on his show, it was noted by the performing rights organization, and royalties were paid. Because Freed was listed as a co-writer and was entitled to performance and mechanical royalties, he received money for giving the record airplay. This is not the same as payola, but it is very close.

Beneath the surface were two issues: the popularity of rock and roll and the feud between the American Society of Composers Authors and Publishers (ASCAP) and Broadcast Music, Inc. (BMI). ASCAP, formed in 1913, and BMI, formed in 1940, are organizations that collect royalties for songwriters and performers based on a system of number of airplays and publications, and license songs to broadcast media for specific negotiated fees. Many adults believed that rock and roll was "bad music," and since their children would not knowingly listen to "bad music," there must be a reason why they did. Led by Congress and the media, the public deduced that DJs were responsible because they played the "bad music" and, since a music professional would not knowingly play "bad music," obviously they were playing it because someone paid them to play it. The basic assumption was that if payola ended, then rock and roll would go away.

Since the birth of BMI, created in response to allegations from ASCAP artists of monopolization and price gouging by their company, ASCAP had charged that there was an inherent conflict of interest when broadcasters owned their own performance rights organization. Conversely, BMI's stance was that ASCAP was a monopoly that needed a competing organization. The issue surfaced in 1959, because during the fifties, BMI's profits were increasing and beginning to worry ASCAP. The reality was that BMI's increasing profits were increasing because ASCAP had previously ignored composers of R&B and country music—the very music that developed into rock and roll. Now that rock and roll was becoming the popular music of the United States, BMI-licensed songs were beginning to get more airplay than ASCAP-licensed songs.

Toward the end of the fifties, the concept of the Top 40 list was spreading, which meant that there was less airtime available for new recordings. Additionally, manufacturers were increasing the number of recordings released each week to between 80 and 125 units. It was becoming more difficult for an independent record label to get its releases noticed by important stations. One method of getting a DJ to notice your record was to include a gift for him. This glut of recordings prompted some stations to offer a form of institutionalized payola. In a "pre-test record plan," seven West Coast stations offered eight plays a day on each station for a ten-day period for $1,200. Several other stations initiated similar plans.[5]

The Harris Subcommittee found that 335 DJs had been paid a total of $263,245 as "consultants."[6] Founding DJ Martin Block (The Make Believe Ballroom) claimed that taking the ten dollars that came with a new recording was like giving a headwaiter a tip for a ringside table.[7] Alan Freed admitted that he took money but claimed it did not influence his decisions; he would take a gift but would not take a dime to plug a record because he would be giving up control of his show. The final 265-page report of the Harris committee was issued in December 1960 and included nine pages addressing "Payola and Song Plugging by Disk Jockeys and Others."

The results of the Committee's investigation were purely cosmetic, but, at least in the eyes of the public, the government had tried to do something about rock and roll. In retrospect, their actions appear to have been flamboyant election-year politics. Several DJs admitted to receiving money and gifts from record promoters, and they were fired by their stations. Alan Freed proved to be the scapegoat for the whole affair, probably because he was rock and roll's most visible proponent, its most infamous DJ (he had gotten too much negative publicity from the "rock riots"), and he was arrogantly unrepentant in his admission of accepting payola. Freed was fired by his station, and, in a 1962 trial, he pleaded guilty to accepting payola. He was fined $300 and was handed a six-month suspended sentence. Adding insult to injury, the IRS claimed he owed $38,000 in back taxes from his payola earnings. Freed never worked in radio again and died of uremia in 1965 at the age of forty-three.

Dick Clark's experience with the committee began with a hostile interrogation and ended with Harris saying, "You are obviously a fine young man . . . . You have made from your own viewpoint, I think, a very good witness . . . . I do not think you are the inventor of the system; I do not think you are even the architect of it, apparently. I think you are the product that has taken advantage of a unique opportunity. . . ."[8]

Dick Clark did not take payola, but he had significant business interests in the music industry, which gave the appearance of a conflict of interest. In 1957, he invested $125 in Jamie Records and made $31,575 profit (11,900%) when he sold it in 1959. He told the committee that anyone could go into the record business for a total outlay of $250, with the chance of making $100,000; this was the hope that drove the industry. Clark had financial interests in Sea Lark Music (BMI), Arch Music (ASCAP), Mallard Pressing Company, Swan Records, and Chips Distributing Company, and owned 160 copyrights. He did not take money to play certain recordings, but he made money legally through performance royalties when he played recordings in which he had an interest. At the beginning of the hearings, ABC network suggested that he divest himself of his business interests. He did and lost eight million dollars as a result, according to his autobiography, *Rock, Roll, & Remember*.

Another basic assumption related to the payola hearings was that a DJ could make a recording a hit simply by giving it enough airplay. Most DJs believe that no amount of airplay can turn a flop into a hit—if it's not in the grooves, you can't make it a hit. As an experiment on November 24, 1959, before the hearings, Dick Clark took a recording that he knew was not a hit, "You Hold the Future" by Tommy Sands, and played it endlessly on his show to prove that "no amount of airplay can turn a stiff into a hit."[9] The record never became a hit.

BRILL BUILDING POP

The professional songwriting center of America was an area of New York City known as Tin Pan Alley. Music publishing houses began gathering on West 28th Street in Manhattan in the 1890s, and by 1904, there were forty-five companies located there. In the beginning, they supplied songs to vaudeville, theater, and cabaret performers in hopes that one would catch the ear of the public and become a hit. When a song became a hit, there was money to be made selling the song in sheet music and piano rolls; both were sold in department and variety stores like F. W. Woolworth. In 1910, the sheet music business was selling about 30 million copies a year; songs like George M. Cohan's "Over There" sold over two million copies. Even at this early stage, people in the music business knew that the way to help make a song popular was through constant repetition and having the song performed by important vaudeville stars. Publishers often persuaded performers to add songs to their act by paying them or giving them a piece of the publishing—in other words, payola existed even before radio.

The R&B songs that became rock and roll were not written by Tin Pan Alley composers (mostly ASCAP members), but were often written by the performers themselves or supplied by the independent record companies who were usually members of BMI. It took only a short while for the publishing industry to catch on and begin to supply songs for the teenage market. By the late fifties, the most active music publishing area was the stretch along Broadway between 49th and 53rd Streets. Most famous was the Brill Building at 1619 Broadway, which in 1962 housed 165 music businesses. Important action also took place at 1650, 1674, and 1697 Broadway. This area was so influential that the pop music of the late fifties and early sixties was often called "Brill Building Pop."

Hits of Aldon Writers

Goffin/King

Will You Still Love Me Tomorrow?; Don't Say Nothin' Bad (About My Baby); Locomotion; Up on the Roof; Chains; Take Good Care of My Baby; Crying in the Rain; One Fine Day; I'm Into Something Good; It Might As Well Rain Until September; A Natural Woman; Hey Girl.

Sedaka/Greenfield

Stupid Cupid; Calendar Girl; Breaking Up Is Hard to Do; Oh! Carol; Happy Birthday Sweet Sixteen; Stairway to Heaven; Another Sleepless Night; Charms.

Mann/Weil

Uptown; He's Sure the Boy I Love; Walking in the Rain; Then He Kissed Me; Who Put the Bomp; You've Lost That Lovin' Feelin'; Don't Know Much; Blame It on the Bossa Nova; Get Ready; Hungry.

Greenwich/Barry

Baby I Love You; Be My Baby; Da Doo Ron Ron; Then He Kissed Me; The Boy I'm Gonna Marry; Chapel of Love; Baby Be Mine; Leader of the Pack; I Wanna Love Him So Bad; Do Wah Diddy Diddy; River Deep Mountain High; Hanky Panky; People Say.

Music publishers in the Brill Building typically employed songwriting teams of two or three people, who crammed themselves into small cubicles with a piano and a typewriter and cranked out songs at an incredible rate. In 1958, Don Kirshner and Al Nivens formed the most important music publishing house of the early sixties, Aldon Music, located across the street from the Brill Building at 1650 Broadway and specializing in teen songs. Aldon assembled a team of writers whose average age was under twenty-five, and eventually produced at least two hundred chart hits.

Several years earlier Don Kirshner had teamed up with Bobby Darin (Robert Cassotto) to write songs, and between 1956 and 1958, they wrote several unsuccessful songs and composed radio commercials. The first important songwriting team to be hired by Aldon was Neil Sedaka and Howard Greenfield, whose first hit was "Stupid Cupid" (1958), recorded by Connie Francis (Concetta Franconero). Francis's association with Kirshner extended back to his commercial-writing days when she was one of the singers he used. Soon, other teams joined Aldon, and together they crafted a large body of music aimed at teenagers. Other important teams were Carole King and Gerry Goffin, and Barry Mann and Cynthia Weil. Ellie Greenwich and Jeff Barry were not employed by Aldon, but their songs, and those of Mort Shuman and Doc Pomus, are also referred to as Brill Building Pop.

AMERICAN BANDSTAND: PHILADELPHIA TEEN IDOLS

Although all rock and roll stars technically were *teen idols*, the phrase is used to refer to a particular brand of non-guitar-playing male singers with pompadour hair styles between the years of 1957 and 1963. The single unifying element of these new teen idols is that they looked good on television. Television, because of its national audience, played an important role in promoting teenage music and, therefore, it became very important for a singer to be telegenic. Increasingly, teen stars were good looking and, because of the homogenizing effect of television, they were also projecting almost identical images. Soon image became more important than musical ability. Television audiences responded to a steady diet of harmless pop music centering on a clean- cut image, cute face, innocent love songs, and slick production techniques that gave the music a polished sound.

Several television actors became singers either out of a desire to perform or as a result of pressure from their producers. Ricky Nelson was in an interesting situation. He had been appearing as a regular on television since 1952, when he began playing himself on the *Adventures of Ozzie and Harriet*. In real life, his father, Ozzie, was a big band leader and his mother, Harriet, was a singer. In 1957, Ricky began singing on the show and releasing records. His first hit was a cover of Fats Domino's "I'm Walking." He continued to release

Dick Clark with Dion and the Belmonts

recordings until his parents' show went off the air in 1966. After his television career ended, he continued singing, but was caught in the area between an "oldies" artist and a current artist. In 1969, he formed the Stone Canyon Band, best described as California country-rock, and in 1971 was booed while performing at a Madison Square Garden oldies concert because he performed new music rather than playing his old hits. In response to this experience, he wrote "Garden Party," which sold a million copies, reached number seven on the charts, and gave his music career new life.

Other television shows followed and had their teen actors release recordings. Both Paul Peterson and Shelley Fabares of the *Donna Reed Show* were successful at placing recordings on the charts, as was Annette Funicello of the *Mickey Mouse Club*. Even film actors Tab Hunter and Sal Mineo tried to launch singing careers.

More influential than any single television show was *American Bandstand* and its surrounding music business atmosphere that caused Philadelphia to became an important teen-pop recording center. Dick Clark was hired by WFIL radio in Philadelphia in 1952 to play adult music. Soon after his arrival, WFIL television canceled their afternoon English movie and filled in the time slot with a music show called *Bandstand*, hosted by Bob Horn. The show was a mixture of interviews and music films, the forerunner of music videos, from the Snader Musical Films Library. The first guest was jazz trumpeter, Dizzy Gillespie. That format was soon changed to feature kids dancing in the studio and singers who lip-synced their latest recording. In the summer of 1956, Bob Horn was having an affair with a fourteen-year-old girl and was arrested for drunk driving. In the resulting turmoil, Dick Clark was moved over from radio to be the host of *Bandstand*. Clark did well, and the local show eventually attracted the attention of the ABC network, which also was thinking of canceling its afternoon English movie. *American Bandstand* began a four-week trial run on ABC on August 5, 1957, and was so successful that it generated fifteen thousand letters a week, more than the number one television program, *Wyatt Earp*. Within two years *American Bandstand* had an audience of twenty million and was broadcast on 101 stations throughout the nation.[10]

American Bandstand became a primary vehicle for promoting and homogenizing teen culture. The show was aired daily during the after-school hours, just before the *Mickey Mouse Club*, and had a tremendous impact on teen clothing, teen attitudes, dance steps, and pop recordings. *American Bandstand's* daily broadcasts instantly spread Philadelphia's teen culture, so that within days, any new fad was embraced by teen viewers throughout the United States.

In his autobiography, Dick Clark mentions an anecdote that illustrates the magnitude of *American Bandstand's* popularity. The police chief of Carbondale, Pennsylvania, told him that one day the police noticed that teenagers had vanished from the streets and sidewalks after school, and they wondered what "evil" all the kids were up to. A house-to-house search revealed that the town's teenagers were all home watching *American Bandstand*.

The show was also important to the business climate around Philadelphia. Before *Bandstand*, there was a small music industry. Dave Miller, of Essex Records, had first recorded Bill Haley and developed the *101 Strings* series, but *Bandstand* greatly expanded the business opportunities. In 1957, local musician Bernie Lowe formed Cameo Records and worked with songwriter Kal Mann and musician Dave Appell and his band, the Appelljacks. Chubby Checker, Dee Dee Sharp, the Dovells, Bobby Rydell, the Orlons, the Skyliners, and the Tymes all recorded for Cameo or its subsidiary, Parkway. Later two local songwriters, Pete DeAngelis and Bob Marcucci, started Chancellor Records and recorded Frankie Avalon, Fabian, and Claudine Clark. Late in 1957, Clark, Bernie Binnick, and Tony Mamarella formed Swan Records, which recorded both Freddie Cannon and the Rebels, and released the Beatles' "She Loves You" in America. Since these Philadelphia labels grew out of the atmosphere that was created by *American Bandstand*, it therefore was natural for local record men to bring their products to Dick Clark to see if they could get airplay.

Frankie Avalon (Francis Avallone), the first of the Philadelphia teen idols, had stage parents who helped him pursue a show business career. Frankie was a trumpet virtuoso who played at local talent competitions and clubs, and was "discovered" in 1951 when he sneaked in to entertain at a party for singer Al Martino. An agent who was at the party took him to New York, where he appeared on several national television shows, including *The Jackie Gleason Show*. After this short bout with stardom, he returned home and joined a local rock band, Rocco and the Saints, and later got his friend Robert Ridarelli (Bobby Rydell) into the band as a drummer. Bobby Rydell, at age nine, had entered Paul Whiteman's local amateur show called *Teen Club* and stayed for three years. Contrary to popular belief, these two teen idols were no overnight-sensation, no-talent bums; they were competent performers who found the door open for them as singers rather than instrumentalists.

In 1958, after two unsuccessful recordings on Chancellor, Frankie Avalon hit with "De De Dinah" (1958), "Ginger Bread" (1958), "Venus" (1959), "Bobby Sox to Stockings/A Boy Without a Girl" (1959), and several others. His local availability and telegenic appearance made it easy for him to appear on *American Bandstand* enough times for writers to refer to him as a *"Bandstand regular."* His television and recording success made him a natural for the movies, and he was paired with Annette Funicello, who by 1960 also had a

Frankie Avalon and Annette Funicello

successful singing career in a series of beach movies, including *Beach Party* (1963), *Bikini Beach* (1964), *Muscle Beach Party* (1964), *Beach Blanket Bingo* (1965), and *How to Stuff a Wild Bikini* (1965). After five beach movies they turned to hot rod movies with *Fireball 500* (1966) and *Thunder Alley* (1967). Their beach movies were so successful and representative of the period that two decades later a retro-sequel, *Back to the Beach* (1987), featured them as parents returning to California with teenagers of their own.

Bobby Rydell was discovered by the bass player for Cameo's house band when they both performed at the same summer resort. He, too, had several flops before finding the right song, "Kissin' Time" (1959), which launched him on a string of nineteen top 30 hits. Like Avalon, his physical appearance and proximity made it easy for him to appear often on *American Bandstand.*

The third Philadelphia teen idol was Fabian Forte, who did fit the description of a pretty face with no particular talent for singing. Frankie Avalon introduced Fabian to Bob Marcucci, who told everyone that he found Fabian sitting on a doorstep. After working with him in the studio, Marcucci took him to Dick Clark, who took him to a record hop and let him lip-sync to his recording, "I'm a Man." The girls at the hop screamed and yelled when he was onstage, indicating to Clark that Fabian might not be a great singer, but his appearance counted more. In 1959, Fabian had hits with "Turn Me Loose," "Tiger," and "Hound Dog Man." The following year, he turned to acting and appeared in *North to Alaska.*

AMERICAN BANDSTAND: DANCE CRAZE

Rock and roll music has always emphasized dancing and rhythm, so the dance craze of the early 1960s occurred naturally as both a response to the new beat and a need for teen social interaction. On television, teen shows like *American Bandstand* were visually oriented and featured lengthy video shots of dancing teens. Many teenagers learned to dance by mimicking the Bandstand kids.

The definitive years of the dance craze were 1960-64, after the Twist, although new dances started appearing in 1957 during the first week of *American Bandstand.* Dances of the 1960s typically featured solo dancing, most often without touching a partner, or doing the same steps in a coordinated fashion. Typically, the songs that accompanied the dances were either twelve-bar blues or a thirty-two-bar AABA form with a I-vi-IV-V chord progression, and usually gave instructions for the dance somewhere in the lyrics. Some of the many dances from this period were the Twist, Pony, Fly, Dog, Madison, Popeye, Watusi, Loco-Motion, Hitch-Hike, Harlem Shuffle, Limbo, Swim, Wiggle Wobble, Bristol Stomp, Cool Jerk, Duck, Mashed Potato, Monkey, Boston Monkey, Hully Gully, Frug, and the Funky Chicken. By the end of the sixties, dances stopped having names until later in the disco era, when dances once again were given names like the Hustle and the Bump. The fact that the dances had names and songs attached to them helped them become part of the cultural landscape of the sixties. Once dances stopped having names and associated songs, they quickly faded from memory.

To a certain extent, the music business was responsible for the strength of the dance craze because it helped supply the songs for the dances. All the dances, except the Bunny Hop (early 1950s), were started by kids who brought the new dance to the show and, if there was not a particular record for that dance, Dick Clark notified his industry contacts and alerted them to the need for a song to accompany the dance. It may appear to some that Dick Clark engineered the dance craze, but he was more of a facilitator, a middleman between the kids on the street and the record industry. Clark told the industry that there was a need and the industry met the need.

The first dance spread by *American Bandstand* was the Bop, which appeared during the first two weeks of the show. Clark, in his conversations with business people on the West Coast, heard of a new dance the kids were doing to Gene Vincent's "Be-Bop-a-Lula." One day on the show, he noticed two teens doing a radically different dance. When he questioned them, he learned they were visiting from California and the dance was called the Bop. Clark asked the kids to stick around after the show and teach the local kids how to do the dance.[11] Later in the fall, Gene Vincent released "Dance the Bop" to answer the need for a record to accompany the already existing dance.

Another dance from 1957 was the Stroll, a line-dance, introduced on *Bandstand* by Chuck Willis. Kids used Willis's "C. C. Rider" for the dance. In November 1957, the Diamonds were on *Bandstand*, when their manager, Nat Goodman, noticed kids doing the dance and asked Clark about it. Clark told him it was the Stroll and that there was "no specific Stroll song"; the Diamonds immediately recorded a song called "The Stroll," and by Christmas 1957, it was in the top five.

The most important dance of the sixties, the Twist (1960), was also helped along by Dick Clark. The Twist was important for two reasons. First, it took the nation by storm. There were books about it and people on television teaching others how to do it—even adults were doing it. Second, it spawned a string of other dances hoping to be the next Twist.

It began in the summer of 1960, when Clark noticed an African-American couple doing a hip-swiveling dance and warned the producer, "Tony! For God's sake, keep the cameras off that couple near the Top 10 Board." He was worried that the hip-swiveling would be too suggestive. Later, he asked the couple what the dance was called, and by the next afternoon the dance was spreading. He called his friend Bernie Lowe at Chancellor Records and alerted him to the dance that was in need of a song. There already was a recording called "The Twist," by Hank Ballard ("Work With Me Annie"); it was on the flip side of his "Teardrops on Your Letter." Ballard's record company, King, had re-released "The Twist" to go with the dance, but for some reason Clark did not use that one. Clark told Bernie Lowe to "turn the song upside down or sideways or whatever" and do the song. Turning the song "upside down or sideways"[12] would make it a new song and qualify it for a new copyright and relieve Chancellor from having to pay mechanical royalties and allow them to collect performance royalties. It turned out the song was too simple to alter, so they just rerecorded Ballard's song with their own singer.

For the new recording, Lowe used the same singer he had used to record Dick Clark's personal Christmas card record, Ernest Evans. According to Clark, during the Christmas recording session, his wife, Bobbie, remarked about Evans, "He's cute, he looks like Fats Domino, like a Chubby Checker." They used the name and it stuck.

Young Ernest Evans probably never dreamed that "The Twist" would be his claim to fame. While hoping for a career in the music business, he worked as an assistant in a butcher's shop where he often entertained clients and friends with songs and impersonations. "The Twist" was so popular that it reached the number one spot on the charts on two separate occasions, in August 1960 and in November 1961. Checker followed this hit with other twist tunes, "Let's Twist Again," and "Slow Twistin'," and introduced several other less successful dances, including the Pony, the Fly, the Hucklebuck, and the Limbo. Many others recorded twist records: "Twist and Shout" (Isley Brothers), "Twistin' the Night Away" (Sam Cooke), "Kissin' and Twistin'" (Fabian), and the "Peppermint Twist" (Joey Dee and the Starlighters).

Another dance was popularized by Eva Narcissus Boyd, better known as Little Eva, a teenage babysitter who happened to be in the right place at the right time. As a domestic worker for songwriters Gerry Goffin and Carol King, Little Eva happened to hear them working on a dance song with instructional lyrics. Little Eva started to sing and dance to the tune, and was asked to record it with the Cookies as a backup group. Although originally intended as a demo recording, her version of "The Loco-Motion" was released and rose to number one on both the pop and R&B charts in 1962. "Keep Your Hands off My Baby," and "Let's Turkey Trot" also reached the top twenty, but by 1965 Little Eva realized that she would never be able to recreate her original success. "The Loco-Motion" was reissued in 1972 and quickly covered by Grand Funk. Covers of this song appeared on the charts as late as 1988.

Dancing continues to be an important aspect of rock; however, this period was unique in the number of dances introduced with accompanying songs. The *disco* era had dancing as a central focus but did not produce the variety of dances that the dance craze of the 1960s had.

GIRL GROUPS

As an outgrowth of the doo-wop style and teen idol phase, girl groups began to appear in 1958 and remained a visible style until 1964. Girl groups, like doo-wop groups, consisted of three to five singers who typically did not play instruments. The most popular groups were the Chantels ("Maybe," 1958), the Angels ("My Boyfriend's Back," 1963), the Shirelles ("Soldier Boy," 1962), the Chiffons ("He's So Fine," 1963), and the Shangri-Las ("Leader of the Pack," 1964). The majority of their material was Brill Building Pop and was aimed at a young teenage audience. The girl-group style used innocent themes that typically emphasized a girl's relationship with a boy and her worthlessness without him. Although innocent lyrics were the norm, the Shirelles recorded songs that discussed sexual issues, such as in "Tonight's the Night," in which they wonder whether tonight is the night that they are going to make love, or in "Will You Love Me Tomorrow," when they sing, "Tonight the light of love is in your eyes, but will you love me tomorrow." Here they ask a serious question about a boy's commitment.

Two producers, Phil Spector and George "Shadow" Morton, became known through their recordings of girl groups. Spector is one the most curious personalities that rock and roll has ever seen. From the Bronx, Spector was of slight build and pale complexion and was somewhat of a loner. As a teen, his father committed suicide and his family moved to California to start a new life. Spector found it difficult to fit in with other teens and often retreated to playing jazz guitar by himself. Being musically talented, he began writing songs and organized a group of high school friends called the Teddy Bears, a female lead and three males (including himself). He wrote and produced their first recording, "To Know Him Is to Love Him" (1958), using lyrics that came from an inscription on his father's tombstone. The recording was a big success and rose to the top of the charts, eventually selling 1.4 million copies, and earned them an appearance on *American Bandstand*. Determined and encouraged by his success as a writer and producer, Spector actively pursued a career in music. Spector then began working under the guidance of West Coast record man, Lester Sill, who previously helped Leiber and Stoller with their careers. At the time, Sill and his partner, Lee Hazelwood, were recording guitarist Duane Eddy, and Sill took Spector to Phoenix to watch the sessions. Spector was fascinated by their technique of building up Eddy's guitar sound by adding reverb—a sound-processing device that makes the instrument or voice sound as if it were recorded in a big hollow room.[13] Later, he used the same technique as the cornerstone of his famous "wall of sound" style. When Spector decided to go to New York, Sill arranged for him to apprentice with Leiber and Stoller, who were then working with the Drifters through an independent production deal with Atlantic Records.

Chubby Checker

In New York, Spector worked with Leiber and Stoller on the new Drifters recordings. He played the guitar solo on "On Broadway," and reportedly co-wrote "Spanish Harlem" with Ben E. King. The Drifters' recordings of this era were unusual because they reduced the presence of the drum set but increased the presence of other percussion instruments, such as the triangle, castanets, tambourine, and timpani. Spector later added elements of this technique to his "wall of sound." While in New York, he produced a handful of hit recordings: "Corinna, Corinna" (Ray Peterson), "Every Breath I Take" (Gene Pitney), "Pretty Little Angel Eyes" (Curtis Lee), and "I Love How You Love Me" (Paris Sisters). Late in 1961, he returned to Los Angeles and with Les Sill formed Philles Records (Phil + Les), which began producing a string of hits with the Crystals.

It was with the Crystals, in Los Angeles at Gold Star Studios, that Spector fully developed his elaborate production techniques, some of which were

The Crystals

copied by others, especially Motown. His style, known as the "wall of sound," was created by overdubbing multiple groups of instruments and bathing them in reverb. He recorded several guitarists and bassists playing the same parts, then played the results back over the studio monitors, and then rerecorded that along with the musicians playing their parts again. Overdubbing was not out of the ordinary, but the process Spector used created a bigger and fuzzier sound. His technique caused a lot of tape distortion that increased with each successive take, and although this technique was technically improper, Spector used it in such a way as to give his recordings a distinctive sound. It's possible to hear the development of the "wall of sound" by listening to the Crystals' recordings in succession, because each recording exhibits a gradual expansion of Spector's technique.

The Crystals' early recordings were somewhat dark compared to other songs for teenagers. Their second release, "Uptown," is about a "little man" who works downtown where "everyone's his boss and he's lost in an angry land, But then he comes uptown to my tenement, uptown where folks don't pay much rent," and there he is a man where he can "hold his head up high" because she'll "be standing by." Although the topic was hard urban living, the singer's only worth is in making her boyfriend feel like a man. Their third recording, "He Hit Me (and It Felt Like a Kiss)" (1962), written by Goffin and King, eventually was pulled from the record bins due to its controversial subject matter.

The Crystals' fourth release, which became their first number one hit and million seller, was "He's a Rebel" (1962), and its story line fits neatly into the lives of many teenage girls who see a spark of something good within their boyfriends even though no one else does. Strangely, it was not the real Crystals that recorded "He's a Rebel." While out of town on a tour, the Crystals were not available when Spector wanted to record the new song. Assuming that his recording technique was more important than the artists, Spector found replacement singers—the Blossoms, led by Darlene Wright—to record the song. It wasn't until the original Crystals heard the song on the radio that they discovered "they" had recorded a new song. Darlene Wright became a solo singer for Philles under the new name of Darlene Love "(Today I Met) the Boy I'm Gonna Marry," and the Crystals (Blossoms) lead was taken over by La La Brooks on songs such as "Da Doo Ron Ron" (1963) and "Then He Kissed Me" (1963).

Spector was involved with other groups, such as the Ronettes, Bob B. Soxx, and the Blue Jeans, but his production techniques reached new heights with the Righteous Brothers' "You've Lost That Lovin' Feelin'" (1964), which used three keyboards and multiple guitars as well as his usual overdubbing. This recording is the best example of Spector's "wall of sound." The instruments in the background are combined and recorded in such a way as to make their individual identities almost unrecognizable.

His final recording in this style, Ike and Tina Turner's "River Deep?—Mountain High," was considered a failure, although it sold well in England. It caused Spector to enter a self-imposed exile. This recording was his biggest and most expensive production yet, with four guitars, four basses, three keyboards, two percussionists, two drummers, two saxophones, two trumpets, and two trombones.

Spector was called out of retirement by the Beatles' second manager, Alan Klein, to remix the hours of tape the Beatles had recorded in 1969 as the *Get Back* project. The results were released in 1970 as the *Let It Be* album, the Beatles' last commercially released album even though it was recorded before *Abbey Road*. Spector continued working with George Harrison on the *All Things Must Pass* and *The Concert For Bangla-Desh* albums in 1971, and John and Yoko's *Some Time in New York City* album. He sporadically resurfaced and has produced artists such as the Ramones and Leonard Cohen. Despite his short career, he was a dominant force in the recording industry and altered the sound of rock and roll for years to come.

George "Shadow" Morton was also an interesting figure in the girls group genre because he created a series of mini-dramas for the Shangri-Las, including "Leader of the Pack," and because his career began as a bluff. Morton went to visit Ellie Greenwich (Gaye), an old friend from Levittown, on Long Island, who was now a famous songwriter. When asked by her partner, Jeff Barry, what he did, Morton said he wrote "songs . . . hit songs." Barry called his bluff and asked him for a slow song, to which Morton replied, "OK, see ya next

Tuesday." Morton went back to Long Island and borrowed a basement studio, found a band, found a girls group from Queens (the Shangri-Las) through a recommendation, and was set to record on Sunday. On the way to the studio that Sunday, he realized that he did not have a song to record, so he pulled the car over and wrote "Remember (Walkin' in the Sand)" in about twenty-two minutes. When he got to the studio, he sang instructions to the band and the girls, because he had no sheet music for them (he was not a musician), and they had a finished product within two hours.[14] On Tuesday, he returned and played the tape for Jeff Barry and Jerry Leiber who liked it, hired Morton as a songwriter for a hundred dollars a week (off the books), rerecorded the song, and released it in August 1964. The song raced up the charts, was number thirteen after three weeks, and then spent six weeks in the top ten.

Their next recording was the quintessential girls group mini-drama of all time, "Leader of the Pack," complete with the sound of a roaring Harley and screeching brakes. The topic is a typical girl's saga of a boy no one understands. Her friends ask, "Is it true you're going out with him?" She responds, "I meet him at the candy store, get the picture," they answer, "Yes, we see." Her parents told her "He was bad," but she said, "He was sad." Her parents forbid her to see him again, and when she tells him, he roars off on his motorcycle and has a fatal accident to the cries of her yelling, "Look out, look out!" The Shangri-Las had several other dramatic hits through 1965, but in the end they wound up as disposable items of the record business. When it was all over, they discovered that they did not even have the right to perform under the Shangri-Las name because they did not own it.

Another recording that was representative of the genre was "My Boyfriend's Back" (1963), by the Angels. The Angels were not quite a one-hit group. They had reached the charts earlier in 1961 with "Till" and "Cry Baby Cry." "My Boyfriend's Back" was number one for three weeks at the end of summer and was perfectly timed for the topic of the song, which is about a girl whose boyfriend went away for the summer and now has returned. During his absence, another boy asked her out. When she turned him down, he "said things that weren't very nice," and was "spreading lies that I was untrue." Now that her "boyfriend's back," he is going to "save my reputation," and she sings warning phrases like "so look out now cause he's comin' after you," "you're gonna be sorry you were ever born, . . . cause he's kinda big and awful strong." Once again, the girl is relying on her relationship with her boyfriend to make things all right; without him she was helpless. These were typical sentiments expressed by girls groups, and few recordings contradicted that message to teenage girls. One of the recordings that did take an opposite stance was Leslie Gore's "You Don't Own Me" (1964), in which she sings, "I'm not just one of your many toys," and, "Don't tell me what to do, don't tell me what to say."

However, songs expressing a woman's independence were rare until society began to change in the 1970s.

The girl groups, like doo-wop, tended to be exploitive of the artists, who typically had short careers. The singers were treated as expendable, as evidenced by the way Phil Spector recorded the Crystals' hits without the Crystals. It is possible that their careers might have been more stable had there been some attention paid to artist development, as was the case at Motown Records.

NOVELTY SONGS

Novelty songs have been part of Tin Pan Alley since the vaudeville days. Novelty music uses popular songs as a vehicle for humor, parody, and social comment, and employs clever lyrics, gimmicks and sound effects to delight the listener. Quite often the most successful of these songs mirror the times in which they are composed in a witty and sometimes silly fashion.

Sheb Wolley's "The Purple People Eater" (1958), Bobby "Boris" Pickett's perennial favorite "Monster Mash" (1962), and "They're Coming to Take Me Away, Ha-Haa" (1966), are examples of the types of novelty recordings that somehow capture the interest of teenagers. Even singers not normally associated with comedy have recorded novelties, such as Chuck Berry's "My Ding-a-ling" (1972). Country artists such as Charlie Daniels and Jim Stafford recorded novelty hits in the 1970s, and pop composer Randy Newman recorded the hit "Short People" (1977). Since the late 1980s, the "king" of novelty songs has been "Weird" Al Yankovich, with his parodies of Michael Jackson's songs, such as "Eat It." It is sometimes difficult to distinguish novelty records from serious pop recordings. The Coasters, with their mini-playlets, came very close to being called a comedy group rather than an R&B group, as did the Hollywood Argyles with "Alley-Oop."

In 1956, rock-era novelty recordings began in earnest when Buchanan and Goodman started their series with "Flying Saucer." These records were comedic interviews that used recorded fragments from other popular recordings as answers to the interviewer's questions. In "Flying Saucer," when asked what he would do if a saucer landed, the interviewee answers, "Jump back in the alley," taken from Little Richard's recording of "Long Tall Sally." When an alien from the spacecraft is asked questions, it replies, "A-wop-bop-a-lo-lop-a-bam-boom." Of course, the prerecorded answers were all previously copyrighted material. Buchanan and Goodman's second hit was "Buchanan and Goodman On Trial" (November, 1956), obviously inspired by the legal problems arising from their first hit. Buchanan and Goodman's style was imitated by others throughout the rock era and also used in local commercials.

Pre-dating Buchanan and Goodman by a few months was "Transfusion" by Nervous Norvus, which told a story of a drunken driver who could not stop having accidents. When in the hospital receiving a blood transfusion he retorts, "Shoot me some juice, Bruce," and, "Pass the claret, Barrett." As tasteless as this recording is by today's standards, it reached number forty-seven on the *Billboard* year-end charts in 1956.

The most successful and longest lasting series of novelty recordings was by Dave Seville and the Chipmunks. Dave Seville was really Ross Bagdasarian, co-writer of "Come On-A My House," a big hit for Rosemary Clooney in 1951, and an actor who appeared in Alfred Hitchcock's 1954 film *Rear Window*. Seville, using simple tape-speed manipulation, built an empire in the music business on this gimmick. His first hit, "Witch Doctor" (1958), featured vocals recorded at half speed and played back at full speed. Seville's true stroke of commercial genius came with his conception of the Chipmunks: Alvin, Simon, and Theodore. This humorous and adorable sped-up vocal trio began covering music from almost every available style, including country, punk, heavy metal, and Beatles songs. Their Christmas novelty tune from 1958, "The Chipmunk Song," sold 3.5 million copies in just over a month, and by 1970, sales were more than thirty million. In the 1980s, Seville's son, Ross Bagdasarian, Jr., carried on the "Chipmunk" tradition.

Another successful novelty entertainer is Ray Stevens, a versatile singer and composer with original hits in country, gospel, novelty, and pop music. While studying music at Georgia State University, Stevens recorded his first novelty hit, "Jeremiah Peabody's Poly Unsaturated Quick Dissolving Fast Acting Pleasant Tasting Green and Purple Pills" (1961), followed by the now politically incorrect, "Ahab the Arab" (1962).

Stevens spent much of the 1960s working in Nashville with Dolly Parton and Waylon Jennings, but returned to novelty music with "Gitarzan" (1969). Stevens also had hits with non-novelty recordings such as "Everything Is Beautiful" and a country swing cover of Erroll Garner's "Misty," which won a Grammy in 1975. His 1974 novelty hit, "The Streak," reflected the mid-1970s phenomena of unexpected naked dashes known as "streaking," and his 1985 hit, "It's Me Again, Margaret," was a humorous piece about bothersome phone calls.

This period of the late fifties and early sixties, which bridges the gap between the heyday of rock's original stars and the period of the British Invasion, has been treated with derision by rock music critics. Although they are somewhat justified in considering this period the doldrums of rock because the Brill Building Pop lacked the fire of early rock, the recordings and television shows produced in this era did accurately reflect the contentment and complacency of American society. As the country was altered by the assassination of President Kennedy, the renewal of the civil rights movement, and the escalation of the Vietnam war, American music gradually responded to the new tensions. The change in music was not sudden, but by the end of the sixties, rock had changed dramatically and, in retrospect, marked this early sixties era as the dividing line between "oldies" and rock.

LISTENING TO THE MUSIC

♪♪ "The Twist"—performed by Chubby Checker

Rhythm and blues vocalist Hank Ballard's 1958 composition, "The Twist," became the definitive tune of the dance craze in the hands of Chubby Checker. Checker transformed this classic twelve-bar blues into something almost magical, and it climbed the charts to number one in 1960, only to return to number one again a year later. Bing Crosby's "White Christmas" was the only other pop song in music history to accomplish this feat. Popularized on Dick Clark's *American Bandstand*, the song spawned many variations and imitations, and was embraced by both teens and adults. Basing the song on a 1953 Drifters tune, "Watcha' Gonna Do," Ballard and the Midnighters first released "The Twist" as a B side in 1959. Their version reached number twenty-eight on the charts in 1962 on the coattails of the Checker version. With its driving beat, vocal breaks, and instructional lyrics, "The Twist" set the stage for the dance craze music of the early 1960s.

Analysis of "The Twist"—2:33 in length, Recorded in thirty-five minutes during July 1959 in Philadelphia and released on Cameo Parkway #811

Possibly one of rock and roll's most famous blues tunes, "The Twist" has all the elements that made its original style, R&B, so important: a honking saxophone, pounding drums, the blues song form and melody, and a blues shouter style. There are two chorus types that alternate in this recording. The first is a classic twelve-bar blues with the repetition of the first line; the second is improvisational lyrics, "twist baby twist," etc., with "round and round" background riffs. The meter is "in four." Personnel: Checker, lead vocals; the Dreamlovers, background vocals; and the Cameo/Parkway studio musicians.

0:00   Introduction (4 measures): Features an opening drum hit and the rhythm section establishing the dance tempo and ending together with a syncopated accent on the "+" of the second beat.

0:05   First Chorus (12 measures): In the classic blues form, this begins "Come on baby . . . ," and repeats in the second line. The background singers riff "oooh . . . bop . . . bop," and the sax growls in unison with their "oooh." The piano plays a squared-off version of one of the many possible boogie woogie patterns. Measure ten of each chorus is a stop-time measure.

0:24   Second Chorus (12 measures): "Twist, baby twist. . . ." The second (fourth, seventh, eighth) verse finds the background vocals singing "round and round . . . ," a catchy line which helps make this blues form more interesting.

0:43   Third Chorus (12 measures): "My daddy is sleeping . . . ." The background returns to the "oooh . . . bop . . . bop."

1:01   Fourth Chorus (12 measures): "Twist . . . baby . . . twist . . . ," and the background returns to "round and round."

1:20   Fifth Chorus, sax solo (12 measures): The wailing sax solo features the same blues form, but this time without the rhythm section break at the end of the phrase. This section is most closely tied to the song's R&B roots, with the background vocalists repeating the "round and round" material.

1:38   Sixth Chorus (12 measures): "You should see my little sis. . . ."

1:56   Seventh Chorus (12 measures): "Twist baby twist. . . ."

2:15   Eighth Chorus (12 measures): Begins "Yea," and Checker improvises lyrics on top of the riff of the background singers.

For Musicians

Never has so much fame and attention come to a simple E blues. Following the drum quarter-note kick used as a pickup, the first three bars of the intro move from the V chord, to the IV chord, and a rhythm break of eighth note, two eighth rests, and an eighth note on the I chord. This last pattern recurs throughout the song, particularly in the sax background riffs and "oo-ahs" of the backup vocals. The effective rhythm break on beat one occurring in the tenth bar of every phrase (except the sax solo) gives this song its unique character and leaves space for the title lyric. The wailing tenor sax solo is typical of this time period: aggressive and blues-oriented. The continuous background vocals add the right thickness to this texture, and the drummer's high hat seems quite persistent, sounding like it is being struck while partially open. Also notable are Checker's final vocal ad libs, which are simple yet give finality and excitement to the finish. The final rhythm lick is the same as in bar four and underlines the piece.

Final Comments

Descriptions of the dance steps involved have been given as "you put one foot out and pretend you are stubbing out a cigarette butt on the floor using your big toe, all the while moving your hands and hips as though you are drying your backside with a towel." In 1961, versions by Johnny Hallyday and Richard Anthony reached number one in France, and in 1988, Checker and the Fat Boys record a contemporary "rap" version entitled "Yo Twist," which reached number sixteen on the charts.

♭♪♪ "My Boyfriend's Back"—performed by the Angels

The 1963 girl-group hit was composed by Robert (Bob) Feldman, Gerald (Jerry) Goldstein, and Richard Gottehrer, and stayed at number one on the pop charts for three weeks.

Analysis of "My Boyfriend's Back"—2:36 in length, released on Smash 1834

This song has a somewhat unusual form and can be described in several ways. The easiest method is to identify three sections (ABC), although the B section is so short it could be called an interlude. The meter is "in four" (four foot taps per measure). The Angels: Peggy Santiglia, lead vocals; Phyllis "Jiggs" Allbut and Barbara Allbut on vocals.

0:00 Introduction (7 measures): The now famous introduction of "My Boyfriend's Back" features two distinctly commercial elements, syncopated hand-claps and spoken voice narrative, similar to the talking bass of the Ink Spots. During this opening, the bass drum establishes the tempo while the lead vocalist sets up the lyrics with this verbal chastising, "He went away and you hung around and bothered me every night. When I wouldn't go out with you, you said things that weren't very nice."

0:12 A Section(16 measures): A drum fill leads in to this section, which is divided into neat four-bar call and response phrases (two-bar singer and two-bar answer). The section begins, "My boyfriend's back." The vocal of the lead singer is interesting in that it is in the gray area between talking and singing, and it is delivered in an emotionless, taunting manner. The response by the background singers is "Hey-la my boyfriend's back."

0:41 B Section (4 measures): This section is in a choral style (everyone singing in a rhythmic unison) and begins. "Hey, he knows what you've been tryin' . . . ," This section has active drum fills that bring in the voices on the second beat. This emphasis of the second beat is basic syncopation.

0:48 A Section (16 measures): This is a return to the style of the first A section, but with new lyrics.

1:16 B Section (4 measures): It begins "Hey, he knows I wasn't cheating," and is the same musical material as the first B with new lyrics.

1:23 C Section (8 measures): This section is in a choral style and begins, "What made you think he'd believe all your lies." Each two-bar vocal phrase is followed by a two-bar instrumental answer.

1:37 A Section (8 measures): This section is half the length of the previous A sections and continues the story with new lyrics, "My boyfriend's back, he's going to save my reputation," answered by, "Hey-la my boyfriend's back."

1:52 B Section (4 measures): This section also has new lyrics and includes the same drum fill leading into the syncopated vocal entrance.

1:58 C Section (8 measures): This instrumental section is the melody from the previous C section. The singers answer its "call" with "wha-ooo."

2:12 A Section (4 measures): A shortened repeat of the A section, "My boyfriend's back, he's going to save my reputation," which leads directly into the final B section.

2:20 B Section (fade): The final section gradually fades out (probably too quickly) to the end of the recording. This section is a good example of the way the call-and-response form can work in improvisation. The solo voice (caller) is improvising lyrics that recap elements of the song, while the background singers (responders) repeat the same phrases over and over. This format is commonly at the end of many R&B recordings.

For Musicians

Basically a I-IV-V adapted AABA song, "My Boyfriend's Back" has some unusual musical features. The seven-bar intro features the song's definitive rhythm pattern built on downbeat, bass drum beat, and offbeat hand-claps, which continue in some form throughout. The narrative introduction is a pop gimmick, which, although sometimes overused, is always dramatic, and here sets up the tune's premise nicely. The responding background vocals occur every third and fourth bar of the two eight-bar verses, and musically highlight this section. The four-bar interlude (B section), found here before the next two verses and also before the bridge (C section), is also of interest, as it uses the earlier harmonic structure but with a different melody and lyric. The bridge goes to the IV chord (Ab), following a similar chord progression as earlier, except for bar eight, which uses a V/V chord going to V, then the tonic for a cadence (F-Bb-Eb). The instrumental horn bridge (C section) features trumpet and trombone in octaves and is simple yet effective as a transition. The most musically spontaneous and exciting moment occurs during the final B section, in which the lead vocalist improvises quite freely as the background vocalists accompany the fadeout.

Final Comments

Girl group songs and their counterpart, the songs of the teen idols, were all pop fare, much of it from Tin Pan Alley–type songwriters more interested in concocting a hit than producing great art. "My Boyfriend's Back" was a functional, well-crafted pop song meant for the many teens searching for personal meaning via radio songs.

[1] Russell Sanjek, *American Popular Music and Its Business: The First Four Hundred Years*, vol. 3 (New York: Oxford, 1988), 442.

[2] John A. Jackson, *Big Beat Heat: Alan Freed and the Early Years of Rock &Roll* (New York: Schirmer, 1991), 245.

[3] Ibid., 244.

[4] Russell Sanjek, *American Popular Music and Its Business: The First Four Hundred Years*, vol. 2 (New York: Oxford, 1988), 321-22.

[5] Sanjek, vol. 3, 445.

[6] Russell Sanjek and David Sanjek, *American Popular Music Business in the 20th Century*, (New York: Oxford, 1991), 177.

[7] Sanjek, vol. 3, 442.

[8] Dick Clark and Richard Robinson, *Rock, Roll &Remember* (New York: Crowell, 1976), 223.

[9] Ibid., 211.

[10] Sanjek, vol. 3, 444.

[11] Clark, 97-98.

[12] Ibid., 100-01.

[13] Alan Betrock, *Girl Groups: The Story of a Sound* (New York: Delilah, 1982), 25.

[14] Ibid., 99.

Chapter Seven

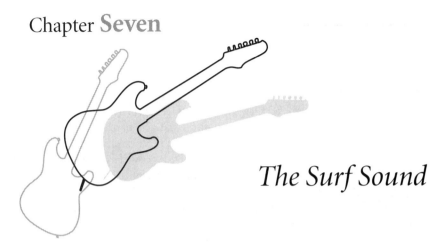

The Surf Sound

Of all strains of rock and roll, none transported the listener to a different place more effectively than *surf* music in the first half of the 1960s. The genre celebrated adolescence and told of the abundance of sun, girls, and cars that were found in California—the "promised land"—where it never snowed and the surf was always up. Surf music began in Southern California and quickly spread all over the country, making those who were not lucky enough to live in California envious of those who did.

The film industry's move to Hollywood was the first signal America received that life was different in California. Film footage of palm trees, ocean waves, orange groves, and adobe-style houses slowly crept into America's consciousness, creating an image of California as something special. The first big California migration occurred during the 1930s when severe drought and dust storms wracked the Arkansas and Red River Basins. That period, known as the Dust Bowl years, saw countless Oklahoma, Texas, and Kansas farmers packing up their belongings, loading them on vehicles, and head west. Folk singer/activist Woodie Guthrie documents this era in Dust Bowl ballads such as "Do-Re-Mi," in which he warns migrants that "California is a garden of Eden, a paradise to live in or see, but believe it or not you won't find it so hot, if you don't have that do-re-mi."

During World War II and the years that followed, Americans migrated to California in record numbers. Unemployment was low because of wartime production; after the war, high-tech jobs, especially in the defense and aerospace industries, remained plentiful. Other things that drew people were California's climate, agricultural potential, and relaxed attitude. By some accounts, California attracted over a thousand new residents a day, with the peak year of 1963 attracting over 600,000 new residents, causing California to surpass New York as the largest state. The most populous area of the state was the southern half, which drew enough from northern California to create a slight decline in population in the north.

California life in the fifties was good, and the economy was prosperous. There was a large middle class, and most families could enjoy life on one paycheck. This economy produced a large number of teenagers who did not have to work part-time jobs as did previous generations and who had a lot of free time and discretionary money. One of the cheapest and most carefree activities one could engage in was to go to the beach, and out of this grew a large beach culture. This culture produced its own language, clothing styles, sports, and new styles of transportation. One of the most popular sports to emerge was surfing.

Surfing developed from the ancient sport "he'e nalu" (wave-sliding) and was perfected by the people of the Sandwich Isles before the fifteenth century. The sport of kings, as it has been called, is mentioned in the writings of Christian missionary William Ellis (1794–1872), who says that Kaumualii, the great mo'i (king) from the island of Kauai, was renowned as an accomplished surfer. Ellis also recalls seeing the elderly Big Island chiefs Karaimoku and Kakioena, both between fifty and sixty years of age, balancing themselves on their long and narrow boards, or splashing about in the foam, with as much satisfaction as youths of sixteen.[1]

Surfing came to America from Hawaii around the turn of the century and was adopted by a few hearty souls. Among them was actor Jackie Coogan, Uncle Fester on television's *The Addams Family,* who surfed using the large, heavy, wooden boards imported from Hawaii. The 1959 movie *Gidget,* and later the television show starring Sally Field, focused on the California surfing culture and brought images of beach life to non-coastal America, renewing its fascination with life in California. Cliff Robertson, one of the stars of *Gidget,* rightly saw that surfing could catch on and formed a partnership to manufacture surfboards in California. Previously surfboards had to be imported from Hawaii and were somewhat hard to get. Once the supply of surfboards increased, because of the new companies, they became plentiful and affordable. Because *Gidget* was successful, other surf movies began to appear and the surf craze was in full swing.

With the new sport came a new subculture, complete with its own dress (madras and Hawaiian shirts, Pendletons, baggies, scandals, white Levis, and blond hair), cars (paneled station wagons known as "woodies," as well as a variety of "muscle" cars), new slang terms (*hang ten, shootin' the curl, pipeline, honeys*), magazines, movies, music, and medical conditions (surfer's knobs). A bevy of movies, starring the teen idols Frankie Avalon and Annette Funicello among others, brought the surf, sand, and sun to millions around the country who would otherwise not know what was "happening" in California. "If everybody had an ocean," sang the Beach Boys in "Surfin' U.S.A.," they would be surfing, but those teens who were landlocked had to settle for sidewalk surfing, better known as skateboarding.

Surf music was not radically different from other rock. It used the same musical forms, chord progressions, and instruments found on Chuck Berry recordings. Its only distinguishing characteristics were its lyrics and the high vocal harmonies that were brought to surf music by the Beach Boys. The development of surf music can be broken down into three basic areas:

- instrumental rock that had no reference to surfing

- instrumental rock with titles that referred to surfing

- vocal rock that had lyrics that referred to surfing

It is this last category that is thought of as classic surf music.

INSTRUMENTAL ROCK

Rock has a small history of instrumental recordings that flow directly into the beginnings of surf music. The reason that surf appears to have developed directly out of instrumental rock is that Dick Dale and the Del-Tones, the first surf band, was primarily an instrumental group, and the Beach Boys' first two albums were filled out with instrumental Dick Dale songs. Instrumental rock borrowed from jazz by incorporating boogie-woogie swing rhythms, by using instrumental improvisation, and by using the saxophone as the primary solo instrument. The saxophone, so common in R&B and doo-wop recordings, was eventually replaced by the guitar because of the influence of performers like Chuck Berry and Scotty Moore. Instrumentals can be traced all the way back to the jump blues bands of the late 1940s and early 1950s, which recorded some strictly instrumental tunes, usually for the "B" sides of their records. The genre never died completely, and instrumental recordings surfaced occasionally as popular hits.

Non-Surf Instrumental Hits

Honkey Tonk	Bill Doggett (1956)
Tequila	Champs (1958),
Rebel Rouser	Duane Eddy (1958)
Rumble	Link Wray (1958)
Sleep Walk	Santo and Johnny (1959)
The Happy Organ	Dave "Baby" Cortez (1959)
Teen Beat	Sandy Nelson (1959)
Guitar Boogie Shuffle	Virtues (1959)
Topsy II	Cozy Cole (1959),
Red River Rock	Johnny and the Hurricanes (1959)
Walk—Don't Run	Ventures (1960)
Wheels	The String-A-Longs (1961)
Green Onions	Booker T. and the MGs (1962)
El Watusi	Ray Barretto (1963)

Duane Eddy

One of the first instrumental rockers to influence surf music was guitarist Duane Eddy. Eddy grew up in Phoenix and, in 1957, began working with producers Lee Hazelwood and Lester Sill, recording a song called "Rebel Rouser." It was released on Dick Clark's Jamie record label and was promoted on *American Bandstand*. The song reached number six in 1958 and spurred other successful collaborations between Eddy and Hazelwood over the next few years, such as "Cannonball" (1958) and "Forty Miles of Bad Road" (1959). Eddy was known for his "twangy" guitar sound, which was created by tuning the guitar lower, turning up the reverb and tremolo, and focusing on the bass strings. Eddy's recordings featured saxophone solos rather than hot guitar-playing. On "Rebel Rouser," for example, Eddy plays the same sixteen-bar melody over and over, to which hand-claps, background singers, upward modulations, and saxophone gradually were added; the high point is the screaming sax solo. His album titles consistently played on the twangy theme: *Have Twangy Guitar Will Travel*, *Twang's the Thing*, *1,000,000 Dollars of Twang*, *Twistin' and Twangin'*, and *Twangy Guitar*. The Eddy recordings were well-produced pop instrumentals by Hazelwood and Sill, and they served as classroom experiences for young Phil Spector, who was attending the sessions with Sill.

The Ventures

The Ventures were the best known of many northwestern rock bands that included the Frantics, Sonics, and Kingsmen. Founded in Seattle by bassist Bob Bogle and guitarist Don Wilson, they hooked up with guitarist Nokie Edwards and drummer Howie Johnston in 1960. Their first recording, "Walk—Don't Run," was their most popular, reaching number two in 1960. It was recorded by the small independent Blue Horizon, which was owned by Wilson's mother, and was distributed nationally by Dolton Records. In 1963, the Ventures jumped on the surf bandwagon and released an album called *Surfing; Let's Go!* even though they had nothing to do with surfing. Their identification with surfing was so strong by 1969 that they recorded the theme song for television's *Hawaii Five-O*. In 1964, they recorded a "surfy" remake of "Walk—Don't Run." A handful of other Venture-type guitar groups such as the Astronauts, Challengers, and Chantays appeared on the surf bandwagon.

Surf Instrumental Groups
Dick Dale

Many of the instrumental groups shared characteristics that became part of the surf sound: twangy guitars, swirling electric organs, insistent drums, and simple, repetitive melodies. One of the most popular groups in Southern California was Dick Dale and the Del-Tones. Dick Dale (Richard Monsour) was an

The Ventures

enthusiastic surfer and guitar player who wed his two passions into a reason-ably successful career. Musically, Dale was admired as a guitarist for the twangy, heavily reverberated sound that he used to convey the experience of the surfer through music. In 1960, he formed a band called the Del-Tones and began play-ing at self-promoted dances at the Rendezvous Ballroom in Balboa. In late 1961, the band recorded several instrumental rock tunes on their own Deltone label; the most popular was "Let's Go Trippin." It hit the charts in September 1961—a few months before the Beach Boys recorded "Surfin"—and reached number one on the local Los Angeles charts, but barely dented the national top 100. His other songs from that year include "Surfbeat," "Surfing Drums," and the instrumental classic "Miserlou." For "Miserlou," a Middle Eastern folk song, Dale drew on his Lebanese heritage and, in doing so, probably was responsible for the style and sound of guitar solos that typified California rock bands later on in the sixties; in fact, he worked with Leo Fender, founder of Fender guitars, on developing amplifiers that could be played very loud without self-destructing. The resulting amp, the Dual-Showman, with two 15-inch speakers, ushered in the beginning of the era of "Loud Rock" bands.

At one point, Dick Dale and his Del-Tones had the top four out of five hits on the Los Angeles radio charts but still achieved only moderate success nationally. When the surfing/beach craze swept the entire country, Dale was rightly seen as an originator of the style and was signed by Capitol Records. Given the label "King of the Surf Guitar" by Capitol Records, Dale still didn't become the national name that he deserved. The reason for this seems to be an audience preference for vocal songs, and vocal groups like the Beach Boys and Jan and Dean were just starting to have national hits at the same time Dale signed with Capitol.

Surfaris

Although drum solo recordings were unusual, "Wipe Out" by the Surfaris (1963) was not the first rock drum solo. Los Angeles drummer, Sandy Nelson recorded several drum solo hits called "Teen Beat" (1959), "Let There Be Drums" (1961), "Drums Are My Beat" (1962), and "Teen Beat '65" (1964). He was part

The Surfaris

of the Los Angeles recording scene and played on Phil Spector's "To Know Him Is to Love Him." Nelson's solos came from the pounding tom-tom solo tradition first established by Gene Krupa's solo on Benny Goodman's "Sing, Sing, Sing," recorded live at John Hammond's famous "Spirituals to Swing" concert. Although "Wipe Out" is not the first drum solo, it became the most famous and is probably the most enduring surf instrumental recording of all time. It is interesting that "Wipe Out" should have had such an impact on rock audiences. The song is actually quite simple: a twelve-bar blues based on a two-bar riff that is repeated on each of the three basic blues chords. On every other chorus is a stop-time, pounding tom-tom drum solo that consists of a repeated two-bar rhythm employing accented notes on a steady stream of sixteenth-notes, all played on one tom-tom. The rhythm is very close to the famous hambone rhythm used in African-American music, except that it omits the one syncopated accent that would require a left-hand accent. For the past thirty years, drummers in bar bands all over the country have had to endure requests to play "Wipe Out" as if it were the supreme test of a "good" drummer.

VOCAL SURF MUSIC
The Beach Boys

Surf music and the Beach Boys are practically synonymous terms. It is unquestionable that surf music would have sounded entirely different without

The Beach Boys

them. While Dick Dale was the first musician to be associated with surfing, primarily because the members of the band were surfers and performed for members of their own surf circle, his recordings did not speak to those other than his own fans or do well on the national charts. The Beach Boys not only created a style of music that identified with those surfer fans but also brought the magic of surfing and California living to America's teenagers wherever they lived. The Beach Boys' recordings were the first vocal surf music and established the "sound" that all future surf music would have. Their instrumental sound was no better than many of the "garage" bands that populated America's suburbs, but their vocal sound was unique, especially when paired with the subject matter. The fact that their subject matter turned out to be surfing was purely accidental and yet had broad repercussions.

The Wilsons were a musical family. Their mother, Audree, had been a pianist and their father, Murry, was an aspiring songwriter. One of Murry Wilson's songs, "Two Step, Side Step," was recorded by the Bachelors and also performed on the radio by Lawrence Welk and his orchestra.[2] Murry hoped for a career as a songwriter, but it never developed beyond those performances. The Beach Boys' family history had a lot to do with the way the band's career developed: A frustrated musician-father became both mentally and physically abusive while watching his sons have the career that should have been his. It was natural that the Wilson brothers—Brian, Dennis, and Carl—would have a love of music and a desire to make their father proud by trying to excel in something he loved, and it was natural for him to want to guide their progress in the industry. However, the quest for his version of perfection gradually pushed Brian over the edge.

Their band developed out of family sing-a-longs around the piano, and soon Brian began to practice piano incessantly. In his book, *Wouldn't It Be Nice,* Brian recounts a story that sheds light on the direction of the future Beach Boys' vocal sound. While riding in the car with his mother one day, he heard the Four Freshmen's "Day By Day" on the radio and was immediately enthralled by their sound, so much so that he had his mother take him to a record store to buy an album. Brian chose *The Four Freshman and Five Trombones* that day but eventually bought all their albums.[3] He also discovered the HiLos. The vocal sound of the Four Freshman and the HiLos grew out of the pop vocal groups of the thirties and forties and, like that of the Ink Spots and the Modernaires, it was typified by tight, closely voiced jazz harmonies, with a high male vocal lead—just like the future Beach Boys. As Brian tried to duplicate the Four Freshmen's vocal harmonies with his family, he was laying the groundwork for the Beach Boys sound. On his sixteenth birthday he received a Wollensak reel-to-reel tape recorder as a present and started taping himself playing and singing, and then sang harmony along with his recorded performance.[4] Although he did not realize it, he was practicing skills that would be useful in the recording studio some day. That same year, brother Carl got a Rickenbacker guitar, and they started adding guitar to their tapes.

Every Christmas, when the Wilsons went to visit their cousins, the Loves, a family sing-a-long would inevitably take place. Soon Brian was teaching his cousins Mike and Maureen to sing Four Freshmen harmonies. Brian also had a musical friend, Al Jardine, who played guitar and sang in a folk group called the Islanders. By the time Brian graduated from high school, the individual pieces of the Beach Boys were in the same general area but were not yet assembled.

While at El Camino Community College, Brian and Al ran into each other and discussed music and how they would like to play together. Soon Brian had assembled Mike Love, Al Jardine, Carl Wilson, Gary Winfrey, and Dennis Wilson into a band; they worked on songs like "Travelin' Man" (Ricky Nelson), "Mama Said" (Shirelles), and "Quarter to Three" (Gary "U.S." Bonds) and were beginning to sound pretty good. They had decided to call themselves the Pendletones, which was derived from Pendleton, the brand name of a woolen outer shirt popular at the beach. When Al and Gary asked Murry Wilson about getting recorded, Murry arranged a meeting with Hite and Dorinda Morgan, who operated several small record labels. The Morgans listened to them sing a traditional folk song and then asked what they had that was original. Dennis answered, "Yeah, we got an original; it's called Surfin.'"[5] Dennis was the only one who surfed, so he explained what surfing was and how popular it was becoming. The Morgans sounded interested and told the group to bring the song in when it was finished. They went home and began writing a song called "Surfin'" and were back at the Morgans in a few days.

The Morgans liked the song and recorded it in their home studio, had some demo records pressed, arranged a distribution deal with a small label, Candix Records, and released "Surfin'" on December 8, 1961. "Surfin'" got airplay on KFWB and KDAY in Los Angeles and became that week's "Pick to Click." The only problem was that instead of using the name the Pendletones, Candix Records issued the recording under the name "the Beach Boys" because they thought it sounded "more surfy." The Wilsons tried to object but it was no use; they would just have to accept being called the Beach Boys. By mid-January, "Surfin'" reached number 118 on the *Billboard* charts, and their first royalty check was a thousand dollars. "Surfin'" eventually peaked at number seventy-five.

The genesis of the Beach Boys' sound was simple and logical: a guitar-based band that used Four-Freshmen–style close harmony in a rock setting, with lyrics about a sport one of the members enjoyed. The one lucky stroke was that the teenagers in Los Angeles were ready for a surf song that was vocal rather than instrumental. A new genre—surf music—was born. Unfortunately, their success set into motion a psychological drama that cast a father, frustrated by the direction of his own songwriting career, against his son, whose psyche was too fragile after years of abuse to handle the tension. Murry Wilson said "Surfin'" was "not good enough" and continued to be overly critical of all Brian's songs.[6] The pressure caused Brian to quit touring with the band in 1965 and eventually to sink into a downward spiral of drugs, alcohol, and mental illness.

The Beach Boys began looking for their next record and wrote "Surfin' Safari," "Karate," "Judy," and "Surfer Girl," the last two modeled on Brian's girlfriend, Judy Bowles. While the Beach Boys were rehearsing, they met Gary Usher. His uncle lived across the street, and he had already recorded two singles on a small label. Gary introduced Brian to the music of Goffin and King, Mann and Weil, and Phil Spector, and soon Gary and Brian became songwriting partners. Brian and Gary quickly collaborated on two good songs, "409" and "In My Room." Murry booked time at Western Studios, where they recorded "Surfer Girl," "Judy," "409," and "Surfin' Safari," and then took the demo to Nick Venet at Capitol Records, who loved them. Capitol released "409," with "Surfin' Safari" on the flip side; "Surfin' Safari" caught on first, but then so did "409," and their second release was a double-sided hit. It sold 900,000 copies and reached number fourteen on the charts.

The early surfing hits were filled with surf and car jargon, as well as famous surfing locations. "Surfin' Safari" mentions "honeys," which was slang for beach girls. "We're loading our Woody," refers to a 1930s station wagon with wood paneling on the side. These cars were perfect because the rear window opened up while the tailgate was still in place, which made it easy to get surfboards in and out. "Walkin' the nose," meant riding up near the front of the surfboard. The beach locations of Huntington, Malibu, and Rincon, as well as international locations such as Hawaii and the shores of Peru were frequently mentioned. The song "409" refers to a 409-cubic-inch engine, the biggest Chevrolet made at that time. The song is essentially a doo-wop–style song with the group riffing "giddy-up, giddy-up, 409" in the background behind lyrics like "She's so fine, my 409," and car lingo like "4-speed, dual-quad, posi-traction 409."

Their next recording was also a double-sided hit. "Surfin' U.S.A," backed with "Shut Down" (1963), was another surf song paired with a hot rod song and filled with more surf and car jargon. Brian decided to write a surf song that mentioned every surf spot in the state just like Chubby Checker sang of all the cities where they were twistin'. One problem with 'Surfin' U.S.A." was that it used the same melody as Chuck Berry's "Sweet Little Sixteen," and when Berry complained, Brian's father gave him the copyright, including the rights to Brian's words.[7] In "Surfin' U.S.A.," the lyrics mention "baggies," which were big, baggy, boxer-style swimming trunks; "Guaraches sandals," which were Mexican sandals made with laced strips of leather; "waxin' down our surfboards," which was applying wax to the bottom of the board to increase traction; and many surfing locations: Del Mar, the Ventura county line, Santa Cruz, Tressels, Australia's Narabine, Manhattan Beach, Domeny, Haggarty's, Swami's, Pacific Palisades, San Onofre, Sunset Beach, Redondo Beach, La Jolla, and Wiamea Bay.

"Shut Down" is a drag-racing song whose lyrics include plenty of car jargon: "tach it up" means running the engine at higher revolutions per minute (RPMs), thus making the tachometer read in the upper numbers; "fuel-injected Stingray" is a Chevrolet Corvette; "413" was a 413-cubic-inch engine found in Chryslers, Dodges, and Plymouths; "slicks" are smooth racing tires with no tread, designed to give more traction; "power shift" is quickly shifting the gears without taking your foot off the accelerator; "ridin' the clutch" is not fully releasing the clutch, thus keeping the wheels from receiving full power; "pressure plate's burnin'" refers to the part of the clutch mechanism that burns out when one rides the clutch. This use of car and surf jargon was a method giving credibility to the artist as one who is well-versed in the art of surfing and drag racing.

The success of the Beach Boys placed continued stress on the father-son relationship, causing enough arguments that Brian finally moved away from home. Murry Wilson did not like Brian's writing partner, Gary Usher, and in the ensuing tension, Brian discovered a new writing partner, Los Angeles DJ Roger Christian, who helped Brian write some of the hot rod songs. About this time, the Beach Boys performed on a show with Jan and Dean, and a friendship developed between them. Brian gave them a song he was working on, "Surf City," which turned out to be a number one hit for them. The Beach Boys' next charted recording was another double-sided hit, "Be True to Your School," backed with "In My Room" (1963). It celebrated high school spirit and the close harmony sounds of the Four Freshmen. In the fall of 1963, Phil Spector invited Brian to visit Gold Star Studios and watch some of the sessions for his Christmas album. Brian had been a big fan of Spector and was able to witness Spector's production techniques, which he increasingly used on Beach Boys' recordings.

The group's success continued and so did the stress on Brian and Murry's relationship until finally, Murry was fired as the band's manager. The older Wilson was convinced that he was responsible for the band's success, so he found another group that he thought might be able to compete with his sons, the Sun Rays. They recorded some songs co-written by Murry and had some success on the charts but ultimately faded away.

When Brian quit touring with the group in 1965, he spent an increasing amount of time writing and polishing his studio production techniques. In 1966 he produced *Pet Sounds* using his more complex version of Spector's "wall of sound," with expanded overdubbing techniques, multiple instruments, and unusual instruments. Brian says that it "represented the maturing of my talent, the single-minded pursuit of a personal vision."[8] The album is generally regarded as darker in tone than any of the Beach Boys' earlier recordings, and with the addition of strings, percussion, and overdubbing techniques, it was their most ambitious project to date. "Caroline, No" was released as a Brian Wilson solo recording, but when it went no higher than twenty-three, they released "Sloop John B" to recapture their audience. Beach Boys fans were not attracted to the group because of their complexity and thoughtful lyrics; they wanted an escape.

On their next project, the Beach Boys were able to combine "good times" and artfully produced rock. The Beach Boys and Brian Wilson's masterpiece, "Good Vibrations" (1966), took over six months to complete, requiring ninety hours of studio time and $16,000 to produce. It includes sleigh bells, strings, harpsichord, exotic instruments such as the theremin (an electronic instrument used in science fiction movies and characterized by slides from note to note), and a huge amount of echo. Unlike *Pet Sounds,* and despite its radio-unfriendly length of three minutes and thirty-five seconds, "Good Vibrations" became a number one hit.

The production of "Good Vibrations" was a masterpiece of studio production techniques that pre-dates the Beatles' *Sgt. Pepper's Lonely Hearts Club Band.* It may have also been the beginning of the end for the Beach Boys. Buoyed by his success, Brian set out to create an album that was more grandiose than *Pet Sounds* or "Good Vibrations." In what was tentatively called *Smile,* Brian collaborated with Van Dyke Parks on an album that was dividing the Beach Boys as to what direction they should go. As the project plodded along, Brian became more withdrawn and depressed until the project was finally dropped. Some of the songs were eventually released, with "Heroes and Villains" getting the most attention (number twelve in 1967), but the album, with changes, was released on Brother Records as *Smiley Smile* and did not sell well. Beach Boys fans are still waiting for Capitol to release the real *Smile* album.

"Good Vibrations" was their last number one recording, although they reached the charts with other recordings, and marked the end of the group as a major recording act. The Beach Boys were able to make an indelible mark on popular music history and accomplish a feat that few groups ever attain, becoming synonymous with an era of American history. It is impossible to think about summer in the 1960s without also thinking about the Beach Boys. They have come to be identified with a period in American culture when summertime meant fun, freedom, and innocence, far removed from the troubles of adult life. Additionally, the Beach Boys' vocal harmonies influenced the development of the California folk rock of the late sixties, including groups like the Byrds, the Mamas and the Papas, and the Eagles.

Addendum

There is a connection between the Beach Boys and mass murderer Charles Manson that offers a possible motive for the Tate–La Bianca murders. Manson was also a singer/songwriter who lived with or frequently associated with Dennis Wilson before the murders. He recorded several songs in Brian's home studio in anticipation of a record deal with record executive Terry Melcher (Doris Day's son). The deal fell through, and some say that Manson sent his followers to terrorize or kill Melcher. In the meantime, however, Melcher had moved from the house he was renting, and Sharon Tate moved in. Manson's followers did not realize this and killed Sharon Tate and her guests instead of Terry Melcher.[9] The songs Charles Manson recorded are available commercially.

Beach Boys 1960s Hits	
Surfin'/Luau	1961
Surfin' Safari/409	1962
Ten Little Indians/County Fair	1962
Surfin' U.S.A./Shut Down	1963
Surfer Girl/Little Deuce Coupe	1963
Be True to Your School/In My Room	1963
Little Saint Nick/The Lord's Prayer	1963
Fun, Fun, Fun/Why Do Fools Fall In Love?	1964
I Get Around/Don't Worry Baby	1964
When I Grow Up/She Knows Me Too Well	1964
Dance, Dance, Dance/The Warmth of the Sun	1964
The Man With All the Toys/Blue Christmas	1964
Do You Wanna Dance?/Please Let Me Wonder	1965
Help Me, Rhonda/Kiss Me, Baby	1965
California Girls/Let Him Run Wild	1965
The Little Girl I Once Knew/There's No Other	1965
Barbara Ann/Girl, Don't Tell Me	1965
Caroline, No/Summer Means New Love	1966
Sloop John B./You're So Good To Me	1966
Wouldn't It Be Nice/God Only Knows	1966
Good Vibrations/Let's Go Away for a While	1966
Heroes and Villains/You're Welcome	1967
Wild Honey/Wind Chimes	1967
Darlin'/Here Today	1967
Do It Again/Wake the World	1968
I Can Hear Music/All I Want to Do	1969

Jan and Dean

Jan and Dean had a music career before the Beach Boys, but as a doo-wop group rather than a surf duo. Jan Berry and Dean Torrence were high school football buddies from Los Angeles when they formed a duo and had some success with doo-wop recordings, such as "Jennie Lee" (1958), under the name of Jan and Arnie, and "Baby Talk" (1959) and "Heart and Soul" (1961), under the name of Jan and Dean. As the surf music craze emerged, they headlined a show on which the Beach Boys performed, when a friendship developed. Brian Wilson, much to the consternation of Murry, gave them one of his unfinished songs on which they collaborated.

"Surf City" was released in 1963, with the Beach Boys doing background vocals, and has the distinction of being the first number one surf hit. The song opens by appealing to teenage-boy fantasies, "Two girls for every boy," and "All you gotta do is just wink your eye." The song has a twelve-bar verse using standard call-and-response patterns with background vocals answering, "Surf City here we come." At the end of the verse is an added one-bar drum fill that leads into the chorus, which is in a standard twelve-bar blues riff. Jan and Dean's friendship with the Beach Boys thrived, and Berry even sang lead on the Beach Boys' hit "Barbara Ann" (1965), although contractual limitations left his name off the credits.

Jan and Dean continued to record surf and hot rod songs until the surf craze dried up around 1965. In 1964, they recorded a novelty song, "Little Old Lady From Pasadena," which played on a phrase made popular by *Tonight Show* host Johnny Carson, in a skit about a used car salesman who offered a vehicle "only used to drive to church on Sunday by a little old lady from Pasadena." In the same year, they recorded "Sidewalk Surfin," which celebrated the growing sport of skateboarding, which was intended to take the place of surfing for teens who could not get to the beach. Early skateboards were nothing more than roller skate wheels fastened to a board, nothing like the technologically advanced boards of the 1990s. Also in 1964, the duo recorded "Dead Man's Curve," about a deadly stretch of California highway. The song proved to be prophetic: In April 1966, Jan ran into a parked truck while going sixty-five miles per hour on Whittier Boulevard. The accident killed his three passengers and left him partially paralyzed, with his speech impaired. The duo makes occasional appearances at oldies venues.

Other Surf Recordings

The surf craze was made up almost entirely of recordings by the Beach Boys and Jan and Dean, but there were a few others. Generally, the other recordings were made by studio groups or groups trying to cash in on the surf sound. It is interesting to note how the recording "Little Honda" (1964) documents the beginnings of Japanese involvement with the American motorcycle and car markets. In 1964, the principle motorcycles were the Harley Davidson, Triumph, Norton, and BSA, all loud and associated with motorcycle gangs and outlaws, as popularized by *The Wild One*. Honda began importing little motorcycles with 50cc and 90cc engines that were slow but perfect for riding around beach communities. The Honda 50 was responsible for changing the image of a motorcycle rider from that of a Marlon Brando–type to that of a more average person.

Other Surf Hits

Surfin' Bird (1963)	Trashmen
California Sun (1964)	Rivieras
Hey Little Corba (1964)	The Rip Chords
Little Honda (1964)	The Hondells

LISTENING TO THE MUSIC

♪♪ "Surfin' U.S.A."—performed by the Beach Boys

Brian Wilson rewrote the lyrics to Chuck Berry's 1958 Chess recording of "Sweet Little Sixteen" and used the song as the basis for "Surfin' U.S.A." Although borrowing the melody was probably unintentional (like George Harrison's problems with the similarity between "My Sweet Lord" and "He's So Fine"), copyright law protected Berry's rights as a songwriter.

"Surfin' U.S.A" reached number three on the 1963 charts, remaining in the top forty for thirteen weeks, and eventually becoming the number two recording on the year-end chart.

Analysis of "Surfin' U.S.A."—2:27 in length, recorded 1963, on Capitol 4932

The form of this recording is a simple verse structure. The A verse is in a stop-time style, and the last four measures of the B verse contain the hook, "Everybody's gone surfin'. . . ." The meter of this selection is "in 4." Personnel: Brian Wilson, high vocals, keyboards, bass; Carl Wilson, guitar; Dennis Wilson, drums; Mike Love, lead vocal, sax; David Marks, rhythm guitar.

0:00   Introduction (2 measures): The opening guitar lick gives us the blues effect Berry intended on his original, but the multi-tracked lead vocal sound of a young California teen announces that a new region is embracing the blues. Wilson's lyrics are a virtual list of Southern California surf and beach spots: a travelogue for would-be surfers.

0:03   First Verse–A (16 measures): The pick-up lyrics to the first sixteen-bar verse begin with the line, "If everybody had an ocean" ("ocean" is the first beat of the sixteen bars). The style of this verse is "stop-time": The "time" stops, the instruments play a bar (4 foot taps), then are silent during the next bar. Every other bar is accompanied only with the sound of the bass drum. The background singing to the syllable "ooh" uses the harmony Brian developed from the Four Freshmen sound.

0:27   Second Verse–B (16 measures): The second sixteen-bar verse is introduced with a drum fill and is in straight-time rather than stop-time. The lyrics of this verse catalog the surfing spots up and down the coast. The background singers riff "inside, outside U.S.A." in their tight vocal harmony. The verse ends with the hook, "Everybody's gone surfin'. . . ."

0:52   Third Verse–A (16 measures): This returns to the stop-time pounding bass drum and "ooh" background vocals. Love lyrically describes his summer surfing plans and give a nod to their earlier hit, "Surfin' Safari," by singing, "We're on safari to stay." A drum fill leads into the next verse.

1:16   Fourth Verse–B (16 measures): Returns to straight-time and the "inside, outside, U.S.A." background riff, while the lyrics return to cataloging surfing spots. The verse again ends with the hook. A drum fill leads into the instrumental solos.

1:40   Solos, organ and guitar (8 measures): Brian Wilson's eight-measure organ solo consists of simple riff-like chordal patterns ascending up the organ keyboard. This is followed by a four-bar surf-style guitar solo, and ends with the established "everybody's gone surfin', surfin' U.S.A." The guitar sound is what is described as surf guitar, although it is also referred to as twangy; it is not Duane Eddy's twangy sound, but that of the Ventures.

2:00   Coda: The group vamps (repeats) on the hook (last vocal phrase) as the music fades.

For Musicians

The introduction's guitar pickups of three eighth notes lead to one full bar of eighths, followed by a downbeat in bar two and silence while the vocal line introduces the verse. This two-bar pattern returns later as a break at the end of every other phrase, and this figure, loosely based on a Chuck Berry guitar riff, helps set up the tune. Recorded in Eb major, this sixteen-bar pop song form follows the I-IV-V blues-chord progression to some extent. A pattern develops of two bars of V chord followed by two bars of the tonic, a repeat of this material, then two bars of IV chord followed by two bars of tonic. The last four bars of the form move from the V chord to the IV, then back to the tonic. This is a simple yet innovative transformation of the blues form into rock and roll (via Chuck Berry). Notice the syncopated electric rhythm guitar and cymbal patterns as they subdivide eighth notes, helping provide musical momentum. The bass drum on every beat in verses one and three is a nice contrast to the freer rock time played during the other sections, and the drum fills at cadence points are even and well conceived. The instrumental break seems superfluous and non-technical, but provides needed vocal relief. The rhythmic highlight throughout is the break that occurs in every other phrase at bar fourteen. This downbeat, followed by silence, save the vocal title line, is a most effective musical device here—well used to emphasize the lyrics. The repeated tag for this song uses the descending V-IV-I pattern found earlier and at the end of more traditional blues songs, and again features the two-bar vocal break already established as the tune fades.

Final Comments

Reissued in 1974, "Surfin' U.S.A." rose to number thirty-six for one week and was also covered by pop vocalist Leif Garret in 1977, who reached number twenty on the charts.

♪♪ "Good Vibrations"—performed by the Beach Boys

Brian Wilson's musical masterpiece, "Good Vibrations," followed on the heels of the Beach Boys' highly influential *Pet Sounds* album, a release that possibly inspired Paul McCartney to create his *Sgt. Pepper's Lonely Hearts Club Band* concept in 1967. Taking six months to record and costing over $16,000 to produce, "Good Vibrations" was an early hint at the psychedelic music era just ahead. Using exotic instruments such as mouth harp, sleigh bells, tambourines, organ, cello, wind chimes, and the electronic theremin (producing the swooping electronic melody line), Brian Wilson created a complex, multi-sectional production that led the way for the emerging directions in rock music: the psychedelic and progressive styles of the late sixties.

Analysis of "Good Vibrations"—3:34 in length, released on Capitol 5676

"Good Vibrations" reached number one on the charts for one week in late 1966, sold one million copies, and became the group's best selling single. The meter is in a fast four foot-taps per measure. The form is an adapted verse-chorus form with two interludes and two additional sections.

Personnel: Brian Wilson, vocals, bass, keyboards, composer; Carl Wilson, vocals, guitar; Dennis Wilson, vocals drums; Mike Love, vocals percussion; Al Jardine, vocals, guitar, bass.

0:00   A Verse (16 measures): "Good Vibrations" starts right on the verse with organ and guitar creating an ethereal texture. The second phrase of this love song adds bass, drums, and tambourine.

0:24   B Chorus (16 measures): The chorus features a contrapuntal choral-style series of background riffs, which, when added together, create a dense texture. A voice or group of voices enter every four bars, first with, "I'm thinking of good vibrations," four bars later "Good Vi-Vi," then "Good-good-good." As each consecutive phrase adds another moving harmony, the texture grows thicker while the music rises.

0:50   A Verse (16 measures): Verse two uses the same musical materials as verse one, with tambourine prominent in the mix.

1:15   B Chorus (16 measures): The second "Good Vibrations" chorus is much like the first, with the use of the theremin and vocal harmony buildup.

1:40   Interlude 1 (12 measures): This new section starts as the vocal line overlaps from the chorus over a new rhythm section feel. This mostly instrumental portion is quite spacey, featuring tack piano, vocal harmony "aahs," lyrical fade-ins, and sleigh bells—all in preparation for the new section ahead.

1:52   C Verse (8 measures): This section grows out of the interlude and begins, "I don't know her where."

2:12   Interlude 2 (24 measures): A church-like organ sound and maracas are the only background for the vocal line in this slower section. Bass and high harmony quickly join, then a simple organ line floats over the top. As the vocal fades, the instruments come to a point of calm. Something is about to happen. Vocal "aahs" ring out in rich harmony, the music abruptly stops as the voices echo, and the chorus lies ahead.

2:53   B Chorus (8 + 2 measures): No theremin is used on this "Good Vibrations." All three layers enter at the same time and quickly fade to an instrumental section.

3:10   D Verse (8 measures): A "Na-na-na-na-na" contrapuntal vocal interplay reminiscent of English madrigals is the highlight of this section. The different low, middle, and high melody lines overlap accompanied only by bass and tambourine.

3:22   B Chorus (6 measures and fade): The theremin and cello used in the "Good Vibrations" chorus returns as the music fades.

For Musicians

Harmonically, "Good Vibrations" is a study in diatonic progressions, ii-V and IV-V cadences, and sophisticated contrapuntal polyphonic vocal textures. The song needs no introduction, and the verse-chord progression moves down somewhat diatonically from Ebm to Db to Cb to Bb for the first phrase, and cadences on Db to end the second phrase. The chorus alternates between the I and IV chords over Gb, and the use of additive textures continues as the first harmony line enters. The chord modulates to Ab and repeats the I-IV pattern as additional harmonies enter. We finally arrive on I and IV in Bb to end the section. The middle, or "C" section, features the instruments mentioned in the time line description above and features a constant bass note on Bb. The free-floating vocals are based on the flatted seven tone and are colorful and dramatic. The last part of this section moves up to Eb as a vocal line fades in but quickly returns to Bb. "Good Vibrations" simply changes tempo at this next new section, with no metric preparation. The lack of vibrato on the organ sound and sustained texture contrast well with the time-keeping maracas as the chords move from F to Gm and C. The tremendously effective vocal "aah" that occurs next is built on Eb/F, making it simultaneously a IV-I and V-I cadence. The last "Good Vibrations" chorus is in Bb and uses the I to IV pattern from earlier, but the progression modulates downward from Bb to Ab to Gb. The vocal fugue at the last new section occurs over bass half-notes playing the roots: Gb to Ab to Bb to Ab. A percussive cello playing eighth notes enters as the Ab chord moves between I and IV, and a last bit of chorus material occurs before fading out.

Final Comments

Brian Wilson's use of studio techniques for "Good Vibrations" helped usher in the era of studio experimentation in which the Beatles and other groups would flourish. The Beach Boys also performed this song live on occasion, as in their well-received live 1969 concert recorded in London.

---

[1] Timothy White, *The Nearest Faraway Place: Brian Wilson, the Beach Boys, and the Southern California Experience* (New York, Henry Holt, 1994), 116.

[2] Ibid., 83.

[3] Brian Wilson and Todd Gold, *Wouldn't It Be Nice* (New York: Harper Collins, 1991), 33.

[4] Ibid., 35.

[5] Ibid., 46.

[6] Ibid., 52.

[7] Ibid., 71.

[8] Ibid., 140.

[9] White, 284; Wilson, 181–83.

Chapter Eight

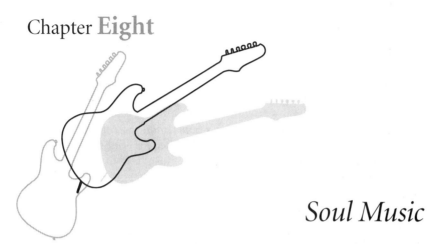

Soul Music

The term "soul" started to appear in reference to music toward the end of the 1950s, when it showed up in album titles like Ray Charles's *Soul Brothers* (1958) and *Soul Meeting* (1962) and John Coltrane's *Soultrane* (1960), and gradually it was also applied to African-American popular music. By the middle of the sixties, *soul* was synonymous with R&B, so much so that Billboard changed the title of its R&B chart to Soul. Soon the term was found in many cultural contexts, such as "soul food" (ribs, chitterlings, and collard greens) and the phrase "soul brother." It is possible that the word "soul" attained its connection to African-American culture because of the title of an important book by African-American scholar W. E. B. DuBois, *The Souls of Black Folk* (1903).

When discussing soul music, it seems that almost everyone has differing definitions. Some would limit the term to the products of certain record companies, such as Stax or Atlantic, and omit Motown because its music is considered too pop, too bleached; others have used the term "sweet soul" when referring to Motown, in an effort to avoid excluding them from soul. When pressed about the term "soul," most will admit that all cultures have soul: There is country soul, Italian soul, Latin soul, and Jewish soul. While it is true that almost all nations and peoples have a form of expression that authentically emanates from the heart and can rightly be called soulful, the use of the term in America in reference to African-American music was so prevalent in the 1960s that the authors will use it to identify most African-American music released during the period.

Soul music of the period was differentiated by geographic location. The two most influential areas were Detroit (Motown Records) and Memphis (Stax Records), although there were other locations. Chicago was home to companies like Chess and Vee-Jay and to performers like Jerry Butler, Curtis

Mayfield, and the Impressions. However, the "Chicago soul" sound was not cohesive enough to be easily defined. From the mid-sixties through the seventies, Philadelphia's Kenny Gamble and Leon Huff created an identifiable sound that laid the groundwork for disco music later in the decade. One of their important recordings was "TSOP" (The Sound of Philadelphia), which became the theme music for television's *Soul Train,* the African-American counterpart to *American Bandstand.* The Philadelphia soul sound includes groups like Harold Melvin and the Blue Notes, the O'Jays, Stylistics, Delfonics, and Spinners. There was also Las Vegas soul sound emanating from polished lounge groups, such as the Fifth Dimension and the Friends of Distinction. None of the other soul music locations were as influential as Detroit and Memphis.

The Detroit and Memphis styles were distinctive and stood in marked contrast to each other. Detroit's Motown Records was an African-American–owned and –operated corporation and was the most influential such organization since Black Swan Records in the 1920s. Motown's owner (Berry Gordy, Jr.), songwriters, and house band were all African-American. Only a few of the upper-management businessmen were European-American. Memphis's Stax Records was owned by European-Americans, had a multiracial house band, and lacked the comprehensive artist-support structure of Motown.

Memphis had a long tradition of both blues and rockabilly recording, and by the mid-sixties its most important label was Stax Records, owned by European-Americans James Stewart and his sister, Estelle Axton. Stax Records was responsible for about half of the twenty million dollars generated by the Memphis recording industry in 1967. Although located in New York, Atlantic Records was another important part of the Memphis sound because of its distribution arrangement with Stax and the amount of recording it did with the Stax house band at the Stax Studios.

The approach to doing business was remarkably different for the two companies. Motown used a corporate-style organization ruled by Berry Gordy, who controlled the "sound" and quality of Motown's product. Many writers have referred to Motown's operation as an "assembly-line" production facility, a veiled reference to Gordy's experience working in Detroit's auto factories. The use of this term seems pejorative because it implies a lack of craft in his productions, but it is also designed to draw an image of Gordy as a "lucky factory laborer" rather than a talented songwriter.

Gordy also realized that the fabricated distinction between R&B and pop music in the minds of radio programmers was costing African-American recording artists, songwriters, and record labels millions of dollars a year in lost revenue from performance and mechanical royalties. To combat this, he developed a style of pop music that transcended the boundaries and served as popular music for both races. In fact, so skillful was his creation that *Billboard* eliminated its R&B charts in 1964, because the music of both races had become inseparable. In 1965, *Billboard* returned to individual charts for reasons that likely were political. The Black Power movement was interested in maintaining racial pride and identity, and having a separate music chart aided those goals.

Gordy's intention was to sculpt his artists so that they were acceptable to European-American culture and therefore able have their recordings played on pop radio and to perform in the most prestigious venues in the country, such as New York's Copacabana, Las Vegas show rooms, and at the White House. To this end, he established an artist development department that schooled his artists in the manners of polite society. Gordy's artists learned how to give interviews without sounding threatening, how to use makeup and wigs, and other general "social graces."

While Motown Records recorded a kind of polite soul with none of the sweating, screaming exhortations associated with the sound of the sanctified church, or any of the energetic dancing of James Brown, Stax Records continued the tradition of raw, unbridled, energetic R&B performances. The best example of this difference is to compare the screams of James Brown with the polite "ahhs" of Smokey Robinson. Brown's scream was raw and sounded like he was doing real damage to his vocal cords, while Robinson's scream was not really a scream but rather a falsetto "ahh." The difference is also readily apparent in the dance styles when comparing Brown's fast footwork and splits to the politely choreographed and understated dance motions of the Temptations or the Miracles.

Another factor that gave the recordings of Stax and Motown their distinctive sounds was their respective house bands. Motown had the Funk Brothers, an all-African-American group, wheras Stax had the Mar-Kays (Booker T. and the MGs), a racially mixed group. Both groups performed on a large percentage of the records released by their respective companies and gave each recording the type of sonic consistency required to craft an identifiable "sound" for the label. Because both were house bands working in the house studio, they had an unlimited amount of time to work out musical arrangements that were tailored for a particular song and artist. This is in marked contrast to a typical music industry producer who schedules studio time for a group, hires the musicians who happen to be available on that date, and proceeds to record as quickly as possible because everything is paid for by the hour. Because of their type of working relationship, both Motown and Stax were able to create some of the most consistent and memorable soul music of the era.

MOTOWN

No single record company in the history of popular music has a sound as identifiable as Motown Records. In fact, the word "Motown" itself defines the genre as much as it identifies the output of a specific record company. Motown was the result of the vision, drive, and dedication of one man—Berry Gordy, Jr.—with the help of a small pool of musical friends. It was also an important source of racial pride for young African-American, Detroit-based talent during the 1960s, because Motown was a visible, successful, African-American–owned business demonstrating that it was possible to "make it" even in segregated society.

After a brief flirtation with a boxing career and working for his father's construction company, Gordy operated a jazz record store for a while and then worked on the Lincoln-Mercury assembly line. In his spare time, Gordy pursued a songwriting career. His first success came in 1957 with "Reet Petite," recorded by Jackie Wilson and released on Brunswick Records. With his foot in the door, Gordy wrote other songs for Wilson, such as the million-seller "Lonely Teardrops," often in collaboration with Wilson's manager, Al Green.

In 1957, Gordy began a relationship with Smokey Robinson that was among the most important events in the formation of Motown Records. During this period, Gordy worked with a small circle of musical friends, including the Five Stars, the Satintones (including Robert Bateman and Brian Holland), Eddie Holland, and Raynoma Mayberry Liles (Gordy's future wife). Raynoma, known as Ray or Miss Ray, had perfect pitch and a traditional musical education. She could write lead sheets, help with harmony and chord progressions, and rehearse background singers. In 1958, Gordy and Raynoma formed the Rayber (a combination of Ray and Berry) Music Writing Company to formalize their musical work and create a cash flow that would someday lead to their own record label.[1] Rayber Music helped people write songs and record demos; they charged one hundred dollars for their service and grossed about fifty dollars per song. It was from this base that they began to sell masters to established record labels and, since Gordy was having trouble getting his royalties from Jackie Wilson, they decided to stop giving him their best material. Their first hint of success was Smokey Robinson's song called "I Got a Job" (1958), an answer to the Silhouettes' "Get a Job," which they recorded with his group the Miracles and sold to George Goldner's End label (see Chapter 3, Doo-wop).

Rayber Music negotiated several other releases, but its first big success came when Marv Johnson asked for help with his song "Come to Me." Rayber helped Johnson with the song, Raynoma added background parts, and they produced a demo recording in their small home studio. They decided the song was too good to give away and that they should produce the master recording themselves. Gordy estimated that it could be done for eight hundred dollars, which they borrowed from Ber-Berry, the Gordy family's savings club. The Gordy family had each member contribute ten dollars a week to a joint account and used the money for investments, usually real estate. A family member could borrow money only after a unanimous vote and repayment terms, with interest, had been agreed upon. Since Gordy's sister Gwen already owned Anna Records, the music business was not considered too risky for investment.

With the eight hundred dollars, Gordy bought recording time at Detroit's United Sound studios, hired studio musicians, and recorded "Come to Me." This session was the beginning of the Motown house band and consequently the Motown sound, because they used Benny Benjamin on drums, James Jamerson on bass, Beans Bowles on baritone sax, and the Rayber Voices (Robert Bateman, Brian Holland, and Raynoma).[2] The Motown sonic elements were now in place. Gordy took the master recording to United Artists in New York where it was very well received. United Artists gave him a three thousand dollar advance and a ten percent royalty, and allowed Gordy to retain the local distribution rights. Having the local distribution rights meant that Gordy and Raynoma would have to form their own record label, so in January 1959 they formed Tamla Records and Jobete Music Publishers. According to Raynoma, both companies were first established jointly; however, Gordy soon suggested that they put everything in his name for "tax purposes."[3] "Come to Me" peaked at number six on the *Billboard* R&B charts, and Motown was off to a good start.

Buoyed by this success, the couple bought a two-story house at 2648 West Grand Blvd. and hung a sign on the front: "Hitsville U.S.A." The first song they recorded at their new three-track studio was "Money (That's What I Want)" by Barrett Strong and co-written by Gordy and crew; it was intended to be similar to Ray Charles's 1959 hit "What'd I Say." Since Barrett Strong was an Anna Records artist, Gordy's sister Gwen wanted to release the song, so they worked out a deal: Tamla Records released the recording in Detroit, and Anna Records, which had a distribution deal with Chess Records, released it nationally. "Money" became the number six R&B recording of 1960 and crossed over to number ninety-seven on the year-end pop charts. Barret Strong eventually moved into songwriting and co-wrote Motown hits like "Ball of Confusion," "Papa Was a Rolling Stone," "Psychedelic Shack," and "I Wish It Would Rain."

Motown's production ethic was similar to that of Phil Spector and Sam Phillips: they continued working on a song until it had the right magic. "Money" took three days of recording before Berry felt the groove was perfect, and then he spent all night in the studio getting the mix right. Motown was able to operate this way because it owned its own recording studio and did not have to worry about paying for expensive time at another studio. Motown's producers could spend countless hours experimenting with different sounds and record multiple takes trying to discover the perfect sound and arrangement. Perfection, along with quality control, was a common theme in Motown's operating procedure.

Gordy used the natural competitive nature of his producers and writers to maintain quality. Songwriters and producers such as Barrett Strong; Smokey Robinson; Norman Whitfield; Mickey Stevenson; and the team of Holland, Dozier, and Holland brought the recordings they hoped to release next to the Friday morning staff meeting, when Gordy would choose, by popular vote, the next week's releases. If a track was voted down, the producer would either have to drop it, try again the next week, or rerecord it. Gordy himself was sometimes in the competition and was not beyond being voted down in favor of a better recording. If a production team had a hit with a particular artist, it had the first shot at producing that artist's next recording. If it flopped, the door was open for another team to work with the artist. This process kept the producers working hard to maintain their quality and to keep the hits coming.

The consistency of Motown's studio musicians was another important key to their success. Although many musicians were involved in the recordings at Motown, there was a core group who were just as much a part of the "Motown Sound" as any artist. The house band—the Funk Brothers—were Earl Van Dyke (leader/piano), Benny Benjamin (drums), James Jamerson (bass), Robert White (guitar), and Thomas "Beans" Bowles (saxophone). The band often worked only from lead sheets (musical notation that included only melody and supporting harmony, leaving the rhythmic interplay up to the musician), and they created their own head arrangements in conjunction with the producer. The results of this rhythm-section freedom is best seen in the bass lines of James Jamerson. These were strongly independent, often highly syncopated, and were so original that a song often could be identified by the bass line alone. Bass-line syncopation was one of Motown's hallmark traits, and it increased in complexity during the decade. Good examples of this element can be heard in both "I Heard It Through the Grapevine" by Gladys Knight and the Pips or Stevie Wonder's "For Once in My Life."

Even though they started simply, Motown's musical arrangements were often more complex than those of other pop music songs. A song usually unfolded with instruments being added to each chorus, making the arrangement build to a climax. Earlier, Leiber and Stoller had used a wide variety of instruments in their recordings with the Drifters, and Motown built on their techniques using strings, flute, oboe, and Latin percussion instruments such as castanets, conga drum, and tambourine. The tambourine first surfaced in R&B in Ruth Brown's gospel-influenced "Mama He Treats Your Daughter

Mean" (1953) and was heard periodically throughout the fifties, but at Motown the tambourine became at staple of most recording sessions. The conga drum had been somewhat rare in pop recordings, but it was regularly heard on Motown recordings, sometimes in solo spots. Motown producers gave recordings a unique quality by trying new and unusual sounds, such as stomping on a piece of plywood placed on the floor ("Baby Love"), dropping chains to make the tambourine sound larger ("Dancing in the Streets"), and knocking on a piano soundboard to create a hollow, knocking sound. Motown also used Phil Spector's "wall of sound" technique on its big productions, with the high point being Diana Ross's recording of "Ain't No Mountain High Enough."

An essential element in any successful recording is the "hook," that part of an arrangement or lyric that gets the attention of listeners and makes them want to hear the rest of the recording. A hook should appear near the beginning, if not in the first groove of the record, and be repeated often. Radio programmers often auditioned a recording by listening to only the first few seconds, and if it did not "hook" their interest instantly, they knew it would not appeal to their audience. Motown producers were masters at creating hooks, whether vocal or instrumental, and generally put them in the first groove of the recording. An example is the opening bass and guitar riffs of "My Girl," the opening bass riff from "You Can't Hurry Love," and the opening vocal hooks of "Stop in the Name of Love," or "Standing in the Shadow Of Love."

Despite the homogenous nature of the "Motown Sound," each artist had his/her own style, as did each producer. Gordy's policy of keeping a successful production team with an artist as long as they had hits was simple and productive; the hit teams remained together and forged an individual sound, and the unsuccessful teams continually reshuffled until a winning combination was found. Production teams with a string of hits that remained together for a long time included Mickey Stevenson with Marvin Gaye, Norman Whitfield with the Temptations, Ashford and Simpson with Marvin Gaye and Tammi Terrell, and Holland, Dozier, and Holland with the Supremes (seventeen consecutive hits).

Brian and Eddie Holland and Lamont Dozier (H-D-H) were Motown's most prolific songwriting and production team and had been with Gordy since the Rayber Music days. Their first hits were "Micky's Monkey" (1963) by the Miracles, and "Come and Get These Memories" (1963) and "Heat Wave" (1963) by Martha Reeves and the Vandellas. A common practice for this team, and one Gordy endorsed, was to quickly record a follow-up recording that sounded very similar to the original; an example is "Quicksand," which was the follow-up to "Heat Wave." In 1964, H-D-H began an association with the Supremes that lasted until 1967, when the team staged a work slowdown to protest their low salary.

By 1968, they decided that they were not earning enough royalties and left Motown to form their own record company, Invictus/Hot Wax.

The most unique component of Motown Records was its attention to artist development. All other record labels simply recorded their artists and left any career development up to their management, if they had any. Once the artist flopped, he/she was abandoned. Since Berry Gordy's artists were mostly young and inexperienced in the ways of show business, Gordy established an artist development department to give them the social and stage skills to help them act like stars both on and off stage. He hired Maxine Powell, owner of a Detroit finishing school, to teach the acts how to behave on stage (walking, talking, and standing) as well as various aspects of off-stage etiquette. If Motown acts were ever going to perform in the finest venues in America, they needed to know how to handle themselves in "polite society." Kids from inner-city Detroit had little concept of, or care for, the subtleties of high society, such as choosing the correct fork in a fancy restaurant or addressing the President. Motown also hired Cholly Atkins, one-time Broadway choreographer, to teach their artists a vocabulary of movement that gave them something more to do onstage than sing. Motown groups developed highly stylized stage routines that included hand gestures as well as elegant dance steps. Their movements were low-key, smooth, and even gracious, and were ideal for network television appearances. Although those stage movements now seem dated and even corny, they set the standard for soul groups everywhere.

Motown's artist development accomplished its function, and its artists had careers that outlasted those of average rock stars. Its biggest success story was Diana Ross, who joined Motown when she was still in high school. Motown developed her career to the point where she was starring in full-length feature films. Ross appeared in *Lady Sings the Blues* (1972) (the Billie Holiday story), *Mahogany* (1975), and *The Wiz*, a remake of the *Wizard of Oz*. Unwisely, Gordy involved himself in the production of the films and, in the case of *Mahogany*, its direction, and placed himself in a field in which he was a complete novice. In his autobiography, Gordy admits that the attention he paid to Ross's career diverted from Motown's other artists, and the power vacuum that it created ultimately hurried the demise of the corporation.

Reports of life at Motown Records were not always positive, and there were constant complaints that Gordy was too paternalistic in his operation of the business and that royalties were both too low and not accurately accounted for. When Motown artists compared notes with other recording stars, they found that their royalty rates were below the industry standard, and they began to rebel. According to Nelson George, when the Jackson Five signed with Motown they got a royalty rate of 2.7 percent, and when they signed with Epic, their rate was 14 percent.[4] When Stevie Wonder turned twenty-one, he voided his Motown contract and renegotiated for a more generous royalty and complete artistic control of his recordings. Another problem was the manner in which Gordy treated female artists, especially Florence Ballard, an original member of the Supremes, who was forced out of the group and died nine years later while living on welfare. In fact, once Gordy became fixated on Diana Ross, the careers of his other female artists, such as Gladys Knight, Kim Weston, the Marvelettes, and Valerie Simpson, languished.

In 1971, Gordy relocated Motown to Los Angeles to be closer to the rest of the recording industry; however, the move took him far from the street-level music scene in Detroit and new talents springing up there. Most of Motown's successful artists were products of Detroit's churches and schools, which gave them a certain similarity in their approaches to music-making and therefore enhanced the unique nature of the Motown sound. After the move, Motown remained successful with artists like the Jackson Five, the Commodores, Lionel Richie, and De Barge, but their share of the top ten never equaled what they had achieved in the sixties. In 1982, Gordy entered into a distribution deal with MCA, ending its status as an independent label and eventually leading to the sale of the company.

Smokey Robinson and the Miracles

Smokey Robinson was probably the most significant factor in Motown's early success. In addition to being a gifted singer with a successful group, the Miracles, Robinson was a skillful songwriter and producer who worked with the Marvelettes, the Temptations, and Marvin Gaye. After the first few Miracles recordings, which Gordy leased to Chess Records, his Tamla label released "Way Over There" (1960). It was Motown's first nationally "noticed" record and, in the true Gordy fashion, a follow-up recording was a high priority.

Robinson was around during the Rayber Music years and therefore was an important contributor to the early Motown sound. Robinson's first major success was "Shop Around," released at the end of 1960. An interesting story accompanies the release of this recording that illustrates how the gut reactions of a producer can be instrumental in creating a pop music hit. After completing the master tape of "Shop Around," something still disturbed Gordy about it, but he wasn't quite sure what it was. That night, he awoke and realized that the tempo was too slow. He immediately went down to the studio, summoned everyone involved, and rerecorded the song at a faster tempo.[5] The new "Shop Around" reached number one on the R&B charts and number two on the pop chart (being beat out for number one by Lawrence Welk); it became Motown's first million-seller. This story illustrates the flexibility of a small company and the benefits of having a recording studio available on a twenty-four-hour basis.

The Miracles were one of Motown's most successful groups, and Robinson was its most impressive male entertainer. Robinson was such an indispensable part of Motown that Gordy made him vice president of the company. His high voice, not quite falsetto but more castrato, was the epitome of sweet soul. An excellent example of Robinson's sweet soul vocal talents is "Ooo Baby Baby" (1965), a ballad that puts him in his upper range (he slips into falsetto a few times) and on which he improvises superb melismas on the syllable "Ooo."

The Marvelettes

Motown's first number-one pop hit came in December 1961, with the Marvelettes' "Please Mr. Postman" (produced by Brian Holland and Robert Bateman). The group, students at Detroit's Inkster High School, was discovered at a school talent show in 1960, where first prize was an audition with Motown Records. The group did not win, but they impressed the talent scout enough that they got the audition anyway. The Marvelettes (Gladys Horton, Katherine Anderson, Georgeanna Dobbins, Juanita Cowart, and Wanda Young) were Motown's only pure "girl group" in the style of the Angels and the Shangri-Las. Motown's other "girl groups" had dominant singers (Diana Ross, Martha Reeves, Mary Wells) whose voices were featured above the background singing of the group. Dobbins and Cowart dropped out soon after "Please Mr. Postman," and the Marvelettes continued as a trio. The song was so wonderfully infectious that the Beatles chose to include it among the American songs on *The Beatles Second Album* (1964). The Marvelettes were not as successful as other Motown girl groups, probably because their style fit an earlier model, but they nonetheless released a respectable number of hits through 1968.

Mary Wells

Mary Wells was Motown's first female solo artist and had her greatest hits with sexy, mid-tempo love songs. Wells was a high school student in 1960, when she tried to sell a song she had written to Berry Gordy. Since she had not written the song down, she had to sing it to him, and he was impressed enough with her voice that he signed her to record the song "Bye Bye Baby." Her song did not sell well, but after she was teamed with writer/producer Smokey Robinson from 1962 to 1965, who found a softer, sexier sound for her, she began to experience chart success.

This production team recorded several hits, including "Two Lovers," "The One Who Really Loves You," and "You Beat Me to the Punch;" but their biggest hit was "My Guy." For some reason, Motown experimented with Mary Wells's career path and paired her with Marvin Gaye in a duo setting, which seems curious considering how big a hit she had with "My Guy." Gordy may have been more concerned with directing Marvin Gaye's career than he was with Wells's. Wells left Motown for Atco Records in 1965, probably sensing Gordy's preoccupation with Diana Ross would hurt her career. She may have intended the move to save her career, but she never achieved the level of success at Atco that she had at Motown.

Stevie Wonder

Born Stevland Judkins (later changed to Stevland Morris), the eleven-year-old prodigy became known as Little Stevie Wonder and developed into one of popular music's most gifted songwriters and producers. Wonder's first hit for Motown, "Fingertips Part II," was a curious live harmonica feature recorded at Chicago's Regal Theater during a "battle of the bands" among various Motown acts. On that night, Little Stevie Wonder was battling Marvin Gaye, and after his performance he was led off the stage, only to turn around and run back on while the audience was still applauding. Stevie broke into another harmonica solo and added another chorus to the song. Part of the band had already changed for the next act, so there was some confusion as to what was going on, and in the background, a musician can be heard asking frantically, "What key? What key?" This spontaneous moment was included on the recording, giving "Fingertips Part II" the kind of excitement generally lacking in pop recordings. The single and the album, *Little Stevie Wonder: The 12 Year Old Genius,* went to number one on the pop charts, the first live recording to do so.

After "Fingertips," Stevie had a long period between hits. In fact, when his name came up at a producers meeting in 1965, no one wanted to work with him. Sylvia Moy, a Motown songwriter, agreed to work with him and help him write songs. As a songwriter, Wonder tended to have about four measures of an idea but needed help to develop that germ into a full-fledged song with a beginning, middle, and end. When Moy listened to Stevie's material, she found a remarkable hook, "Baby, everything is alright, uptight, outa sight," and worked with him to complete it. Gordy loved the song but, probably because of his chauvinistic attitudes, did not allow her to produce it. He told her it was a great song but said, "It's going to take a real pro to produce this record the way it should be done,"[6] and "Up Tight" was given to Mickey Stevenson and Hank Crosby to produce. The song was a success, and Moy and Wonder continued their writing partnership until 1970.

Stevie Wonder's vocal style, based somewhat on Ray Charles's, is a unique blend of gospel melismas, the division of words into extra syllables, and accenting normally unaccented syllables. For example, in "I Was Made to Love Her" (1967), he divides the word *year* in half by singing, "ye-HEAR," and in "If You Really Love Me" (1971), the word *kissin'* is accented "kiss-IN." Wonder has a great facility with a variety of song types and a way of rendering them to fit his unique style. His harmonica-playing is also unique. He uses a chromatic harmonica rather than a blues harmonica. This instrument is featured on several recordings, especially "For Once in My Life" (1968) and "Alfie" (1968).

As Wonder matured as a musician, he was allowed to become more involved in the production of his recordings. The first solo production was "Signed Sealed Delivered" (1970). In 1971, Wonder turned twenty-one and was shocked to find out that the earnings held in trust for him amounted to only a million dollars, despite having earned over thirty million dollars for Motown. Because he had been a minor when he signed with Motown, he was able to get out of his contract and renegotiate a new one giving him more money and total control of his recordings. Wonder then built a recording studio in his home where he could work on his songs independently. The first solo production to come from him was the album *Where I'm Coming From* (1971).

After he assumed artistic control, Wonder produced some of the finest popular music of the early 1970s, including seven number-one hits. Following a tour with the Rolling Stones, which gave him more visibility among European-Americans, he released "Superstition" (1972) and "You Are the Sunshine of My Life" (1973); both became number-one hits. In "Superstition," he began using new keyboard technology, beginning an involvement with synthesizers and creating a new style of synthesizer-funk that influenced jazz artists such as Herbie Hancock *(Head Hunters,* 1973). With various electronic keyboards, he was able to play most of the parts himself, and on albums such as *Talking Book* (1973) and *Innervisions* (1974), he played almost all the instruments.

Martha Reeves and the Vandellas

Martha Reeves started out at Motown as a secretary for producer Mickey Stevenson, although earlier, as a member of the Dell-Fis, she had recorded for the Chess label. One day Mary Wells could not make it to a recording session, and Reeves got a chance to record "I'll Have to Let Him Go" in her place. Later, Martha and her backup group, the Vandellas, sang for a couple of Marvin Gaye sessions and finally, after they teamed up with Holland, Dozier, and Holland, recorded a succession of hits like "Heat Wave" (1963), "Come and Get These Memories" (1963), and "Dancing in the Street" (1964).

"Heat Wave" was one of the most exciting recordings of the early Motown era. It grooves along with a shuffle rhythm at a tempo of 169 beats per minute, is filled with gospel call-and-response, and has an important syncopated accent that falls between the second and third foot tap (under the lyric "heat wave"). Although their harmonies were not as polished as those of other groups, the Vandellas sang with more fire than any other Motown girl group.

The Supremes

In 1960, Diana Ross, Mary Wilson, and Florence Ballard were still in high school when they first came to ask Berry Gordy for a recording contract. Gordy wisely told them finishing school was more important and to come back after they graduated. They showed up the day after graduation. They got their start at Motown singing background vocals, and when Gordy finally signed them in 1961, he changed their name from the Primettes to the Supremes (the old Temptations were called the Primes, and the Primettes were their sister group). The Supremes had no success until 1963 when, after nine attempts, the writer/producer team of Holland, Dozier, and Holland found the right formula with "Where Did Our Love Go." That combination of the Supremes and H-D-H had a head-spinning run of seventeen hits in a row and ten number-one hits in four years.

Launching a recording by an unestablished act is more difficult than releasing a new recording by an established act; the audience needs a visual image to place what they hear in context. Initially, "Where Did Our Love Go" went nowhere on the charts until Gordy booked the Supremes on Dick Clark's traveling "Caravan of Stars" show. They had bottom billing when the tour began—Motown's headliner on that tour was Brenda Holloway ("Every Little Bit Hurts" and "You've Made Me So Very Happy")—but as the tour progressed, "Where Did Our Love Go" steadily rose to number one, and by the end of the tour the Supremes were its headliners. It is possible that without the exposure provided by Dick Clark, the Supreme's new recording would have disappeared unnoticed. "Baby Love," their follow-up single, had no trouble reaching number one in both the United States and England, and today is probably the recording most associated with them. On December 27, 1964, the Supremes appeared on *The Ed Sullivan Show* and fulfilled Gordy's goal of creating a sweet soul music for mainstream America. Motown's artist development department had done a good job, and the Supremes were such a musical and visual success that they were asked back by Sullivan for eighteen more appearances.

From the beginning, the focus had always been on Diana Ross, but in 1967 it was made official when Ross was given top billing over the other Supremes. That was also the year that Smokey Robinson was given top billing over the Miracles, the year that Florence Ballard was replaced by Cindy Birdsong, and the year that H-D-H left Motown over a financial dispute. The departure of H-D-H left the Supremes without a writing team and Motown without its most successful production team.

The loss of the H-D-H team was troubling, but Gordy had been developing the Supremes' career in another direction: He intended to get the Supremes on the supper club circuit, where Sinatra and other big-name entertainers performed, ultimately Las Vegas. They began by adding popular standards like "You're Nobody 'Til Somebody Loves You" to their act and worked small clubs until finally, in 1965, they got a chance at the most important club in the country—the Copacabana in New York. From there they became an established act in Las Vegas and the most visible of all Motown artists.

In 1970, Ross left the Supremes and was replaced by Jean Terrell; their last performance together was on January 14, 1970, at the Frontier Hotel in Las Vegas. Ross's first solo recording was a moderate success with "Reach Out and Touch (Somebody's Hand)," but she reclaimed her chart-topping status later that same year with "Ain't No Mountain High Enough."

With "Ain't No Mountain High Enough," Motown had finally out-Spectored Phil Spector. It was an extravagant wall of sound production with mini-drama pathos surpassing even the Shangri-Las. The song alternates between Ross's soaring melismatic "Aahs" over strings and a sexy, spoken, romantic "I-still-love-you" lyric. Two minutes and twenty seconds into the track, the song starts to build with an instrumental stop-time, and the background singers syncopatedly riff "Ain't No Mountain High Enough . . . " behind Ross's polite yet sexy screams. Then, after an instrumental interlude, the singers again riff while Ross improvises over a highly syncopated bass line. This was the production high point of the 1960s Motown girl-group sound.

Temptations

In 1960, a combination of several groups, the Distants and Elgins, came together to form the Primes (Paul Williams, Eddie Kendricks, Otis Williams, Melvin Franklin, and Eldridge Bryant) and were signed by Motown in 1961. Soon, Bryant quit and was replaced by David Ruffin, an Anna recording artist, and they changed their name to the Temptations. Although they were a versatile group with three strong lead singers, they did not have much success until Smokey Robinson began producing them. Their first success was with "The Way You Do the Things You Do" in 1964, but they did not have a number-one hit until "My Girl" a year later. "My Girl" was an answer song to Mary Wells's "My Guy," and both were written and produced by Smokey Robinson. The Temptations developed into one of Motown's most successful male groups and eventually recorded over twenty top-ten hits over twenty-five years.

Norman Whitfield began producing the Temptations when Robinson failed to get a hit with "Get Ready" (1966), and this, according to Motown policy, opened the door for other Motown producers. The first hit for the new team was "Ain't Too Proud to Beg" (1966), which was followed by a series of hits that lasted several more years. Whitfield's style of producing was different than H-D-H's. Instead of trying to follow up a hit with a sound-alike song, Whitfield tried to make the next recording completely different. In 1968, the

The Temptations

Temptations began to update their style to a more contemporary psychedelic sound with "Cloud Nine," a drug-related song that departed from Gordy's original tenet of creating recordings that were the "Sound of Young America." This was an attempt to get their sound more in line with the changes in the recording industry brought about by acid rock bands, Sly and the Family Stone, and the Beatles. In 1969, "Cloud Nine" became the first Motown recording to win a Grammy. Many of the Temptations' subsequent songs also dealt with more unusual topics: "Don't Let the Joneses Get You Down," "Message From a Black Man," "War" (the popular version was recorded by Edwin Starr), "Psychedelic Shack," and "Ball of Confusion."

Ruffin left the group when he was denied top billing and more money, and was replaced by Dennis Edwards. In May 1971, Eddie Kendricks also left the Temptations for a solo career. The last vintage Temptations recording with Eddie Kendricks singing lead was "Just My Imagination (Running Away With Me)" (1971). The new Temptations lineup had several more hits, such as "Papa Was a Rolling Stone" (1972), but by the mid-1970s they had left Motown.

Four Tops

When the Four Tops were signed by Motown in 1963, they already were seasoned professionals who, as the Four Aims, had recorded for Chess Records and were fairly successful in Las Vegas and on the supper club circuit. The Four

Tops (Levi Stubbs, Lawrence Payton, Renaldo "Obie" Benson, and Abdul "Duke" Fakir) got off to an uncertain start because Motown first tried having them record jazz standards for an experimental record label. However, the H-D-H team was able to find a sound that was right for them, and beginning in 1964, they had a steady progression of hits, including "Baby I Need Your Loving" (1964), "I Can't Help Myself" (1965), "Its the Same Old Song," "Standing in the Shadows of Love," "Bernadette," and, their masterpiece "Reach Out I'll Be There" (1966). Motown had their first back-to-back number-one hits when the Four Tops' "I Can't Help Myself" knocked the Supremes' "Back in My Arms Again" out of the number-one spot in 1965. "I Can't Help Myself" went on to be *Billboard's* number-one R&B recording of 1965. The Four Tops' sound was tailored to fit in with Motown's other male vocal groups in a three-tiered lineup: the Miracles were the softest, sweetest; the Temptations were in between with a combination of sweet soul and hard soul; and the Four Tops had a rougher, hard-soul sound featuring the lead vocals of Levi Stubbs.

Marvin Gaye

Marvin Gaye got his early musical training singing and playing organ at his father's church in Washington, D.C. In 1958, he joined the Moonglows, a well-known doo-wop group led by Harvey Fuqua. Fuqua and Gaye signed with Motown, Fuqua as a writer/producer and Gaye as a session drummer; he played on "Please Mr. Postman" by the Marvelettes. Gaye later established himself as a singer and worked with most of Motown's great producers: H-D-H, Smokey Robinson, Norman Whitfield, and Ashford and Simpson.

Gaye's first hit was "Stubborn Kind of Fellow" (1962), and he subsequently recorded over twenty hits during the decade. His voice was capable of singing in a sweet soul vocal style, as in "How Sweet It Is to Be Loved By You," and a harder soul style such as "I Heard It Through the Grapevine." In the beginning, Motown had trouble developing a direction for him. Gaye wanted to sing jazz standards, but once they convinced him to try a funkier style, he began to experience success. Motown tried several approaches with him and, in the mid-sixties, began pairing him in duets with female singers— first Mary Wells until she left Motown, then Kim Weston. However, his most successful partner was Tammi Terrell in 1967–68. Their work together ended when Terrell was diagnosed with the brain tumor that eventually killed her.

In 1971, Marvin Gaye got complete control of his recordings and persuaded Gordy to let him do a jazzy protest album. The result was the concept album *What's Going On*, which included two other hits besides the title track: "Mercy Mercy Me (The Ecology)" and "Inner City Blues." In 1972, he contributed the score to the feature film *Trouble Man* and also had a hit with the title cut. Both of these albums moved closer to pop jazz, were well received by musicians, and aired topics about inner-city life that had been ignored by pop music. In 1982, Gaye left Motown and signed with Columbia Records, which proved to be good for his career. He was able to reach the number one position with "Sexual Healing" (1982), from his Grammy-winning *Midnight Love* album. Despite his talent, Marvin Gaye had personal problems likely resulting from the clash between his lifestyle as a star and his religious upbringing. On April 1, 1984, he was shot to death in an argument with his father.

The Jackson Five

The Jackson Five (Jackie, Tito, Marlon, Jermaine, and Michael) were a Gary, Indiana, family act coached by their father, who performed at amateur contests around the country, including the Apollo Theater. Father Joe had once been a manager and guitar player for the Falcons, a group that included Wilson Pickett ("In the Midnight Hour") and Eddie Floyd ("Knock on Wood"). For Motown, the Jacksons filled the void left by Stevie Wonder as a child-prodigy act. Their debut single, "I Want You Back" (1969), hit number one in January 1970, and so did the next three singles: "ABC," "The Love You Save," and "I'll Be There." It was the first time in the history of Hot 100 (the *Billboard* chart featuring the top 100 singles based on sales information and national radio airplay), that a group had four consecutive number-one hits in their first four tries. Because their first album was called *Diana Ross Presents the Jackson Five,* it is commonly believed that Ross discovered the group, but she had nothing to do with their discovery. She did, however, take an active role in supporting Michael's talent.

The Jackson Five was led by the dynamic singing and dancing of Michael Jackson, who was eleven years old at the time of their first hit. (Stevie Wonder before him was also eleven at the time of his first hit.) Michael's singing and dancing during this period were extremely powerful, influencing future styles. (He was so popular that he had his image portrayed in a popular Saturday morning cartoon show.) By the early 1970s, he was beginning to develop into a solo act.

In 1976, the group left Motown and signed with Epic Records but had to change their name to the Jacksons because Motown owned their original name. Unlike many of the artists who left Motown, the Jacksons continued to record hits with Epic, and Michael had two extremely successful albums: *Off the Wall* (1979) and *Thriller* (1982), one of the best selling albums in record history. The albums produced several hit singles, and the record sales helped Columbia, Epic's parent company, repair from the financial disaster caused by the disco bust. Michael's work in music videos, particularly *Thriller,* may have been his most important contribution to popular music. His concepts about music and film influenced the direction of the infant music video industry.

Prior to *Thriller*, music videos, except for the Beatles' work, were little more than a collection of shots of bands performing their hit singles. Michael's work clearly set a new standard for music videos.

THE MEMPHIS SOUL SOUND

Motown's soul music rival was the Memphis sound, dominated by Stax Records and its New York distributor/partner, Atlantic Records. Stax Records' vision of soul music was not a result of the careful crafting of a determined visionary leader but rather the result of pure luck. The Stax story began in 1958 when Jim Stewart, a white Southern country fiddler and banker, tried his hand at producing music and formed Satellite Records with his sister, Estelle Axton. In 1960, they moved their Satellite recording studio to the vacant Capitol Theater on East McLemore Avenue in the heart of an African-American neighborhood in Memphis. No one is certain what style of music he intended to record at Satellite, but Stewart is quoted in Phyl Garland's *The Sound of Soul* as saying, "We didn't even know what R&B was then. We just happened to move into a colored neighborhood."[7]

Their first hit recording found them and determined the future direction of the new label's product. In 1960, Rufus Thomas, a DJ at WDIA, and his daughter Carla, on vacation from college, walked into Satellite and wanted to record a song he had written called "Cause I Love." Thomas was an experienced performer, having spent years on the vaudeville circuit, and had recorded several hits, including "Bear Cat" (1953), Sun Records' first hit, which made it to number three on the R&B charts. "Cause I Love You" sold thirty thousand copies and caught the attention of Jerry Wexler of Atlantic Records, who paid Stewart a thousand dollars to lease the song for national distribution.[8] This was the first money Satellite earned. The only reason that Wexler even noticed the small Satellite release was that the pressing plant owner, Buster Williams, called Wexler when he found himself pressing "enormous quantities" of the record.[9]

Wexler flew down to Memphis and was impressed with the Memphis sound and the way the band worked out energetic arrangements by improvising in the studio. At Atlantic in New York, they tried for what Wexler called "immaculate funk," like the Drifters, but he realized that their New York arrangers and musicians were running out of ideas and that the Memphis system produced recordings with more fire. This was the beginning of a productive association between Atlantic and Stewart that guided the future of the Satellite/Stax label as an R&B label. Although no one realized it at the time, the Atlantic deal was also the beginning of the end for Stax Records, because buried in the fine print was a clause that gave Atlantic control of not only "Cause I Love You" but also all of Stax's future masters.[10] Stax's founders did not discover that they did not have any ownership rights of their past releases until the two companies parted in 1967.

Atlantic issued Carla Thomas's next recording, "Gee Whiz" (1961), and it reached number five on the R&B charts. The success of this recording was a good indication to Stewart that Stax was going to be a soul music label. Later, in 1963, Rufus Thomas had two dance hits, "The Dog" and "Walking the Dog," and still later in the 1970s, he had several more dance hits, such as "Do the Funky Chicken" (1970).

The development of the Stax house band, the Mar-Kays, was also purely accidental. There was a European-American R&B band from Messick High School in Memphis that called themselves the Royal Spades (Charlie Freeman, Steve Cropper, Donald "Duck" Dunn, Wayne Jackson, Don Nix, and Packy Axton). Packy was the son of Estelle Axton, part owner of Satellite, so the band used her studio to record.[11] In 1961, they changed their name to the Mar-Kays and recorded "Last Night" on Satellite; to the surprise of everyone, it reached number three on the charts. The success of this record prompted Stewart to change the name of the label to Stax (St = Stewart plus Ax = Axton), to avoid confusion with a California label with the same name. The Mar-Kays became Stax's house band because they were in the right spot at the right time, and soon afterward Al Jackson, Jr. (drums), and Booker T. Jones (organ), both African-Americans, joined the rhythm section.

In 1962, another accidental occurrence shaped the band's future. During a Rufus Thomas recording session, the musicians had some free time and were "just messing around" with a little riff tune, when Jim Stewart heard it and recorded it. He released the song, calling it "Green Onions," and called the band Booker T. and the MGs (Memphis group or MG sports car, depending on the source). "Green Onions" became a number-one hit on the national R&B chart and solidified the group's position as Stax's house band. Over the years, Booker T. and the MGs recorded a series of funky instrumental hits, such as "Boot Leg," "Groovin'," "Soul Limbo," "Hip Hug Her," "Hang 'Em High," "Time Is Tight," and "Melting Pot." The band was known by two names: When the rhythm section recorded, they were known as Booker T. and the MG's, and when they added the horns, they were called the Mar-Kays.

By 1962, all the pieces were in place. Stax had a few hits, a cohesive house band, and a distribution deal with Atlantic Records. Jerry Wexler liked the sound produced in the Memphis studio and by its house band so much that he began recording Atlantic artists there instead of in New York City. Stax, in addition to a good sound, also had a strong stable of songwriters, including house-band guitarist Steve Cropper and the team of Dave Porter and Isaac Hayes. Cropper's songwriting collaborations produced "634-5789," "FA-FA-FA-FA-FA Sad Song," "Going Back to Memphis," "Green Onions," "In the

Midnight Hour," "Knock on Wood," and "(Sittin' on) The Dock of the Bay." Porter and Hayes wrote "Soul Man," "Hold On I'm Comin'," "When Something Is Wrong With My Baby," "You Got Me Hummin'," "I Thank You," and "Wrap It Up."

Otis Redding

Otis Redding was the next big discovery for Stax Records. In 1962, Joe Galkin, an Atlanta record man, called Jerry Wexler and wanted him to front two thousand dollars so the group he was managing, Johnny Jenkins and the Pinetoppers, could record at Stax. Wexler agreed and flew down for the sessions. After Jenkins recorded his instrumentals, there was less than an hour of studio time remaining, and one of his sidemen (and driver) was allowed to try recording some songs. The first was a Little Richard–type song, "Hey Hey Baby," and the second was "These Arms of Mine." The sideman/driver was

Otis Redding

Otis Redding. Wexler was impressed with the second song and wanted to sign Redding, but so did Stewart. Although Atlantic had financed the recording session, because of the close relationship between the two companies and because Atlantic would end up owning the masters anyway, Wexler allowed Stax to sign Redding. "These Arms of Mine" reached number twenty on the R&B charts.[12]

Redding had previously released recordings in California—" Shout Bamalama" (1960) on Confederate and "Gettin' Hip" on Alshire—but his association with Stax, Steve Cropper, and the house band proved most successful. They turned out a string of hits, such as "Mr. Pitiful" (1965), "I've Been Loving You Too Long" (1965), "Respect" (1965), "I Can't Turn You Loose" (1965), "Fa-Fa-Fa-Fa-Fa" (1966), "Satisfaction" (1966), and "Shake" (1967). Otis Redding was the archetypal Memphis soul singer, a sweating, pleading, screaming "Gotta-gotta-gotta" gospel performer, but he never sold well on the pop charts until he performed at the Monterey Pop Festival in 1967 and exposed the European-American rock audience to the power of soul music. In December 1967, four days before his death in a plane crash in Wisconsin, Redding recorded "(Sittin' On) The Dock of the Bay," which was released posthumously and became his first million-selling recording. This recording was different from his other soul ventures. It was softer—without the sanctified gospel pleading—a perfect pop crossover recording that eventually became the number four recording of 1968. Many of his new listeners were unaware of Redding's earlier style because all they knew was his last recording, and his death prevented any future discovery. His earlier music experienced a resurgence when it was included in *The Commitments* (1991), a movie about an Irish R&B band. The Commitments' hit single from the movie, "Try a Little Tenderness," was a note-for-note copy of Redding's earlier version.

Sam and Dave

Sam Moore and Dave Pratter were a popular Miami act that Jerry Wexler brought to Stax in 1965. To prevent what had happened with Otis Redding, Wexler worked out an unusual deal. Sam and Dave signed with Atlantic but their recordings were issued on the Stax label. Later in 1967, when the two companies stopped working together, Wexler pulled Sam and Dave off Stax. While at Stax, they had great success with songs written by Dave Porter and Isaac Hayes, starting with "You Don't Know Like I Know" (1966), which reached number seven on the R&B charts. Later, in the same year, they crossed over to the pop charts with "Hold On! I'm Comin.'" Their biggest hit, "Soul Man" (1967), the number-two R&B record of the year, came in the year of the split, and when Sam and Dave returned to Atlantic, they never again attained the same level of success they had at Stax. "Soul Man" was revived over a decade later when it was performed in the 1979 movie *The Blues Brothers,* and since then has come to be regarded as one of the quintessential soul recordings of the 1960s.

Wilson Pickett

In 1965, Jerry Wexler brought Wilson Pickett, another Atlantic artist, to Memphis to record. In 1962, Pickett had some success with a Detroit group called the Falcons and as a solo singer for Lloyd Price's Double L label, but Atlantic could not find the right formula for him until Wexler brought him to record at the Stax studios. In Memphis, Wexler put him in a hotel room with Steve Cropper and a bottle of Jack Daniel's, and told them to "write."[13] One of the songs they wrote was "In the Midnight Hour. When recorded with the house band, it became the number-two R&B record of the year and since has become a bar-band standard.

A few months later, Pickett and Cropper wrote and recorded another hit, "634-5789," but by the end of 1965, relations between the two companies had become strained and their collaboration ended. The catalyst for the breakup was the personality of either Wilson Pickett or Don Covay, but tension between Atlantic and Stax had been building for some time because of the amount of time Atlantic spent recording at Stax's studio. Atlantic's producer/engineer, Tom Dowd, was in Memphis fifteen to twenty weekends a year, and Stewart felt that Atlantic was overworking his house band and, more importantly, stealing his sound. Atlantic was, in fact, stealing his sound. Atlantic was making the transition from its overproduced 1950s-style R&B recordings, as exemplified by the Drifters, to the funkier soul sound of the 1960s.

Aretha Franklin

When Jerry Wexler was no longer able to record at Stax Studios, he looked for a new place to get the Southern sound he was after. He found it in Muscle Shoals, Alabama, at Rick Hall's FAME Studios It was there that he recorded Wilson Pickett's next hits, such as "Land of 1,000 Dances," "Mustang Sally," and "Funky Broadway," as well as Percy Sledge's "When a Man Loves a Woman." While Wexler was in Muscle Shoals, he got a call from Aretha Franklin, a Columbia Records artist, saying that she was interested in recording for Atlantic.

Aretha grew up surrounded by gospel music. Her father, Rev. C. L. Franklin, was a nationally known gospel singer and leader of the 4,500-member congregation New Bethel Baptist Church in Detroit. As a teenager, she toured the gospel circuit with her father and sisters and first recorded at the age of fourteen. In 1960, she was signed to Columbia Records by the legendary John Hammond, who saw her as another Billie Holiday. Although he had some small success with her, he was not steering her career in the right direction. When she contacted Wexler in 1966, he thought the best thing for her would be to send her to Memphis to work at Stax. Wexler offered her to Stax in the same type of deal he had worked with Sam and Dave: Atlantic would sign her, but the recordings would be released on Stax. However, Stewart was not interested.[14] The next best thing was to take her to Muscle Shoals to record with the FAME rhythm section.

Aretha arrived at FAME studios in Muscle Shoals in 1967, with her husband/manager Ted White, and recorded "I Never Loved a Man (The Way I Love You)." There was a racially instigated problem with the all–European-American backup band, and Aretha left the next day, having finished only one song and part of another. A few weeks later, Aretha resurfaced and completed the recording in New York, and it became her first million-seller. Later Wexler recorded her with a band made up of musicians from Memphis, Muscle Shoals, and New York.

Her second release was a version of Otis Redding's "Respect" (1967), which eclipsed the original version. Aretha sang the song with such emotion and authority that most listeners have forgotten that Redding wrote and recorded the song first. Wexler's instincts about the type of sound Aretha needed were correct, and she became the most important female singer of the style. Franklin experienced continued success with Atlantic and the studio musicians they assembled for her. They produced some of the most memorable soul music of the period, such as "Baby, I Love You" (1967), "A Natural Woman" (1967), "Chain of Fools" (1967), "(Sweet Sweet Baby) Since You've Been Gone" (1968), "Think" (1968), "Eleanor Rigby" (1969), "Spirit in the Dark" (1970), "Bridge Over Troubled Water" (1971), and "Spanish Harlem" (1971). Aretha's style was the closest melding of rock and fervent gospel music since Ray Charles in the fifties. She improvised long melismas as naturally as breathing and set the standard by which future female soul singers would be judged.

The End of Stax

The sound of soul music aimed at the African-American community was dominated by Stax and Atlantic in the sixties, and Atlantic relied on the Stax sound for much of its success. The sound of the rhythm section (Booker T. and the MGs) along with the horn section (Mar-Kays) gave the recordings an individual sound that was truly distinctive. Their horn sound, a blend common in jazz's hard bop era (a blend of jazz, R&B, Gospel and Blues often featuring sax), gave the recordings a gritty, hard edge that was only available in clubs. The two companies existed in a delicate balance. Atlantic needed Stax's sound to get out of the New York studio rut it found itself in, and Stax needed Atlantic's money and distribution system. Stax's demise was most likely an outcome of the contract it had signed at the beginning, giving Atlantic ownership of everything recorded at Stax. However, without Atlantic it might never have developed beyond its initial Carla Thomas hit. In 1968, Gulf and Western bought Stax Records for $4.3 million and ran it as an independent subsidiary, but in 1970 it was repurchased by Jim Stewart and Al Bell. Stax continued to place recordings on the charts, including the number-one R&B recording of 1971, "Mr. Big Stuff" by Jean Knight, and the number-two, -three, and -four recordings of 1972; but there were other problems involving new faces in the company and white-collar crime. Stax began having legal problems in 1973, with a grand jury investigation into kickbacks and other malpractice. In 1975, there was an indictment for bank fraud and an IRS investigation. Stax finally gasped its last breath in 1976.

LISTENING TO THE MUSIC

♪♪ "My Girl"—performed by the Temptations

"My Girl" was composed backstage at Harlem's Apollo Theater by William "Smokey" Robinson and Ronald White of the Miracles during 1964. This fine example of the Motown soul sound features Berry Gordy's pop production values. "My Girl" reached number one on the pop and R&B charts in 1965, staying there for eleven weeks. It is considered a masterpiece of mid-sixties sweet soul music.

Analysis of "My Girl"—2:55 in length, recorded on Gordy (Motown) #7038

The form is a verse-chorus with an A section of two four-measure phrases and an eight-measure B section, called the chorus, which repeats unchanged, except for orchestration, throughout. The meter is "in 4." The Temptations: David Ruffin, lead vocal; Eddie Kendricks, vocal; Paul Williams, vocal; Otis Williams, vocal; and Melvin Franklin, bass vocal. The rhythm section includes Robert White on guitar with the Hitsville U.S.A. House Band.

0:00   Introduction (4 measures): The opening bass guitar riff, the heartbeat of "My Girl," is doubled by the bass drum and is quickly joined by the electric guitar counter-line, which holds this piece together. The finger snaps add just the right backbeat feel as the drums play a fill into the first verse.

0:09   A Section (8 measures): Opens with David Ruffin's wonderfully emotional voice delivering the first line of Robinson's lyrics, with its contrasting images: "I've got sunshine . . ." This section of the verse is accompanied by finger snap, staccato guitar backbeat, and the guitar counter-line. The background singers add a harmonized "Ooh."

0:28   B Section (8 measures): Begins "I guess . . . ," and builds through a thick, polished sound of vocals, horns, and violins to the vocal release of the title line, "My Girl," sung in masterful call-and-response fashion.

0:46   A Section (8 measures): Begins "I've got so . . . ," and speaks of the "birds" and the "bees," as this romance tune unfolds, now accompanied by rich string counter-melody with call-and-response answers, first from the trumpets, then the lower brass. As in the blues, the vocal line takes up the first two bars (8 foot taps), and the answer fills the third and fourth bars

1:05   B Section (8 measures): The chorus is repeated with a different orchestration, and this time the string counter-melody begins immediately.

1:23   Instrumental: After a repeat of the introductory bass riff played under a falsetto melismatic "hoo," the guitar counter-line enters with the strings, followed by an instrumental solo section featuring the string section with horns and band in the background. Vocal "hey, hey, hey" background harmonies help highlight this section. Use of strings, rather than saxophone or guitar, for the instrumental became a common Motown production technique. This section changes key toward the end (1:46).

1:51   A Section (eight measures): Begins "I don't need no . . . ," and the presence of the strings is stronger than in the earlier verses.

2:09   B Section (8 measures): Instruments and vocal backgrounds become more intricate and exciting. The saxophone now doubles the words "My girl."

2:21   Coda: A descending bass line at the end of this B section helps mark the closing section (coda) as Ruffin repeats the opening lines and the background singers enter falsetto range singing "Talking 'bout my girl."

For Musicians

Built on a standard four- and eight-bar pop format, "My Girl" opens with a classic two-bar bass riff, establishing the pulse of the song. The electric guitar riff in the following two bars is built on the notes C, D, E, G, A, C of a pentatonic scale, and returns throughout the song on both the I and IV chords and in both guitar and bass. The last eight bars of the verse move diatonically as the music cadentially approaches the tonic: I-ii-IV-V-I-ii-IV-V (in C). The title lyrics feature the tonic major-seventh chord, and the song progresses through the ii and V chords before the second verse. The interjecting "My Girl" vocal responses effectively lead to the vocal "My Girl" harmony break in the last bar of the phrase.

The second verse features string patterns turning to lines, with rhythmic horn fanfares in bars three and four, and seven and eight. This texture increases in thickness throughout the phrase. Next, an instrumental interlude begins with two bars of the intro music, then is repeated with the addition of gliding string chords. The next four bars feature the opening bass line "pulse," the electric guitar pentatonic line, horn background figures, a "pseudo-classical" string melody, and vocal "hey, hey, hey" interjections, all over the alternating I and IV chords. The next four bars are quite modulatory: ii—V—iii-V/ii into the key of D major. The iii chord in C also cross-functions as ii in the new key, so consequently the V/ii A major chord in C cross-functions as V in D, setting up the new tonality for verse three. The same combination of musical elements continues, with additional instrumental background fills and guitar riffs through the title line vocals. The descending riff is quite rhythmic, using a repeated eight-note pattern on the notes A, G, F#, E as a harmonic turnaround. As the vocalist frees up the rhythm of the lyrics, the song fades over a thickly textured repeat of the four-bar I-ii-V chord progression.

Final Comments

White and Robinson wrote "My Girl" in response to Smokey's prior hit, "My Guy," sung for Motown by Mary Wells. "My Girl" has often been covered, first by Otis Redding in 1966, and next as part of a 1968 medley recorded by Bobby Vee, which made the pop charts for four weeks. Another medley version of the song was recorded live by Daryl Hall, John Oates, David Ruffin, and Eddie Kendrick at the reopening of New York's Apollo Theater in 1985. The RCA recording of this version remained on the charts for over seven weeks. A 1988 Capitol recording of "My Girl," covered by Los Angeles male vocalist Suave, also reached the top forty, staying there for seven weeks as well. Most recently, a 1992 Macaulay Culkin film with the same name as the song included it as the title song.

♪♪ "Respect"—performed by Aretha Franklin

Although Memphis soul singer Otis Redding's original version of his song "Respect" made the top forty in 1965, it was Aretha Franklin's 1967 version of the song that was number one for two weeks and remained on the charts for eleven more weeks after that. This song was her biggest selling single. It also reached number one on the R&B charts and sold one million copies in ten months.

Analysis of "Respect"—2:20 in length, released on Atlantic 2403

The form of this recording is surprisingly simple: a ten-measure structure that can be divided into a six-measure A section, a four-measure B section that returns unchanged, and a stop-time C section. Aretha Franklin, vocal; with the Muscle Shoals Sound rhythm section and horns. Backup vocals by the Sweet Inspirations, featuring Aretha's sister Carolyn Franklin.

0:00 Introduction (4 measures): Opens with a somewhat country-sounding guitar riff over long-note chords by the saxophones.

0:08 A Section (6 measures): Begins "What you want..." over a syncopated bass line, strong tambourine and snare backbeat, and background vocal interjections of "oohs" on the first beat of each measure. The bass line uses syncopation by emphasizing the notes between foot taps on every other measure. If you count 1 + 2 + 3 + 4 +, the notes fall on the "+s."

0:21 B Section (4 measures): Begins "Respect when you..." and effectively uses the call-and-response technique with the response "just-a-little-bit." Over this response, Aretha improvises a few lyrics.

0:30 A Section (6 measures) Begins "I ain't gonna do ...," the background singers return in bar four, and Aretha winds her way through long phrases of lyrics set to gospel-derived blues notes in her unique, rough style. It is interesting to speculate why the background vocals do not enter until bar four. In the first verse, the "ooh" is very weak in the second bar, indicating that the singers were unsure if they should continue the pattern. It is possible that the background may have been improvised.

0:43 B Section (4 measures): This is a return of the previous B section.

0:50 A Section (6 measures): Begins "I'm about to ..." and is delivered in a more personal plea-style without the background singers.

1:03 B Section (4 measures): A variation which begins "When you get home...." The background enters with "just-a, just-a" lyrics, and two bars later returns to "just-a-little-bit" as in the previous B sections.

1:11 Sax Solo (8 measures): Changes keys briefly for a tenor saxophone solo over two-bar chords and the rhythm section.

1:27 A Section (6 measures): Begins "ooh your kisses ...," once again accompanied by the "oohs."

1:41 B Section (4 measures): Another variation beginning with "when you get home ...." The background is "re-re-re-re," and in two bars returns to "just-a-little-bit."

1:48 C Section (four measures): Aretha spells out the title word in a syncopated fashion: "R-e-s-p-e-c-t," and mentions a popular slang expression, "T-C-B," i.e., take care of business.

1:56 B Section (12+ measures): The remainder of the recording is a coda using the material from the B section and is a good example of how call-and-response works. While the saxophones riff, Aretha (call) is improvising lyrics while the background singers (response) are singing responses in four-bar sections. The first four-bar section begins with "sock it to me, sock it to me" (a very percussive use of the lyrics, another African characteristic) for two bars and then "just-a-little-bit" for two more. The second four-bar section continues with "just-a-little-bit." In the third four-bar section, they sing "re-re-re-re" for two bars and then return to "just-a-little-bit," and the recording fades out at the end of the third section. In a live performance, this type of call-and-response pattern could go on indefinitely.

For Musicians

A "loose" blues form in C major, "Respect" opens with an instrumental four-bar introduction alternating between the I and V chords and featuring sustained horns and riffing rhythm section, establishing the time feel. The first six bars of the verse alternate from V to IV under Aretha's gospel vocal, followed by four bars of I and IV alternating like the introduction. Verse two also follows this ten-bar pattern with additional background vocals and horns. Verse three features little vocal harmony, and leads to an abrupt, unprepared modulation at the instrumental bridge section. This eight-bar section progresses harmonically in this fashion: ii/iii-V/iii (played three times) to V for two bars, or F#m-B7 (played three times) to G7. This apparent move to the tritone is disguised by the parallel horn pads under the ad lib tenor, and the third relation between the B7 and the cadencing G7 makes a smooth transition back to C. Aretha really delivers her emotion-laden message in the last verse, with the vocal background in full response. The unique "hook" of this song occurs after this verse, with an instrumental stop-time isolating the spelled-out title lyrics. For four bars, beat one is hit, then the "and of four" and the downbeat of the next bar are accented between the solo vocal line. The tonic seventh chord alternates with the IV chord in a thick vamp of horns, lead and backup vocals, and rhythm section as the song fades.

---

[1] Raynoma Gordy, *Berry, Me, and Motown: The Untold Story* (Chicago: Contemporary, 1990), 49.

[2] Ibid., 72.

[3] Ibid., 73.

[4] Nelson George, *The Death of Rhythm and Blues* (New York: Penguin, 1988), 149.

[5] Gordy, 97.

[6] Ibid., 185.

[7] Phyl Garland, *The Sound of Soul* (Chicago: Henry Regnery, 1969), 123.

[8] Dorothy Wade and Justine Picardie, *Music Man: Ahmet Ertegun, Atlantic Records, and the Triumph of Rock n' Roll* (New York: Norton, 1990), 129.

[9] Jerry Wexler and David Ritz, *Rhythm and the Blues: A Life in American Music* (New York: Knopf, 1993), 169.

[10] Wade, 131.

[11] Stanley Booth, *Rhythm Oil: A Journey Through the Music of the American South* (London: Jonathan Cape, 1991), 119.

[12] Wexler, 194–95.

[13] Ibid., 175.

[14] Ibid., 204.

Chapter Nine

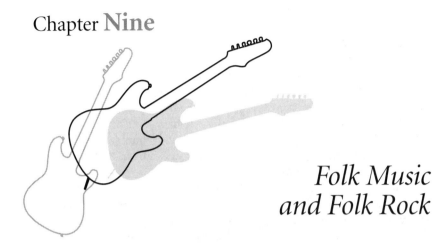

Folk Music
and Folk Rock

In the late 1950s through the 1960s, there was a trend toward acoustic music, sung by solo singers or small groups and known as *folk music*. The use of this term differs significantly from the way it is used by ethnomusicologists in describing the traditional music found in every nation. True folk songs are usually handed down from generation to generation, with each listener adding to or adapting it in some way, and, since the music is not written down, the original composer is unknown. The folk music of the 1950s and 60s began as this type but developed into a type of music that was written down, with a known composer, and concerning contemporary subjects.

The world of folk music is very broad, partly due to the many varying styles of different communities and partly due to the variety of subject matter. There are folk songs about work, family, drinking, patriotism, government, and topics appealing to children, etc. It is music sung by and for ordinary people about everyday occurrences, joys, and hardships. Before the 1920s, folk songs were usually passed down without the use of a recording or written music, much the way Americans learn songs like "Happy Birthday," "A Hundred Bottles of Beer on the Wall," and "Rock a Bye, Baby"—these songs are part of the culture. Although these are not folk songs, their method of transmission is similar to that of folk music.

The development of folk music in North America began immediately after Europeans and Africans began settling the continent. Native Americans had folk songs, but their effects were negligible to the developments chronicled here because the melodic structure and language were so different from the music brought to America by Europeans. Most early American folk songs were derived from songs brought over by English, Scottish, or Irish immigrants, and the lyrics were gradually adapted to fit contemporary American events. Immigrants who settled in rural areas, especially the Blue Ridge and

Appalachian Mountains, were isolated from the rapid style changes of the cities, and so the melodies of these early songs were preserved intact. When electricity, followed by radio and the phonograph, was introduced into rural areas, those old songs began to be influenced by commercial music and professional musicians. The British folk songs preserved in these mountain regions became the foundation for the music known as *hillbilly* music in the 1920s and, later *country and western*. Early hillbilly (country) music singers were, therefore, the original American folk singers with an impact on future musical development in this country.

African-American music, because of its close Southern and rural geographic proximity, influenced folk and country music, especially with the characteristics of call-and-response, syncopation, and blues notes. Although blues is not generally thought of as country music, it was probably the first folk genre developed in America and, as such, was part of the repertoire of Greenwich Village folk singers. African-American country music and Anglo-American folk music of the nineteenth century have at least two common elements: the instrumentation and vocal range. The instrumentation was typically guitar, banjo, harmonica, and fiddle (a string band), and the vocal range was narrow to accommodate untrained voices.

Folk music serves as an important outlet for social commentary and protest; in the mid- nineteenth century, the Huchinson Family Quartet sang about the dangers of alcohol, the abolition of slavery, and women's rights. At the beginning of the twentieth century, union organizers from the International Workers of the World (IWW), known as the Wobblies, used songs published in their *Little Red Songbook* (1909) to spread their message. In the 1930s and 1940s, folk singers like Woody Guthrie and Pete Seeger continued this organizing tradition by singing at union meetings and rallies, and in the 1960s, Joan Baez and Peter, Paul, and Mary used folk songs at civil rights marches and anti-war demonstrations.

Music called "folk music" has appeared on popular music charts at various times, often in the form of polished songs, either based on real folk music or fabricated to sound folk-like. The success of the quasi-folk music may have influenced the industry to record more folk-like songs and, furthermore, may have sensitized audiences to the sound of simple music. In 1949, "Riders in the Sky" by Vaughn Monroe and "Mule Train" by Frankie Laine reached the popular music charts and, although they may have been based on folk songs, they were presented in a polished professional music industry format.

During the next two years, a real folk group, the Weavers, had great popular success with "Goodnight Irene," "Tzena, Tzena, Tzena," and "On Top of Old Smokey." Their first two recordings were released under the name Gordon Jenkins and the Weavers, and the last recordings were released under the Weavers alone. Gordon Jenkins was a record company executive who added himself to the songs for business purposes and claimed writer's credit for "Tzena, Tzena, Tzena," as well as "Silent Night," "Adeste Fideles," and the "Allegro" movement from Mozart's *Eine Kleine Nachtmusik*. How could he do it? This was public domain music, and performance royalties are paid to the arranger of public domain music. Some writers have speculated that this 1950s appearance of public domain folk music on the charts was intended to start a trend of royalty-free music. This early folk music did not develop into a trend at that time, possibly because of the Weavers' connection to the labor movement and its ties to the Communist Party.

Woody Guthrie

Woody Guthrie (Woodrow Wilson Guthrie) was probably the most influential folk singer of the period leading up to the folk music of the sixties. While most folk singers of his period tended toward the academic pursuit and preservation of ancient ballads, Guthrie's life was the model for the "freight train-hopping, hobo-troubadour with a guitar on his back" folk singer image of the 1950s and 1960s. Many of Guthrie's songs were political and commented on the struggles of the common man and the need for people to join together to fight exploitation. In the 1930s, union organization was a prominent cause among radical intellectuals, and in the 1960s the cause became the civil rights and anti-war movements. Nevertheless, the music's function was to raise individual consciousness and sway public opinion.

Woody Guthrie was born in Okemah, Oklahoma, and after a series of financial setbacks, his family moved to Pampa, Texas, where his musical experience began with a Western band called the Corncob Trio. In 1937, after dust storms had devastated the financial climate in the region, Guthrie left Texas to look for work and became part of the Dust Bowl migration to California. When he arrived in California, he found that it was not the "promised land" everyone thought it was, and that the only jobs most immigrants could find were as agricultural workers who often were exploited by the large growers.

Songs like "The Great Dust Storm," "Do Re Mi," and "Talking Dust Bowl Blues" are a few of his many "Dust Bowl ballads" about the plight of those searching for a better way of life. Guthrie developed a particularly interesting style of half speaking and half singing over a guitar accompaniment. That became known as the "talking blues style." Guthrie used this style in songs like "Talking Dust Bowl Blues," and it was adopted by the next two generations of folk singers, such as Pete Seeger, Phil Ochs, and Bob Dylan.

When Guthrie arrived in California in 1937[1] and talked his way into a radio show on KFVD, he received no salary but sold mimeographed copies of his songs to listeners.[2] Although Guthrie sang on the radio in the 1930s, his first recordings were not made until 1940, when Alan Lomax recorded him for the Library of Congress. Guthrie is said to have written over one thousand songs, including "This Land Is Your Land," "Do Re Mi," "Billy the Kid," "Pretty Boy Floyd," "Roll On Columbia," "So Long It's Been Good to Know You," and "Tom Joad." Most Americans know "This Land Is Your Land," but usually the sanitized version. The original version was more radical, and ironically, included verses considered too unpatriotic for publication.[3]

The 1930s was a time of great social unrest in the United States. The Great Depression had widened the gap between the rich and poor, and working people needed the representation of unions to protect their interests. During the same period, the Communist Party was organizing workers to combat the same social problems that Guthrie sang about. Because both were working on the same side of the cause, Guthrie accepted invitations to sing at workers' rallies and, in so doing, became associated with the American Communist Party. Guthrie never officially joined the ACP as he refused to denounce his religion as they requested. When asked about his politics, Woody often said, "Some people say I'm a Communist. That ain't necessarily so, but it is true that I've always been in the red."[4]

After he moved to New York in 1939, he continued his labor organizing with members of the East Coast folk community such as Pete Seeger and Lee Hays, both members of the Almanac Singers. Guthrie often wrote songs to suit a particular problem or event. For example, while he and Seeger were singing at a union meeting in Oklahoma City, feminist Communist organizer Ina Wood criticized them for their lack of women's songs. That night, Guthrie wrote what became one of his best known union songs, "Union Maid," about how a woman should not be a "servant of the male elite" and should stand on "her own two feet."

Woody continued traveling and singing for union organizers and eventually ended up back in California where he joined a project to write music for a film documenting the construction of the Grand Coulee Dam. "Roll On Columbia" is from this period. After he returned to New York, he resumed singing with Seeger and the Almanac Singers.

In October 1947, the House Committee on Un-American Activities opened its hearings into Communist influence in the movie industry and promptly denounced nineteen prominent "leftist" directors, producers, and screenwriters as enemies of the state. Soon they searched for Communists everywhere. Many performers were publicly accused of being Communists or Communist sympathizers, and an informal list, known as the blacklist, began to be used to identify suspicious persons. Once someone was accused of having "left-wing" associations, employers stopped hiring them for jobs in the industry. Actors like Will Geer and Zero Mostel were among those blacklisted, and folk singers like Woody Guthrie, Pete Seeger, and members of the Almanac Singers were easy targets for Communist-hunters.

During the 1950s, Guthrie began exhibiting signs of Huntington's chorea, a genetic nervous system disease that had killed his mother, and he was hospitalized. By 1954, he needed constant care, so he checked himself into the Brooklyn State Hospital, and in 1959, he was transferred to the Greystone Hospital in New Jersey. In the early 1960s, Bob Gleason, a fan of Guthrie's since the 1930s, began bringing Guthrie to his apartment for weekend visits and played host to Greenwich Village folk singers who came to pay tribute to Woody.[5] Among those folk singers was young Bob Dylan, who spent much of his early career emulating Woody's musical style, dress, posture, and even his Okie accent.

Pete Seeger

Pete Seeger, one of the father figures of the Greenwich Village folk scene, had a unique music education: His father, Charles Seeger, was one of America's foremost ethnomusicologists, and his mother, Ruth Crawford- Seeger, was a composer and violinist. Working with musicologist Alan Lomax, and later with Woody Guthrie, Seeger became a repository of American folk music and one of its earliest popular successes. In the 1940s, Seeger led a group called the Almanac Singers, who were heavily involved with social causes, including union organizing. Their Almanac House on West 10th Street in New York City became a gathering place for left-wing Bohemian poets, musicians, and intellectuals.[6] His "Talking Union Blues" was patterned after Guthrie's talking blues style and was used at union rallies during the 1940 Ford Motor Company strike. One of Seeger's most famous songs, "If I Had a Hammer," was originally intended as a union song; however, its lyrics were easily reinterpreted to fit the message of the civil rights movement.

At some point in the late 1940s, the Almanac Singers evolved into the Weavers, who, in the early 1950s, reached the popular music charts with several innocent top ten folk songs: "Goodnight Irene," "Tzena, Tzena, Tzena," and "On Top of Old Smokey." Soon after that success, however, they found it difficult to book performances because they were blacklisted for their labor-organizing activities.

In 1950, *Red Channels: The Report of Communist Influence in Radio and Television* was published. It identified over 130 writers, composers, and performers who were allegedly pro-Soviet. The publication served as an entertainment industry blacklist, and those identified had problems finding work. Seeger was identified as the National Chairman of People's Songs; as a song leader for the Henry Wallace Presidential Campaign, the American Committee for Yugoslavian Relief, the Committee for a Democratic Far Eastern Policy,

Voice of Freedom Committee, and the American Youth for Democracy; and as an instructor at the Jefferson School of Social Science, School for Political Action Technique.[7] Though some of these organizations were considered subversive by government Communist-hunters, these groups were more Socialist than Communist, and Seeger's participation varied from leadership positions to simple concert and promotional appearances.

Seeger's songs were an important part of the 1960 folk repertoire and include "Turn, Turn, Turn," "Bells of Rhymney," "Guantanamera," "Kisses Sweeter Than Wine," "Where Have All the Flowers Gone?" "If I Had a Hammer," and "We Shall Overcome." In the 1990s, Seeger remained politically active and focused his energies on a campaign to clean up the Hudson River. Pete Seeger still performs occasionally in public, and had a 2006 appearance at the MerleFest Folk and Bluegrass Festival in Wilkesboro, NC. In March of 2007, the 88-year old Pete Seeger performed with his brother Mike and sister Peggy and several other Seeger family members at the Library of Congress in Washington, D.C.

FOLK REVIVAL
Phase One: Pre-Folk
In the mid-fifties, folk music began a revival at about the same time R&B crossed over to the pop charts. By 1957, folk music, viewed as the "good music" alternative to rock and roll, was the favorite of college students, as opposed to rock and roll, which was viewed as suitable only for juvenile delinquents.

It is difficult to pinpoint the beginning of, or the reason for, the folk revival in the mid-fifties, but two possible sources might be the *Sing Along With Mitch* series and *calypso* recordings. In 1955, Mitch Miller, foe of rock and roll and the A&R director of Columbia Records, began a series of choral recordings, generically known as "Sing Along With Mitch," which were "community sing-a-long good-time" songs, similar to the Weavers' earlier hits but without the "left-wing" affiliation. Miller had the number three recording of 1955, "Yellow Rose of Texas," which was a folk-like song sung in an acoustic style. Also in 1955, the Walt Disney movie *Davy Crockett* was so popular that its title song, "Ballad of Davy Crockett," had two versions on the year-end charts: Bill Hayes's version at number six and Fess Parker's (the star of *Davy Crockett*) at number twenty-two. All three recordings had a folk quality very much like "On Top of Old Smokey" and possibly exposed a market for folk-like material, which other artists exploited.

In 1956, three folk-like recordings appeared on the charts, "Rock Island Line" (Lonnie Donegan), "Cindy Oh Cindy" (Vince Martin and the Tarriers), and "Mary's Boy Child" (Harry Belafonte). Donegan's recording is interesting because it made him the father of the English *skiffle* movement. In England, skiffle bands performed acoustic American folk songs, both African-American and European-American, and inspired many British teens to form bands of their own; among them were the Quarrymen led by John Lennon. It is possible that "The Rock Island Line" encouraged other folk-like recordings; however, the only other skiffle-inspired recording to reach America was Laurie London's "He's Got the Whole World in His Hands" (1958).

In the same year, Harry Belafonte's recording of "Mary's Boy Child" started a short-lived trend in calypso music. Calypso was a rhythmic acoustic folk music from the Caribbean island of Jamaica. Belafonte's success inspired three more calypso recordings the following year, "Banana Boat Song (Day-O)," "Marianne," and "Mama Look-A-Booboo." The calypso trend never developed into a full-blown craze, but it exposed teens to simple music that was playable by anyone who could sing and knew a few guitar chords.

On the surface, the connection between the calypso music and the folk revival seem unrelated. However, the basic aesthetic of those recordings reveals that they had qualities similar to those of later folk music, and they primed audiences for that type of acoustic sound. The first generally accepted recording of the folk revival was by the Kingston Trio. The Kingston Trio was not a calypso band, but they were somewhat influenced by those recordings, naming themselves after the capital of the island of Jamaica, the home of calypso music.

Phase Two: Good Clean Pop
Kingston Trio

The Kingston Trio (Bob Shane, Nick Reynolds, and Dave Guard), the first successful folk group of the late-fifties, formed in 1957 and performed around San Francisco. They dressed in matching striped shirts, had crewcut hairstyles, sang in a pleasant vocal harmony with clearly enunciated lyrics without a trace of "Womp-bomp-a-loo-bomp," and appealed more to college-age students than to high school students. In 1958, they reached number one with "Tom Dooley"—an old ballad about Tom Dula, a convicted murderer who was sentenced to die by hanging in 1866—which was first recorded by G. B. Grayson in the 1920s.[8] Serious stuff, to be sure, but the airy arrangement, bouncy vocal harmony, and light guitar accompaniment made it seem like good fun.

In 1959, they recorded a light-hearted protest song, "M.T.A.," about a five-cent rate hike by the Metropolitan Transit Authority in Boston, which told the tale of an unwitting passenger who boarded the train with the usual fare, but did not realize he needed another nickel to get off. Although this was technically a protest song, it did not have the feel; in fact, it had the sound of a novelty recording such as the Playmates' "Beep Beep." In the same year, they released a more serious song, "A Worried Man," with serious lyrics such as, "It takes a worried man to sing a worried song." However, the way these lyrics were delivered did not give the impression that they were worried but rather that they were having a songfest around a campfire.

Hootenanny

The Almanac Singers picked up the term *hootenanny* in the Pacific Northwest, where it described a union meeting sing-a-long, and brought it to New York where it came to refer to a gathering of folk singers. To the mainstream audience, hootenanny groups were large folk ensembles of around ten members, such as the New Christy Minstrels ("Green Green," 1963), the Rooftop Singers ("Walk Right In," 1963), and the Serendipity Singers ("Don't Let the Rain Come Down," 1964).

Hootenanny groups were the epitome of the sitting-around-the-campfire type of singing—they were "good clean" kids having "good clean fun." During the summer of 1963, the ABC network aired a show called "Hootenanny," which attempted to be the *American Bandstand* of folk music. However, they ran into trouble when their version of folk music encountered real social-protest folk music. The network refused to book Pete Seeger unless he signed a loyalty oath (his old Communist problem resurfacing) and, because he was the living spiritual father of the folk movement, performers like Joan Baez, Peter, Paul, and Mary, and Bob Dylan thereafter refused to appear on the show.

The New Christy Minstrels, formed in 1961, survived the longest of the hootenanny groups and provided a valuable training ground for future singers. Although the group was named after the Christy Minstrels, a famous minstrel show that helped popularize the songs of Stephen Foster, they had nothing to do with minstrel music. The group had significant, albeit subtle, influence on future music trends: Kenny Rogers had a major role in combining country and rock in the 1970s; John Denver was very successful as a solo artist, although by the time he surfaced as a solo act, the term folk singer was outdated and he was referred to as a "singer/songwriter"; Gene Clark and the Byrds had the most immediate influence by merging folk with rock; and Barry McGuire helped launch the Mamas and the Papas. Barry McGuire reached the top ten in 1965 with a protest song called "Eve of Destruction," which was so blatantly prefabricated that no true folkie took it seriously. Nevertheless, he used the Mamas and the Papas during one of his recording sessions and helped launch their career.

Phase Three: Folk Turns Serious

During the 1950 and 60s, New York's Greenwich Village was the home of serious folk music. The folk scene was divided along two lines, high folk and low folk. High folk artists were dedicated to preserving old folk songs as they were first collected; low folk artists sang a variety of songs, including their own, that were intended to entertain their audience. High folk was represented by the performances of Pete Seeger, Theodore Bikel, Josh White, and Odetta, while low folk was exemplified by the Kingston Trio, Peter, Paul and Mary, and the electric Bob Dylan.

The songs of the union activists were an important part of the folk repertoire, and folk singers generally believed that folk songs should address society's ills and protest injustice. The new generation of folk singers continued the Guthrie-Seeger tradition of music as social protest and using that style for 1960s causes. The decade was a time of increasing activity in the civil rights movement, culminating in a march to Washington in August 1963. At the same time, Americans were beginning to notice the increasing body count in the Vietnam War. The assassination of President Kennedy on November 22, 1963, changed the political and social climate in the United States, and the complacency of the fifties instantly disappeared. The younger generation realized that not all was right with the world and made a concerted effort to make a change; the call for change first came in the music of folk singers.

This generation of folk singers probably did not start out intending to be "protest singers," but that role gradually grew on them as they discovered the problems of the world. Some sang songs with poetic messages that could be applied to the civil rights or anti-war movement, and some wrote songs directed at particular problems, such as Phil Ochs's "Draft Dodger Rag" and Country Joe and the Fish's biting satire, "Feel-Like-I'm-Fixin'-to-Die Rag."

Peter, Paul, and Mary

In 1961, Chicago folk club owner, Albert Grossman (later Bob Dylan's manager) organized a group to take advantage of the growing number of folk venues around the country.[9] The members came from diverse backgrounds. Peter Yarrow was a folk singer, Paul Stookey was a stand-up comic and singer in a rock band, and Mary Travers was an off-Broadway singer who sang a little folk material as well. They debuted at the Bitter End, a New York coffeehouse, after rehearsing for several months with arranger Milt Okum. The trio became known for their intelligent, topical songs and their clean vocal arrangements. Peter, Paul, and Mary were visible members of the sixties counterculture, participated in the civil rights march on Washington—the same event that produced Martin Luther King's inspiring "I Have a Dream" speech—and were without doubt the most successful folk group of the decade.

In addition to their success as a folk trio, their physical appearance set the direction of future styles. At the time they became popular, hair styles for women were the beehive and bouffant style, which required dedicated preparation, and men adhered to a closely cropped, clean-shaven look. Mary's long, straight, blond hair was meant to convey a plain disregard of fashion. Many teenage girls unfortunately born with curly hair spent hours straightening it in an effort to mimic her hair style. Peter and Paul sported a look that was associated with the intellectuals of the beat generation. Both singers wore a neat little chin beard called a goatee, which began a trend toward facial hair that endures today.

Their first recording, "Lemon Tree" (1962), reached number thirty-five, and their first top-ten hit was Pete Seeger's old union song, which now was used as a civil rights song: "If I Had a Hammer" (1962). During the next year, they gave Bob Dylan a boost in popularity by recording his "Blowin' in the Wind" (1963), the number seventeen song of the year, and "Don't Think Twice It's All Right" (1963).

On the lighter side, they recorded a children's song called "Puff the Magic Dragon" (1963), which later was interpreted as a drug song by social censors. "Puff the magic drag-on" was interpreted as "smoke the magic joint." The phrase "Little Jackie Paper loved that rascal puff . . . sealing wax and other fancy stuff," furthered the impression. "Jackie Paper" was taken to refer to cigarette papers and "sealing wax" as the glue. Many songs of this period were filled with drug references, but some identified by censors often had nothing to do with the subject.

Peter, Paul, and Mary recorded twelve top-forty songs during the sixties, ending with John Denver's "Leaving on a Jet Plane" (1970), which became their only number one recording. They had signaled the end of the acoustic folk era years earlier when they recorded "I Dig Rock and Roll Music" (1967), a title that would have been unthinkable five years earlier except as a novelty-folk song. Today, Peter, Paul, and Mary have a solid reputation as acoustic folk singers, and their "reunion" concerts have been broadcast on public television.

Joan Baez

Joan Baez was the first important solo folk singer of the period, and her image embodied the folk movement. She was sincere, authentic, and traditional; her physical appearance captured the folk ideal; she became deeply committed to social causes; and she was a talented singer and guitarist. Baez attended Boston University and performed regularly at Cambridge's Club 47. She received national attention when Bob Gibson, a Chicago folk singer, invited her onstage to sing "Virgin Mary" and "We Are Crossing Jordan River" with him at the first Newport Folk Festival in 1959.[10]

Baez's early albums included traditional folk music, African-American folk songs, Carter Family favorites, and Woody Guthrie songs. In the early sixties, she was known for her version of Pete Seeger's "We Shall Overcome," which she sang at the 1963 march on Washington and effectively turned into a civil rights anthem. The song was developed by Seeger and Zilphia Horton of the Highlander Folk School and was introduced into the civil rights movement by Guy Carawan during a workshop at the school.[11] Baez was instrumental in exposing Bob Dylan and his songs, thereby helping him attain credibility within the folk community. Baez and Dylan were romantically involved for a while and were often referred to as the king and queen of folk music. In 1965, Baez began the Institute for the Study of Non-Violence in Carmel, California, which was heavily involved in protesting the Vietnam War. In 1969, she performed at Woodstock and, soon after, received anti-war publicity when her husband, student activist David Harris, was jailed for refusing to subject himself to the draft. Baez did not reach the top ten until 1971, when she recorded a pop-ish version of "The Night They Drove Old Dixie Down." After a brief flirtation with pop music, she returned to her previous mix of authentic folk and protest songs.

Bob Dylan

Of all the folk singers, Bob Dylan has proved to be the most enigmatic yet influential songwriter of the decade, possibly in all of rock history. His songs were responsible for the combining of folk and rock, and they inspired other songwriters, such as John Lennon and Paul McCartney, to write lyrics that were poetic and obscure. Dylan was not a skillful guitarist or harmonica player, and his singing style was not like that of any folk singer of the period. Yet, by the end

Joan Baez and Bob Dylan

of the 1960s, he had assumed the status of a rock icon. Today, his reputation remains substantial enough to endure embarrassing performances like those on the Grammy Awards (1991) and *The David Letterman Show* (1994).

Born Robert Zimmerman, Bob Dylan came to New York from a middle-class home in Hibbing, Minnesota. While in high school, he discovered R&B via the "No Name Jive" program hosted by Frank "Gatemouth" Page on station KWKH in Shreveport, Louisiana.[12] At around this time, he organized a rock band called the Golden Chords. When he entered the University of Minnesota in 1959 and discovered that college students respected folk music more than rock, he began performing in that style at coffeehouses in the Dinky-town section of Minneapolis. Dylan moved to New York City in late January 1961, and immediately went to Greenwich Village and worked his way into the folk community. While in Minnesota, Dylan had been in awe of Woody Guthrie and did his best to emulate him, including adopting an Okie accent and even fabricating stories of his hobo travels. One of the reasons he went to New York was to visit Guthrie, so at the first opportunity, he traveled to Woody's New Jersey hospital and often visited him at Bob Gleason's apartment.[13]

During this early period, Dylan performed for tips at various Greenwich Village coffeehouses, such as the Gaslight, Bitter End, and especially Gerde's Folk City. In fact, his only paying engagements in the Village were at Gerde's where he opened for John Lee Hooker and, on another occasion, for the Greenbriar Boys. Other Greenwich Village singers, like Joan Baez and Carolyn Hester, began performing Dylan's songs and often invited him onstage to sing a few songs, which helped introduce him to a wider audience. Success happened quickly for Dylan. Robert Shelton gave him a great review in the *New York Times* (September 29, 1961), saying "A bright new face in folk music is appearing at Gerde's Folk City . . . there is no doubt that he is bursting at the seams with talent."[14] Carolyn Hester had him play harmonica on her first album for Columbia Records (September 30, 1969). He played harmonica on a Victoria Spivey and Big Joe Williams session (*Three Kings and a Queen*, October 21, 1961). Finally, John Hammond arranged for a contract with Columbia Records in November 1961.

His first album for Columbia, *Bob Dylan* (1962), was not commercially successful but introduced two original songs: "Song to Woody" and "Talkin' New York." "Talkin' New York" is an autobiographical account of Dylan's first days in New York delivered in Guthrie's talking-blues style. It includes an account of the coffeehouse criticism he evidently received for his fake Okie accent, in which people tell him he sounds like a "hillbilly." The first album also includes "Baby, Let Me Carry You Down" and Dave Van Ronk's version of "House of the Rising Sun." It is interesting to note that the Animals, a British Invasion group, chose these two songs for their first recordings.

Dylan's second album, *Freewheelin' Bob Dylan* (1963), included "Blowin' in the Wind," which made a favorable impression on the Village folk community and was a huge hit for Peter, Paul, and Mary. It is a remarkably subtle song that is soothing for the listener. It has a great hook; however, the audience had to listen to and understand the lyrics to perceive the song's civil rights and anti-war stance. The song might not have been as popular as it was had the mainstream audience understood Dylan's controversial message that the country needed to respond to these injustices.

As Dylan became more visible to the pop audience, he was invited to appear on *The Ed Sullivan Show*, but he walked off the show when CBS lawyers refused to allow him to sing "Talkin' John Birch Society Blues." His 1964 album, *The Times They Are A-Changin'*, established him as a major folk songwriter and featured social commentary in songs such as "The Times They Are A-Changin'," "With God on Our Side," "Only a Pawn in Their Game," "The Lonesome Death of Hattie Carroll," and "Ballad of Hollis Brown." "Only a Pawn in Their Game" is a powerful song immortalizing assassinated NAACP leader Medgar Evers and accurately pointing a finger at the "race-card" tactics so often used by politicians. It portrays poor European-American Southerners as victims of the system.

"The Times They Are A Changin'" is also a remarkable song in that it called for a change from the status quo and adequately expresses the feelings of the sixties generation. The sixties did bring change, some good and some bad; however, the most positive change was forcing all Americans to rethink their attitudes about race, the war in Vietnam, and the damage both were doing to the nation's psyche. Musicians, first folk and then later rock, played an important role in bringing about this social awareness. In the song, Dylan asks politicians to wake up and respond to the plea for change.

At some point, Dylan distanced himself from folk purists and even stated in interviews that he was not a protest songwriter. During 1965, he released *Bringing It All Back Home*, an album that featured traditional folk instrumentation on one half and an electric, rock-oriented band on the other. At this point in his career, Dylan's use of amplified instruments was drawing criticism. Furthermore, after he became heavily involved with drugs, especially LSD, his lyrics took a turn toward the obscure.[15] This is especially noticeable in his first charted single, the electric "Subterranean Homesick Blues" (1965). Lyrically, the song was a collection of vague images that needed to be interpreted by the listener. Also on the album was an acoustic version of "Mr. Tambourine Man," which was subsequently recorded by the Byrds. These two Dylan songs mark the beginning of *folk rock*.

The folk world was badly shaken at Newport Folk Festival on July 25, 1965, because that was the day electricity reached folk music. During the evening show, Dylan used an amplified band to accompany him in a rock version of "Maggie's Farm" and was booed off the stage after three selections. Peter Yarrow (of Peter, Paul and Mary) talked him into going back and doing an acoustic set. Dylan went back and played "Mr. Tambourine Man" and "It's All Over Now Baby Blue," signaling his intent to depart from the acoustic folk scene. The yells from the audience apparently began in the press section but were only a call to readjust the balance of the instruments so they could hear Dylan. The audience further back, however, mistook the yells for negative criticism and joined in with boos. The resulting pandemonium was interpreted as the audience's rejection of Dylan's use of amplified instruments.

The following month (August 27, 1965), he performed at a concert at the Forest Hills Tennis Stadium, in Queens, New York. This time he opened with an acoustic set but followed it with an electric. As soon as the group began the electric set, the yelling started with shouts of, "We want the old Dylan," but Dylan stood his ground and finished the set with his new recording, "Like a Rolling Stone."[16] The audience at his Carnegie Hall concert the following month knew what to expect, and he was warmly received by his new non-folk audience.

Dylan's 1965 album, *Highway 61 Revisited*, included his first popular music hit, "Like a Rolling Stone," which reached number two on the pop charts. The song was unique in several respects. First, it was one of the longest recordings of its time to get radio play (5:59). Typically, singles were no longer than three minutes long so radio stations could surround them with enough commercials to pay the bills. Second, its lyrics were wonderfully obscure and, for the first time, made the pop audience really listen to figure out what the song was about—knowledge of these lyrics was a 1965 "hipness" test.

Dylan's next album, *Blonde on Blonde* (1966), was recorded in Nashville using country-music studio musicians. The sessions were sparsely rehearsed and extremely loose, to the extent that the musicians had to watch Dylan's fingers to determine the chord changes. On "Rainy Day Women #12 and 35," the musicians switched instruments with each other to intentionally sound bad; the musicians thought it was all a joke, but instead the recording became Dylan's second million-selling single. By this time Dylan had sold over ten million records worldwide, and his songs had been covered by over one hundred other artists.

On July 29, 1966, Dylan suffered injuries from a motorcycle accident near his home in Woodstock, New York, and spent almost eighteen months recuperating. Recordings emerged from this period featuring new songs by Dylan and the Band, which were widely bootlegged until Dylan released them himself under the title of the *Basement Tapes* (1975). When he reemerged after the accident, he went to Nashville to record *John Wesley Harding* (1968), which marked a new Dylan phase by moving a little closer to *country rock*.

John Wesley Harding resembled his earlier work: gone were the "surrealism and drug imagery" which had been replaced by "a belief in God, with self-discovery and compassion."[17]

The Byrds' country rock album, *Sweetheart of the Rodeo*, was released in 1968, and there may have been some mutual influence encouraging the move further toward country rock. *Nashville Skyline* (1969) completed Dylan's move toward country and featured artists like Johnny Cash, a more mellow vocal style, and a radio hit, "Lay Lady Lay." At this point in his career Dylan was losing his pop support because country music was "unhip." In retrospect, Dylan had succeeded in returning folk music to its country music roots.

In 1970, Dylan entered a period of unsuccessful contract renegotiation, and Columbia Records hurriedly released several albums designed to discourage other labels from signing him. The first was *Self-Portrait*, which contained remakes of songs by the Everly Brothers ("Let It Be Me"), Paul Simon ("The Boxer"), Gordon Lightfoot ("Early Morning Rain"), and Rodgers and Hart ("Blue Moon"). The second, *New Morning*, was made up of studio scraps. The third was his *Greatest Hits Vol 2*. Although Dylan eventually returned to Columbia, he signed with Asylum; his first album for them was *Planet Waves* (1974).

In 1971, Dylan performed at George Harrison's Concert for Bangladesh, but he did not resume touring until 1974, when Phil Ochs persuaded Dylan to perform at a benefit for the people of Chile. The hootenanny nature of the performance made such an impression on Dylan that he organized a touring version known as the Rolling Thunder Revue (1975–76), which included Joan Baez, Ramblin' Jack Elliott, Arlo Guthrie, Phil Ochs, Joni Mitchell, Allen Ginsberg, and the Byrds' Roger McGuinn. The tour was a quest to relive the fun days of Greenwich Village in the early sixties when everyone was filled with the spirit of camaraderie, traded songs, and performed for each other.

In 1979, Dylan shifted both his musical and religious interests to Christianity with the album *Slow Train Coming*, and toured with born-again material, which confused many of his fans. Despite this, his recording "Gotta Serve Somebody" (1979) was a hit and earned Dylan his first Grammy award. Tours through the early 1980s saw Dylan moving away from his religious phase, and his 1983 release *Infidels* proved to be his best-selling album of the previous four years. In 1988, Dylan was a member of the Traveling Wilburys, which included Tom Petty, George Harrison, Jeff Lynne, and Roy Orbison, and in 1989 he was inducted into the Rock and Roll Hall of Fame. Dylan's songwriting skills have earned him a place in rock history. However, his recordings and performances had suffered from a lack of attention and rehearsal, which sometimes conveys the impression that he does not care and has taken his loyal audience for granted.

FOLK ROCK

California Sound

The *folk rock* style generally begins with the Byrds, but includes such diverse groups that any one definition seems impossible. The list includes the Turtles; Barry McGuire; the Mamas and the Papas; Sonny and Cher; the Lovin' Spoonful; the Stone Ponies (Linda Ronstadt); Simon and Garfunkel; Donovan; Buffalo Springfield; Spanky and Our Gang; Country Joe and the Fish; Jose Feliciano; Glen Campbell; Kenny Rogers and the First Edition; Crosby, Stills & Nash; Poco; the Flying Burrito Brothers; the Eagles; Pure Prairie League; Jefferson Airplane; the Grateful Dead; the Fugs; the Holy Modal Rounders; the Jim Kweskin Jug Band; the Nitty Gritty Dirt Band; and Jackson Browne. Some of these performers, such as the Jefferson Airplane and

Lovin' Spoonful

Grateful Dead, seemingly have nothing to do with folk music, but their roots are firmly planted in the San Francisco folk scene.

The Byrds

In the summer of 1964, singer and guitarist Jim (later renamed Roger) McGuinn, a former accompanist for the Limeliters and Chad Mitchell Trio, was working as a single at the Troubadour in Los Angeles, where he met Gene Clark, who had just left the New Christy Minstrels. Clark liked the combination of folk and rock that McGuinn was performing, and they decided to work together. Soon afterward, David Crosby, a member of Les Baxter's Balladeers, joined them and the nucleus of the Byrds was in place. Crosby had a friend, Jim Dickinson at World Pacific Studios, who let them use the studio after hours without charge. Dickinson became their manager and got them a contract with Electra Records. Recording under the name the Beefeaters, they released "Please Let Me Love You." The record was not successful, and when Dickinson suggested that adding a drummer and a bass player might help, they asked Chris Hillman and Mike Clarke to join. Chris Hillman was a bluegrass mandolinist, so playing the bass was not a big switch. Clarke, although a good conga drummer, did not even own a drum set and at rehearsals played along on cardboard boxes.

Although the Byrds had strong folk roots, they were operating more under the influence of the Beatles when they organized their group. The Byrds modeled

The Byrds

their instrumental setup based on what they had seen the Beatles play in *A Hard Day's Night* and even costumed themselves after the Beatles; later they were billed as "America's Answer to the Beatles." The new Byrds signed a one-record contract with Columbia, and Dickinson made them record Dylan's "Mr. Tambourine Man."[18] Initially the Byrds did not like Dylan's song. Crosby said it was "too folksy," but they adapted it to sound like a Beatles song, complete with Rickenbacker twelve-string guitar and four-part harmony. This polished folk-rock version combined the best of both musical worlds, folk music and a Beatles sound. The recording shot up to number one on the *Billboard* charts.

The Byrds followed "Tambourine Man" with Pete Seeger's "Turn! Turn! Turn!" (1965), which also was a big hit. Their 1966 album, *Fifth Dimension*, began a "space-rock" phase that was likely influenced by experimentation with hallucinogenic drugs. The title song, although sounding like past folk rock, seemed to be describing an LSD experience. The album's hit single, "Eight Miles High" (1966), is often identified as a drug song. The Byrds claim, however, that it was about their flight to England.

What gives "Eight Miles High" the psychedelic drug-related sound is the *raga-rock* guitar work. Jim (Roger) McGuinn is sometime credited with coining the term "raga-rock," which identifies a style of guitar-playing that emulates the sound of the sitar, an Indian instrument. The sitar was brought to popular music by Beatle George Harrison, who used it on "Norwegian Wood" (1965), and sparked an interest in the instrument, leading to a performance by Ravi Shankar, an Indian classical musician, at the Monterey Pop Festival in 1967.

Later, the Byrds experienced personnel changes that led to a new musical direction. Gene Clark left in 1965 because of his fear of flying, and David Crosby, unsatisfied with the musicianship of the other members, left in 1967 to perform with Stephen Stills, Graham Nash, and later Neil Young. After the changes, and the addition of Gram Parsons, the Byrds moved in a country music direction culminating in the release of *Sweetheart of the Rodeo* (1968), one of the first recordings to indicate the future direction of California folk rock. After Hillman and Parsons left the Byrds, McGuinn kept the group together with shifting lineups, although the original members reunited for an unsuccessful reunion album in 1973. From 1975 through 1976, McGuinn toured with Dylan's Rolling Thunder Revue, and later in 1977, he formed the Thunderbyrds.

Buffalo Springfield

Buffalo Springfield's reputation as a band is larger than their accomplishments would indicate; they had one hit recording, "For What It's Worth" (1967). Their reputation exists primarily on the strength of the musicians, especially Neil Young, Stephen Stills, and Richie Furay, who significantly influenced the development of the California folk rock sound. The group, formed in 1966 and named after a brand of steamroller, was like the Byrds in that its members came from the folk music tradition.

With Jim McGuinn's (Byrds) enthusiastic support, they quickly developed a reputation, signed with Atlantic, and released an album in 1967, featuring original songs by both Stills and Young, including their hit single. "For What It's Worth," the band's only major hit, was written by Stills in response to what he saw during the Sunset Strip riots, although "riots" is probably too strong a word. What took place was a police action to clear the sidewalks of long-haired kids, freaks, and hippies between the Whisky A-Go-Go and Pandora's Box, two L.A. rock clubs.[19]

During 1966, the group was the house band at the Whiskey-A-Go-Go and toured with the Byrds. This began the association among Stills, Young, and David Crosby. In 1967, Neil Young quit just before the Monterey Pop Festival, and later Jim Messina and future Blood, Sweat, and Tears bassist Jim Fielder joined. Buffalo Springfield finally disbanded in 1968, and its members formed other groups that continued in the California folk-country rock direction. Stills and Crosby (Byrds), joined by Graham Nash (Hollies), formed Crosby, Stills, and Nash (CSN). Young, who always relished his individuality, split time between his band Crazy Horse and CSN, which then became Crosby, Stills, Nash, and Young (CSN&Y). Richie Furay and Jim Messina formed Poco (1968), and later in 1970, Jim Messina joined Kenny Loggins to form Loggins & Messina.

The California folk/country rock scene was influenced by members of the Byrds and Buffalo Springfield as they formed and reformed in various combinations. The style was typified by laid-back tempos and very clean multi-part vocal harmonies. The interconnections and shared personnel between the groups help explain the similarity in approach these groups exhibit.

Crosby, Stills, Nash and Young (CSN&Y)

Crosby, Stills, Nash, and Young was America's first "super group," a name given to groups composed of important members of other famous groups. They were a unique combination of talented singers and songwriters known for their close harmonies and a mixture of acoustic and electric sounds. They were influential in the country and Southern rock styles of the 1970s. The group formed in 1968 with David Crosby from the Byrds, Stephen Stills from Buffalo Springfield, and Graham Nash from the British group the Hollies.

Their first album, *Crosby, Stills and Nash*, was released in 1969 by Atlantic Records and included the hit singles "Marrakesh Express" and "Suite: Judy Blue Eyes." In 1969, Young joined for their next album, *Deja Vu*, adding his distinct vocal and songwriting abilities. It was a critical and commercial success, with the hit singles "Woodstock" (number eleven) and "Teach Your Children" (number sixteen).

The group's most memorable performance was at Woodstock in 1969; it was only their second live performance. CSN&Y broke up in 1971 shortly after recording their third album, *Four Way Street*. A reunion album called *CSN* was released in 1977, but they broke up again shortly thereafter. Other reunions have taken place in 1982, 1987, 1990, and 2000.

Other Folk Rock Groups

The remaining folk rock groups are an interesting blend of eclectic styles. The Mamas and the Papas and the Turtles focused on the close harmony sounds that were so common in California folk rock. The Mamas and the Papas grew out of the New York folk scene that included their good friends, Jim McGuinn and Barry McGuire, who both found earlier success in California. John Phillips, the leader of the Mamas and the Papas, was singing in a folk group called the Journeymen when he married an aspiring model-turned-singer, Michelle Gilliam. The other two members, Cass Elliot (Mama Cass) and Dennis Doherty, came from a New York electric folk group called the Mugwamps, which also included Zal Yanovsky and John Sebastian (Lovin' Spoonful).

Once they were rehearsed, Phillips moved them to California, and their first recordings came with the help of Barry McGuire, (ex–New Christy Minstrel), who let the group use some of his remaining recording studio time to record their songs. One of the songs they recorded was "California Dreaming," which featured McGuire. After the recording was pressed, the producer, Lou Adler, decided to remix it without McGuire, leaving only the choral backing of the Mamas and the Papas. Over the next two years they had several hit recordings: "Monday, Monday" (1966), "I Saw Her Again" (1966), "Words of Love" (1966), "Dedicated to the One I Love" (1967), and "Creeque Alley" (1967). In retrospect, the sound of the Mamas and the Papas did not necessarily relate to folk music and was similar to other non-folk vocal groups like the Association, the Hollies, and the Fifth Dimension. It was their previous New York folk associations and their folksy appearance that link them to the folk rock category.

The Turtles began as a California surf band called the Cross Fires, performiing regularly at the Rebellaire Club in Manhattan Beach. In 1965, they were signed by White Whale Records, which wisely turned them into a folk rock group because the surf trend was on the way out. In 1965, they had a hit with Dylan's "It Ain't Me Babe," and in 1966 recorded "Happy Together," which was a number one hit. They had several other top ten recordings, but disbanded in 1970 when the two singers, Mark Volman and Howard Kaylan, left and assumed the identities "Flo and Eddie" (for contractual reasons) and became part of Frank Zappa's show. They performed with Zappa until 1972 and appeared on his *Just Another Band From L.A.* album, where they parodied their previous Turtles hit "Happy Together."

Singers Sonny and Cher also assumed folk rock identities for their first hit recordings. Sonny (Salvatore) Bono and Cherilyn Sarkasian LaPier met when she was a background singer for Phil Spector. Sonny had been working with Spector and trying to make it as a songwriter. In 1957, his song "High School Dance" was on the flip-side of Larry Williams's "Short Fat Fanny," and in 1964 he co-wrote "Needles and Pins," which became a hit for the Seekers. Sonny and Cher were married in 1964 and, after some false starts under the name of Caesar and Cleo, recorded their first hit, "I Got You Babe" (1964). They positioned themselves as a folk duo, with Sonny wearing a furry vest and Cher with long straight folk-singer hair, and both in very colorful "hippie" clothes. They had a series of hits: "Baby Don't Go" (1965) and "The Beat Goes On" (1967), plus solo recordings by Cher, "All I Really Wanna Do" (1965), "Bang Bang (My Baby Shot Me Down)" (1966), and "You Better Sit Down Kids" (1967). After numerous television appearances,

Sonny and Cher

they repositioned themselves as a young adult act, which led to their own highly rated television comedy-variety show (1972–1974). In 1974, they were divorced and went on to very separate and interesting careers. Cher has had great success as a solo recording artist and an actress (she won an Oscar for Best Actress in 1987), while Sonny entered the political arena by winning election as the mayor of the wealthy desert community of Palm Springs, and later being elected to the U.S. House of Representatives. Sonny died in a skiing accident in 1998. In 2000, Cher won a Grammy for Best Pop Dance Recording.

Another folk duo, Simon and Garfunkel, emerged as an important act through the intercession of Columbia Records producer, Tom Wilson, who was also Dylan's producer. In 1957, recording under the name Tom and Jerry, Simon and Garfunkel had a top fifty hit "Hey, Schoolgirl," which landed them an appearance on *American Bandstand*. They had no follow-up hit and disbanded, only to reunite in 1962. In 1964, Wilson signed them to Columbia Records, and they recorded the *Wednesday Morning, 3 A.M.* album, which was a pure folk duo with two singers and one guitar. Columbia shelved the recording until the second part of 1965, when Wilson added electric guitar, bass, and drums and remixed it to fit the "new" folk rock sound started by the Byrds and Dylan. It was successful, and "The Sound of Silence" (1965) reached number one on the charts. Simon, who was in England at the time performing a solo act, returned to the United States and reformed the duo. They had a series of successes with Simon's songs from 1962 to 1965: "Scarborough Fair/Canticle" (1966), "Homeward Bound" (1966), "I Am a Rock" (1966), "At the Zoo" (1967), "Mrs. Robinson" (1968), and "The Boxer" (1969). Their final effort before splitting again was the album *Bridge Over Troubled Water* (1970), which sold nine million albums and contained three hit singles "Bridge Over Troubled Water," "Cecelia," and "El Condor Pasa." The group's success was the result of Simon's skill as a songwriter and the sweet harmony their two voices produced. Simon has since had great success as a singer/songwriter, and in the 1990s wrote songs with a world music sound; his *Rhythm of the Saints* features the performance of Brazilian musicians, and *Graceland* uses the background singing of the South African group Ladysmith Black Mambazo.

Good-Time Music, Jug Bands, and Poets

At the edge of the folk music scene was something called *jug band* music, or *good-time* music, which included early twentieth-century jazz, blues, and pop music, as well as newly composed songs written in an earlier style. The two most visible groups in this style were the Jim Kweskin Jug Band and the Lovin' Spoonful. Jug bands in the 1920s played jazz and blues on homemade instruments like a bottle/jug (as a substitute for a bass), kazoo, harmonica, and washtub bass as well as more traditional manufactured instruments like violin and guitar. The Jim Kweskin Jug Band never made it to the charts but they were well known among fans of eclectic folk music and several of their members made substantial contributions in other groups, such as fiddler Richard Greene. Their singer, Maria D'Amato, married guitarist Geoff Muldaur and became the Maria Muldaur who recorded the top ten hit "Midnight at the Oasis" (1974). She was never able to build her career on that hit because her musical tastes were far too eclectic for the normal pop audience.

The Lovin' Spoonful also grew out of the New York folk scene and were organized by John Sebastian (autoharp and harmonica) and Zal Yanovsky, both former members of the Mugwamps (Mamas and the Papas). In 1965, they began appearing at the Nite Owl Cafe and attracted a large following. Their first recording "Do You Believe in Magic" (1965) hit the top ten and was followed by "You Didn't Have to Be So Nice" (1965), "Daydream" (1966), "Did You Ever Have to Make Your Mind?" (1966), "Summer in the City" (1966), and "Nashville Cats" (1966). Their approach to good-time music, with colorful clothes and the autoharp, gave them the appearance of being carefree hippies until their dark hit "Summer in the City." They disbanded in 1968, and Sebastian later became famous for writing and singing the theme music for the seventies television show *Welcome Back Kotter*.

The Holy Modal Rounders, formed in the early 1960s by Peter Stampfel and Steve Weber, were also part of the New York folk scene but they, along with the Fugs, leaned toward the conceptual side of music-making. The *Rolling Stone Encyclopedia of Rock* does a good job of trying to describe their music, saying they were "gonzo traditionalists who mix old folk and bluegrass tunes with their own bouncy, absurdist free association." Their music truly defies words. The Rounders' brush with popularity came when their recording "If You Want to Be a Bird" was included in the movie *Easy Rider* and its soundtrack.

The Village Fugs, formed by poets Ed Sanders and Tuli Kupferberg are also too unusual to go unmentioned. Their initial recordings were released by ESP Disk, and they tested the limits of censorship by writing about sex, drugs, and assorted deviations before anyone else. They recorded the Rounders' "Boobs a Lot" and other interesting but humorously filthy songs such as "Slum Goddess," "Kill for Peace," "I Couldn't Get High," and "Saran Wrap," a song about safe sex. On their more commercial album for Reprise, *It Crawled Into My Hand, Honest*, they sang the many terms for marijuana in a medieval polyphonic chant style. The Fugs were more outrageous than Frank Zappa, although their music was far less complex.

LISTENING TO THE MUSIC

🎼♪♪ **"Blowin' in the Wind"—performed by Peter, Paul and Mary**

Bob Dylan's "Blowin' in the Wind" became an anthem for the civil rights movement of the 1960s. It was a song that reflected the attitude of the youth of the time and the optimism of social change. Peter Yarrow, Paul Stookey, and Mary Travers brought early commercial success to Bob Dylan's music, covering "Blowin' in the Wind" in 1963. Their pure folk voices, acoustic instruments, and variety of harmonic combinations helped Dylan's song to number two on the pop charts. Dylan's lyrics stand out over the simple chords and colorful harmonies using the image of wind for social change. The question-and-answer format of the lyrics and intricate harmonies of Peter, Paul and Mary is accompanied nicely by the smooth, continuous acoustic guitar and bass parts.

Analysis of "Blowin' in the Wind"—2:56 in length, recorded in 1963 on Warner 3568

This is a thirty-two bar form (A-A-A-B; 8+8+8+8). The meter is "in two." Because the folk trio has very simple instrumentation—guitar and bass—variety is achieved by changing the style of each section. Listen to the sound of the voices as they change from solo voice, to duo harmony, two voices in unison, two voices in unison with another in harmony, and full three-part harmony. Also notice how there is no call-and-response or any instrumental answers from the guitar.

0:00   Introduction (8 measures): An instrumental folk music introduction, established by the acoustic guitars and acoustic bass, uses music from the B Section section, "the answer my friend." There are two different guitar styles represented on this recording, although the recording mix makes it difficult to distinguish between them. One style, in which each finger plucks a different string, is called "finger-picking," and the other is "strumming," in which all six strings are struck with an up-and-down arm motion.

0:11   A Section (8 measures): Begins with "How many roads." The lyrics are delivered in two-part harmony with Mary's voice on top. This is a choral style with each voice moving in rhythmic unison.

0:24   A Section (8 measures): Begins "How many seas." This phrase continues the two-part harmony, male voice changes.

0:36   A Section (8 measures): Begins "How many times." The sound texture of this verse expands with the addition of the third voice.

0:49   B Section (8 measures): The sound texture of the phrase, "The answer my friend," returns to two-part harmony, this time with two male voices.

1:02   A Section (8 measures): Mary sings a solo verse beginning with "How many years."

1:14   A Section (8 measures): A second voice joins Mary singing in unison.

1:27   A Section (measures): Two unison voices and the other in harmony sing "How many times."

1:37   B Section (8 measures): Mary sings this verse by herself.

1:52   A Section (8 measures): "How many times" is a three-voice texture.

2:04   A Section (8 measures): There is no change in texture in the phrase "How many years."

2:15   A Section (8 measures): With the phrase, "How many deaths," the volume of the three-voice texture increases.

2:28   B Section (8 measures): Mary sings the final B Section section solo.

2:40   Coda or Tag (8 measures): The guitar repeats the B Section section alone for the first four bars and is joined by the voice for the last four.

For Musicians

Less raw and skeletal than Dylan's original version, Peter, Paul, and Mary's recording of "Blowin' in the Wind" brings clever, well-conceived vocal harmonies to the new "traditional" folk music of the 1960s. Performed in E major, this song follows a strict thirty-two-bar form (AAAB), with four eight-bar phrases as the interior framework for each verse. The eight bar introduction is taken directly from the last eight-bar phrase of the verse and follows a IV-V-I-vi-IV-V-I pattern. During the next three verses, the melodic and harmonic material will vary during each four-bar phrase as the lyrics progress, with the vocal contrasts becoming the musical highlight. These harmonic changes are quite effective in breaking up the monotony of the static thirty-two-bar form. The final eight-bar phrase relies on the intro music for four bars and is completed with a final vocal answer of the title line at the end.

Final Comments

"Blowin' in the Wind" won Dylan the Grammy award in 1963 for Best Folk Music Record, and he later performed the song with Peter, Paul, and Mary at that year's Newport Folk Festival. Contemporary Soul and Pop musician Stevie Wonder recorded a version of the song in 1966, reaching number nine on the pop charts.

♪♪♪ "Mr. Tambourine Man"—performed by the Byrds

The transition from folk to folk rock came with the addition of electric instruments and Dylan's acoustic folk song "Mr. Tambourine Man." The Byrds' electrified, updated version from 1965 set the folk rock trend in motion. The Byrds' debut single, "Mr. Tambourine Man" remained at number one on the pop charts for a week, sold one million copies, and established a musical formula the group would follow on subsequent releases, such as Pete Seeger's "Turn! Turn! Turn."

Analysis of "Mr. Tambourine Man"—2:16 in length, recorded in early 1965 in Hollywood, released on Columbia 43271

This is a verse-chorus form, beginning with the chorus. Dylan's recording had four verses; the Byrds shortened theirs to one of his verses, divided into two parts. The construction of the chorus (16 measures) is normal; however, the twenty-five-measure verse (14 + 11 measures) is unusual. Dylan's lyrics are fleeting images placed side-by-side with little breathing room for any instrumental responses. The meter is "in four" (four foot taps per measure). Personnel: Jim (Roger) McGuinn, vocals and electric twelve-string guitar; Hal Blaine, drums; Jerry Cole, rhythm guitar; Larry Knechtal, electric bass; Leon Russell, electric piano; and (Byrds) Gene Clark, vocals and tambourine, and David Crosby, vocal harmony.

0:00   Introduction (4 measures): The distinctive finger-picking pattern of the Rickenbacker twelve-string electric guitar establishes the tempo for two measures, and then the electric bass and tambourine enter. Notice that the reverb used in the recording process tends to muddy up the clarity of the background instrumental parts.

0:08   Chorus (16 measures): The chorus is four lines' long with an ABAC lyric structure beginning with "Hey, Mr. Tambourine man." The guitar accompaniment has two layers: (1) a one-bar riff using the "Charleston rhythm," which is usually doubled by the bass guitar, and (2) a finger-picking line common to acoustic folk music. The Byrds sing the chorus in a choral style harmony (unison rhythm).

0:41   First Verse (14 measures): The verse, sung by McGuinn is Dylan's second verse, which tends to emphasize the psychedelic drug trip interpretation, "Take me for a trip upon your magic swirlin' ship. . . ." A drum fill leads into a shortened second verse. (Note: When the lyrics are printed, they appear in one twenty-five-measure verse.)

1:08   Second verse (11 measures): Begins with "I'm ready to go anywhere. . . ."

1:31   Chorus (16 measures): A repeat of the original musical material.

2:05   Coda (8 measures): The band vamps on the finger-picking pattern of the introduction, and the sound fades. This is called a "board fade," because the recording engineer gradually lowers the volume, and the song is over when it becomes inaudible. The board fade serves two purposes: (1) It fills in the need for an ending. (2) It allows the radio DJ to talk over the record as it fades out.

For Musicians

The four-bar introduction alternates between a D chord and an A chord, and features two bars of solo twelve-string electric guitar rhythm followed by the addition of electric bass on sliding pitches, tambourine, and drums for two bars. This musical texture became a sonic model for many later folk rock and country rock bands, and a musical formula for the Byrds. The chorus moves through the following pattern, with one chord per bar: IV(G)-V-I-IV-I-IV & ii (two beats each) and two bars of V. This repeats, then proceeds to the first verse, which follows an unusual chord sequence with internal repeats relating to the lyrics: IV-V-I-IV-I-IV- I-IV-I-IV-I-IV-V-V (two bars). This sets up an extended fourteen-bar phrase for verse one. The second verse similarly follows the lyrics, but is shortened to eleven bars: IV-V-I-IV-I-IV-I-IV-I-V-V (two bars). These twenty-five bars make up the entire main body of the song, and successfully combine Dylan's abstract and creative lyrics with Beatles-esque harmonies. The last four bars of the chorus return to the instrumental intro material and repeats this once again as the song fades.

Final Comments

This recording features only McGuinn prominently, the others singing harmony, and studio musicians providing most of the other instruments. Within two years of this recording, the Byrds moved into a more psychedelic, less commercial phase while losing several key members, including Crosby.

---

[1] Ed Robbin, *Woody Guthrie and Me: An Intimate Reminiscence* (Berkeley, California: Lancaster-Miller, 1979), 87.

[2] Ibid., 26.

[3] Ibid., 111.

[4] Ibid., 133.

[5] Anthony Scaduto, *Bob Dylan* (New York: Grosset & Dunlap, 1971), 53-54.

[6] Robert Cantwell, *When We Were Good: The Folk Revival* (Cambridge, Massachusetts: Harvard University Press, 1996), 4-7.

[7] American Business Consultants, *Red Channels: The Report of Communist Influence in Radio and Television* (New York: American Business Consultants, 1950), 130.

[8] Cantwell, 4-7.

[9] Fred Goodman, *The Mansion on the Hill: Dylan, Young, Springsteen, and the Head-On Collision of Rock and Commerce* (New York: Random House, 1996), 88.

[10] Cantwell, 297.

[11] Ray Pratt, *Rhythm and Resistance: The Political Uses of American Popular Music* (Washington: Smithsonian Institution Press, 1990), 177.

[12] Scaduto, 6.

[13] Ibid., 54-56.

[14] Robert Shelton, "Bob Dylan: A Distinctive Folk-Song Stylist," *New York Times*, 29 September 1961, 31.

[15] Scaduto, 155.

[16] Ibid., 215.

[17] Alan Rinzler, *Bob Dylan: The Illustrated Record* (New York: Harmony, 1978), 249.

[18] Ed Ward, Geoffrey Stokes, and Ken Tucker, *Rock of Ages: The Rolling Stone History of Rock & Roll* (New York: Rolling Stone Press, 1986), 304.

[19] Goodman, 68-69.

Chapter Ten

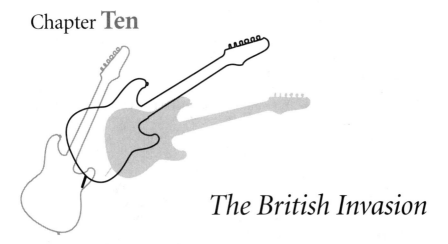

The British Invasion

The British Invasion refers to the period of time beginning in 1964 when America's pop charts seemed to be dominated by English bands. While, in fact, British bands did not dominate the charts, after years of very few English artists making the charts at all, the numbers that began appearing in 1964 represented an increase of several hundred percent. British bands placed twenty-seven recordings in the 1964 year-end *Billboard* top one hundred; although this was not a majority, capturing 27 percent could be described as becoming a driving force in the music scene.

Although they were not the first British bands ever to appear on the charts, beginning in January 1964, the Beatles were the first of a long string of British bands. The appearance of British bands seemed like an invasion to Americans: Non-American bands had never sold well to American teens and, since Americans had "invented" rock and roll, it was expected that the best any foreign group could hope to do was serve up a pale imitation of the music. The Beatles did, in fact, begin by copying American rock. However, they synthesized it and developed their own style, which, when coupled with their hair and clothing styles, appeared to be new and different to American teens.

In the early years, British Invasion bands could be divided into two types: the first were clean-cut, clean-harmony bands like the Beatles, Gerry and the Pacemakers, and Peter and Gordon; the second were bands with a "scruffy" appearance who leaned toward music more closely related to the blues, like the Rolling Stones, Animals, and Them.

Early English Crossovers

Between 1955 and 1963, most of the English musicians who made the American charts were products of the *trad jazz* movement. The English, among other Europeans, developed a fascination for American music but took an academic approach that was determined to preserve its purity. English trad jazz bands performed American jazz during the period 1917 to 1930. This was known as traditional jazz, New Orleans jazz, or sometimes Dixieland, and these bands prided themselves on their dedication to preserving "authentic" African-American music. For some reason, English trad jazz band recordings found their way onto American pop charts: "Petite Fleur" (Chris Barber's Jazz Band, 1959), "Midnight in Moscow" (Kenny Ball and his Jazzman, 1962), "Stranger on the Shore" (Acker Bilk, 1962), "Alley Cat" (Bent Fabric, 1962), and "Washington Square" (Village Stompers, 1963).

The trad jazz bands were responsible for sensitizing English audiences to traditional American music and providing an aesthetic for the next generation's blues musicians to pursue. When young trad jazz musicians tired of performing the "preserved" African-American music of their elders, they made the next logical step by finding "their own" African-American music to preserve— blues and, later, R&B. The first musical trend to develop from trad jazz was *skiffle,* and the second was blues or rhythm and blues. Skiffle was American folk songs, both African-American and European-American, accompanied by simple instruments, the most expensive being a guitar. The instrumentation of skiffle bands had an American antecedent in the jug bands and spasm bands of the early jazz period; they often used a washtub bass (the English called it a tea-chest bass) and a washboard in place of drums. The simple and inexpensive instrumentation of skiffle music made it accessible to British teens.

The most famous skiffle artist was Lonnie Donegan, whose recording "Rock Island Line" (1956) reached the American top fifteen and finished the year at number fifty. Lonnie Donegan was a guitarist/banjoist with Chris Barber's Jazz Band. During the band's intermissions, he entertained the audience with American folk songs. Barber included Donegan's version of Leadbelly's "Rock Island Line" on his 1954 album, *New Orleans Joys,* and it became an international hit, selling three million copies. Donegan did not have another American hit until "Does Your Chewing Gum Lose Its Flavor (On the Bedpost Overnight)?" (1961), but in England he became the undisputed "King of Skiffle." Although the Skiffle trend in England did not last more than a couple of years, it encouraged the next generation to form bands. Among those hopeful musicians were John Lennon and Paul McCartney.

In 1961, Cyril Davies and Alexis Korner, both members of Chris Barber's Jazz Band, left to form the group Blues Incorporated, which became an influential training ground for other English musicians. Among the musicians who performed in their band over the years were Mick Jagger, Charlie Watts, and Brian Jones, all of whom later became the Rolling Stones; Jack Bruce and Ginger Baker of Cream; Danny Thompson, John Renbourn, and Terry Cox of Pentangle; and Graham Bond. Blues Incorporated was one of the favorite bands at London's Marquee Club, and it was there, as a replacement for Korner's group, that the Rolling Stones first performed. In 1962, Cyril Davies left Korner to form the Cyril Davies All-Stars, which at one time included guitarist Jeff Beck (Yardbirds). Another important early English blues group was John Mayall's Bluesbreakers, which formed in 1963, and at various times included the talents of Eric Clapton, Mick Taylor, Jack Bruce, Mick Fleetwood, John McVie, Aynsley Dunbar, Jon Mark, John Almond, and Jon Hiseman. They may not have made the American charts, but the Bluesbreakers, Cyril Davies All-Stars, and Blues Incorporated made their contribution to the British Invasion by starting a blues movement that served as a training ground in American roots music for English musicians.

The Beatles

The Beatles (John Lennon, Paul McCartney, George Harrison, and Ringo Starr) were one of the most popular and influential groups in all of rock history during the seven years of their professional recording career and long afterward. Why were they so successful? There are is number of possible reasons for their phenomenal popularity: their showing up at the right moment in time, clever packaging and marketing, an expert support staff, and their physical appearance, charming personalities, songwriting talent, instrumental talent, singing style, and conceptual ability. However, no single explanation seems to fully answer the question. Many of these elements were possessed by other artists, but none became as influential as the Beatles.

The most remarkable part of the Beatles' success was that although they had no formal training, they evolved musically from album to album and carried their audience with them to each new level; in fact, their audience eagerly awaited the release of each recording to find out in what new direction the Beatles were headed. This was truly remarkable because, as a general rule then and now, pop artists are seldom permitted the freedom to evolve from their original style and are expected to maintain and build upon their original audience. The usual game plan for a band is to gradually broaden their appeal by homogenizing their musical features. Developing beyond the original sound is usually a fatal mistake because audiences will not tolerate a change in the sound that attracted them to the group in the first place. The Beatles' style evolved into new areas and continued to please the band's original fans. It is remarkable enough when an artist makes a contribution to music such that it defines its own particular style. It is extremely rare for an artist to do so in several styles.

Did the Beatles arrive at the right moment in history?

American listeners are always ready for something new. However, at the exact moment the Beatles arrived, the foundations of the nation had been shaken by the assassination of President Kennedy (November 22, 1963). It is possible that when the Beatles first began to appear on American radio (December 1963–January 1964) and on *The Ed Sullivan Show* (February 1964), Americans were subconsciously searching for some novelty to distract their attention away from the serious implications of the Kennedy assassination. The assassination was not the only event to put pressure on the American psyche. The change in the status of African-Americans was happening too quickly for some segments of society, and America's involvement in Southeast Asia as a result of the Vietnam war was steadily increasing. It may be that "Beatlemania," as it was called, helped the country forget the serious problems that confronted it.

The Beatles also arrived during a time when the music industry needed fresh ideas. The original stars of rock and roll—Elvis, Chuck Berry, Buddy Holly, Little Richard—were gone and had been replaced by teen idols who satisfied the love-projection fantasies of teenage girls but failed to provide the exuberant rock energy required by teenage boys. America's newest musical styles were Motown, folk, and surf. In 1963, it appeared that Motown had the greatest potential to develop into a vibrant musical style. Folk music did not satisfy the urge for energetic music, and surf music could not go on much longer with songs about beach life. Clearly, the time was ripe for something new, and the Beatles apparently had the perfect combination, a re-synthesis of America's rock styles grafted onto new song forms.

Was the Beatles' sudden success a result of clever marketing and packaging by an expert manager?

It is possible that the sudden publicity surrounding their arrival in America and the fact that Americans discovered them at this same time made it appear as if they were an overnight sensation. While they required no period of gradually building an American audience, they did have to spend years attracting their British audience. Their manager, Brian Epstein, had no particular expertise in artist management, and his only music business experience was as a record store owner. While it may be educational to work at the point where the recorded product changes hands to the consumer, this experience does not prepare one to be a rock manager. If he had been an experienced record man, he probably would have given up and moved on after the Beatles were rejected by all major English labels. Epstein's inexperience, combined with his work ethic, enabled him to take a product that he believed in, the Beatles, and continue knocking on doors until he found recognition for their talent. And then he followed through enough to make it pay off.

The Beatles were not an instant success in England because they were quite ordinary, even substandard, by some accounts. It was only after their performing experience in Hamburg, Germany, that they became successful in

England and, at the point of their return, it is possible that marketing and packaging played some role. Their engagement in Hamburg both improved their musicianship and altered their appearance, making them appear exotic to English teens. In Hamburg, they developed a friendship with art students Astrid Kirchherr and Klaus Voorman, who pushed the Beatles to adopt some of the styles of those who involved in German existential culture—"exis" as they were called. Astrid developed a relationship with Stu Sutcliffe (the Beatles' bass player at the time), styled his hair in what was called the French cut, and made him a leather "exi" stage outfit.[1] (Astrid and Stu later married.) Eventually, the other Beatles also succumbed to the French cut and leather stage clothes. Their adopted German look, along with the wild stage act they developed while performing for Germans, was very un-English, so when they returned to England, they stood out among the English bands. During one of their first performances upon returning from Germany, at Litherland Town Hall on December 27, 1960, the agent billed them as "Direct from Hamburg," and the girls who chased them after the show commented on how well they spoke English, indicating that they believed the Beatles were a German band.[2] It is apparent that their initial English popularity in 1960 had something to do with their exotic foreign appearance and stage demeanor.

It is difficult to determine whether marketing had any significant influence on their popularity in America, because it was the radio audience's response that drove the record company rather than the reverse. Capitol Records reluctantly agreed to release "I Want to Hold Your Hand" on January 13, 1964; but a DJ on WWDC began to play a copy that his girlfriend, a BOA stewardess, had brought from England. The response was positive, if not overwhelming. The DJ evidently sent a tape to another DJ in Chicago, then to one in St. Louis, and in this manner American DJs and their audiences discovered the Beatles before Capitol's advertising campaign had begun.[3] Based on this audience response, Capitol Records rushed to manufacture one million copies of the recording. Capitol was so unprepared for this response that it had to use the pressing facilities of their rivals, CBS and RCA, to press enough records to meet the demand.

The marketing of Beatles' licensed products began in England under the control of Brian Epstein, although it soon became such a burden that he handed the responsibility over to others toward the end of 1963. Nicky Byrne, chosen to handle the licensing, formed a company called Stramsact for Britain and Europe, and a subsidiary called Seltaeb, Beatles spelled backwards, to license the American rights. In England there were Beatles corduroy collarless jackets (like the one Astrid had made for Stu), sweaters, aprons, boots, guitars, belts, badges, handkerchiefs, bedspreads, shoulder bags, pencils, buttons, and even candy (the Ringo Roll). Byrne came to America to assign the rights to various manufacturers shortly before the Beatles arrived, and it was he, upset over Capitol's lack of promotion, who worked out a deal to give a free Beatles T-shirt to every teen who showed up at the airport on February 7, 1964, to greet the Beatles on Pan Am flight 101.

Capitol finally got into the spirit and committed fifty thousand dollars for a rush promotion program. They printed five million posters and stickers, a four-page life story, promotional recordings for DJs, and an open-ended interview tape. The interview tape, previously used by Elvis, was a wonderful promotional tool for both the DJs and the record company. The tape contained only the Beatles' answers, which allowed local DJs to insert the questions and make it appear as if the DJ were personally interviewing the Beatles. On February 7, DJs prepared their audiences for the Beatles' arrival by announcing the time as "6:30 A.M. Beatle-time," and the weather as "forty-three Beatle-degrees outside," and noting how long it would be before they touched down at the airport.

Was it their physical appearance?

Appearance and sex appeal is important in the popularity of most public figures, and it must have played some role in that of the Beatles. Just as their German look helped them in England, their exotic British appearance helped them gain attention in America. The French-cut hairstyles were the first thing Americans noticed about them, and discussion about the length of their hair filled media commentary. At first, most Americans thought their hair was too long, but gradually the Beatles influenced American styles, and teens began growing their hair Beatle-length, much to the chagrin of parents and teachers. The Beatles' stage costumes—matching collarless suits and Beatle boots—were also different from what Americans were accustomed to, so this also attracted attention. Americans were accustomed to country artist's cowboy boots and motorcyclists' boots, but the smooth-toed, Cuban-heeled, ankle-high Beatles boots were new to Americans. Above all, each Beatle had a distinct visual personality, each attractive to teenage girls on some level. George was the quiet one with the guitar skills, Ringo was the cuddly one that girls wanted to mother, Paul was perky and cute, and John was the good-looking wise guy.

Was it their charming personalities?

The Beatles' personalities caught American journalists completely off-guard. Judging by the length of their hair, journalists expected the Beatles to be ignorant cavemen, but instead they found the Beatles witty, charming, and capable of constructing appropriate answers to reporters' insipid questions. When asked "Will you sing something for us," John said, "We need money first." When John was asked, "Was your family in show business," his reply was "Well, me dad used to say me mother was a great performer."[4] When asked,

"Are you going to get a haircut," George singled out one strand of hair, pointed to it, and said that he had already had one cut. They handled the press with the skill of a great comedy team, and in that first interview insured the future co-operation of the media. Journalists were shocked by their intelligence and wit, because they never expected anything more than one-syllable responses from rock stars; Americans had been trained by Elvis's simple "Yes-maam, No-maam" answers to expect nothing more.

Was it their musical and songwriting talent?

As songwriters, Lennon and McCartney were as prolific and creative as any past songwriters, and listening to their songs in succession makes one aware of how remarkable their development really was. Although they used American rock and roll as a model, they were able to progress beyond its standard musical forms (twelve-bar blues and thirty-two-bar AABA) and predictable chord progressions (twelve-bar blues and I-vi-IV-V) to the point where serious music critics took notice. English critics, such as William Mann, registered favorable comments on Beatles' music and called them the "outstanding English composers of 1963." He spoke of their "pandiatonic clusters" and their "aeolian cadences," and treated their music with the respect rarely accorded popular music.[5]

The Beatles were not virtuoso instrumentalists but rather solid club-level musicians. George Harrison was a proficient guitar player who had command of the styles of Carl Perkins and Chuck Berry and was open to learning new styles such as those of the Indian sitar. Ringo Starr was a solid rock drummer who kept "good time," had a "good groove," and played what was appropriate, while never showing off. Paul McCartney played active, creative, and unusual bass lines because he was a guitar player, thought like a guitar player, and therefore conceived bass lines that were atypical. John Lennon was a capable rhythm guitarist but never developed his technique beyond what was needed to deliver his songs.

The Beatles used their instrumental skills in a remarkably inventive manner, and they displayed great creativity in conceiving new sounds. John recorded the first intentional guitar feedback on "I Feel Fine" and recorded the first backwards guitar solo on "Rain." Feedback is created when a microphone or guitar pickup receives its own amplified sound coming from a speaker and reamplifies it. The resulting circuit creates a distorted squealing sound. Lennon's discovery of the backward sound was purely accidental, but his application of the technique was unique and inspired others to do the same; it even inspired searches of recordings looking for backward messages. They used other forms of tape manipulation as well. On "In My Life," the piano is recorded at half speed and one octave lower. When replayed at the normal tempo, it sounds to be in the correct range and similar to a harpsichord. On "Being for the Benefit of Mr. Kite," they cut various taped performances of calliope music into small pieces and then spliced them together, creating the sound of a macabre psychedelic merry-go-round. On "Revolution Number Nine," John and Yoko created an eight-minute tape collage, similar in concept to the music of serious electronic composers. "Strawberry Fields" was a combination of two separate recordings in different keys and at different tempos which, when combined, created a surreal sonic portrait.

The Beatles often used instruments that were not typically part of rock records: a string quartet and octet ("Yesterday" and "Eleanor Rigby"), baroque trumpet ("Penny Lane"), and sitar ("Norwegian Wood" and "Love to You"). Of course, attributing these advances solely to the Beatles would ignore the essential contributions of their record producer, George Martin, who made suggestions (string quartet on "Yesterday") and made their other ideas technically possible (combining the two "Strawberry Fields" tapes).

Probably the single most unique aspect of the group was the incredible variety of styles they were able to perform. They could be all things to all people. John and Paul were the principal lead singers, although George and Ringo sang lead occasionally. They could sing in a blues-shouter style like Little Richard and Chuck Berry, a close harmony "country-brothers" style like the Everly Brothers, and a multi-part harmony like the Beach Boys. No other popular rock group ever approached the type of versatility demonstrated by the Beatles. Although their versatility was similar to nightclub cover bands who perform music designed to appeal to a variety of musical tastes, the Beatles eclipsed the club-band model by writing better songs with the same broad appeal and performing them with a unique flair.

Was it their conceptual abilities?

The Beatles were not the originators of any contemporary social concepts, although they brought those once fringe ideas (peace and love, etc.) to a general audience in such a way as to give them vitality. The ideas they espoused were adopted by their generation. Their most powerful cause was their anti-war stance. They were not the first artists who opposed the war in Vietnam (folk singers had taken up that cause much earlier), but their songs and "happenings" were influential enough to help shift public opinion against the war. In that way they contributed to its end by the early 1970s. John and Yoko's "bed-in for peace" in Amsterdam and Toronto drew the attention of the media, which reported it because they expected to be covering a "between-the-sheets" sex story about the Beatles. One Christmas, John rented a billboard in New York and other cities that carried the simple message "WAR IS OVER IF YOU WANT IT HAPPY X-MAS from John & Yoko."[6]

The Beatles also gave birth to the modern music video. Early music videos, called soundies, were around in the 1930s and 1940s on special juke boxes, but few were more than films of the artist performing a song. The two Beatles films, *A Hard Day's Night* (1964) and *Help* (1965), contained musical segments that showed them doing more than holding instruments and moving their lips. The segments were a collage of "cute" Beatles antics performed over the music, and evolved artistically and technically over the years to the point where they established a new format for viewing music that eventually developed into music videos and the MTV cable network. The content of their movies also increased expectations for other rock movies. Previously, rock movies had been either scripted around a collection of various rock performances, such as Alan Freed's movies, or included the stiff acting of a rock star, such as Elvis. *A Hard Day's Night*, a pseudo-documentary, was a different type of rock film that showed typical events in the Beatles' daily lives. In some of the scenes, they really were being chased by fans. The Beatles played themselves, and their characters were central to the plot by initiating most of the action. They proved themselves fully capable of sustaining the interest of an audience. *Help*, a parody of the James Bond spy film *Dr. No*, was unlike their earlier films or any other rock film because it was entertaining, despite the fact that it had rock stars playing the main characters. Of course, they did not write, direct, or have anything to do with the production of the films. They were, however, allowed to improvise some of the action and their approaches to the characters.

It is difficult to define the elements that made the Beatles as popular and socially powerful as they were. Their kind of popularity went beyond the screaming bobby-soxers who fainted for Frank Sinatra in the 1940s or the generation that elevated Elvis to sainthood; their cultural concepts helped shape the actions of a generation. Other performers may have possessed the same or even superior abilities but none have approached the kind of international stardom experienced by the Beatles.

The Beatles History

The Beatles' story can be broken into four phases, although the lines dividing these phases are sometimes obscured by overlapping events.

Phase One (1957–62):	the years before their recording contract
Phase Two (1963–65):	the years of initial success marked by boy/girl love songs
Phase Three (1965–68):	the experimental years (song forms, studio techniques and drugs)
Phase Four (1968–1970):	the final years leading to the breakup

Phase One

The progression of bands that ended with the Beatles began in 1957 with John Lennon (1940–1980) and a skiffle group called the Quarry Men. Inspired by Lonnie Donegan and the apparent simplicity of skiffle, John bought a guitar. His mother taught him some of the basic chords she knew on the five-string banjo. He formed a group with some of his friends from the Quarry Bank School (Nigel Whalley, Ivan Vaughan, Pete Shotton, Rod Davis, and Colin Hanton), and they began playing for school and church functions. The Quarry Men performed a typical skiffle repertoire, including songs such as "Rock Island Line," "Cumberland Gap," "Railroad Bill," "Maggie May," and "Don't You Rock Me Daddy."

The dynamics of the Quarry Men changed on July 6, 1957, when Ivan Vaughan introduced Paul McCartney to John Lennon while they were playing for the St. Peter's Parish Church Garden Fete in Woolton. Paul impressed them by writing out the words to "Twenty Flight Rock" (Eddie Cochran) and "Be-Bop-A-Lula" (Gene Vincent), and by playing Little Richard's "Long Tall Sally" and "Tutti Frutti."[7] Paul became a member of the band, and soon he and John were spending hours practicing together and performing at St. Peter's and St. Barnabas's church dances, and at other functions such as the Broadway Conservative Club. At this point in their career, the Quarry Men were wearing black pants, white cowboy shirts with fringe along the sleeve, and bola ties.

The next member to join was George Harrison, who attended the same school as Paul, the Liverpool Institute, a year behind him. They became friends and regularly practiced guitar together. Eventually, Paul introduced George to the Quarry Men, and he "auditioned" for them sometime in late 1957 at a club called the Morgue with "Raunchy" and "Guitar Boogie Shuffle."[8] George was not asked to join then, but he followed the band around and was asked to sit in on occasion. His image as the "quiet one" probably came from the insecurity of his having to stand around waiting to be asked to perform, never quite sure of his standing with the group.

During the next two years John, Paul, and George performed under several different names: Johnny and the Moondogs, the Nurk Twins, and Long John and the Silver Beetles. In 1959, they added Stuart Sutcliffe, a friend of John's from the Art College who had a perfect sullen James Dean look, but he was not a musician. Regardless, he wanted to play and looked the part, so he bought a bass guitar and began to perform with John, Paul, and George.

The next major step in their career was meeting Alan Williams, owner of the Jacaranda coffee bar, who became their manager, and Bob Wooler, his assistant, who later helped publicize their German recording. In 1960, Alan Williams began furnishing bands for Bruno Koschmider, a Hamburg night-club owner. The first groups he booked were Tony Sheridan and Derry and the Seniors. In August 1960, Koschmider needed a third group for the Indra club. Williams wanted to send Rory Storm and the Hurricanes or Gerry and the Pacemakers, but they were both working elsewhere, so his third choice was the

Beatles. The Beatles had been performing without a drummer and asked Pete Best, whose mother owned the Casbah Coffee Club, if he would like to join for their Hamburg engagement. The original Beatles were then in place: John Lennon, Paul McCartney, George Harrison, Stu Sutcliffe, and Pete Best.

The Beatles opened at the Indra on August 17, 1960, where their contract called for them to perform for four and one-half hours each night and six hours on weekends. The nightly performance schedule helped them improve their musical skills and develop a style that would satisfy a variety of audiences. During the first night, the crowd of about half a dozen, mostly prostitutes and their customers, was not impressed with their versions of "Honey Don't" (Carl Perkins) and "Too Much Monkey Business" (Chuck Berry). This prompted Alan Williams to shout at them from the bar, "Make it a show, boys!" Bruno joined in and shouted, "Mak show boys."[9] The Beatles responded to this prodding by jumping around in their best imitations of Elvis and other rockabillies. On October 4, 1960, they were moved to another of Koschmider's clubs, the Kaiserkellar, where they became acquainted with Astrid Kirchherr, Klaus Voorman, and their existential crowd.

Toward the end of November 1960, a rival club, the Top Ten, persuaded the Beatles to ignore their contract with the Kaiserkellar and perform there for more money. Just as they were about to open, Bruno Koschmider tipped the local police that George was seventeen years old, too young to be working past midnight, and he was deported on November 21, 1960. The other Beatles stayed and performed without him for a short time but returned to Liverpool in December.

After performing at several Liverpool clubs, they returned to Hamburg for an engagement at the Top Ten Club beginning in April 1961. At the Top Ten Club, they alternated with Tony Sheridan's band from 7 P.M. until 2 or 3 A.M., and it was during this time that Stu decided to quit and pursue studies at the Hamburg State Art College. Paul had always thought that he could do a better job than Stu, so he took over on bass guitar.

Their first professional recording session took place during this period. Bert Kaempfert, a bandleader and producer for Polydor Records, signed Tony Sheridan to a contract and hired the Beatles as his backup band, calling them the Beat Brothers. It was Kaempfert's idea to have them play old familiar songs with a rock beat. He recorded Sheridan singing "My Bonnie" and "When the Saints Go Marching In," and he let the Beatles record "Ain't She Sweet" and an original instrumental, "Cry for a Shadow."

When they returned to Liverpool, they began their famous engagement at the Cavern Club, where Bob Wooler, a DJ and columnist, urged patrons to purchase their German recording. Raymond Jones has been recorded in history as the person who, on October 28, 1961, walked into NEMS (North End

Music Store) and asked its proprietor, Brian Epstein, for "My Bonnie" by the Beatles.[10] Epstein had never heard of it and asked the boy which label it was on. On November 9, 1961, Brian visited the Cavern Club and was amazed at what he discovered. Besides the fact that the Beatles, alias the Beat Brothers, were just a backup band for Tony Sheridan, and in spite of the fact that he was a classical music fan, he found the Beatles' music to be fresh and different. He liked it. Upon questioning them, he found out that they were not under contract to anyone, so he told them that they needed a manager. They agreed, and Epstein and the Beatles worked out a contract.

The combination of Epstein and the Beatles may have occurred at just the right moment in time to spark their rise to fame. Epstein made corrections in their stage behavior that made them, in his eyes, appear more professional. He told them to be punctual, not to eat, drink, or belch onstage and, if they had to smoke, it should be "high-class" cigarettes like Senior Service rather than their workingman's smokes. He made them abandon the black leather, still associated with Nazis in the British mind, and outfitted them in matching suits. It is interesting to note that the first time they returned from Hamburg, they were mistaken for a German group by the girls at the Litherland Hall. Their exotic look played some role in their initial popularity, and if at that point they had been wearing matching suits like every other English band, it might have destroyed one of the early elements of their popularity. Epstein was right, however. If they were to reach the next level of success, some changes needed to be made.

Toward the end of April 1962, after being rejected by England's major recording labels, Brian was directed to George Martin at EMI's subsidiary, Parlophone. George Martin had been a bandleader and was knowledgeable about music. Most of all, his company needed something to change its image as EMI's junk label whose only success came from comedy albums. He heard something in those tapes that showed promise and offered the Beatles an audition on June 6, 1962. At the audition, he decided that the group might be successful if they could find the right songs. He rightly thought the rocked-up standards were too corny and did not like any of the original songs they played. At that point, Martin also tried to determine who should be the focus of attention (lead singer) but could not reach a decision because John and Paul complemented each other so well. Conventional musical wisdom said that a band should have only one leader, but he ignored that, and the risk paid off. Spreading the attention around gave the Beatles the kind of versatility that other groups lacked. Having John and Paul out front and responsible for the direction of the group created a balance of power, a yin and yang force that kept each of them from going too far. Paul's proper, obedient personality was offset by John's acerbic wit, predilection for basic rock and roll, and arty experimentation.

After the audition, Martin told Epstein that if he decided to offer the Beatles a contract, he wanted to use his own drummer (Andy White) in the studio, because Pete Best's studio skills were weak. It did not matter to him if they used Pete on live performances. The Beatles decided to replace Pete Best and had Brian fire him on August 16, 1962. He was replaced by Ringo Starr, Rory Storm's drummer. On September 11, 1962, they recorded two original songs, "Love Me Do" backed with "P.S. I Love You." The record was released to the public on October 4, 1962.

In an effort to "manufacture a hit," Brian ordered ten thousand copies for NEMS, and although it was a small number, it guaranteed that the recording would make the British top twenty. The decision by Brian was a wise one because EMI, Parlophone's parent company, put no effort into promoting the recording. In their corporate wisdom, they, like Decca, believed that "guitar groups were on the way out."[11] The first airplay of "Love Me Do" came on Radio Luxembourg because their fans called in so many requests. It is possible that without Brian's record order or the requests of their fans, the Beatles' recording would never have been heard and EMI's prophesy would have been self-fulfilling. "Love Me Do" reached number seventeen by December. On November 26, 1962, the Beatles recorded their second single, "Please Please Me." Martin instinctively knew it would be a number-one hit.

The next step was to follow the success of "Please Please Me" with an album, and George Martin again made a decision that was at odds with conventional music industry wisdom. Traditionally, an album contained only the hit and was surrounded by filler songs designed to earn mechanical royalties for the record company's publisher. Martin decided to put together an album of quality songs, and since then, Beatles albums have been characterized by having several hits. In fact, many of their early singles were double-sided hits. On February 11, 1963, in a thirteen-hour recording session, the Beatles recorded a fourteen-track album containing their originals "I Saw Her Standing There" and "Do You Want to Know a Secret?" several American rock songs from their nightclub act, and even songs sung by George and Ringo.

Phase Two

George Martin had tried to get Capitol, EMI's American subsidiary, to release the Beatles' recordings several times. When "Please Please Me" went to number one, he sent it to Jay Livingstone in New York, who said, "We don't think the Beatles will do anything in this market."[12] Martin then arranged to have both "Please Please Me" and "From Me to You," their third British hit, released on Vee Jay, a Chicago independent record label. When "She Loves You" was a hit in August 1963, he again offered it to Capitol, but he had to settle for a release on Swan, a Philadelphia label. None of the three recordings made it to the charts. On November 5, 1963, Brian Epstein flew to New York and successfully persuaded Brown Meggs, Capitol's director of Eastern operations, to release "I Want to Hold Your Hand." The release date was set for January 13, 1964, but Epstein was warned that Capitol did not expect it to be successful.

While in New York, Epstein also visited Ed Sullivan, who hosted America's most important television variety show. Luckily for the Beatles, Sullivan had been at Heathrow Airport when they returned from their Swedish tour and had seen, firsthand, the response they elicited from British teenagers. Sullivan booked them for two shows, February 9 and 16, and also had them make a tape that could be used later. Because Epstein was desperate for American exposure, Sullivan got them for only $3,500 per show and $3,000 for the tape. Brian also made a deal with Sid Bernstein, an agent for General Artists Corporation (GAC) for a Carnegie Hall performance on Lincoln's Birthday, February 12, 1964. Bernstein had been taking evening classes in British government for several years and, as a result of reading English newspapers, was aware of the Beatles' enormous popularity. When he could not get GAC to book the Beatles, he booked the concert himself. Later, in January while the Beatles were performing in Paris, GAC booked them for a concert in Washington, D.C.

In America, events started happening quickly after a Washington DJ began playing "I Want to Hold Your Hand" in December and its popularity quickly spread. Beatlemania hit America. Certainly, the mania was assisted by the radio reports that it was "6:30 A.M. Beatle time" and the promise of free T-shirts for those who showed up at the airport. But once the Beatles were seen and heard by the American public in interviews and on *The Ed Sullivan Show,* their personalities and talent took over. For whatever reason, in February 1964, America was now ready for the Beatles. The streets in front of the Plaza Hotel in New York, where they were staying, were clogged with teenagers trying to catch a glimpse of them. Ed Sullivan had fifty thousand requests for tickets for his theater's 728 seats, and his show earned the highest rating of any previous show, capturing seventy-five million viewers.

In the months that followed, the Beatles' earlier recordings, once turned down by Capitol, were being rereleased on various labels and finding new popularity. Vee-Jay rereleased "Please Please Me" and "From Me to You," and released an album called *Introducing the Beatles* before Capitol managed to release their first album, *Meet the Beatles.* Swan rereleased "She Loves You" in January. MGM got the rights to "My Bonnie" and released it in February; and "Twist and Shout," and "Do You Want to Know a Secret?" were released by Tollie. In April, the Beatles held positions one through five on the *Billboard* charts and had recordings on five different labels. This whole scenario was a record executive's worst nightmare: a group his company had rejected had become an international success and the recordings it had rejected were being released by competitors and becoming hits.

Phase Three

The third phase of the Beatles' professional life was marked by continued experimentation with lyrics and recording techniques, fueled partly by curiosity and partly by their experimentation with drugs. In a 1968 interview with *Rolling Stone* magazine, John said of their lyrics, "We've gone past those days when we wouldn't have used words because they didn't make sense. . . . Dylan taught us a lot in this respect."

The *Rubber Soul* album (December 6, 1965) is usually thought of as the beginning of this experimental period, the end result being the Beatles' decision to stop touring. Their final American performance was at Candlestick Park in San Francisco on August 29, 1966. The generally accepted explanation for their decision to stop doing concerts—that the songs they were recording in the studio were impossible to do live (i.e., backwards guitar and tape manipulation effects)—is certainly true, but the fatigue they were experiencing from almost constant performing since Hamburg (1960) also played a role in their decision. Furthermore, they had no private lives. Their personal lives and words were subjected to the kind of close scrutiny usually reserved only for presidential candidates. For example, in an interview with Maureen Cleave published in *London's Evening Standard*, John happened to say that "most young people are more interested in rock 'n' roll than in religion . . . We're more popular than Jesus now."[13] The English audience did not really notice, but Americans went crazy. Religious leaders spoke out against the Beatles, and there were Beatles record–burning parties all over America, so John had to issue an apology/clarification to finally get the situation neutralized. This type of scrutiny, combined with the inability to live a somewhat normal life, helped the Beatles make the decision to stop touring.

Rubber Soul is often called their acoustic album because, although there are electric guitars, the predominant tone is one of acoustic string instruments. Several of the songs have a distinctly country feel, which may have influenced the later California country-rock trend. There is also subtle experimentation with different instruments and recording techniques:

- On "Norwegian Wood," George uses a sitar to play the melody, and John's lyrics are beginning to become more obscure.

- On "Think for Yourself," Paul alters the sound of the bass by adding distortion, calling it a "fuzz bass."

- "Michelle" contains bilingual lyrics, French and English.

- "Girl" has an exotic sound reminiscent of the soundtrack to the movie *The Third Man,* using a string sound resembling that of a mandolin and zither.

- "In My Life" includes George Martin playing piano recorded at half-speed, so that when it is played back at full speed, it sounds similar to a harpsichord.

- "Wait" has a guitar effect that uses a volume pedal to hide the attack sound. After the strings are struck in the normal manner with the volume down, the volume is then raised, thus allowing the already vibrating strings to be audible.

Revolver (August 8, 1966) was the next major step in their experimentation phase and was so filled with unique sounds and variety that some consider it the best Beatles album. The album begins with some unidentified sounds and talking. A count-off starts the first song.

- "Taxman" is a Beatles "protest song" about tax rates, with a very gritty guitar sound. The guitar solo is an early metal blend of blues riffs with sitar-like ornaments.

- "Eleanor Rigby" is a narrative song by Paul accompanied by a string octet.

- "Love You To" features the sitar, which George continued to study. Here it is used in a more traditional Indian style than on "Norwegian Wood."

- "Here, There, and Everywhere" is another one of their clean vocal harmony recordings. This came closer to the Four Freshman sound than the Beach Boys. It also used the guitar volume pedal "hide-the-attack" effect.

- "Yellow Submarine" used externally taped sounds, such as the gurgling of water and other submarine sounds, as well as the sound of a brass band. Although it sounds like a children's song, it is also very psychedelic. "Yellow submarines" was also the street name of a type of prescription pill. Later, a movie of the same name satisfied the band's three-movie contract with United Artists.

- "She Said She Said" is a drug song based on a tripping experience John had in California when someone (he thinks it was Peter Fonda) kept whispering in his ear, "I know what it's like to be dead."[14] The B section uses an interesting variety of meter changes.

Their next album, *Sgt. Pepper's Lonely Hearts Club Band* (June 2, 1967) again revolutionized the record album. The first Beatles' album in 1964 was revolutionary in that it contained more than one hit song. *Sgt. Pepper* was revolutionary because it was the beginning of the concept album, a recording whose songs were interconnected by some overriding idea, similar to the song cycle of "classical" music. Frank Zappa's *Freak Out* album actually pre-dated *Sgt. Pepper* as a concept album, although it slipped unnoticed into record store bargain bins. *Sgt. Pepper* was a major leap in the way musicians used the recording studio; they stretched the limits of four-track recording beyond mere overdubbing. The use of tape loops on "Being for the Benefit of Mr. Kite" is but one example.

The "concept" of this album was that it had been recorded by a fictitious band, not by the Beatles. To this end, they created a unique album package that included a sheet of cardboard cut-outs, similar to paper dolls, of a Sgt. Pepper mustache, picture card, stripes, badges, and stand-up portrait. Another first was that the lyrics were printed on the back of the album.

The recording begins with sounds of the audience talking and a band tuning up (violin and accordion), segueing into a song introducing the band, which includes an interlude by a brass band, presumably Sgt. Pepper's band. The title song flows seamlessly into the next song, "With a Little Help From My Friends." Although each selection is separated by an ending and a traditional visual space, the effect upon listening is of one continuous musical work because the real-time space between the tracks was reduced to a "breath" and some cuts cross-fade the ending of one with the beginning of the next. The album continues through a series of "musical acts" by the band, ending with "Good Morning, Good Morning," which then flows seamlessly into a reprise of the title song using the sounds of a fox hunt, horses, barking hounds, and a hunting horn.

After the obvious end of the album is one more remarkable song, "A Day in the Life," which was a true collaboration between John and Paul. John had been writing songs based on current events, and Paul often wrote descriptive "travelogues" such as "Penny Lane." John had written the first part of the song based on the newspaper report and the death by auto accident of Tara Browne, the Guinness family heir. When Paul was asked to contribute to the song, he submitted a "bus trip scene" that began, "Woke up, fell out of bed. . . ." These two segments were connected by the sound of a forty-one-piece orchestra improvising a crescendo from the bottom to the top of their instrumental range. The return to the A section is accomplished after Paul's line, "Somebody spoke and I went into a dream," whereupon the orchestra enters a psychedelic, dream-like section and returns to John's section. The final sound on the recording is another long orchestral crescendo, twenty-eight seconds, followed by a final explosive chord and its reverberation, which lasts forty-three seconds. The final chord "slammed the album shut"[15] and gave listeners forty-three seconds to reflect on what they had just experienced.

Sgt. Pepper's Lonely Hearts Club Band was a critical and commercial success. *The New York Times Review of Books* said it represented "a new and golden renaissance of song," and acid guru Dr. Timothy Leary said the Beatles were "prototypes of evolutionary agents sent by God." The album may have been the last time the group was of a like mind, all contributing to the success of the concept. After this, the slide toward dissolution began.

Magical Mystery Tour (November 27, 1967), their next album, was supposed to be the soundtrack of a film/television special of the same name. The recording was well received, but the movie, considered a cult classic, was the Beatles' first failure since their Decca audition. Paul had developed the idea based on Ken Kesey's "merry pranksters," who tripped through California in a "magic bus," dispensing LSD. The Beatles went along with the idea, thinking it might be an artistic follow-up to *Sgt. Pepper.* Paul thought it would be fun to load up the bus with people, tour British seaside towns, and film what happened. Nothing did. It was an ill-conceived venture that was doomed for lack of organization and content.

Phase Four

The last phase of the Beatles begins about the time of *Magical Mystery Tour,* and their disintegration was so gradual that it went unnoticed by the public until near the very end. What happened? Most likely the stress of being together and successful as long as they had been was beginning to be felt. Members of a band usually feel this type of stress much earlier in their career, but the Beatles' phenomenal success and sense of direction kept them together much longer than most. Typically, bands struggle and perform together trying to make it for several years before they finally achieve initial success, and so it was with the Beatles. Success places added stress on any band just at the point when they have successfully accomplished their number-one goal—a hit record. The continued stress of touring, performing, and having to write material for the next album, combined with the ego-overinflating that grows out of the constant adulation from fans is too much to handle for all but the heartiest musicians. John and Paul were two distinctly different personalities who held each other in the state of dynamic tension, successfully combining the best of both for ten years. Once the force that bonded them disappeared, they slowly began to drift apart.

There were two forces holding the Beatles together. The first was the quest for success and the second was their manager, Brian Epstein. Once their quest for success was over, one element of that dynamic tension was gone. On September 8, 1967, Brian Epstein accidentally overdosed on Carbatrol, an anti-seizure medication. Although he had tried to commit suicide on several other occasions, his death was considered accidental as the coroner found that the drug had been ingested over a period of two or three days.[16] Even though it is generally believed that the Beatles had outgrown Epstein, he still played an important role as organizer, facilitator, and catalyst for John and Paul.

The Beatles released three albums of new material between *Magical Mystery Tour* and their breakup: *The Beatles* (*White Album*), *Abbey Road,* and *Let It Be.* Meanwhile, they also were working individually on other recording projects. Before the final Beatles album, John and Yoko Ono released *Unfinished Music No. 1—Two Virgins, Unfinished Music No. 2—Life With The Lions, The Wedding Album,* and *Live Peace in Toronto 1969.* George released *Wonderwall Music* and *Electronic Sound.* Paul released *McCartney,* and Ringo released *Sentimental Journey.*

The Beatles, better known as *The White Album,* reflected appeared to be a collection of individual projects rather than the work of one band. The Beatles entered the recording sessions with songs that each had written individually, and each had preconceived ideas about how they should sound. This was a change from the way they had worked in the past, because it precluded input from the others. Without the yin and yang relationship at work, John's songs turned out cynical and biting, while Paul's were overly cute and sentimental. Most writers generally regarded the album as the Beatles "paying tribute" to their varied influences, but others take the stance that this was the Beatles' final statement about their individuality before going their separate ways. *The White Album* was the Beatles' most eclectic collection of songs:

- Paul's "Back in the U.S.S.R." is a rocking parody of a Chuck Berry song, "Back in the USA," with a center section about "Russian girls" with a Beach Boys' falsetto background.

- "Ob-La-Di, Ob-La-Da," also by Paul, has a reggae groove and a generally happy tone.

- "Martha My Dear," written by Paul for his sheepdog, Martha, has the sound of a ragtime parlor orchestra.

- Paul's "Blackbird," with its acoustic guitar finger-picking, became a standard for 1970s lounge guitarists.

- "Mother Nature's Son" is in the same vein as "Blackbird," and is one of Paul's most beautiful and simple compositions.

- George wrote "Piggies," with John's help on the lyrics. It is a seemingly comical song, was given a murderous interpretation by Charles Manson. He seemed to know who needed "a damn good whacking."

- "Rocky Raccoon," written by Paul, has the feel of an early Dylan ballad and even has a harmonica part in Dylan's style. It was the ballad of Hollis Brown meets Marty Robbins.

- "Don't Pass Me By" is an old-time country song composed and sung by Ringo, with a scratchy old-time fiddle accompaniment.

- Paul's "Why Don't We Do It in the Road" is a very simple twelve-bar blues (three choruses with the same lyrics) and likely a parody of what was passing for blues in the rock world.

- "Yer Blues," by John, is another blues, complete with guitar answers and a stop-time chorus.

- Paul's "Helter Skelter" has a very heavy (slow), almost dripping, metal sound, and Charles Manson also got some inspiration from this one. In 1969, members of Charles Manson's communal family committed the Tate-LaBianca murders. Evidence at the scene suggested that they were inspired by several Beatles songs.

- "Revolution 1," by John, starts out with a distorted guitar sound but quickly turns into an anti-revolution folk doo-wop song with horn riffs.

- "Honey Pie" is a cute 1920s song from the English music hall tradition composed by Paul.

- "Revolution 9," credited to John and Yoko, is eight minutes of various tape loops, backwards and forward. This was John and Yoko's project and was so avant-garde that the others tried to keep it off the album.

- "Good Night," written by John for Ringo to sing, is a lovely, sweet pop, à la 1950, that has been interpreted as them saying "goodnight, sweet dreams" to the Beatles-era.

In January 1969, the Beatles tried to record a soundtrack for their movie *Get Back,* but the sessions dragged on without direction amid fights and walkouts. They finally gave up on the project, but it later was resurrected by Alan Klein, their manager for a time, who brought in Phil Spector to recut and remix the tapes. The results were issued as *Let It Be* (May 18, 1970), the last album *released* by the Beatles. The last album *recorded* by the Beatles, *Abbey Road* (October 1, 1969), was a final attempt to get back together and record an album like they used to, all collaborating in the same room. They called George Martin, and he agreed to produce it. The album, like all the Beatles albums, was filled with unique songs, such as "Come Together," "Something,"

"Here Comes the Sun," and "Because." This album is sometimes viewed as the Beatles getting together one last time to prove that they were the best band of the sixties and could still work together.

The Beatles' final appearance together was May 20, 1970, at the premiere of the movie *Let It Be*. Their death was slow, and no one agrees who walked out first or what the final "straw" was. Many blame Yoko Ono. Others blame their financial plight, all but ignored until after Brian's death, and the ensuing conflict it caused between Paul's business manager/father-in-law, Lee Eastman, and the other Beatles manager, Alan Klein. In reality, the sixties were over and it was time for them to move on.

Paul Is Dead and Backward Masking

At the end of the Beatles' career, two curious and intertwined rumors began to spread: that Paul McCartney was dead and that the Beatles had put secret messages on their recordings, some of which were backwards. Placing backwards messages came to be known as "backmasking" or "backward masking" There are two types of backwards messages. The first is a phrase that is recognizable in English when played forward, yet seems to say something else when played backwards. The second type is a phrase that is intentionally placed on the recording backwards that sounds like gibberish when played forward, but is recognizable in English when played backwards. Backmasking was connected to the "Paul is dead" theory because some of the "clues" surrounding his "death" were supposedly hidden on recordings with backmasking. (Backmasking had a life beyond the Beatles, as other groups, principally Led Zeppelin, have been accused of placing satanic messages on their recordings.)

The "Paul is dead" rumor was fascinating because it held America's interest for so long, evidencing the inordinate amount of attention given the Beatles by their fans. The rumor was thought to have originated in Midwestern college newspapers in 1969 and then spread further by Russell Gibb, a Detroit DJ. The story even drifted into the academic world in the journal article "The Curious Case of the 'Death' of Paul McCartney," in *Urban Life & Culture*.[17] The story was that Paul had been killed in an automobile accident around November 1966 and was replaced by William Campbell (whose passport photo is on the poster that came with the *White Album*), and the remaining Beatles had been secretly hiding clues.

There are approximately seventy clues. The major ones are:

On *Sgt. Pepper's Lonely Hearts Club Band*

1. On the cover, the Beatles are standing over a grave with the word "Beatles" spelled out in flowers along Paul's left-handed bass. The three strings on the bass symbolize the three remaining original Beatles.

2.   Inside, Paul is wearing an arm-patch with the letters "OPD," which supposedly stand for "officially pronounced dead" in Canada. The partially hidden patch actually contains the letters "OPP" for Ontario Provincial Police.

3.   On the back cover, Paul is facing backwards while the others are faced forward, and directly over his head are the lyrics to "Within You Without You."

On *Magical Mystery Tour*

1.   At the end of "Strawberry Fields," just as the music is fading out, John says, "I buried Paul." John maintained that he said "cranberry sauce."

2.   On page three of the booklet, a sign on Paul's desk reads, "I was."

3.   On page thirteen, Paul is not in his shoes; they are next to him, empty, and apparently covered with blood.

4.   On page twenty-three, the Beatles are wearing red carnations, except for Paul, who is wearing a black one.

On the *White Album*

1.   The opening phrase of "Revolution 9" is "number nine, number nine, number nine." When played backwards it says, "turn me on, deadman."

2.   At the end of "I'm So Tired," the words at the end played backwards say, "Paul is dead now, miss him, miss him."

On *Abbey Road*

1.   The cover shows a "funeral procession" walking toward a cemetery. Paul is in his bare feet, out of step with the others, his eyes are closed, and he's wearing a burial suit. John is the preacher, Ringo is dressed in black as a mourner, and George, wearing workclothes, is the grave digger.

2.   The license plate on the Volkswagen in the background reads "28 If," meaning that Paul would have been twenty-eight years old had he lived (actually, Paul would have been twenty-seven).

The "Paul is dead" rumors were so pervasive that Paul had to come out of semi-exile and deny the accounts of his death personally. The fact that this legend assumed so much media time attests to the news value the Beatles still had in 1969.

Life After the Beatles

Beatles fans had a difficult time believing that the best band in the world would break up while they were so popular and an influential musical force. Most believed that the band would someday reunite, and indeed several of the Beatles performed together in various combinations at certain events. Concert promoters offered them millions of dollars for one more tour, or even a single performance. Any hopes of that eventual reunion were dashed on December 8, 1980, when John Lennon was assassinated by Mark David Chapman outside Lennon's apartment building.

Lennon, with his collaborator-wife Yoko Ono, was fairly successful in his post-Beatles years. Lennon met Ono in 1966 at a showing of her art work at the Indica Gallery. They developed a relationship and were married in 1969. Lennon and Ono's musical collaboration began almost immediately, and through her, he was able to explore the musical *avant-garde*. Their work found its way onto the Beatles' *White Album* on the eight-minute, 15-second tape collage, "Revolution 9." Their relationship caused considerable strain within the Beatles, and some blame Ono for the group's breakup.

After several *avant-garde* albums, Lennon returned to the charts in 1971 with "Power to the People" and *Imagine* (#1). He reached the charts several more times, including a number-one hit with "Whatever Gets You Through the Night," on the number-one album *Walls and Bridges* (1974). His last release before becoming a house-husband was a collection of fifties rock songs called *Rock n' Roll*. In 1980, Lennon and Ono returned to music. They signed a record deal with Geffen records and released *Double Fantasy* less than one month before he was murdered. The first single from the album, "(Just Like) Starting Over," reached number one and was reminiscent of the Beatles' early work; it quoted fifties rock melodies and included a rockabilly hiccup at the beginning. After Lennon's death, two other singles, "Woman" and "Watching the Wheels" made it to the charts, and the album won the Grammy for Album of the Year (1981).

Paul McCartney's post-Beatles life was more successful than that of any of the others, possibly because of his penchant for writing good pop songs. His first solo release, *McCartney,* came two weeks before the release of *Let It Be* and contained his first solo number-one hit, "Maybe I'm Amazed." A year later, he reached number one again with "Uncle Albert/Admiral Halsey." After these hits he, along with his wife Linda (the former rock photographer, Linda Eastman), formed the band Wings and began to tour.

Throughout the seventies, McCartney continued to experience success, releasing more number-one recordings, including: "My Love" (1973, "Band on the Run" (1974), "Listen to What the Man Said" (1974), "Silly Love Songs" (1976), and "With a Little Luck" (1979). In the early eighties, he took part in two successful collaborations, one with Stevie Wonder ("Ebony and Ivory," 1982) and another with Michael Jackson ("The Girl Is Mine," 1983). McCartney was not as successful at recording number-one hits during the rest of the eighties, but he continued to write and tour.

As a songwriting team, Lennon and McCartney were a unique balance for the other. On their own, John was too inaccessible with his *avant garde* explorations and simple fifties rock, while Paul was too commercial, with pleasing pop songs that lacked the hard edge of their earlier collaborations.

George Harrison and Ringo Starr continued to record and perform during their post-Beatles lives, although with less success than John and Paul. Harrison reached number one with "My Sweet Lord" (1970), however that success was tempered by a lawsuit that proved that the song bore a striking resemblance to "He's So Fine" (1963) by the Chiffons. In 1971, Harrison organized one of the first and most important benefit concerts in rock history: the Concert for Bangladesh raised money for UNICEF to help feed the war victims in that new country. The concert featured guest performances by Eric Clapton, Bob Dylan, Ravi Shanka, Ringo Starr, and Leon Russell, and was made into a three-album set that won a Grammy for Album of the Year (1972) and was released as a movie.

Harrison joined the Traveling Wilburys and won a Grammy for Best Rock Performance by a Duo or Group (1989). Ringo Starr managed to place some recordings in the top ten, including the number one "Photograph," "Your Sixteen" (both in 1973), "It Don't Come Easy" (#3, 1971), and "Back Off Boogaloo" (#9, 1973). Ringo had more success with his acting career, appearing in the films *Candy* (1967), *The Magic Christian* (1969), *That'll Be the Day* (1973), *Caveman* (1981), and a hit children's show on PBS, *Shining Time Station.*

Beatles Imitators: The Monkees

The Monkees were specifically created to be a television version of the Beatles. The show's producer, Don Kirshner, advertised for actors in *Variety* and eventually selected Davy Jones, Micky Dolenz, Michael Nesmith, and Peter Tork for the roles of the Monkees. Davy Jones was an English actor and had the all-important accent; Micky Dolenz had been a child star, appearing in *Circus Boy* in the 1950s; and Nesmith and Tork had worked as musicians. Their first single, "Last Train to Clarksville," was released before the television show aired, and upon first hearing, many American teens thought that it was a new release by the Beatles because it featured the same peppy harmonies as the Beatles' second-phase recordings.

Their show ran from 1966 to 1968 and successfully combined TV sitcom material with Beatles-like music video vignettes. During the music video segments, the Monkees engaged in cute antics similar to those of the Beatles in

A Hard Day's Night and *Help.* They lip-synched to their records on the show, not unusual for television, but many have suggested that they did so in their live performances as well. They were capable of playing musical instruments but not at the same level as the studio musicians who recorded their songs. However, the fraud aspect of pretending to play distressed them, and they eventually learned to play well enough to perform for themselves. One of the most unusual concert-tour pairings ever was the Monkees and their opening act, Jimi Hendrix. The Monkees' young fans did not understand Hendrix, and he left the tour after a few shows.

The television audience enjoyed the Monkees, and their recordings are still played on oldies radio. The Monkees were not the only television band. *The Partridge Family* (1970) was the story of a fatherless family who earned money by performing as a rock band and starred Shirley Jones, David Cassidy, Susan Dey, and Danny Bonaduce. The story was inspired by a real family band, the Cowsills ("The Rain, the Park, and Other Things"), and David Cassidy (Shirley Jones's son on the show and in real life) was able to launch a brief career as a teen idol in the 1970s.

POP GROUPS OF THE BRITISH INVASION

In 1964, the Beatles opened the door for other English groups. The first, known as Mersey Beat groups, came from Liverpool and the Mersey River area, but later in the summer of 1964, British blues-inspired groups like the Animals began to appear. The first groups that arrived immediately after the Beatles were bands that used a pleasing vocal sound and clean vocal harmonies—the first style trait listeners associated with the Beatles. At first, the perverse media habit of building up artists into idols and then quickly tearing them down seemed to be operating. In January 1964, when the Beatles' number-one English recording "I Want to Hold Your Hand" was replaced by the Dave Clark Five's "Glad All Over," newspapers quickly claimed they had "crushed" the Beatles. The media fully expected the Beatles to be just one of many short fads soon to be replaced by another. After a while, the media realized that the Beatles would be popular for a longer period and they stopped billing new groups as Beatle-killers.

Gerry and the Pacemakers

Gerry Marsden led a popular Liverpool skiffle group at the same time as the Quarry Men, and initially they were more successful than Lennon and McCartney. When Alan Williams, the Beatles first agent/manager, needed a group to send to Hamburg, he first wanted Gerry and the Pacemakers, but they were already working, so he had to settle for the Beatles. After the Beatles began experiencing success, the Pacemakers were the next logical Liverpool group for

Brian Epstein to sign. Their early career was similar to that of the Beatles, with performances at Hamburg and Liverpool clubs like the Cavern Club.

Gerry and the Pacemakers reached American charts in June 1964 with "Don't Let the Sun Catch You Crying," and "Ferry Across the Mersey" (1965). During their two years of American visibility, they reached the top fifteen with several other recordings, but they disappeared after their sound wore out. The length of their American career was probably what the media initially expected for the Beatles.

Herman's Hermits

In October 1964, Herman's Hermits began a series of top-ten hits with "I'm Into Something Good" (1964). Their last hit was in 1967. At first, Americans thought they resembled the Beatles because they dressed in a similar fashion, they had long hair, and they sang with the expected clean vocal harmony. The lead singer, Peter Noone, was attractive and had extremely pronounced dimples, which made him successful with younger female fans. The Hermits were successful until the blues-inspired British bands achieved dominance; the Hermits were just too cute for their own good. Their two most popular recordings, "Mrs. Brown You've Got a Lovely Daughter," and "I'm Henry the Eighth, I Am," emanated directly from the English music-hall tradition; the former even used a ukulele-like guitar sound to heighten the old-time effect.

Other Early Groups

Also appearing in the first few months of the British invasion were solo singers and folk-like duos. Cilla Black (Priscilla White), a hat-check girl at the Cavern Club, reached the American charts in July 1965, with "You're My World" and later, in 1966, with "Alfie." Dusty Springfield, another solo singer, had a quick succession of hits such as "I Only Want to Be With You" (February 1964), "Stay Awhile" (April 1964), and Wishin' and Hopin'" (June 1964), and remained successful in England after she faded in America. "Little Children," by Billy J. Kramer, a close friend of Brian Epstein, reached the charts in May 1964. However, like the other solo singers, he had no lasting impact on the shape of the British invasion.

The duos Peter and Gordon ("A World Without Love," "Nobody I Know," "I Go to Pieces," "True Love Ways," and "Woman") and Chad and Jeremy ("Yesterday's Gone," "A Summer Song," and "Willow Weep For Me") had a period of success on the American charts. Both groups recorded songs with a very smooth vocal sound that could have fit neatly into the yet-to-be-invented *folk rock* category. It is possible that the sound of these two groups influenced other American folk singers to consider a more electric sound. Peter and Gordon got their break because Paul McCartney, who was dating Peter's sister, Jane Asher, gave them "World Without Love" to record.

The Zombies had several hits but did not experience much success because of the timing of the recordings. "She's Not There" (1964) hit the American charts about the same time as Herman's Hermits first hit, and it reached number two. The following January, "Tell Her No" reached the charts, but that was all they had for a long time. In 1967, they recorded an album called *Odyssey and Oracle* but disbanded several weeks after its completion. Their third American hit, "Time of the Season," came from that album, but because they were no longer together, they were not able to benefit from its success. The Zombies' recordings had an interesting soft, jazzy, instrumental sound, along with pleasant vocal harmonies and, of all the first-wave British bands, they were probably the most unique. Their keyboardist, Rod Argent, formed his own band named after himself, and in 1972 had a hit with "Hold Your Head High."

BRITISH INVASION GROUPS

Although the first groups of the British invasion were pleasant vocal, clean-harmony bands, the rougher, blues-shouter-inspired groups had the most lasting influence on rock. The seeds of the blues revival that began with purists Alexis Korner and John Mayall were beginning to sprout and regenerate the blues feeling in new contexts. The first significant blues-shouter recording appeared in the summer of 1964 when the Animals' "House of the Rising Sun" made the charts. It is difficult to imagine the type of cross-fertilization of blues and folk music that took place during the skiffle movement, but the result was a shouting folk-blues style. One possible explanation is the influence of Ramblin' Jack Elliot, a Woodie Guthrie disciple. He left New York for England around 1955 because of the McCarthy hearings, and stayed there until 1961. Elliot was influential in the skiffle movement because he introduced an American folk-guitar style (flatpicking) to England, performed regularly at London's Roundhouse club (also a favorite spot of Korner), and recorded several albums that sold well enough to remain in print for a decade. In a radio interview, Elliot told of entertaining a group of British schoolchildren on a railway platform one day, and years later one of the children, Mick Jagger, told him that performance had inspired him to play guitar. Lonnie Donegan recorded several of Woody Guthrie's songs, and one must presume that he was introduced to Guthrie and the New York folk repertoire by Elliott.

The Animals (Eric Burdon, Alan Price, Chas Chandler, John Steel, and Hilton Valentine) began as the Alan Price Combo, a jazz trio, but their focus shifted toward blues with the addition of Burdon. Their first two recordings, "Baby Let Me Follow You Down" and "House of the Rising Sun," were both from Bob Dylan's first album, and the likely reason the songs appeared on Dylan's recording was that they were staples of the Greenwich Village folk

The Animals

repertoire. The connection between the Animals and the Greenwich Village folk scene was Jack Elliot. "House of the Rising Sun" reached the American charts in August 1964, and since Dylan was unknown to most teenagers at this time, the music was not received as a folk song but rather as an English song. The recording was important because it prepared the American ear for the sound of the British blues shouter, and it may have influenced Dylan to move back to his rock roots. Dylan heard the Animals' version of "House of the Rising Sun" during his May 1964 English tour and told his friends, "My God, ya oughtta hear what's going down over there. Eric Burdon, the Animals, ya know? Well, he's doing "House of the Rising Sun" in rock. Rock! It's fuckin' wild! Blew my mind."[18]

Them, featuring Van Morrison, also used the raspy vocal sound similar to that of the Animals. They reached the American charts in 1965 with "Here Comes the Night" and "Mystic Eyes," and hit again in 1966 with "Gloria." "Mystic Eyes" was an unusual recording for pop radio because it was basically a blues jam. The song began with a very bluesy harmonica solo over an up-tempo walking-bass line that eventually evolved into the hambone/Bo Diddley rhythm. The lyrics are sparse and have an improvised quality to them.

There is a mention of a graveyard and then just the repeated words "mystic eyes." Their next recording, "Gloria," was also based on simple musical material (two riffs) and lyrics that were delivered in a blues-shouter, talking-blues style. "Gloria" has an interesting history. It was not a hit for Them, but it was for a suburban Chicago group called the Shadows. of Night. It also was used by Jim Morrison (Doors) in live shows to act out a sexual encounter. The fact that censors did not ban the song, as they had earlier rock songs, like "Louie, Louie," is an indication of society's increasing tolerance of suggestive lyrics.

"Gloria" has a talking-blues section in which the singer follows Gloria's action. In the final section, the singer spells out of the name G-L-O-R-I-A, and then goes into a double-time ring-shout section. The form of Them's recording of "Gloria," and some of their other songs, is the one-chord blues vamp, like Muddy Waters's "Mannish Boy" and John Lee Hooker's "Boogie Children." Them disbanded in 1966, but Van Morrison began a solo career and reached the top ten in 1967 with "Brown-Eyed Girl." Both the Animals and Them were influential in preparing audiences for the sound of gravel-voiced blues shouters.

The Kinks, who reached the American charts first in October 1964 with "You Really Got Me" and later in January 1965 with "All Day and All of the Night," have a long history, but their influence is difficult to interpret. Their early hits used basic blues riffs and a very distorted guitar sound, which qualifies them for status as the early roots of *heavy metal*. However, their attitude, behavior, and general delivery is suggestive of an early appearance of the *punk* aesthetic. Their later songs are interpreted as chronicling the woes of the crumbling British Empire and middle class. "All Day and All of the Night" was a simple, even corny, love song that probably would not have sold well had it not been for the distorted fuzz-tone guitar riff that permeated the whole song. That riff, probably played by a pre-Zeppelin Jimmy Page, prepared the audience for future distortion-laden power-chord groups. The song's guitar solo was an exciting clone of the Kingsmen's "Louie, Louie" solo, complete with the scream, "Get 'em!" preceding it. Their vocal sound was, at the same time, disaffected, whiney, and sneering, which, when combined with those innocent love lyrics and power chords, created a hybrid pop sound: the incessant one-chord vamp of the Delta blues grafted onto pop love lyrics.

The Kinks had trouble in the United States because their rude behavior caused them to be barred by AFTRA for "unprofessional conduct," and that meant that they were not able to tour in support of their recordings. In 1966, they turned away from the distorted riff sound and released "A Well Respected Man." Some suggest this was an answer to the Beatles' "Nowhere Man," and it began a path that led them to a series of concept albums and theatrical presentations, such as *Arthur*, the *Decline and Fall of the British Empire, Preservation Acts 1 and 2,* and *Schoolboys in Disgrace.*

Rolling Stones

The Rolling Stones were part of the second generation of British blues bands, the first generation being Alexis Korner and Cyril Davies. They were the most successful English group other than the Beatles, and represented, as rock critics generally comment, the opposing musical viewpoint. The Rolling Stones were managed by Andrew Loog Oldham, a former publicity man for Brian Epstein's NEMS, who carefully crafted their image to occupy the position opposite the Beatles. While the Beatles were polite, witty, and polished, the Rolling Stones were aggressive, sexually suggestive, and raw. While the Beatles presided over the love generation, the Stones orchestrated the unruly Altamont concert. The Beatles personified the colorful *mod* culture, while the Stones were the rockers. Of course, this was all image. The Beatles were a rough Hamburg band who dressed in black leather and were only molded by Brian Epstein into the polite moptops, and the Rolling Stones were a purist blues band fronted by Mick Jagger, a student from the London School of Economics, shaped by Oldham into the satanic Stones. Their divergent marketing strategies placed the two bands in such opposing musical positions that, in the 1960s, American teens identified their musical tastes by asking the question "Are you a Beatle or a Stone?"

The band formed amid the excitement for R&B caused by the Alexis Korner–inspired blues revival. Mick Jagger and Keith Richards attended the same grammar school, but their exam results sent them in different directions: Mick to college and Keith to a trade school. One day they met on the train and discovered their mutual love of the Chicago blues, so they began meeting for listening/jam sessions at Dick Taylor's house. The three of them formed a band called Little Boy Blue and the Blue Boys. Around the same time, Brian Jones, who had been a trad jazz sax and clarinetist, began working with Korner's band under the stage name Elmo Lewis as a blues guitarist in the slide-guitar tradition.

The first edition of the Rolling Stones included Ian Stewart (piano), Dick Taylor (bass), Tony Chapman (drums), along with Mick Jagger, Keith Richards and Brian Jones; later Taylor and Chapman were replaced by Bill Wyman (bass) and Charlie Watts (drums).[19] Jones was the best musician of the group, and his superiority made him the leader; his contract with Oldham even included an extra leader's fee. Their first performance as the Rolling Stones (their name came from a Muddy Waters recording) was at the Marquee Club as a substitute for Alexis Korner, who had an engagement elsewhere. Soon the early Stones were befriended by Giorgio Gomelski, owner of a blues club called the Crawdaddy in the Station Hotel, who helped them improve their performance and let them play at his club when he felt they were ready. There were only sixty-three people at their first Crawdaddy performance, but within weeks the audience grew to over four hundred.[20]

Andrew Loog Oldham and his partner, Eric Easton, signed the Stones to a management contract in 1963 and arranged for a recording contract with Decca Records. Decca was an easy target because earlier it had rejected the Beatles and did not want to let the next big group slip through its fingers. The Stones entered the Olympic recording studio nine days later and began working on their first single, "Come On," by Chuck Berry. From the beginning, Oldham was concerned with the group's image: He had Ian Stewart expelled from the band because he had the "wrong look" (although he took part in most of the Stones' recording sessions) and suggested that Charlie Watts grow his hair longer because he looked too respectable. Oldham coolly calculated their "bad boy" image. After the band's first television appearance, on *Thank Your Lucky Stars,* he reacted to the negative adult response by telling the Stones that "the more the parents hate you, the more the kids will love you."[21]

The "bad boy" image was a new twist for the Stones because they began as reverent protectors of the blues and R&B tradition; their early albums attest to their dedication. Their first album, *England's Newest Hit Makers,* had Buddy Holly's "Not Fade Away"; "Route 66" from the smooth West Coast blues of Nat King Cole; Willie Dixon's Chicago blues, "I Just Want to Make Love to You"; Motown's Marvin Gaye classic by Holland-Dozier-Holland, "Can I Get a Witness"; Chuck Berry's "Carol"; and Rufus Thomas's "Walking the Dog," plus a few originals. The second album, *12 x 5,* had a few more originals but still included standards like Chuck Berry's "Around and Around"; Ray Charles's first hit, "Confessing the Blues"; the Drifters' "Under the Boardwalk"; and Dale Hawkins's rockabilly hit "Susie Q." Gradually, they added more and more original material until they established their own identifiable style built on a foundation of African-American music. Their reverence for the Chicago blues was such that, during their first tour of the United States, they stopped at Chicago's famous Chess studios and recorded several songs.

The Stones were not an instant success, but their popularity in America grew steadily until the summer of 1965 when "(I Can't Get No) Satisfaction" hit the charts. Their second single, "I Want to Be Your Man," was given to them by the Beatles and reached the British top fifteen. Their next recordings, "Not Fade Away" (Buddy Holly), "It's All Over Now" (the Valentinos), and "Little Red Rooster" (Willie Dixon) were also successful in England, but they did not reach the American top ten until "The Last Time" in April 1965. Their 1964 American tour was not a big success and drew as few as six hundred fans at some locations. Rather than taking America by storm, as the Beatles had, their success slowly grew until "(I Can't Get No) Satisfaction" peaked in June 1965. Thereafter, all their recordings were hits. It's difficult to know whether their bad-boy image drove them or if they drove it, but by the end of the sixties, in the mind of the public, they were agents of the "forces of darkness."

Their drug and alcohol use haunted them from the beginning, starting with Brian Jones, who was so incapacitated that he finally was asked to leave the band. Jones's legendary bouts with drugs and alcohol, complicated by his mutually destructive relationship with actress and occult enthusiast Anita Pallenberg, made him useless as a band member. He did not participate in the recording of "Satisfaction" because he was asleep, or unconscious, and missed the session, and he was often so incapacitated that, during recording sessions, the Stones pretended to record his playing. Eventually, in 1969, he was replaced by Mick Taylor. Brian accidentally drowned on July 2, 1969, after ingesting quantities of downers, brandy, vodka, and whiskey.

Mick Jagger and Keith Richards were also deeply involved with drugs and alcohol, yet they were able to control their use enough that they could still show up and perform. Their drug use affected their lifestyle and brought them into contact with people who helped solidify their bad-boy image. They became involved with filmmaker Kenneth Anger, a follower of Aleister Crowley (1875–1947), who was the leader of a cult called the Hermetic Order of the Golden Dawn. Anger wanted to cast Mick in the role of Lucifer in a film called *Lucifer Rising*, but Mick limited his contribution to writing the film's music. His girlfriend, Marianne Faithful, and his brother Chris appeared onscreen. Adding further to their growing satanic image was the album *Satanic Majesties Request*, an attempt to compete with the Beatles' *Sgt. Pepper's Lonely Hearts Club Band*, and the song "Sympathy for the Devil." Their fans' behavior also fueled their image because Stones' concerts were often scenes of chaotic disturbances. In Paris, police had to use tear gas; in Marseilles, Mick was hit by a chair thrown onstage; a London concert was stopped after three minutes because of a mad dash toward the stage; and the infamous Altamont concert ended with three accidental deaths and one murder.

Regardless of the origins of their image, by 1970, in the minds of the public, the Rolling Stones *were* sex, drugs, rock and roll, and Satan. The Stones were the first band to purposely cultivate an evil image and thereby opened the door for other bands to try to exceed it. Since that time, many other groups, especially *heavy metal* ones, purposely employ occult iconography to associate themselves with and extend rock and roll's connotation of evil. Music history frequently tells stories of performers who allegedly have sold their soul to the devil to achieve musical success, such as violinist Niccolo Paganini (1782–1840), whose enormous technical powers were thought by many to have come from the devil. The legend most rock fans are familiar with is the story of blues singer Robert Johnson selling his soul to the devil at the "crossroads" one night. These stories became so influential that audiences have come to view such satanic deals with a touch of romanticism.

The Stones' efforts to keep up with, and outdo, the rock world led to a disastrous free concert at the Altamont Raceway in San Francisco on

December 6, 1969. Earlier in the year, a large successful rock festival had been held near Woodstock, New York, which produced a feeling that all of America's youth were united in the spirit of peace and love. The festival attracted an audience of about 450,000 who coexisted peacefully without major incident; it was the zenith of the peace and love generation. The Stones' concert at Altamont was exactly the opposite–it single-handedly brought an end to the sixties' spirit of peace and love.

The Stones' 1969 tour of America had created bad publicity because of high ticket prices and late performance times, sometimes by several hours. The tour was being filmed by Albert and David Maysles to be released as a Stones live-concert movie. When the Stones reached Los Angeles, Jerry Garcia (of the Grateful Dead) suggested that a gigantic free concert in San Francisco would make a great ending to the film, plus give them some positive publicity. The owner of the Altamont Raceway offered free use of his track, and the deal was signed only twenty-four hours before the concert was to begin. The details for the concert were hastily drawn and many mistakes were made in the planning of sanitation facilities, parking space, and security. The most grievous error was using the motorcycle gang the Hell's Angels as a security force and paying them with five hundred dollars worth of alcohol, thereby assuring that they would be drunk and dangerous.

By noon, the concert site was already crowded with 250,000 people who were drinking and ingesting bad acid. Fights broke out, and the Angels enforced order by using pool cues as riot batons. Even the performers were not immune to the violence that erupted. Marty Balin of the Jefferson Airplane was knocked unconscious when he jumped off the stage to try to stop the Angels from beating someone. Although the Stones arrived at the site on time, they appeared onstage an hour and a half late because Mick felt that his costume would look better after dark. When they started their third number, "Sympathy for the Devil," Mick thought he saw someone pointing a gun at him, so the Angels leapt into action. Mick tried to calm the ensuing chaos by announcing, "Brothers and Sisters, come on now. That means everybody cool out." He never regained full control of the situation, but continued with the song anyway and remarked about their satanic tribute, "We always have something funny happen when we start that number." As the Stones performed "Sympathy for the Devil," the Angels beat and knifed to death Meredith Hunter, the African-American who had supposedly pointed the gun at Jagger. The Stones had finally taken their bad-boy image too far, unleashed the forces of evil, and brought the generation of peace and love to a crashing halt.

The Stones survived the concert at Altamont (Mick immediately left for Switzerland with a suitcase full of cash), but the "Age of Aquarius" was not so lucky. The events of the day made Woodstock seem like a faded dream and forced the unwanted realization that America's youth were not all united in the spirit of peace and love. The concert also brought an end to large rock festivals in America, and any future concerts were weighed down with concerns about security, billing, film rights, insurance and performance fees.

As a band, the Rolling Stones survived the decade and outlived the Beatles; however, their chart successes began to occur less frequently. Their 1971 hit, "Brown Sugar," reached number one, but came under attack by various groups because its lyrics touched on sensitive issues by using phrases such as, "Gold coast slave ship bound for cotton fields," "Brown sugar, howcome you taste so good," and "Whip the women just around midnight." The Stones' continued success has been remarkable, particularly because they have never altered their musical style to appear contemporary, except for a short disco flirtation with "Miss You" (1978), and yet they have never been thought of as an oldies act. Perhaps their reverence for the basic R&B characteristics that they built their style upon never went out of style with the audience.

BRITISH RHYTHM AND BLUES: OTHER DIRECTIONS
The Yardbirds

While the Rolling Stones' version of the blues led them to develop their own particular musical style, the Yardbirds developed a style that can be considered a precursor to heavy metal. Originally called the Most Blueswailing Yardbirds, they replaced the Rolling Stones at the Crawdaddy Club and performed a repertoire also derived from Chess Records Chicago blues recordings. The band at one time or another included three of the top guitar players of the era: Eric Clapton, Jeff Beck, and Jimmy Page. Clapton later became part of the power trio in Cream, Page formed Led Zeppelin, and Beck formed the Jeff Beck Group (with Rod Stewart and Ron Wood). The early Yardbirds were known for their "rave ups," which were sections of open improvisation within a song, just like jazz, which led to their use of extended guitar techniques like feedback, distortion, heavy bass, muted-string strumming, a background of short riffs, and ending with a double-time ring-shout rhythm. The implicit freedom of these rave-up sections gave the Yardbirds the opportunity to experiment with this new vocabulary of techniques, which were further developed by *metal* bands.

Their first hit, "For Your Love," was a very popish, unblues-like song that featured the sound of an electric harpsichord, bongo drums, and vocal harmonies. Despite their move to psychedelic pop, their first album contains enough R&B to give some insight into the way they used the rave-up format in live performances. The second selection on the album, Mose Allison's "I'm Not Talking," features a blues-shouter vocal over a fuzz-tone guitar riff and also has several jump-blues style guitar solos by Clapton. The last song on the second side is a five-and-a-half-minute version of "My Girl Sloopy," better known as "Hang On Sloopy," a typical American garage-band song. The Yardbirds start with a typical performance, complete with background falsetto call-and-response parts, but about two minutes into the selection they sing "ah" and build a major chord note by note, like the Beatles' version of "Twist and Shout." When they get to the top of the chord, they scream wildly and the guitars quickly "power strum" one chord, creating a metallic wall of sound. This happens several times, and four minutes into the song they break into double-time ring-shout rhythm placed over a jazzy walking bass line.

Their third American single, "I'm a Man," is a one-chord blues vamp originally recorded by Bo Diddley as "I'm a Man," and by Muddy Waters as "Mannish Boy." Toward the end of the album version is an open solo section with a call-and-response between the guitar and harmonica, which leads to a "noise" section where the guitar rapidly strums the strings. These rave-ups were the beginning of extended improvisations in rock and, in the next decade, gave rise to the creation of guitar superstars.

While the Yardbirds were exciting and improvisational in live settings, their move to popish psychedelic songs was too far away from the blues for Eric Clapton's taste, so he quit the band in 1965, opting to work as a laborer rather than play pop music. Clapton soon joined John Mayall's Bluesbreakers and resumed playing the music he loved. Jeff Beck replaced Clapton, who still appeared on four songs on the second American album, *Having a Rave Up* (1966). In 1966, Jimmy Page replaced the bass player, but within a short time Page and Beck were trading lead guitar spots. The band stayed together until 1968, although their last American hits, "Shapes of Things" and "Over Under Sideways Down," were in 1966. After they broke up, Jimmy Page formed Led Zeppelin to play the remainder of the Yardbirds' performance obligations. Led Zeppelin established a format from which other metal groups could grow: a heavy reliance on distorted blues riffs, the blues-shouter style—which became closer to screaming than shouting—prominent bass lines, and a dose of the occult.

Cream

When Eric Clapton quit the Yardbirds in March 1965, he joined John Mayall's Bluesbreakers for a short time and then, in 1966, formed a group called Cream. At the time Cream was referred to as a "supergroup," an all-star band made up of the best members from other groups, and it lived up to that expectation for two years. The other players, Ginger Baker (drums) and Jack Bruce (bass), had earned their blues credentials with Alexis Korner and the Graham Bond organization. All three had powerful reputations as technically superior musicians. Cream has also been referred to as a "power trio," a small group whose musicians are able to make up for the missing members with skill and heavy amplification; they were the forerunners of *heavy metal.*

Cream's live performances were exciting and filled with lengthy improvisations from Clapton, Bruce, and Baker. Baker's drumming was extremely powerful and he, along with Keith Moon (the Who), was considered one of the best drummers of the era. The group was an instant success at live performances, but they did not make an impression on the American charts until February 1968 with "Sunshine of Your Love."

"Sunshine," one of the recordings from this period that could be considered a starting point for heavy metal, is a twelve-bar blues built on one riff that permeates the entire recording. Clapton's guitar solo shows his mastery of B. B. King's style. It uses long tones that draw attention to the sound quality of the distortion, string bending, and the finger vibrato that King developed because he was not comfortable with a bottleneck. Baker's drum style on the recording also was revolutionary in that he did not use cymbals in their normal time-keeping role. Instead, he used pounding tom-toms to propel the music. On other recordings, even though Baker used cymbals in the typical manner, he increased the presence of toms and made the drum sound an important element in the overall music mix.

After Cream folded, Clapton formed another supergroup called Blind Faith, with Ginger Baker, Steve Winwood, and Rick Grech, who stayed together for one album and one tour. Shortly after the demise of Blind Faith, Clapton joined Delaney & Bonnie, another short-lived band that at one time included Leon Russell, Dave Mason, and George Hamilton. Delaney and Bonnie Bramlett developed a combination of gospel, country, and R&B that would have been interesting to any English musician who had been through the skiffle craze. Bonnie had previously worked as a backup singer for Ike and Tina Turner and had developed a better-than-usual African-American vocal imitation that was closer to the "real thing" than that of any other English band.

In 1970, Clapton began to emphasize his singing and recorded a solo album that contained his first solo hit single, "After Midnight." Soon after that success, he organized Derek and the Dominos with former Delaney & Bonnie sidemen and recorded one album that contained one of his most notable recordings, "Layla." The song is propelled by a wonderful guitar riff that underlies a set of lyrics delivered in a blues-shouter style, but the only guitar solo comes at the end when the record is fading out.

Derek and the Dominos broke up in 1971, and Clapton did not perform often due to his increasing heroin habit. He began a comeback with the album *461 Ocean Blvd.* (1974), which reached number one, and during the seventies, he reached the top ten several times: "I Shot the Sheriff" (#1, 1974), "Lay Down Sally" (#3, 1978), and "Promises" (#9, 1979). By the eighties, Clapton's recordings had become a staple of AOR radio (Album Oriented Radio or Album Oriented Rock, featuring longer, live clips), and his legendary status, "Clapton as God," was intact. Clapton won his first Grammy in 1991 for Best Rock Vocal Performance for *Bad Love*. In 1991, his four-year-old son, Connor, fell to his death out a fiftieth-story window. The tragedy inspired the song "Tears in Heaven" (#2, 1993). The heartfelt acoustic song won the Grammy in 1992 for Best Pop Vocal Performance. Since that year, Clapton has won, or shared, seven other Grammies, with the latest in 1999 for *The Calling* by Carlos Santana, featuring Eric Clapton.

Clapton remains an important guitarist, and others are rated according to the standard he established through his work with the Yardbirds and Cream. Clapton's guitar style has remained rooted in the blues, with his country-blues-style accompaniment riffs and his single-line solo style reminiscent of both T-Bone Walker and B. B. King.

The Who

The place of the Who (Peter Townshend, Roger Daltrey, John Entwistle, Keith Moon) in rock history is a curious one because they grew out of the same R&B movement as did other British rock bands but became best known for their barbaric destruction of instruments onstage and for their rock opera *Tommy*. Although both are theatrical events, they seem incompatible. The Who first gained popularity through their identification with a British youth movement called the mods, a movement that had little impact in the United States other than in fashion styles.

In England in the early sixties, there were two popular youth types: mods and rockers. (in America, the choices were hippies, greasers, or preppies.) The rockers wore black leather jackets, jeans (sometimes leather pants) and cowboy boots or motorcycle boots, had Elvis (Teddy Boy) hairstyles, and rode motorcycles. The mods, short for modernists, chose a continental Italian appearance with short hair, rounded-collar Italian shirt, bell-bottomed pants, and pointed-toe shoes; they rode Italian motor scooters, preferably Vespas. The girls were frail and elfin-like and wore short dresses, high-heels, and seamless stockings, and had a pale face color with lots of mascara. An entire fashion industry developed, centered around Carnaby Street and King's Road in London, by catering to the mods. Those clothing styles gradually infiltrated the United States in the mid-1960s. During this period, male clothing became more colorful and was characterized by flowered and paisley shirts and ties, combined with brightly colored bell-bottomed pants. Women's styles were also influenced along the flowered and paisley lines. Women were also placed in the position of having to adhere to the mod female body type because a model named Twiggy ruled the fashion world. Twiggy was extremely thin, with a distinctly pre-pubescent figure, and had heavily made-up eyes; her effect on the fashion industry and feminine body image never entirely wore off.

In 1963, the Who acquired a manager/public relations man named Pete Meaden who wanted them to appeal to the mod audience. Meaden changed their name to the High Numbers, after a current mod fad of wearing T-shirts with numbers on them, and crafted their repertoire to suit the mods' tastes, which were Motown and R&B. Meaden booked them into a mod hangout called The Scene, where they were unusually successful, especially since the mods generally preferred recorded music. On the strength of their popularity with the mods, the High Numbers recorded "I'm the Face" (face was also mod slang) and "Zoot Suit," although the recordings did not sell well. After their recordings flopped, the High Numbers found new managers, Kit Lambert and Chris Stamp, and changed their name to The Who to distance themselves from the failure of their previous mod recordings.

In 1964, Pete Townshend had an accident and damaged his guitar on the low ceiling above the stage at the Railway Hotel and, in a temper tantrum, beat the guitar to death by smashing it on the floor. The audience loved it so much that the Who began adding orchestrated violence to their act. Sociologists are better equipped to deal with the questions of why their instrument-smashing became so popular, but it worked for them and became a Who trademark. In 1964, they signed a contract with Decca and recorded "I Can't Explain," which was released in January 1965. Their first single using the Who name did not sell well until they appeared on the television show *Ready, Steady Go,* where Townshend smashed his guitar and Moon overturned his drums. The audience loved it and rushed out to buy their recording. By the time they reached America two years later, their stage act was a well-developed routine, with Townshend using big full-circle arm motions to pound out guitar power chords, Moon behaving like a wild man behind the drums, Daltrey confidently strutting around the stage, and Entwistle calmly laying down intricate bass lines. The impact of their stage act seemed to define the rebellious defiance of rock's sound in visual terms.

The Who's first American success (number seventy-five) came in late 1965 with "My Generation," a song about teenage angst that seems to be as meaningful now as it was then. The song was in a stop-time call-and-response format that included vocal stuttering by Roger Daltrey, and it mentioned three common teen phrases: "put us down," "dig," and "fade away" (from the Stones' song "Not Fade Away"). Earlier, Bill Haley had said that he tried to write songs that included popular teen expressions, so Townshend was continuing a longstanding tradition in rock and roll by using popular slang. The fourth line of the song contains their most famous lyric, "Hope I die before I get old," which seemed to echo the sentiment expressed in that era's American saying, "Don't trust anyone over thirty." The stuttering, however, drew the most attention from critics, who said it reflected the neurotic state of teenagers in modern society.

In 1967, they reached the top ten with "I Can See for Miles," number twenty-four with "Happy Jack," and they preceded Jimi Hendrix at the Monterey Pop Festival. At Monterey, they tossed a coin with Hendrix to see who would go on first because both of their stage acts involved instrumental destruction; Hendrix lost and followed the Who, but he one-upped them by squirting lighter fluid on his guitar (in a very suggestive manner) and setting it on fire. Rock and roll had always been a theatrical production, but the Who and Hendrix brought it to new levels.

Conscious of the role of theatrics in popular music, the Who innovated a new rock convention by composing a rock opera, *Tommy* (1968), about a deaf, mute, and blind youth who excels at playing pinball. The music intelligensia were thrilled because rock had adapted itself to an accepted musical form, the opera. Furthermore, acknowledgment of that form demonstrated that rock itself had matured into a serious art form. In reality, it meant that by calling the production an opera, rock was somehow elevated so as to be acceptable to audiences at the Metropolitan Opera House, and there was now a way to attract teens to "classical" performances. The Who performed the opera twice during the period. The song "Pinball Wizard" became a pop single in the United States, and Ken Russell made a film version (1975) of *Tommy,* featuring Tina Turner and Elton John.

In 1973, Peter Townshend completed another rock opera, *Quadrophenia,* dealing with the mod culture, but it did not have much impact in the United States because the mod lifestyle had no American counterpart. In 1979, a film version of *Quadrophenia* was released, but the most popular Who movie was *The Kids Are All Right* (1979).

In 1978, Keith Moon died of an overdose of Heminevrin, a sedative prescribed to help him cure his alcoholism. Moon along with Zeppelin drummer, John Bonham, Stone's guitarist Brian Jones, and many other rock stars, had lived a dangerous lifestyle filled with sex, drugs, and alcohol to such an extent that their escapades were known throughout the rock world. Despite these problems, the Who were one of the best English rock bands of the period, but they seemed to be trapped between "just playing good rock and roll" and making a kind of music that was culturally meaningful.

LISTENING TO THE MUSIC

♪♪ "Satisfaction"—performed by the Rolling Stones

Keith Richards's aggressive fuzz-tone guitar riff sets the pattern for this classic rock song, whose lyrics reflect the anger and frustration of teens everywhere during the summer of "protest music." During the first week of May 1965, while the Rolling Stones were touring Florida, Richards conceived this famous lick while working with a new Gibson distortion device. A late-night visit to Jagger's room with this musical idea inspired Mick, and the group started recording the new song within a week. First working out of Chess Records in Chicago, they finished the recording in Los Angeles at RCA. "Satisfaction" reflects R&B styles as performed by these mid-sixties British youth in a most original way. Richards later claimed that the riff was based on the Martha and the Vandellas' tune "Dancing in the Streets," and the title line most likely had its origins in the Muddy Waters song "I Can't Be Satisfied." The Rolling Stones' seventh U.S. single became their first number-one hit in the United States, spending twelve weeks on the charts and selling one million copies.

Analysis of "(I Can't Get No) Satisfaction"—3:40 in length, released in England in June 1965 (London 9766), and in the United States in July 1965 (Abkco 6667-1)

This is a verse-chorus form with a sixteen-bar chorus (A) and an eighteen-bar verse (B). The A section is referred to as the chorus because it repeats relatively unchanged, and the B is the verse because the lyrics change each time. The famous fuzz-tone riff occurs during the B section and also the last four bars of the A-section, helping to sonically link the A section to the B section. The meter is in four (4 foot taps per measure). Interestingly, the combination of drums and tambourine produces the cha-cha rhythm from the fifties (1 − 2 − 3 + − 4). Personnel: Produced by Andrew Loog Oldham, featuring Mick Jagger, lead vocals; Keith Richards, guitar & vocals; Brian Jones, rhythm guitar (rumored to have missed this recording session); Bill Wyman, bass; Charlie Watts, drums.

0:00   Introduction (8 measures): The fuzz-tone riff begins by itself in the first bar, with the bass entering in bar two and drums following in bar three. An acoustic guitar and tambourine enter in bar five.

0:14   A Section (16 measures): Jagger's vocal lines are accompanied by a non-fuzz guitar that also adds an answer to each space in the vocal line. Much like the classic vocal blues, the lyric repeats the first line and then climbs in excitement with the lyrics "'cause I try, and I try, and I try, and I try," coming to a climax on the title line. Some rough-edged background vocals can also be heard. The return of the opening guitar riff helps add momentum to the last four measures of the A section.

0:42   B Section (18 measures): Begins with the lyrics "When I'm drivin'" and is accompanied by the fuzz-tone guitar riff. The use of the incessant riff is reminiscent of one-chord vamp blues songs like "I'm a Man." After twelve bars, a drum and tambourine break (with the same rhythms used during the lyric) interrupt, followed by four more measures of "No no no, that's what I say."

1:14 A Section (16 measures): The first A section repeats.

1:42 B Section (18 measures) Begins "When I'm watchin'," and is again accompanied by the fuzz-tone riff. The structure remains the same, with the drum break after twelve measures and "That's what I say" lyrics filling the final four measures.

2:14 A Section (16 measures): A return of the A section, except that this time the second line is changed to "Can't get me no girlie action."

2:43 B Section (18 measures): Begins with "When I'm ridin' 'round the world" and continues with the same format.

3:15 Coda: The final section features the recurring guitar riff. Here Jagger improvises, using the title line in various low and high ranges as the song quickly fades.

For Musicians

The opening guitar figure is based on the fifth, sixth, and flat seventh notes of an E major scale, infusing this simple pattern with important blues notes. The contrapuntal, almost free-moving bass line makes the chord progression ambiguous, but most often E to D are used for this eight-bar intro. The distorted guitar texture continues as this motive recurs frequently throughout the song. For the choruses, the guitar and tambourine play figures at the ends of the bars, punctuating the lyrics, while the bass line remains syncopated under Jagger's "giant triplet" melodic figure. This vocal phrasing technique gives great forward momentum to the melodic material. The chord progression for these eight bars uses two measures of E followed by two bars of A. The ascending melody on "'cause I try" is enhanced by the alternating E to B chords below, and the title line climax is accentuated by the returning guitar riff. The background harmonies are rough and free-sounding, with the title line sung in group fashion. The remaining two choruses and verses follow the same musical formula, with sixteen bars for the chorus and eighteen for the verse. The final coda section returns to the intro material, with Jagger exploring his vocal range accompanied by the guitar riff.

Final Comments

"Satisfaction," a hit huge for the Rolling Stones, was voted Best Record of the Year in the annual *New Music Express* reader's poll in 1965. Singing it as a regular feature during concert tours, Jagger frequently pointed at audience members during the "'cause I try, and I try" section, and late 1960s tours often featured a large inflated phallus during this song. Soul artists Otis Redding and Aretha Franklin both recorded the song, with Redding's version reaching the charts in 1966. A highly syncopated tongue-in-cheek version by the emerging New Wave group Devo hit the charts in early 1978, helping establish them as recording artists.

𝄞♪♪ "Lucy in the Sky With Diamonds"—performed by the Beatles

Lennon's ability to compose psychedelic music invoking images of other realms is highlighted on the 1967 album *Sgt. Pepper's Lonely Hearts Club Band* in "Lucy in the Sky With Diamonds." The often-told history of the song's origin reports an encounter between Lennon and his four-year-old son Julian, who showed his father one of his paintings, to which he had given this unusual title. Musically inspired, Lennon's sense of poetic imagery resulted in the fanciful word play heard in this song. Much has been made of the correlation between the drug LSD and the capital letters of the song title, but until the day he died, Lennon denied that this song referred to the hallucinogen. The influence of such substances on the Beatles has been well chronicled, and the song has become a musical journey on various levels to all types of listeners. Studio rehearsals for "Lucy in the Sky" began in the early winter of 1967. Lennon had composed the psychedelic masterpiece "Strawberry Fields Forever" the year before, but its release was delayed by this new album. "Lucy in the Sky" showcased the Beatles' studio ingenuity, George Martin's open-minded production concepts, and the new emerging sound of *psychedelic rock*.

Analysis of "Lucy in the Sky With Diamonds"—3:22 in length, recorded at London's Abbey Road Studio A, February 28th and March 1, 1967 (from 7, P.M. to 3 A.M.)

This song has two tempos, one triple (groups of three), the other duple (groups of two). The triple can most easily be counted with three fast foot-taps per measure and counted 123-123-123-123, with the duple counted 1 + 2 + 3 + 4 +. At the change of tempo, your foot-taps slow down to about half the previous foot-tap number. The song is divided into three sections: A-B-C, with the C-section functioning like a chorus. The Beatles: John Lennon, lead vocal, piano, acoustic guitar; Paul McCartney, vocals, electric bass, Hammond organ; George Harrison, vocals, electric guitar, tamboura; Ringo Starr, drums, maracas.

0:00   Introduction (4 measures of 3 beats): McCartney's opening organ melody is filtered to resemble a celeste as this dreamy waltz begins.

0:06   A Section (9 measures of 3 beats): Begins "Picture yourself . . . ," as John's echoing voice paints a colorful image of this new world over

McCartney's simple bass line (one note per bar until the end of the phrase), and Harrison's sustained tamboura (an East Indian instrument somewhat like a sitar).

0:18 A Section (10 measures of 3 beats): Begins "Somebody calls you," with no changes made in the texture.

0:32 B Section (12 measures of 3 beats): Begins "Cellophane flowers of yellow and green . . . ." The song smoothly changes key upward. The tamboura now doubles Lennon's voice, and the bass line plays on all three beats of the measure. Counting along with the bass will help you count the tempo change. On the word "gone," the music suddenly changes tempo, indicated by the four heavy drumbeats. The feel of the music is now a heavy, slow four. The bass line is playing two notes per beat, $1+2+3+4+1$.

0:47 C Section (Tempo change, 8 [1 measure drums, 7 vocal] measures of 4 beats, count $1+2+3+4+$): Begins "Lucy in the sky . . . ." The vocal harmony "ahhs" help smooth out the tempo change and lead back to a dream-like verse.

1:08 A Section (9 measures of 3 beats, go from $1+2+3+4+$ to 123123): Begins "Follow her down . . . ." The texture is just like the first section, tamboura drone and one bass note per measure.

1:20 A Section (10 measures of 3 beats): "Everyone smiles . . . ."

1:33 B Section (12 measures of 3 beats): Begins "Newspaper taxis appear . . . ." The music again rises for the next phrase in the new key.

1:47 C Section (8 measures count $1+2+3+4+$): As before, the word "gone" signals the four drumbeats and new tempo as the hard rock chorus music returns. The ethereal vocal "ahhas" end this section and bring the song back to the verse.

2:06 A Section (9 measures of 3 beats): Begins "Picture yourself . . ." Lennon sings in the last verse before moving directly to the chorus, after the lyric "the girl with kaleidoscope eyes."

2:20 A Section (8 measures of 3 beats): Begins "Suddenly someone . . . ."

2:30 C Section (9 measures): "Lucy in the Sky with Diamonds," lyric repeats.

2:52 C Section (8 measures) repeats again.

3:12 C Section: The track fades as the C section repeats.

For Musicians

This art piece alternates between a lyrical, triple-meter feel on the verses and a hard rocking duple feel for the chorus. The opening organ melody arpeggiates the basic chord progression of the verses, A-A/G-F#mF+1, a brilliantly conceived third-related descending sequence, especially for rock and roll. The timbre of the transformed organ is bell-like, resembling a celeste. This texture combines with the droning tamboura and simple bass line to accompany Lennon's double-tracked vocal. The verses are a superb example of musical imagery, with sounds and words creating a unique musical experience, one conjured from Lennon's imagination via tonality. The first phrase is eight bars long, followed by one instrumental bar and a six-bar phrase, using the following progression: I-IV/IV-vi-bVI+ (aug. sixth chord)-I-IV/IV-ii-bVI. The last four bars of this phrase are modulatory, moving from the vi chord on the word "eyes" to two bars of Dm (with the second bar Dm/C), functioning as the iii of the approaching key, Bb major. The new verse continues in Bb with this progression on the words "cellophane flower": I-V/V-V-I-V/V for ten bars, and then modulates to G major for the last two bars of the phrase, cadencing to the chorus on I-V7, and vi (G-D7-Em). The song lands on the V chord on the word "gone," and a metric modulation occurs, approximately a dotted half note equals a half note, to the meter of "four four" time for the rock and roll chorus. The repeated chords here are I-IV-V, or G-C-D7, played over a melodic bass line, heavy drum backbeat, and organ chords, while the famous chorus is sung for six bars. Bar seven of this section, on the word "aah," is on the V chord and takes the song back to the triple-time verse material. This entire form repeats again back to the opening key of A major for the second and last verses. But after the fifteenth bar of the final verse, on the word "kaleidoscope," the song goes to a coda on the chords A and F#m for the word "eyes." The metric modulation from before returns here, and the song ends with the repeated chorus, including the sustained vocal "aahs" at the end.

Final Comments

As well received as "Lucy in the Sky With Diamonds" was by Beatles fans, Lennon always felt it was poorly recorded, and the BBC banned the song from British airwaves because of the "drug references." Lennon's reaction might have something to do with the various production techniques used, including speeding up and slowing down the song's tempo for the vocal parts, or the fact that it was so quickly recorded, in only two nights. But Lennon also stated that this was the Beatles' version of Dylan's "Mr. Tambourine Man," and its impact has been felt by a generation of listeners.

British rocker Elton John recorded a reggae-flavored cover of "Lucy in the Sky" in 1974, featuring Lennon—credited as Dr. Winston O'Boogie—on electric guitar. Elton John reached number one on the charts with his version, and it remained on the charts for ten weeks, selling a million copies. Lennon joined him onstage at New York's Madison Square Garden for a performance of "Lucy in the Sky" on November 28, 1974. It was John Lennon's last public performance.

[1] Hunter Davies, *The Beatles* (New York: McGraw Hill, 1978) 81-86.

[2] Ibid., 92.

[3] Philip Norman, *Shout: The Beatles in Their Generation* (New York: Simon and Schuster, 1981) 215-16.

[4] Ibid., 221.

[5] Nicholas Schaffner, *The Beatles Forever* (New York: McGraw–Hill, 1977), 23.

[6] Ibid., 130.

[7] Davies, 32.

[8] Norman, 53-54.

[9] Ibid., 90.

[10] Ibid., 134.

[11] Ibid., 144.

[12] Ibid., 202.

[13] Ibid., 256.

[14] Schaffner, 63.

[15] Norman, 290.

[16] Ibid., 305.

[17] Barbara Suczek. "The Curious Case of the 'Death' of Paul McCartney," *Urban Life & Culture*, vol. 1, no.1 (1972).

[18] Anthony Scaduto. *Bob Dylan* (New York: Grosset and Dunlap, 1971) 176.

[19] Tony Sanchez, *Up and Down with the Rolling Stones* (New York: William Morrow, 1979) 16.

[20] Ibid., 18.

[21] Ibid., 22.

Chapter **Eleven**

Road to Modern Rock-San Francisco: The Counterculture and Acid Rock

Up until the late sixties, AM radio airplay was the single most important vehicle for the success of a rock recording. Thus, most artists crafted their singles to fit that format. In 1967, a new radio format, called free-form, and later known as AOR (album-oriented rock), changed the rules for success by creating another path for music to reach an audience. The emergence of AOR meant that music not designed for the demographics of top-forty radio could receive airplay, reach an interested audience, and thus sell enough copies to recoup the record label's expenses. Parallel to this development were some serious challenges to American society. The Vietnam War caused a deep division in America's population, recreational drugs were beginning to creep into mainstream culture, and a youth movement known as the counterculture (hippie culture) began to emerge.

The easiest way to explain the change in music is to simply say that rock got harder in the following ways:

- The instrumental sound became more aggressive.

- Short blues riffs assumed a more important position in the structure of a song, sometimes serving as its only melodic aspect.

- Singers increased their intensity, moving from a blues-shouter style to what could be called a screamer style.

- The guitar sound almost always included some distortion.

- Instrumental solos became more important and longer, giving rise to "guitar heroes" and extended "jams."

- The bass guitar became louder and bass players became more active.

- Drummers played more aggressively, no longer relegated to the role of quiet accompanist, and drum sounds were recorded louder and in more detail

- Drug-inspired imagery became more prominent, eventually including occult or satanic imagery.

The first name applied to the new sound was *acid rock*, which later became *hard rock* and still later, *heavy metal*. In the seventies, this new music fragmented into myriad subgenres, most of them fitting the above descriptions in one way or another. By the late seventies, these styles had developed to such a point that clear distinctions could be drawn. Heavy metal had taken on a look and attitude that was easily discernible from *punk, progressive rock, art rock, Southern rock, boogie, pomp rock, anthem rock*, and *glam rock*, among other variations.

Although these changes were taking place throughout the country, the most visible sources of change, at least to the American public, were English groups and San Francisco bands. Because of the Beatles' French haircuts, English musicians were the originators of long hair. Other English groups, such as the Rolling Stones, Yardbirds, Led Zeppelin, and Jimi Hendrix, established part of the future metal aesthetic by using blues riffs played with a distorted guitar sound. It is likely that the use of distortion was an attempt to emulate the sound of early blues artists' poor and broken equipment. The San Francisco Bay area was the first place where the existence of a youth-oriented counterculture was first noticed. The social climate in the city allowed a musical scene to develop that associated hippies and drugs with bands like the Grateful Dead, Jefferson Airplane, Quicksilver Messenger Service, and Janis Joplin.

FM Radio

In the fifties and sixties, AM (amplitude modulation) radio was the way most Americans received radio signals. FM (frequency modulation) radio had been around since the 1930s but was not used for popular music. The principle advantage of AM radio was the wide coverage of its signal, which could bounce off the ionosphere and be heard for hundreds, even thousands, of miles. In fact, its coverage was partly responsible for spreading rhythm and blues to areas outside those with large African-American communities. FM's disadvantage is that its signal travels in a straight line and cannot bounce off the atmosphere and therefore has a shorter range. The advantage of the FM signal is that it is not affected by atmospheric disturbances such as lightening. This makes it an excellent vehicle for music with a high sound quality.

In 1961, the Federal Communications Commission (FCC) began licensing FM stations to broadcast in stereo, possibly with the idea that those stations would be a home for "good" music (FM = fine music)—in other words, the early 1950s popular music style that had been pushed off of AM radio by rock and roll. A survey of station programming in 1967 by the National Association of Broadcasters (NAB) found this mix of music on FM radio:

- 61% middle of the road (a popular radio format featuring more orchestration, strong melodies and harmonies, but not hard-edged or heavy in nature. A forerunner of Smooth Jazz and Adult Conte mporary genres.)

- 16% easy listening

- 7% classical

- 5% country

- 4% rock and roll

- 3% light classical

- 3% Broadway/Hollywood

Additionally, 60 percent of the 990 FM stations merely duplicated the broadcasts of their AM sister stations.

On October 15, 1965, the FCC ruled that jointly owned FM and AM stations serving a market of 100,000 could not broadcast duplicate programming for more than half of their broadcast hours. This ruling created an instant need for additional radio programming and more DJs. The next step in making FM radio the primary delivery system for rock was when Tom Donahue, San Francisco DJ, promoter, and record label owner (Autumn Records) invented underground radio.

In 1967, while listening to the radio with his wife, he had a brilliant idea: There was so much good rock in San Francisco that everybody *he knew* liked, yet none of it was being played on the radio, so surely there must be *some* market for it. His next step was to find a station manager who would let him experiment with a new format and build an audience. First, he identified a station that was in financial trouble by calling stations out of the phone book until he found one with a disconnected phone—a station that could not pay its phone bill was in financial trouble. Then he sold the station manager his idea for a new format. The station manager at KMPX agreed to let him have the 8 P.M. to midnight slot to experiment with an eclectic mix of music. He began broadcasting the first underground radio on April 7, 1967.[1]

Donahue sold advertising time to the small shops that catered to San Francisco's growing counterculture, and the new format became successful within a short time. The station owner changed the format of the entire station, changed the call letters to KFRE, installed Donahue as the manager, and allowed DJs to program any music they wanted, such as Jimi Hendrix, the Grateful Dead, and Jefferson Airplane. The station was so successful that the owner transferred Donahue to his Los Angeles station, KDOM, to duplicate the success. Later, after a disagreement with the owner, Donahue approached the corporate radio giant Micromedia, Inc., and convinced executives there to adopt the new format. They subsequently changed their stations, KHIP in San Francisco and KOAS in Los Angeles, to the new free-form format.[2] Donahue was one of the major figures in elevating the status of FM radio to the point where it became an essential vehicle for album rock. Without the album rock format, there was no way for record companies to expose music by groups like Hendrix, Led Zeppelin, Pink Floyd, and Black Sabbath.

SOCIAL PRESSURES AND THE COUNTERCULTURE

There were philosophical differences in American society that grew out of the 1950s lifestyle and fostered the development of the 1960s counterculture. In many ways, the sixties counterculture was an extension of the 1950s Beat Generation philosophy, and many Beat Generation personalities guided its thinking.

Vietnam

During the late sixties, the most serious division in American society was caused by the war in Southeast Asia, which was more divisive than any other war in the twentieth century. This division was more complex than the simple generational issues that separated parents and their children. American attitudes about the war were diverse, and there were divisions between various groups—for example, college students vs. high school graduates, urbanites vs. rural dwellers, and Northerners vs. Southerners. Of course, the divisions were not as simplistic as they seem, because within each group were various of subgroups. For example, among college students there was a division between "jocks" and "hippies" (long-hairs vs. crew-cuts).

In 1965, the Selective Service began drafting young men, especially teenagers, to help supply soldiers for the war. As the war claimed more and more draftees, Americans' awareness of the war increased, and people began to choose sides. Adults who had lived through World War II typically supported the war in order to be patriotic, but many younger Americans did not believe that the issues involved were worth the cost of their lives. As the war escalated, college campuses became a focal point of anti-war protests, and by 1967, the protests had grown large enough to receive national attention. Some of the more visible protests were at Columbia University (1968), where students seized the administration building to protest the war; the 1968 Chicago Democratic National Convention, which was the scene of a bloody battle between the police and war protesters; and at what became known as the Kent State University "massacre" (May 4, 1970), where National Guard troops fired into a crowd of stone-throwing war protesters, killing four students.

Students opposing the war became part of the counterculture and responded to the draft in a variety of ways. Some publicly burned their draft cards, some fled to Canada, some disappeared into the hippie subculture, some attempted to fail their physical by inhaling aluminum foil and other medical subterfuges, and some applied for Conscientious Objector status. Students enrolled in college received draft deferments; however, by the end of the sixties, the need for troops was so strong that the government began revoking the deferments of those students who had failed courses, because that rendered them unable to graduate within four years, a requirement for the deferment.

Civil Rights

The civil rights movement was another social pressure that divided Americans into opposing camps, with the counterculture supporting equal rights for African-Americans. The modern civil rights movement began with the 1954 *Brown v. Board of Education* Supreme Court decision. This decision reversed the "separate but equal" interpretation of the law, which held that separate facilities for African-Americans and European-Americans were legal as long as those facilities were equal. In reality, facilities were separate but seldom equal. Despite the ruling, many communities refused to change.

In 1955, Rosa Parks was arrested for failing to relinquish her bus seat to a European-American, and the resulting protests catapulted Reverend Dr. Martin Luther King to the forefront of the civil rights movement. In 1957, the governor of Arkansas used the Arkansas National Guard to prevent African-American students from attending Little Rock Central High School. President Eisenhower responded by sending in federal troops to ensure compliance with the Supreme Court ruling. The ultimate result was a clash within society and also between society and its government.

The violent resistance to change by some European-Americans precipitated numerous arrests of civil rights demonstrators, cross-burnings by the Ku Klux Klan, and the assassinations of Medgar Evers (1963), Malcolm X (1965), and Dr. Martin Luther King (1968). At the time, there was speculation that the 1963 assassination of President John F. Kennedy had been motivated by his enforcement of the civil rights laws. Kennedy was, in fact, sympathetic to the movement, and his murder was thought to be another setback for civil rights. Robert Kennedy, his brother, the former attorney general and 1968 presidential candidate, was assassinated in 1968. These were troubled times.

As African-Americans pushed to protect their rights under the Constitution, as affirmed by the Supreme Court, they sought equal entry into such public places as restaurants and lunch counters, bus and train stations, and public schools. Often the attempts to integrate these facilities were met with arrests, and, at times, tensions inflamed to the point where riots broke out; the most infamous were in Newark, Detroit, and Watts. Riots usually occurred in response to some situation in which people believed that the police had overstepped their bounds. The famous Watts riot broke out on Wednesday August 11, 1965, in response to the arrest of an intoxicated driver. The arrest attracted a large crowd of onlookers, and when police reinforcements arrived they were pelted with rocks and bottles. The riots escalated to the point where Molotov cocktails (gasoline bombs) were being thrown and looting was taking place. The National Guard was called in, and it took six days to restore order. The final count was thirty-four people killed (twenty-nine African-American residents of Watts), four thousand arrested, and $200 million in property damage.

Drugs

The use of recreational drugs also divided Americans, but not in the same way as the Vietnam war or the civil rights movement. There were no large demonstrations, but those who used recreational drugs saw themselves as a separate class known as "heads" (potheads, acid-heads). In the past, America's drug problem had been with heroin and its associated crimes, but in the sixties, the counterculture began using marijuana and LSD. Prior to this, drug use was a simple problem because it was associated only with the underclass and jazz musicians, but in the mid-sixties drug use became a problem in mainstream society. Marijuana use began to creep into the middle class, and knowledge of LSD expanded beyond government-financed researchers.

The drugs of choice in the 1960s were undoubtedly marijuana and d-lysergic acid diethylamide, better known as LSD or acid. Marijuana had long been used by jazz musicians but had not previously crossed over into general use. LSD was introduced into the culture through university and government experimentation. LSD was first discovered in 1938 by Dr. Albert Hoffmann, a researcher for Sandoz Laboratories but did not become known widely until Dr. Timothy Leary, a Harvard psychologist, began experimenting with it and came to believe it could be a wonder drug used to unlock the human mind. Leary's advice, "Tune in, turn on, and drop out," became the buzzwords of the sixties counterculture and were so well known that they became comic phrases on television's *Laugh In*. (Timothy Leary's Website continues to espouse the virtues of LSD today. He has updated his imagery for the computer age by stating that "Neuro-transmitter chemicals are information codes which allow us to activate and boot up circuits in our brains. Young adults should be taught how to use info-chemicals in order to navigate their brains." He has added a new catch phrase, "Just say know," to counter First Lady Nancy Reagan's advice to "just say no.")

The U.S. government assisted the spread of LSD through its various research programs. Indeed, it is ironic that the government played such an important role in the emergence of acid rock. By 1951, the CIA was experimenting with LSD in a variety of settings as well as financing scientific research on it. CIA researchers tested it on each other and on unsuspecting citizens. At some point prior to 1955, the CIA used George Hunter White, an employee of the Federal Narcotics Bureau, to operate a safe house in Greenwich Village, where he dispensed LSD to unsuspecting visitors. In 1955, they transferred White to San Francisco, where he hired prostitutes to lure men into his CIA-funded brothel and gave them doses of LSD. This operation lasted into the 1960s. This research, as well as the funded scientific research at universities like Stanford University, near San Francisco, was probably responsible for introducing LSD into the San Francisco Bay area.[3]

Author Thomas Wolfe, in his book *The Electric Kool-Aid Acid Test*, chronicles the adult life of Beat Generation author Ken Kesey (*One Flew Over the Cuckoo's Nest*, 1962). Kesey first became aware of LSD in late 1959 when Vic Lovell, a graduate student in psychology at the Veterans Hospital in Menlo Park, California, paid willing subjects to take hallucinogenic drugs for the Stanford Research Institute. Intrigued with the drug, Kesey took LSD out of the hospital and shared it with his friends. Constantly experimenting and sharing their newfound "freedom," Kesey and his followers (eventually called the "Merry Pranksters"), were in the San Francisco Bay area before the explosion of San Francisco rock bands occurred in the mid-1960s. As its popularity spread, LSD was made readily accessible by Augustus Owsley Stanley III, a chemist who synthesized the drug and dispensed it, often for free.

Kesey and his Merry Pranksters held gatherings called "acid tests," similar to the New York "happenings" of Andy Warhol, except these were scripted only by the effects of the acid. The first acid test, held on December 4, 1965, at a house in San Jose, featured the music of the Grateful Dead and other San Francisco bands, as well as orange Kool-Aid spiked with LSD. To the experienced, acid may have been a way to further explore the mind and to have all of the senses heightened to an extraordinary degree, but for the inexperienced, acid could either be a new experience in self-discovery or a "bad trip" that could make a person "freak out" with wild hallucinations and experience uncontrollable paranoia. Kesey's acid tests eventually led to a three-day extravaganza called "The Trips Festival," held at the Longshoremen's Hall, January 21–23, 1966. The event, produced by Bill Graham, featured the Grateful Dead, Big Brother and the Holding Company, the Loading Zone, and a synthesizer-light show by Donald Buchla.

SAN FRANCISCO AND ACID ROCK

The combination of drugs and the desire for peace, a synthesis of the anti-war and civil rights movements, came together and was expressed publicly first in San Francisco, a city with its own identity, separate from the glitzy image of Los Angeles or Hollywood. In the 1950s, it had become a center for Beat Generation writers and poets like Jack Kerouac, Neal Cassady, and Allen Ginsberg, who became known as "beatniks." Their intellectual and artistic activities gave San Francisco a distinct appetite for alternative art forms and lifestyles and influenced the thinking of young college students at San Francisco State University and the University of California, Berkeley.

In the mid-sixties, when young followers of beatniks began to take over the Haight-Ashbury district, a San Francisco newspaper writer, Michael Fallon (September 5, 1965), used the term "hippies," derived from the jazz word "hip," to describe them. Haight-Ashbury attracted hundreds of young, mostly college-educated adults, promising the good life—one of cooperation, freedom, love, and mind expansion. Hippies were the core of the youth counter-culture movement of the sixties, and their effects are still with us. Long hair and a late-nineties return to hippie clothing are the most visible remnants of their style; however, the movement ran much deeper than fashion.

The hippies' intent was to drop out of the wealth-seeking "rat race" they saw their parents engaging in and to enjoy the subtleties of the simple life. Hippies avoided the accumulation of wealth and the personality traits that quest encompasses. Many lived in communes where people performed needed chores based on their desire to assist the community. There was even a hippie subclass called the Diggers, who took it upon themselves to provide food and clothing for anyone who was in need. The hippies lived an idyllic lifestyle until word spread, and the Haight became inundated by teens from other parts of the country who lacked the philosophical underpinnings of the San Francisco experience. In 1967, running away to San Francisco was the equivalent of an earlier generation's running away to "join the circus," and the Haight became a circus of drug pushers, pimps, and other criminal types who preyed on the innocent. By 1968, the original Haight-Ashbury scene was over, and serious hippies were beginning to leave and establish communes in rural areas of America, thus forming the core of the "back to the land" and "self-sufficiency" movements. The most well-known association of individuals from this period is the Rainbow Family.

The Music

The music of this period distinguished itself with long instrumental solos, the content of which eventually developed into a variety of future styles. The music was first called *acid rock* and *psychedelic* music because of its association with LSD. The same music later evolved into *heavy metal*, a name taken from the lyric "heavy metal thunder" in Steppenwolf's "Born to Be Wild." Now the term "heavy metal" has a much broader connotation than acid rock, but at the time, journalists were looking for something that would describe the music that was evolving out of the San Francisco counterculture.

The San Francisco music scene was too diverse to be described by any one term: It was a fusion of "roots music" (blues and folk), amplification, and LSD. With bands as diverse as the Grateful Dead, Jefferson Airplane, Big Brother and the Holding Company, Santana, and Sly and the Family Stone, the difficulty of defining the music by such terms as "acid rock," "psychedelic rock," or the "San Francisco sound" becomes obvious. The latter designation is perhaps the most restrictive, because it leaves out bands with a similar purpose and sound, such as the Doors, and previously discussed bands such as the Byrds (raga rock and "Eight Miles High"), and the Beatles who, during this same period, performed a style of rock that could also be called "psychedelic."

Many early San Francisco bands grew out of the folk scene and were influenced to move into rock by the success of the Beatles. The first band usually identified in this lineage was the Charlatans, who also were one of the first bands to dress in thrift-store chic. Their first professional engagement was out of town at the Red Dog Saloon in Virginia City, Nevada (June 1965). However, when they returned to San Francisco, they found themselves in an entirely new music scene, and failed to have much impact outside of the area. The Charlatans' drummer, Dan Hicks, later became popular with his own drummer-less group, Dan Hicks and his Hot Licks.

The diverse music scene was further encouraged by the addition of performance venues, the most important being Bill Graham's Filmore West, which grew out of dance-happenings held by the Family Dog collective (a loose conglomeration of free spirits managed by Chet Helms, a peer of Bill Graham, who hosted dances and social gatherings at the Avalon Ballroom in the early 1960s), at the Longshoreman's Hall. Bill Graham entered the music business by organizing dances to benefit the San Francisco Mime Troupe's legal defense fund and by helping plan Ken Kesey's Trips Festival.[4] The success of those dances prompted Graham to rent an aging ballroom called the Filmore and fill it with the new rock. Its success encouraged him to find a similar space in New York and call it the Filmore East. At first, Graham shared bookings at the venue with the Family Dog, but a disagreement sent the Dog to the rival Avalon Ballroom for their dances. Both venues were important to the growing San Francisco music scene.

Monterey Pop and Other Rock Festivals

The first American psychedelic rock festival was the Monterey Pop Festival held on the weekend of June 16–18, 1967. The festival was organized by record man Lou Adler (Dunhill Records) and John Phillips (Mamas and the

Papas), although many others (Bill Graham, Johnny Rivers, Terry Melcher, and Abe Somer) were asked to contribute money and sit on a board of directors that also included Paul McCartney, Mick Jagger, Smokey Robinson, and Brian Wilson.[5] Many record executives attended, including Columbia's Clive Davis, to check out the new sound of West Coast music. The Monterey Pop Festival included performances by Jefferson Airplane, the Grateful Dead, Big Brother and the Holding Company, Country Joe and the Fish, Electric Flag, the Byrds, the Mamas and the Papas, Buffalo Springfield, Ravi Shankar, Otis Redding, the Who, and Jimi Hendrix, plus seventeen other well-known bands.

The Monterey Pop Festival was the first of a series of sixties rock festivals (the most famous being Woodstock) that culminated in the tragic murder at the Rolling Stones' concert at Altamont Raceway. Rock festivals served the same purpose as Alan Freed's shows and the Dick Clark Caravan of Stars. They made it possible for fans to see a variety of performers in a short span of time. In the early days of rock, such shows were fairly easy to produce because performers usually shared a backup band. Since the Beatles, however, most bands had become self-contained, and promoting rock festivals proved to be a logistical nightmare. Big rock festivals required an area large enough to contain the crowd and far enough away so that noise did not disturb anyone yet close enough to be easily accessible; enough parking and surface transportation; enough financial backers to put up enough advance money to reserve the groups who were advertised as performers; enough support services to supply food, shelter, rest

---

Woodstock Performers

Friday	Saturday	Sunday
Richie Havens	Quill	Joe Cocker
Country Joe and the Fish	Keef Hartley	Country Joe and the Fish
John Sebastian	Santana	Ten Years After
Incredible String Band	Mountain	The Band
Sweetwater	Canned Heat	Blood Sweat and Tears
Tim Hardin	Creedence Clearwater Revival	Johnny Winter
Bert Sommer	Grateful Dead	Crosby, Stills, and Nash
Ravi Shankar	Janis Joplin	Paul Butterfield Blues Band
Melanie	Sly and the Family Stone	Sha Na Na
Arlo Guthrie	The Who	Jimi Hendrix
Joan Baez	Jefferson Airplane	

room facilities and medical treatment; and enough security to prevent gate-crashers from entering free and to prevent violent confrontations.

By 1969 rock festivals were beginning to experience crowd-control problems. Festivals at Palm Springs, Newport, and Denver ended in violence, property damage, and arrests, and just as it appeared that large-scale rock festivals were not feasible, the Woodstock Music and Art Fair (August 15–17, 1969), held on Max Yasgur's farm in Bethel, New York, proved that it could be done—or so it appeared. Crowds of more than 300,000 showed up at Woodstock and braved rain, inadequate sanitary facilities, and bad acid in perfect peace and harmony. Its success was held up as an example that the world had finally changed and a nation of people—the Woodstock Nation—could coexist peacefully with each other. It appeared as if the Age of Aquarius had arrived. For that short period of time, the citizens of the rock world were in universal harmony. Additionally, the capitalist world was happy because both Monterey and Woodstock were financially successful; their promoters had negotiated music and movie rights that made up for the thousands of gate-crashers.

Grateful Dead

The Grateful Dead (Jerry Garcia, Bob Weir, Ron "Pigpen" McKernan, Phil Lesh, and Bill Kreutzmann), was one of the first and longest-lasting bands to emerge from San Francisco's new rock culture. Like many of the area's bands, they had been an acoustic group—Mother McCree's Uptown Jug Champions—and performed what is today called *roots music*, a blend of bluegrass, blues, and folk. They electrified around 1965 and renamed themselves the Warlocks. The jug band included blues singer and piano player Ron "Pigpen" McKernan, bluegrass banjo and guitarist Jerry Garcia, and guitarist Bob Weir. When they electrified, they added drummer Bill Kreutzmann and bassist Phil Lesh. The Warlocks/Grateful Dead were the house band for Ken Kesey's acid tests, and they were financed by Owsley, the LSD chemist. Later, when Owsley and the Dead parted ways, Owsley financed a California acid-power trio, an early-metal band called Blue Cheer.

More than any other band, the Grateful Dead represented the spirit of San Francisco during the sixties, never altering their style to make pop recordings. For this they were rewarded with the undying loyalty of their fans, known as Dead Heads. The Dead were present at nearly every major event at the beginning of psychedelic rock and the peace/love movement. They were the main attraction, along with Big Brother and the Holding Company, at the Love Pageant Rally, at Ken Kesey's Trips Festival in 1966, at Graham's Fillmore Auditorium concerts, and at the "First Human Be-In," organized by Allen Ginsberg at Golden Gate Park. This event also featured the Quicksilver Messenger Service, Jefferson Airplane, poetry readings by Ginsberg, prayers from Eastern religions, and the presence of LSD guru Timothy Leary. They also appeared at more mainstream events like the Monterey Pop Festival (1967) and Woodstock (1969). The Dead epitomized the idealism that many bands of this era felt. They were non-commercial, featured long jazz-like improvised solos, operated the group as a cooperative unit instead of having a leader, and even lived communally at 710 Ashbury Street.

The Grateful Dead was a live act that did not translate well to recordings. However, it is fair to say that their performances were more than the sum total of the music they performed. The Grateful Dead were notoriously particular about their recordings and tried to capture the spirit of their live performances. Their first album, *The Grateful Dead* (1967), left them $100,000 in debt to their record label, Warner Brothers, which did not recoup the money until years later. Their recordings sold steadily but never at the level of a hit recording. The length of many of the Dead's songs made it difficult for them to get AM radio airplay, and only a handful of their songs were popular hits ("Truckin'" and "Touch of Gray" among them). In the early 1970s, their recordings began to sell more copies due to the new power of FM radio and their expanding family of fans.

Despite the lack of mainstream commercial success, the Dead achieved true cult status, complete with a cadre of Dead Heads who followed the band from performance to performance, stereotypically in Volkswagen vans, living on the bare essentials—some never missed a performance. The Dead Heads created a psychedelic communal ambiance surrounding the performance that was just as important as the music itself, by selling tie-dyed clothing, incense, handicrafts, and LSD. This following helped the band become one of the longest lasting bands in rock history. Their only time off in over thirty years was between 1974 and 1976. The layoff was probably due to McKernan's 1973 death from liver disease, and it gave band members time to pursue outside projects. The group permanently disbanded in 1996 after the death of their most popular member, Jerry Garcia.

Jefferson Airplane

When the new San Francisco Haight-Ashbury scene began to get national attention and record companies flocked to the city searching for new acts, the first band to sign with a major label was Jefferson Airplane. Jefferson Airplane formed in 1965 when Marty Balin organized a folk rock band for the Matrix, a club he managed on Filmore Street. The original band included Marty Balin (vocals), Paul Kantner (guitar and vocals), Jorma Kaukonen (guitar), Jack Casady (bass), Skip Spence (drums), and Signe Toly Anderson (vocals). Like the Grateful Dead, the band started out as a folk group but soon developed a psychedelic rock sound. They both were products of the San Francisco environment.

By the time their first RCA album, *Jefferson Airplane Takes Off* (1966) was released, Anderson was too pregnant to continue and was replaced by Grace Slick, formerly with a band called the Great Society. Slick had a much stronger voice that added a sense of urgency to their sound, and her appearance (she had been a model) gave the band a striking presence. Their second album, *Surrealistic Pillow* (1967), was classic psychedelic rock and included two giant hits, "White Rabbit" and "Somebody to Love." "Somebody to Love" was the perfect song for the period (1967 has been dubbed the "Summer of Love") and "White Rabbit," inspired by Louis Carroll's *Alice's Adventures in Wonderland* (1865), included references to pills, hallucinogenic mushrooms, and the hookah-smoking caterpillar.

Although Jefferson Airplane, or some form of it, has been around for nearly as long as the Grateful Dead, its road was quite a bit rockier. Between 1970 and 1980, the band went through serious personnel changes. In 1970, the band slowed down after Slick became pregnant by Kantner, although Slick and Kantner worked as a duet on two additional albums, *Blows Against the Empire* (1970) and *Sunfighter* (1971). Several years later, Slick and Kantner resurrected the band, but the only original member it included besides themselves was Balin, who joined them a year later. They took the name Jefferson Starship and had their first number-one album (as Airplane or Starship) with *Red Octopus* (1975) and a hit single in "Miracles." In 1984, Kantner broke off from Slick and the others, causing a dispute over the ownership of the band's name. The result was the continuation of the band under the name Starship. In 1989, most of the original band reformed as Jefferson Airplane, while all the rest continued as Starship.

Janis Joplin and Big Brother and the Holding Company

In 1965, Chet Helm was booking bands for the Family Dog collective, first trading weekends with Bill Graham at the Filmore and later on his own at the Avalon Ballroom. Big Brother and the Holding Company (Peter Albin, bass; Sam Andrews, guitar; Dave Getz, drums; Jim Gurley, lead guitar) began as a group of musicians at one of the loose jam sessions held just as the music scene was beginning to develop. Their first engagement was the Trips Festival (1966), and Helm used them as the house band at the Avalon when he started booking dances. They were a popular blues band but lacked any strong personality in front. Helm remedied that situation in 1966 by asking Janis Joplin, an acquaintance who was performing in her home state of Texas at the time, to join Big Brother.

Janis Joplin was a gutsy blues singer who packed her performances with a variety of emotions and was able to communicate them to the audience. They signed with Bob Shad's Mainstream Records in San Francisco, but Shad planned only to release their demo tape rather than spend money rerecording them. Before Mainstream released the recording, the group made a favorable impression on the second day of the Monterey Pop Festival. Most of the bands were hoping to give strong performances, since this was the first big showcase for West Coast rock bands and a film was being made of the festival. Clive Davis, president of Columbia Records, and Albert Grossman (Dylan's manager) were in the audience and were impressed with the way Janis commanded the stage and reached the audience; they both signed the band. The only problem was that Columbia had to buy out their Mainstream contract, which was now worth much more after their successful Monterey performance.

Columbia finally released their album, *Cheap Thrills*, and it has since become a rock classic, containing both "Piece of My Heart" and "Summertime." Davis had to edit down "Piece of My Heart" because, like most San Francisco bands, Big Brother tended to engage in long improvisations. The shortened recording was a commercial success, and when the reviewers singled out Joplin for praise, she began to have thoughts of a solo career. She decided to leave Big Brother and find a backup band with stronger musicianship. Columbia split their contract and agreed to continue recording Big Brother and the Holding Company but, according to Clive Davis, the band did not want to do the types of things—like touring—required to launch their act.

Joplin's new band was called the Kozmic Blues Band and included Big Brother guitarist Sam Andrews, backup singers, and horns. The resulting album, *I Got Dem Ol' Kozmic Blues Again, Mama*, was released in 1969 and featured the song "Try." Like many musicians, Janis made the mistake of letting her stage persona take over her life. Her image was that of a hard-living, hard-drinking, hard-loving red-hot mama. She was "one of the guys," and the lifestyle killed her. Just as her career was in full swing, she was found dead in a hotel room on October 4, 1970, as a result of a heroin overdose. Janis had been working on a new album, *Pearl*, with a new band called the Full Tilt Boogie Band. After her death, Columbia released "Me and Bobby McGee," which became her first number-one hit and the recording for which most of America will remember her. Interestingly, this song, like Otis Redding's final recording "(Sittin' on) the Dock of the Bay," was atypical in that it was more mellow than her usual recordings.

Other San Francisco Bands

Several other bands associated with the San Francisco music scene landed record contracts but never became as popular nationally as the Dead, Airplane, or Janis. Quicksilver Messenger Service, formed in 1965 by a group of roommates, became a favorite around the area and signed a recording contract with Capitol in 1967. They had a strong local reputation and, like other area bands, their early repertoire featured blues and long instrumental solos. Their recordings did not sell well until 1970, when "Fresh Air" from the album *Just for Love* got some airplay and moved the album up to number twenty-seven.

Moby Grape, formed in 1967 in San Francisco, included Skip Spence (the original Jefferson Airplane drummer) on guitar and also became a popular local band. Despite their following, they were not able to succeed on a national level. The credit for their failure is usually given to Columbia Records, whose overkill advertising hype actually worked against them. Columbia released a beautiful package that included a full-color poster of the band and simultaneously released eight singles from it. The major-label hype either turned off its core of hippie followers or created an expectation that was impossible to meet. They entered San Francisco rock history as the most famous unsuccessful band.

Blue Cheer is another group that sometimes gets overlooked because of their short recording life and the various methods of cataloging bands. When bands are listed as power trios, Blue Cheer is usually mentioned because there were so few. However, in the category of heavy metal, Blue Cheer is usually overlooked because they did not attain the stature of Led Zeppelin and Black Sabbath. The band grew out of the San Francisco acid culture and rose to prominence after Owsley, the acid chemist, left the Grateful Dead. Blue Cheer, named after a type of LSD, was probably the first American heavy metal band, but this was before anyone used the term. At the time they became popular, rock bands were just starting to turn up the volume, and Blue Cheer was reputedly the loudest band of the era. (Photos show them in front of a stack of Marshall amplifiers.) They formed in 1966, and in 1968 released "Summertime Blues," an old Eddie Cochran rockabilly hit. "Summertime Blues" used ponderous tempo, extremely distorted guitar riffs, and the drummer kept time on the tom-toms rather than on the cymbals—all the sonic elements of heavy metal. The album also included the famous blues "Rock Me Baby" and their own version of a love-doctor song called "Doctor Please." Both of these cuts are valuable in demonstrating the way classic blues-guitar riffs, combined with electronics and feedback used for its sustaining power, provided the basic vocabulary of heavy metal. Blue Cheer was one of the bands that bridged the gap between San Francisco acid rock and heavy metal.

Other San Francisco bands were part of the counterculture's musical stew but are generally omitted from the history of San Francisco bands because of their racial identity. Santana, the first important Latin rock band, was formed in 1967 and first became popular in San Francisco's Mission District. The band, beginning as the Santana Blues Band (1966), featured Carlos Santana's guitar skills blended with fiery Latin rhythms. Santana is usually omitted from lists of San Francisco bands because the music is pigeonholed as "Latin rock" rather than "psychedelic rock." However, this distorts the aesthetic of "hippie music." The San Francisco hippie community intended to be color-blind and embraced all cultures and their music.

Santana's popularity spread to the mainstream San Francisco culture after the group was booked into the Filmore West in 1968, but they were not signed to a record contract until their impressive appearance at the Woodstock Festival in 1969 attracted Columbia Records. Their first album, *Santana*, easily soared to the number-one position and eventually went double-platinum (sales of two million). Their second album, *Abraxas*, is considered a classic and contained their two most famous hits, "Black Magic Woman" and "Oye Como Va." Carlos continued to evolve as a musician and, in the 1970s, recorded albums with jazz artists like John McLaughlin (Mahavishnu Orchestra), Alice Coltrane, and Dave Holland. Today, Carlos Santana's guitar skills are still respected (he won a record-setting eight Grammy awards in February 2000), and he still holds his status as a great rock guitarist even in the first decade of the twenty-first century.

Sly and the Family Stone is another frequently omitted San Francisco area band, probably because they are more easily identified as *funk* rather than psychedelic. Although Sly, along with James Brown, is rightly considered one of the originators of seventies funk, omitting them from San Francisco bands on racial grounds again would disrespect the counterculture's aesthetic of universal racial harmony. At the time, Sly's music was viewed as the sound that would appeal to both rock and R&B cultures, and their record sales support this: "Dance to the Music" (number eight on the pop charts, number nine on R&B), "I Want to Take You Higher" (number thirty-eight pop, number twenty-four R&B), "Hot Fun in the Summertime" (number two pop, number three R&B), "Thank You (Falettinme Be Mice Elf Agin)" (number one on both charts), "Family Affair" (number one on both charts). Additionally, the band crossed gender boundaries with singer/trumpet player Cynthia Robinson, who served as a role model for other female brass players. The band also included bassist Larry Graham Jr. (Graham Central Station), whose vocabulary of bass pops, slaps, and thumps established the techniques that later funk players used.

Creedence Clearwater Revival (CCR) is another Bay Area band that achieved huge success (with seven gold singles and ten gold albums, including collections) yet does not fit neatly into the hippie niche. Their music has often been described as *swamp rock*, because their lyrics revolved around bayou themes and their pronunciation led listeners to believe they were from Louisiana. Although they played at the Filmore and appeared at Woodstock, they are generally omitted from discussions of the San Francisco scene. The band formed as early as 1959 by students at El Cerrito Junior High School and performed under a variety of names, such as the Blue Velvets and the Golliwogs. They signed with a local San Francisco label, Fantasy, and released the single "Suzy Q" (1968), an old rockabilly song by Dale Hawkins, which was popular enough to earn a gold record for the album. Their subsequent hits—"Proud Mary," "Bad Moon Rising," "Green River," "Down on the Corner," "Travelin' Band," "Up Around the Corner," and "Looking Out My Back Door"—all occurred over a period of two years (1969–70) and made them one of the most important "above ground" rock acts in the country. Internal disputes in 1971 led to their breakup in 1972.

A note regarding hippie and psychedelic music. History is often reinterpreted by contemporary media, and so it is with San Francisco rock. Record collections offered on television as "not available in stores" often provide a faulty image of the demographics of certain recordings. Collections describing themselves with words such as "psychedelic" or "flower power" combine recordings that on the surface appear to be psychedelic or hippie music but were not truly part of that subculture. Recordings like the Lemon Pipers' "Green Tambourine," Strawberry Alarm Clock's "Incense and Peppermints," and John Phillip's "Creeque Alley" represent hippies and the psychedelic experience in the same way that Stephen Foster's plantation songs represent African-American slave songs—that is, as an outsider looking in.

Other California Acid Bands

There were other significant California bands that sometimes fall through the cracks because they were not from San Francisco or did not fit into the surf or folk rock category. Iron Butterfly was one of the most influential because of their huge pre-heavy-metal hit "In-A-Gadda-da-Vida" (1968), which became a mainstay of the new FM rock format. The title is said to come from the alcohol-slurred pronunciation of "In the Garden of Eden." The band grew in San Diego but moved to Los Angeles in 1966 and secured an extended engagement at the Whiskey-A-Go-Go. Later at the Galaxy, they developed enough of a following to attract Atlantic Records (Atco) and began touring nationally. Their first album sold well enough, combined with their audience's response, to warrant a second album, *In-A-Gadda-da-Vida,* which sold three million copies and stayed on the charts for 140 weeks. "In-A-Gadda-da-Vida," like Cream's "Sunshine of My Love," was built on a wonderful two-measure heavy riff that permeates the entire song. As an added plus, it features a two-and-a-half-minute drum solo by Ron Bushy. Also like the Cream recording, the tempo is slower than the average rock song and there are more "pounding tom-toms," which gives it a ponderous feeling that contributes to the "heavy" in the "heavy metal" label that eventually came to describe this type of music.

Steppenwolf, formed in 1967, was another short-lived band that pre-dates the term heavy metal. The first musical use of the term ("heavy metal thunder") was taken from their first hit "Born to Be Wild." (An earlier use of the term is found in a character, the Heavy Metal Kid, created by beat writer William Burroughs in *Nova Express.*) The band had a great deal of visibility during the period because two of their songs were included in the cult film classic *Easy Rider* ("Born to Be Wild" and "The Pusher"), and another in the film *Candy* ("Rock Me"). Although only two of their singles went gold ("Born to Be Wild" and "Magic Carpet Ride"), they had six gold albums, which serves as an indication of the growing strength of the FM album-oriented rock format.

The Doors (Jim Morrison, vocal; Ray Manzarek, organ and keyboard bass; Robby Krieger, guitar; John Densmore, drums) formed in 1966. They were a Los Angeles band and are perhaps the hardest to classify because their sound did not fit into any ready-made musical category. This difficulty is compounded by the premature 1971 death of Jim Morrison, which deified him in the eyes of the rock world and created a larger-than-life image of the band. Their instrumental sound featured the thin sound of the electric piano Vox organ, (unlike the full-bodied Hammond organ used by other groups), and a keyboard bass, and it was not overly guitar-heavy like other psychedelic bands. The main attraction of the Doors was Morrison's lyrics, emotion-charged voice, and movie star appearance.

The band members attended the University of California Los Angeles (UCLA), where both Morrison and Ray Manzarek were film students. Morrison had planned to go to New York but instead ended up living with a friend near the beach, ingesting large quantities of LSD, and writing songs. Manzarek was also a musician and played in a band called Rick and the Ravens with his brothers. A few months after graduation, Morrison and Manzarek met on Venice Beach, and Jim sang Ray some of his lyrics. The lyrics impressed Manzarek, so they decided to form a band called the Doors. That name is said to have come either from a quote by William Blake—"If the doors of perception were cleansed, everything would appear as it is, infinite"—or from the title of Aldous Huxley's book, *The Doors of Perception,* about the drug mescaline. Ray eventually enlisted John Densmore and Robbie Krieger, whom he knew from transcendental meditation classes. After four or five months, they found a gig at the London Fog on the Sunset Strip. Later they performed as the house band at Whiskey A-Go-Go, where they were signed by Jac Holzmann of Electra Records.

Their first album contained the hit single "Light My Fire" by Robbie Krieger and also the disturbing "The End" by Morrison. Morrison's lyrics were dark and perhaps foreshadowed his future behavior, but they were brilliant when compared to other pop music from the era. The Doors followed with a series of hit singles, including "People Are Strange," "Love Me Two Times,"

"Unknown Soldier," "Hello, I Love You," "Touch Me," "Love Her Madly," and "Riders in the Storm."

The Doors' audience behavior was unlike that at a typical rock concert. The *New York Times* reported that at one performance at the Winterland Ballroom in San Francisco, when the Doors came onstage "there was a sudden silence and the crowd sat as if it were about to hear a chamber music concert."[6] Although he would sing or speak each lyric "as if it were poetry,"[7] Morrison became a possessed performer on stage. Other members of the group have described his behavior in this way:

> Shamanistic ecstasies took over. Dionysus was on stage, dancing wildly, madly. He was capable of anything on stage and would do anything as we all know by Miami, New Haven.[8]

In New Haven (1968), Morrison was arrested onstage for resisting arrest when during a song, he began a monologue in which he told the audience how he and a girl had just been sprayed with Mace by the police in a backstage shower stall.[9] After that publicity, the authorities began waiting for trouble at the Doors' concerts, and they found it in Miami in 1969. Morrison frequently drank too much and often performed drunk. At the Miami concert, he again was drunk and missed some cues, causing a song to break down. He started talking to and teasing the audience, saying, "You haven't come to see a good rock and roll band play music. You've come to see something greater than you've ever seen before . . . What do you want? I got it . . . how about I show you my cock?"[10] He then took off his shirt and waved it in front of himself like a bullfighter's cape, saying, "Did you see it? There it is." According to the band, after the concert they were in the dressing room with the police drinking beers and joking, but "about a week later we get the news that there's a warrant out for Jim's arrest." The charges were eventually dismissed because no one had seen anything and there were no pictures. (The band members still claimed many years later that they did not see anything.) After the Miami incident, the Doors' engagements were canceled, and they did not perform onstage for some time. When they did return, the auditorium was filled with police.

The Doors released two successful albums after Miami, but Morrison took an extended leave from the group soon after *L.A. Woman* was recorded and moved to Paris with his wife. He died in Paris of heart failure in his bathtub on July 3, 1971. There were rumors that he did not really die, because only his wife saw the body and the death certificate was signed by an unknown doctor. A Morrison cult developed, and his gravesite in Paris became a popular mecca for rock fans. Thanks to books, movies, and Doors Web sites, the cult of Morrison is still going strong and the band's recordings continue to sell well.

It is indeed a challenge to try to sort out the diversity of music from this period in rock history. Bands like Jefferson Airplane, Santana, Blue Cheer, and Creedence Clearwater Revival seemingly have nothing in common save their geographic location. As it turned out, their location in San Francisco with its new FM radio format and counterculture audience gave all of these bands the freedom to explore new styles without concern for AM radio or its listeners.

LISTENING TO THE MUSIC

♪♪♪ "Riders on the Storm"—performed by the Doors

Jim Morrison's eerie poetic images fit well with the minor jazz-rhythm-section feel on the Doors' eighth hit, "Riders on the Storm." It was released one month after Morrison's death and became their classic bestseller. Its lyrics take on special irony and profundity because of Morrison's demise. Recorded in the group's workshop, their last single hit combined a relaxed, jazzy groove with surreal lyrics and instrumental solos.

Analysis of "Riders on the Storm"—7:01 in length, released on Elektra #45738 in July 1971

This song reached number fourteen on the charts and stayed there for nine weeks. The song appeared on the *L.A. Woman* album, which reached number nine. The form is a minor blues, and the meter is "in four" (four foot-taps per measure). The Doors: Jim Morrison, vocals; Ray Manzarek, keyboards; Robby Krieger, guitar; John Densmore, drums.

0:00   Introduction: The opening thirteen seconds of "Riders on the Storm" features rain and storm effects (without the band or any tempo), creating a spacy quality that is most effective as an opening to the intro.

0:14   Introduction continues (13 measures): Time starts in a subtle fashion, first with the keyboard bass line, then with the right hand electric piano fills played freely with rhythm section. The descending high-register piano pattern, which has become a trademark sound of this song, establishes the tempo. The last bars of the intro are very sparse, setting up the verse to come.

0:42   First Chorus (12 measures): Morrison incants, "Riders on the storm," as this mysterious song begins to take form. His lyrics, though free form, set the mood of self-discovery, rebirth, and death through metaphors and poetic images. The bass line is constant and, as in the classic blues, Morrison's vocal line is given a guitar answer in one-measure exchanges, rather than the typical two-measure answer. The choruses are linked by a unison rhythm in measures 9 and 10.

1:09   Second Chorus (12 measures): Begins, "There's a killer," and in this chorus the guitar and piano join in background riffs.

1:38   Instrumental Solo (12 measures plus 2 measure vamp): Krieger's guitar solo sticks fairly close to the melody, but with tremolo and reverb effects, rhythm section, and storm noises. The last part of this section returns to the vamp used in the intro and prepares the listener for the next chorus.

2:11   Third chorus (12 measures): Begins "Girl, you gotta love your man" and continues like the previous choruses. The guitar tone returns to its previous jazzy sound.

2:38   Instrumental Solo (50 measures): Manzarek's lengthy electric piano solo never bogs down, but builds and churns forward. Drawing from both minor modes and the blues scales, the solo includes the use of several blues riffs. Accompanied by the rhythm section and storm noises, this section is quite atmospheric, showing off Manzarek's keen sense of melody and timing, while the guitar provides background ostinato. The solo ends with the descending piano pattern (at 4:19) from the introduction.

4:28   Interlude: The piano returns to the intro music, but very gently, as the rhythm section drops out below. A moment of musical silence follows as the storm noises envelop the listener and time seems to float.

4:37   Drum Fill: A drum fill brings us back to the tempo, and the intro music featuring piano, guitar, bass, and drums returns to reestablish the groove.

4:56   Fourth Chorus (12 measures): A repeat of the first verse, but without guitar responses.

5:25   Coda (8 measures): Krieger plays a guitar riff (later used vocally by Morrison) accompanied by the rhythm section and storm sounds during this brief instrumental section.

5:42   Coda continues (8 measures): Morrison sings the title line using Krieger's guitar melody, repeating it three more times.

6:10   Coda continues (8 measures): Awash with the storm sounds, Manzarek plays a riff based on his well-known intro figure, this time not descending but ascending, and Krieger plays freely behind him.

6:20   Coda continues: This relaxed final section features both keyboards and guitar playing out-of-time fills, delicately combining with the storm noises to create a picturesque texture as the drums fade.

6:39   Coda continues: The storm sounds finish the piece alone and subside as the music fades.

For Musicians

"Riders on the Storm" is basically a twelve-bar minor blues form based around E Dorian and using both the Dorian and E blues scales. The effective opening (and tag) of storm noises permeates this piece, giving the song's rather sparse rhythm section textures more breadth. Time starts with a keyboard bass line that functions as an ostinato throughout most of the song. Manzarek's descending eighth-note piano pattern in bars seven through ten of the intro is based on thirds, starting on A to F#, then G to E, and so on down the E Dorian scale. This musical device gives the impression of falling rain as well as any musical technique conceived, and gives this song a unique signature lick while establishing the piano style. The rhythm section also relies heavily on eighth-note subdivisions to create the groove, and the last four bars of this thirteen-bar intro return frequently throughout the tune as an interlude. During the two twelve-bar phrases of verse one, the call-and-response technique is used as Morrison sings and Krieger responds on guitar. Krieger's twelve-bar guitar improvised solo is melodic but filled with surprise stops and starts and tremolo. The basic structure of theses verses is as follows: four bars of E minor, two bars of A with no third, two bars of E minor, one bar of D, one bar of C, and two bars of E minor.

The interlude returns before the piano solo, where the song's improvisational boundaries are effectively explored. Manzarek opens these forty-four bars of E minor with pentatonics, works with the Dorian scale, and ends with a rhythmic touch of the blues, all created with a firm sense of direction, content, and form. His return to the descending third pattern in bars forty-five through forty-seven of this section does not seem abrupt or surprising, but the relief provided by the four empty measures of sparse piano and storm sounds is most welcome. Densmore's drum fills restart the tempo as the interlude returns for eight bars. After Morrison repeats the first twelve-bar phrase of verse one, the song makes its way for twenty bars on E minor, with guitar and vocal riffs interrupting the rhythm section and storm textures. The last six metered bars of the song feature a variation of the descending-thirds piano figure, this time played more freely. As the drums fade, piano and guitar play rubato arpeggios in the upper register as the storm abates.

Final Comments

It is interesting to note the popularity of the Doors' music decades after their demise. In 1980, almost a decade after Morrison's death, the Doors had their top-selling year, and record sales and airplay continue.

𝄞♪♪ "Sugar Magnolia"—performed by the Grateful Dead

Singer/guitarist Bob Weir collaborated with lyricist John Barlow to create this gentle, hippie love song for the Grateful Dead. Combining pop and country rock styles with pervasive vocal harmonies, "Sugar Magnolia" is simplified psychedelic rock with folk elements. Rather than showing the Dead's improvisatory nature, this song follows its own unique, deliberate form filled with syncopation, guitar riffs, subtle chord shifts, and poetic lyrics.

Analysis of "Sugar Magnolia"—3:12 in length, released on Warner Brothers, *American Beauty*

The album reached number thirty in 1970, with the song peaking at number ninety-one in 1973. The meter is in a fast four foot-taps per measure but can be counted in a slower two. The Grateful Dead: Jerry Garcia, vocals and lead guitar; Bob Weir, vocals and rhythm guitar; Ron "Pigpen" McKernan, organ and harmonica; Phil Lesh, vocals and bass; Bill Kreutzmann, drums; Mickey Hart, second drummer.

0:00 Introduction (10 measures): Any Dead Head will recognize "Sugar Magnolia" from the opening sliding-pedal steel-guitar chord and bouncy rhythm section. The bass part moves freely, with drums and guitars setting the tempo and feel. The last two bars of this section function as a "tag" for each verse and return throughout the recording. This feature is common in older country music.

0:15 A Section (10 measures): Verse one begins "Sugar magnolia," and Weir sings of his new love, whose "head's all empty and I don't care." Vocal harmonies occur frequently yet unpredictably, and Weir, Garcia, and Lesh provide remarkable vocals similar to those of Crosby, Stills & Nash in style. In the first ten-bar phrase, vocal harmonies accompany all but measures 5 and 6.

0:30 A Section (10 measures): Begins "Sweet blossom come on," and only measures 7 and 8 use vocal harmonies.

0:46 B Section (10 measures): Begins "She's got" and could be called a chorus because the music and lyrics return later. This section features smooth country-rock harmonies and syncopation. The lyrics are autobiographical, reflecting the unique nomadic subculture of the Grateful Dead family and followers.

0:59 Instrumental section (10 measures): This is based on the harmony from the A section. The first four bars feature steel guitar accompanied by bass and guitar, and in the second four bars, the guitar and bass play a unison line, providing a counterpoint to the steel guitar.

1:14 A Section (10 measures): Begins "Well, she comes" and continues without vocal harmony.

1:31 A Section (10 measures): The second phrase uses vocal harmony in a reverse call-and-response pattern with the harmony preceding the solo voice. A maraca rhythm is added to the texture.

1:44 C Section (11 measures): Begins "Sugar magnolia" and is unusual in that it introduces new material. The background singing now takes the form of a riff and is even more reminiscent of Crosby, Stills & Nash. There are an extra two beats after measure 8, which is best described as a measure of 6/4 (six foot taps). This section also has the two-measure tag, which gives the listener a familiar landmark in the musical sound-scape.

2:00   B Section (10 measures): Begins "She's got everything" and continues to restate the lyrics and vocal harmony.

2:16   A Section (11 measures): Begins "Sometimes" and resembles the A section; however, it modulates upward after four bars, includes background choral-style harmonies, and includes the same 6/4 bar of six as does the C section.

2:31   False ending (6 beats): Two beats of silence followed by a four-beat drum fill into the Coda.

2:35   Coda (16 measures and fade): This is a reprise of the C section and begins with the "De-de-de" vocal harmony riff. The maraca rhythm returns, and Weir sings lyrics around the riff as the song fades.

For Musicians

"Sugar Magnolia" sets a fine balance between a throughly composed nature and a recurring two-bar tag. The ten-bar instrumental introduction features pedal steel guitars and contrapuntal bass lines. Each verse (A section) is ten measures—a standard eight-measure phrase plus two measures serving as a "tag." The chords shift with the lyrics, the text painting in a subtle way as A moves to C#m, F#m, E, and A. The bridge moves to E and B, and this section seems more energetic in lyrics and rhythm. The instrumental section is polyphonic, with each instrument providing its own unique texture. The "Sugar Magnolia" section is characterized by a chord progression built on A, G, D, and A and features a 6/4 bar interjected seven measures in, followed by two vocal bars and the interlude. Here the freely composed nature of the song steps forward, even as the bridge returns, with a modulation occurring (at 2:26) for a new version of the chorus. The eighth bar of this phrase has no activity, save the held instruments and voices, obfuscating time before the bar of drums indicates both tempo and cadence. The last section is an eight-bar repeat. The "daydream" atmosphere mentioned in the lyrics is effectively created here, combining dotted quarter, eighth-note, and quarter-note block harmonies that provide momentum, much rhythm section interplay, and an ethereal solo vocal line.

Final Comments

"Sugar Magnolia" became part of the Grateful Dead's concert material and received FM radio airplay along with other songs from the *American Beauty* album.

[1] Jim Ladd, *Radio Waves* (New York: St. Martin's Press: 1991), 7.

[2] Ibid., 36.

[3] Martin A. Lee and Bruce Shlain, *Acid Dreams: The CIA, LSD and the Sixties Rebellion* (New York: Grove, 1985), Chapter 1.

[4] Jim Marshall, Baron Wolman, and Jerry Hopkins, *Festival: The Book of American Celebrations* (New York: Macmillan, 1970), 17.

[5] Ibid., 36.

[6] Robert Windeler, "Doors, a Way in and a Way Out, Rock on Coast," *New York Times,* 20 November 1967, 61.

[7] Ibid.

[8] Ray Manzarek, Interview by Robin Denselow, 2 November 1983, "The Doors Press Conference," Institute of Contemporary Arts, London.

[9] New Haven Police 'Close the Doors'," *New York Times,* 11 December 1967.

[10] Manzarek interview.

Chapter Twelve

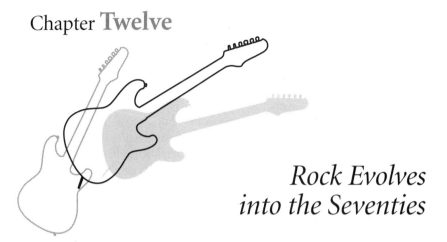

Rock Evolves into the Seventies

Once again, there is no clear distinction between the music at the end of the sixties and the beginning of the seventies, because cultural events rarely divide themselves into neat decade-long packages. In some respects, trends in rock are shorter because they often break down by high school generations; by the time one class graduates, the music they preferred as freshmen has become passé. Although it was not apparent at the time, rock was fragmenting along new stylistic lines that would eventually be collected under several broad titles like *metal, dance music, punk,* and *listening music.* The rock that developed as a result of the British Invasion and San Francisco scene gradually became hard rock, and eventually it fragmented into *art* and *progressive* rock, *heavy metal, Southern rock, blues* and *boogie* bands. African-American styles explored the rhythmic *funk* started by James Brown and Sly and the Family Stone, while continuing the vocal group traditions developed by Motown, and never lost the connection between dance and music. The function of music as a companion to the collective dance experience was reaffirmed as it developed into *disco* in the second half of the seventies and then *dance music* in the eighties. *Folk* music became *folk rock* and broadened to a listening genre now referred to as *singer/songwriters.*

As the new FM radio format established by Tom Donahue grew, it became the primary vehicle for rock that was too hard for the AM top-forty format. The new format fostered two major musical divisions, *pop music* and *album rock.* Pop music was the tuneful "lite" music aimed at those members of mainstream society who were thought to be "too shallow to understand serious music," while album rock was for those who were "serious about their music." FM's superior sound quality, the growing number of radios, and the development of FM stereo gradually resulted in its rise to the position previously held by AM radio as the main vehicle for pop music. By the end of the eighties, FM's rule was so complete that a role reversal had taken place, with AM radio being the vehicle for the music called *alternative rock.*

Early Metal

It is as impossible to identify the first heavy metal band as it is to identify the first rock and roll band because, as the authors have tried to demonstrate, all music evolves in a natural and logical progression from the music that preceded it. Most, if not all, of the early metal bands had their roots in the blues and continued to propagate many of the African musical characteristics on which American popular music is based. The authors have suggested that English bands such as the Rolling Stones, the Yardbirds, and John Mayall's Bluesbreakers were natural outgrowths of the preservationist tendencies of the trad jazz movement, and that they developed a vocabulary of guitar riffs learned from old American blues records. This vocabulary of blues riffs became the guitar lesson material of the following generation, who, in turn, used them as the building blocks of future rock styles.

It may be useful to listen to some early blues recordings again and notice the basic elements that form the common ground between blues and metal:

- Muddy Waters's recording of "Mannish Boy" uses a one-chord vamp (riff) style that most likely pre-dated the three-chord blues form. The use of the one-chord riff as the building block for a song is evident in scores of pre-metal rock, like the Stones' "Satisfaction," Cream's "Sunshine of Your Love," and Iron Butterfly's "In-A-Gadda-Da-Vida."

- Almost any Blind Lemon Jefferson recording will reveal a number of short guitar riffs that can be excised and used as the basis for a new song. There are very few schools today where one can study rock guitar, and in the sixties there were none. Musicians learned guitar patterns either by persistent and repeated listening to a particular recording or by watching the fingers of someone who had.

- Listen to the distorted sound of the guitar in "Rockett 88," or a similar early-fifties blues recording, and imagine yourself a musician who wanted to duplicate that sound with a state-of-the-art 1966 amplifier. That search led some sixties musicians to puncture their amplifier's speaker with knitting needles to produce a distorted sound. Electronically minded musicians discovered ways via circuitry to get that sound without destroying a speaker. With today's technology, in what was once an oxymoronic situation, a guitarist can get a big, distorted guitar sound at extremely low volume levels.

- Listen to the way Muddy Waters's bottleneck slide guitar style gives a sustained, wailing sound to certain notes. That sound is evident in the playing of many guitar players like early Eric Clapton and Jimi Hendrix. Also imagine what one would do to sustain that sound even longer than the natural vibration of a guitar string. It is possible that this search led to the use of guitar feedback as a sonic device. John Lennon claimed to have been the first to record feedback ("I Feel Fine"), and it is also evident on early Yardbirds rave-ups.

- Listening to the gruff vocal sound of 1930s blues singers like Charlie Patton, the 1950s recordings of Howlin' Wolf, the sanctified pleadings of early gospel groups, and early James Brown will suggest to the listener possible role models for musicians wanting to emulate the sound and tone of African-American blues. It is easy to see the similarities between these sounds and the shouting/screaming style of metal singers. For example, an attempt to emulate the emotion of singers like James Brown is readily heard in the singing of Led Zeppelin's Robert Plant.

Jimi Hendrix

Jimi Hendrix is one possible starting place when examining early metal, although this approach is not without flaws. Hendrix's often-touted image as "psychedelic voodoo child" ties him to the acid rock of the period, while his earlier performances with R&B artists on the chitlin' circuit tie him to the African-American blues tradition. It is precisely these contradictions that make him an excellent starting place. Hendrix was an evolutionary figure who combined previous musical elements in such a way as to create a new musical compound, a recombination of blues with its stepchild, rock and roll. This new musical compound provided the individual building blocks of the music of the future. It gave music a new collection of guitar techniques, a new method of using the amplifier as part of the instrument, and it set the stage for the flamboyant theatrical antics of future bands.

Like Blind Lemon Jefferson, Robert Johnson, T-Bone Walker, Chuck Berry, and Bo Diddley, Jimi Hendrix was one of a long line of guitar virtuoso-innovators who developed new approaches and techniques for the instrument. While most musicians in any era spend their time copying the styles of others and "reinventing the wheel," Hendrix developed techniques that brought the guitar and amplifier to a new plateau and set the standard for future guitar heroes. He mastered the instrument to such an extent that it seemed to be nothing more than a toy to him, playing behind his back and even with his teeth. Furthermore, he learned to use the amplifier as part of the instrument and developed a vocabulary of feedback techniques that amazed other guitarists.

Hendrix, an American guitarist, seemed to appear out of nowhere, because he was not well known in America until his performance at the Monterey Pop Festival (1967). Even then, Americans believed he was part of the British Invasion. He began his music career as a backup guitarist for well-known R&B artists such as Little Richard, the Isley Brothers, Wilson Pickett, and King Curtis. He eventually settled in Greenwich Village with his own band called Jimmy James and the Blue Flames (1965). His amazing technique impressed other guitar players, like Mike Bloomfield, but he was not noticed beyond musical circles. In 1966, the Animals' bassist Chas Chandler heard him and believed that he could make Hendrix a star in England, so Chandler left the Animals to become Hendrix's manager.

Chandler formed a power trio around Hendrix, the Jimi Hendrix Experience, with bassist Noel Redding and drummer Mitch Mitchell. The Experience was an exciting group that helped alter the roles of the bassist and drummer. Drummer Mitch Mitchell played with a loose, relaxed, almost jazz-like feel, and incorporated all the drums, instead of just snare drum and cymbals, into his time patterns. The group's first album, *Are You Experienced?* (1967), contained songs that reflected the Kesey acid-induced experiences of San Francisco bands: "Manic Depression," "Purple Haze," and the title track. The drug references were abundant. The question, "Are you experienced?" in the counterculture meant "Have you dropped acid?" and Purple Haze was a type of acid—it was a brand name like Blue Cheer, Windowpane, or blotter acid. Although Hendrix and the Experience was still unknown in the United States, Paul McCartney, a Monterey Festival board member, recommended them, along with the Who, to perform at the Monterey Pop Festival.

Since both the Who and Hendrix included demolition of the stage as part of their acts, they argued over who would perform first at Monterey, and decided to settle it with a coin toss. The Who went first and proceeded to destroy everything in sight: amps, mikes, guitars, and drums. When Hendrix followed them—reminiscent of Jerry Lee Lewis's actions when forced to precede Chuck Berry—he set his guitar on fire before smashing it on the stage. But there was more to it than a simple torching. Hendrix simultaneously made love to, exorcised, and sacrificed his guitar. Then, in a highly sexual manner, he squirted lighter fluid from a can onto the guitar and lit it.[1] The concert did wonders for Hendrix's career, and the Experience eventually released two more successful albums: *Axis: Bold as Love* (1968) and *Electric Ladyland* (1968).

By the time Hendrix got to the Woodstock Festival in 1969, he had disbanded the Experience and performed with a hastily assembled group called Electric Sky Church. The most memorable part of his Woodstock performance was his version of "The Star Spangled Banner," which then was taken as a musical anti-war statement. When he got to the part of the song with the lyrics "bombs bursting in air" he painted a sonic portrait in feedback resembling aerial warfare. It was a very political moment for those in the audience.

During this period, Hendrix was under pressure from militant African-American groups to be "more Black" because his music was associated with the hippie movement, and he was performing with "White" musicians. The irony was that Hendrix already was playing "Black" music and, more importantly, was using it to shape the future of rock. Responding to this pressure, he formed a new African-American power trio called the Band of Gypsies, with Billy Cox on bass and Buddy Miles (Electric Flag) on drums. The only recording of the band was a live performance at Fillmore East. Hendrix's death on September 18, 1970, less than a year later, was another in a series of drug-related deaths around the same time (Janis Joplin died on October 4, 1970, and Jim Morrison on July 3, 1971). The official cause of Hendrix's death was choking on vomit induced by an overdose of barbiturates. Hendrix's influence on rock was enormous, such that he easily could be called the most influential guitarist of the sixties.

Led Zeppelin

Another starting point in the development of heavy metal is Led Zeppelin (Jimmy Page, Robert Plant, John Paul Jones, and John Bonham), who formed in 1968 to honor contractual engagements in Sweden left by the dissolved Yardbirds. Their original name was the New Yardbirds. The Yardbirds was one of the first English blues rock bands to gain popularity in America, and during its existence it included three early guitar heroes: Eric Clapton, Jeff Beck, and Jimmy Page. Although Clapton left because the band had strayed too far from the blues, the Yardbirds' blues rave-ups remained an important part of their live performances. When Led Zeppelin formed, the blues and rave-ups were an important element in their musical heritage.

When he joined the Yardbirds in 1966, Jimmy Page was one of the busiest studio session guitarists in England, recording as many as three sessions a day. He had appeared on recordings by Mick Jagger, the Kinks, Joe Cocker, and Donovan. His knowledge of the recording process and his skill as a guitarist were indispensable to the success of Led Zeppelin.

The band's albums were instantly successful and remained on the charts for long periods. Although singles from their albums, such as "Good Times Bad Times" and "Whole Lotta Love," were successful, all songs from their albums became regulars on the FM radio format. As with other early metal bands, like Blue Cheer, their blues roots are evident on early recordings. Listening to them "with those ears" will be instructive in demonstrating the way blues riffs developed into metal. On "Good Times Bad Times," which opens with two stark power chords, Page's solo begins like the famous "Louie Louie" solo, and then takes on a bluesy sound with long notes that are reminiscent of Muddy Waters's bottleneck guitar sound. With the benefit of years of studio experience, Page colored each selection of the album with unique guitar sounds.

Zeppelin's albums also had an acoustic element that remained an underreported element of metal bands. Their first album contained "Babe I'm Gonna Leave You," "Your Time Is Gonna Come," and "Black Mountain Side," on which Page's acoustic guitar–playing sounds like a cross between Ravi Shankar (Indian sitarist) and Blind Lemon Jefferson. Their most famous acoustic-style recording, "Stairway to Heaven," from their fourth album, is one of the most popular and controversial recordings in rock history. At one time, the song was the most performed recording on FM radio and received added publicity when, in the late seventies, it was discovered that it contained satanic messages when played backwards. Sound files of these backward messages can now be found on the Internet.

Led Zeppelin has remained popular among rock fans, and their recordings, unlike those of other bands, have a timeless appeal to them. As such, they have a permanent home on FM AOR radio formats. The end came for Led Zeppelin when their drummer John "Bonzo" Bonham died from excessive alcohol intake on September 25, 1980. After his death, the other members issued a statement saying they could not go on without Bonzo because it would not be the same band. Since that time, Page and Plant have released albums and toured, and there have been at least seven "reunion" concerts.

Black Sabbath

By the time the band Earth changed their name to Black Sabbath (1969), they had developed the classic heavy metal format. Earth was basically an English blues band that evolved out of a series of other bands; Tony Iommi (guitar) and Bill Ward (drums) both played in Rest and Mythology, and Ozzy Osbourne (vocals) and Geezer Butler (bass) belonged to the Rave Breed. Those bands combined to form a band called Polka Tulk, which became Earth and finally Black Sabbath, a name inspired by the title of a 1935 Boris Karloff movie. Their sound was derived from the previous blues rock tradition—they made use of the same blues riffs as earlier bands—but the content of their lyrics signaled a break from the past. Black Sabbath sang about gloom, doom, the breakdown of society, and the fight between good and evil.

They financed their first album, *Black Sabbath*, themselves; it was rejected by fourteen record labels before the band found one willing to release it. Received successfully, the album reached number eight on the British charts and remained there for eighteen weeks. Their second album, *Paranoid*, entered the charts at number one and replaced Simon and Garfunkel's *Bridge Over Troubled Water*. Despite the album's success, the band was criticized by rock journalists and DJs for their "bone-crushing volume," ponderous tempos, and satanic imagery. A reviewer for the *Los Angeles Times* said of their performance at the Forum (March 15, 1972) that the songs "consisted of anguished screeching about war pigs, rat salads, iron men and similar gloomy topics set to an endlessly repeated two-chord riff."[2] The fact that they replaced Simon and Garfunkel on the charts but were rejected by the critics illustrates the gap that existed between the rock power structure and the audience.

It is difficult to assess the extent of Black Sabbath's satanism because of the difficulty encountered in interpreting any lyrics and the menacing power of the band's visual image. Their detractors lean toward the devil-worshipper interpretation while their fans see them warning listeners about the consequences of society's current path. Aside from their lyrics, their reliance on satanic imagery is strong. For example, the cover of *Sunday, Bloody Sunday* (another movie title) prominently features the "mark of the beast," the number 666. Black Sabbath is the godfather of all metal bands and retains a loyal following.

Ozzy Osbourne left the band, or was fired, after their 1979 tour. He was replaced by Ronnie James Dio from Ritchie Blackmore's Rainbow. Osbourne had serious problems with substance abuse, and during one period he was consuming four quarts of cognac per day, plus assorted drugs. His behavior during this period could be described as colorful. During a meeting with Columbia Records executives, his wife suggested that he release two white doves into the room as a peace offering. Ozzy released one dove and bit the head off the other.[3] In a later concert in Des Moines, fans threw a live bat on stage, and thinking it was one of those Halloween rubber bats, he bit off its head. Osbourne continues to be a concert attraction, and in 1996 he instituted a yearly Ozz-Fest tour featuring metal bands.

Theatrics in Rock

Theater and image has always been an important factor in rock and roll success, from Elvis's lip-curling, hip-swiveling television appearances to the Beatles' carefree music videos. By the seventies it became increasingly important for rock acts to infuse their live appearances with increased attention toward the theater of the event. This trend may have begun with Andy Warhol and the Velvet Underground's multimedia presentations in New York, and with the LSD-inspired San Francisco Trips Festival (1966), with its "Sound-Light Console" performance by Donald Buchla. Soon after these events, acid rock bands began including a light show with their performances, first by projecting blobs of light (colored oils in water and an overhead projector) and progressing to sophisticated laser light shows.

Alice Cooper (Vince Furnier) added more theatrics with macabre makeup and a live stage show that featured a mock hanging, electrocution, chopping up dolls, and a live boa constrictor. Adults throughout America cringed and did not approve of the implications of Cooper's performance as theater for teens. He was as much an actor playing a role as any *West Side Story* gang member. Cooper's recordings in the early seventies were very popular, and his single "School's Out" (1972) reached number seven on the charts.

The theatrical ante was upped by Kiss, formed in 1972, who costumed themselves as fantasy cartoon characters with Kabuki-like face paint and science fiction costumes. Their stage show was huge, and by the late seventies it required seven semi-trailers to haul it around. Their performance was filled with menacing theatrics designed to thrill its audience and repel adults. Gene Simmons spit blood, breathed fire, and wagged his long tongue at the audience. As with Black Sabbath, critics and DJs hated them and refused to play their recordings until 1976, when their single "Beth" reached number seven on the charts. They became so popular that Marvel Comics published a Kiss comic book (the red ink supposedly contained their blood), and NBC aired a full-length cartoon, *Kiss Meets the Phantom of the Park*. Kiss faded during the eighties, but their 1996 reunion tour was the surprise hit of the North American summer concert of the season, earning more money than any other act. They toured again in 1998, and in 2000 they began their "farewell tour."

Progressive Rock

As rock recordings lengthened beyond the standard three-minute radio format, musicians were faced with an ancient musical question: how does one sustain the listener's interest over a long period? There are several choices: (1) continue to repeat the melody and constantly change the instrumentation, like Ravel's *Bolero;* (2) improvise new melodic material over the song's harmonic foundation, like jazz musicians do; or (3) write multi-sectional compositions that can move from section to section, much like the symphonic composers of the eighteenth and nineteenth centuries. Acid rock, blues, and boogie bands chose the second solution and tried to sustain the audience's attention with long improvisations. Progressive rock tried the third option and emulated the forms of classical music (referring to the broad range of European art music): the symphony, tone poem, suite, and opera.

Sociologists approach these musical choices with a discussion of social class: Metal and punk are blue-collar music for the lower classes, while progressive rock is aimed at the upper classes. There is a certain amount of truth in this approach; however, it is more applicable with a British audience where there is a more formalized distinction between the classes than in the United States.

Another method of approaching the choices between classical forms and extended improvisation would note the differences between the cultures of Europeans and Americans in the twentieth century. Americans created the blues, jazz, and improvisation, the skill of spontaneous composition, which became a highly developed art form used to lengthen performances of a song. American acid and blues rock musicians who developed a higher level of instrumental expertise tended to use this jazz model when adding length to a composition. The use of classical forms tends to be a choice of European bands, and this is likely a result of greater exposure to classical music, both in the media and in private music lessons. Because of cultural differences and the financial structure of the media, classical music is more available in Europe via live performances and European state-owned radio and television stations than it is in the United States. Although a music education in both cultures includes an exposure to the "classics," American public school musicians have been exposed regularly to jazz performance traditions since the sixties. It is logical that European rockers chose European musical forms when they sought to maintain interest in extended compositions, while Americans and those blues-rock musicians influenced by American music chose the jazz model.

Art rock was the first label given to this unconventional style, because it obviously included classical structures. As the style entered the seventies, however, it tended to be called *progressive rock*. Although there are some differences, one would be hard pressed to divide late-sixties and early-seventies bands into these two styles. The term "progressive" was probably preferred in the long run because it sounded less pretentious and was more inclusive than *art rock*." The music of 1950's modern jazz artists Stan Kenton and Dave Brubeck was also described as "progressive," even though both of them used elements of classical music to extend their compositions.

One of the earliest appearances of art rock was the 1967 Procol Harum hit "A Whiter Shade of Pale" which used a melody from Bach's *Suite No. 3 in D major*. It was a pop song rather than an extended composition, but it suggested the possibilities in combining rock and classical music. Around the same time, the Moody Blues began working in extended forms on a series of albums such as *Days of Future Passed* (1967), *In Search of the Lost Chord* (1968), *On the Threshold of a Dream, To Our Children's Children's Children* (1969), *A Question of Balance* (1970), *Every Good Boy Deserves Favour* (1971), and *Seventh Sojourn* (1972). At the time, these recordings were not so much thought of as progressive rock as they were psychedelic fantasies. However, in retrospect, they were a beginning of progressive rock.

There was a sort of musical confusion at the beginning of the seventies as bands searched for an identity. This confusion is exemplified by Deep Purple (formed in 1968). They recorded three top-forty American hits in 1968

("Hush," "Kentucky Woman," and "Smoke on the Water"); they were listed as the loudest rock band in the *Guinness Book of World Records;* and they recorded with the *Royal Philharmonic Orchestra*—a pop, metal, art rock band. Their *Concerto From Group and Orchestra* (1970) was well received by critics from both sides, rock and classical, and inspired another extended composition, *The Gemini Suite.* As with the Who's rock opera *Tommy* (1968), there was great excitement in the classical world now that rock was "respectable" and now that the two musical traditions were joined. There was no reason for the excitement, because the "rock band and orchestra" genre never developed beyond a few experimental efforts. The main problem was that although the works were well-received by critics, record buyers were not as enthusiastic.

Emerson, Lake and Palmer (ELP) formed in 1970 after jamming together at the Fillmore West and were instantly met with praise from critics. Keith Emerson had classical music training, Greg Lake was a founding member of King Crimson and, together with Carl Palmer, they created a unique approach to blending the two musical styles. ELP had some success with radio airplay ("Lucky Man," 1971, and "From the Beginning," 1972), but they made their biggest impact with albums and stage shows that involved smoke, lights, and a huge cast. Their extended compositions were interesting, in a variety of styles, and did not water down their rock aesthetic. A significant accomplishment was their arrangement of Modest Mussorgsky's composition *Pictures at an Exhibition* (1970), which gave a popular, well-known orchestral composition a rock interpretation. The composition is filled with bombast in its original orchestral setting, so it was a perfect choice for the addition of more rock bombast.

Yes, formed in 1968, was another very successful progressive rock band that used extended forms without overtly bowing to classical music. They tended to be on the edge of jazz fusion and might have crossed over to jazz if vocals had not been so important to their performance. Their first engagement was opening for the Cream Farewell Concert in 1968, and they made a favorable impression on critics who hailed them as the next supergroup. The group's style was typified by displays of instrumental virtuosity, abruptly shifting meters, and clear vocal harmonies.

Genesis has turned out to be one of the more curious of the progressive bands, from their start as a "songwriters collective" in 1966, to the emergence of Peter Gabriel and Phil Collins as solo acts. The group began as the Garden Wall (Peter Gabriel, Tony Banks, Mike Rutherford, Anthony Phillips) at the Charterhouse School for Boys. After graduation, they remained together and released their first album *From Genesis to Revelations* in 1969. Their first real success came in 1971 with the release of their third album, *Nursery Cryme,* which included their new drummer Phil Collins. They tended to be more literary than other groups, with Peter Gabriel telling "mysterious" stories between songs and wearing masks and costumes to help create a mood; their instrumental sound served only to enhance the story rather than to impress the listener with their instrumental skills. Gabriel left for a solo career in 1974, and Collins took over as lead singer.

Gabriel began exploring technology and third-world musics, and maintained his visibility as well as his credibility among musicians. He placed recordings on the charts sporadically beginning with "Shock the Monkey" (1982), and he reached number one in 1986 with "Sledgehammer." At this point, Gabriel was in the unique position of having a hit recording without selling out. In 1989, Gabriel won a Grammy for Best New Age Performance for his score for *The Last Temptation of Christ*.

Phil Collins and Genesis continued recording and became more successful at reaching the charts, finally earning a platinum record with *And Then There Were Three* (1978). In 1981, Genesis reached the top ten with *Abacab* and thereafter attained considerable commercial success. However, Phil Collins found the most success with solo projects and reached the year-end top 100 ten times during the eighties. He also won a Grammy for Best Pop Vocal Performance (1984) for "Against All Odds (Take a Look at Me Now)."

King Crimson, formed in 1969 around the conceptual talents of Robert Fripp, tended toward an avant-garde, dissonant type of rock—it was very interesting and jazz-like at times. The band went through a series of personnel changes and were unified only by the vision of Fripp. In 1974, Fripp disbanded King Crimson because of a desire to perform for smaller audiences composed of serious listeners. Along with Brian Eno, he combined the latest electronic developments into a system he called "frippertronics." In 1981, Fripp revived Crimson with Adrian Belew, Tony Levin, and Bill Bruford, and they remained fairly stable during the decade.

Pink Floyd formed in 1965 as a blues band. They used a variety of different names before settling on Pink Floyd, a combination of Syd Barrett's favorite blues singers, Pink Anderson and Floyd Council. Although they began as a blues band, they quickly got involved in London's psychedelic scene. In 1965, the International Poetry Festival was held at Royal Albert Hall, featuring Beat poets Allen Ginsberg and Lawrence Ferlinghetti. Its success led to other Beat events at clubs like the Marquee Club. A similar Beat/music cross-fertilization was happening in San Francisco at the same time. Pink Floyd became part of this scene and developed its quirky music mix out of it.

In 1969, Syd Barrett became incapacitated by his LSD use and left the band to check into a hospital. His departure changed the music mix, and in 1973, they released the extremely popular album *Dark Side of the Moon*. The album stayed on the *Billboard* charts for thirteen years. They remained an important cult band, and in 1979 released *The Wall*. This album contained a hit single,

"Another Brick in the Wall." The tour in support of the album involved the building of a huge wall on the stage between the audience and the band. The concept was well received by a multi-generational audience. In the mid-eighties, the band was thrown into turmoil again when Roger Waters quit and sued the others for the rights to the band's name. As with the other progressive bands, their longevity and personnel changes resulted in a history/discography that divides into different eras and styles, with fans preferring one or the other.

Frank Zappa

Frank Zappa is probably the most enigmatic figure in the annals of rock and roll and he, more than any other artist, defies any sort of classification. Zappa is a product of the mid-sixties Los Angeles hippie scene and might have been discussed in the previous chapter except that he was unlike any of those musicians and did not become famous during that era. In fact, he never really became famous aboveground. Instead, his cult following grew slowly over a number of years, until at some point he ended up being well known by a multi-generational audience. Zappa's music was not typical of any other art or progressive rock bands. While British art rock bands typically used elements of eighteenth and nineteenth century art music, Zappa worked in the musical language of twentieth century composers, particularly Edgard Varèse. As a teenager, Zappa's first record album purchase was the music of Edgard Varèse; the second was Stravinsky's *Rite of Spring*. Zappa was so impressed by Varèse's music that he used money from his fifteenth birthday to place a long-distance call to Varèse in New York.[4] (Readers are encouraged to seek out the music of Varèse and Stravinsky at the public library to discover the music that helped shape Zappa's output.) Zappa's music was a mix of the sonic clusters that are also found in Varèse's music, acid rock, and wry social satire.

In 1964, Zappa was playing in a bar band called the Soul Giants and talked them into doing original music and changing their name to the Mothers (later changed to the Mothers of Invention because of record company pressure). The Mothers' first album, *Freak Out* (1966), was rock's first double album. It was a commercial failure but an artistic success, as the wealth and variety of music on it was astonishing. There were doo-wop and psychedelic songs mixed together in such a way that the listener had trouble knowing if the Mothers were a doo-wop band making fun of hippies or a hippie band making fun of old rock and roll—they were both. On the second disk were two extended compositions that defy description except to say that they were improvisational fantasies. Their next albums, *Absolutely Free, We're Only in It for the Money,* and *Lumpy Gravy,* were filled with social satire like "Brown Shoes Don't Make It" and "Plastic People." *We're Only in It for the Money* was a parody of *Sgt. Peppers Lonely Hearts Club Band,* complete with art work and cardboard cut-outs. These albums were funny, but they also contain sections of the most original instrumental rock ever recorded. In 1967, Zappa recorded *Cruising With Ruben and the Jets,* which was either a satire of or a tribute to doo-wop.

Zappa continued on his course through the seventies and eighties (he died in 1993), recording a quirky combination of humor, satire, and serious compositions. After 1970, the personnel of his bands constantly changed, and at times included Howard Kaylan and Mark Volman (Turtles), Jean-Luc Ponty, Don "Sugarcane" Harris, Jack Bruce, Terry Bozzio, and Adrian Belew. By the eighties it had become an honor to play in one of Zappa's bands, because it was an indication you were a disciplined musician and had achieved a high level of technical proficiency on your instrument. Zappa even cracked the pop charts in 1979 with his disco satire "Dancin' Fool," from his *Sheik Yerbouti* album, and again in 1982 with "Valley Girl," which poked fun at the speech patterns of his daughters' friends. Zappa stands out as the most unique and original rock musician of the era.

In 1985, Zappa testified before a Senate subcommittee in an effort to counteract the influence of the Parent's Music Resource Center, which was attempting to increase the amount of censorship already felt by rock musicians. The end result was that the recording industry agreed to place parental advisory labels on recordings that might be offensive. The labels were in fact censorship because chain discount stores refused to carry albums with warning labels. This forced record labels to release censored versions of the recording. Ironically, Zappa's album *Jazz From Hell,* a Grammy winner for Best Rock Instrumental Performance (1987), carried a parental advisory label even though it had no vocals, because of the title of one track, "G-Spot Tornado."

Zappa's most unusual role came when President Vaclav Havel asked him in 1990 to serve as Czechoslovakia's trade, tourism, and cultural liaison to the West. However, under pressure from Secretary of State James Baker, Havel changed the appointment position to an unofficial cultural ambassador. In 1991, Frank Zappa was diagnosed with prostrate cancer, and he died on December 4, 1993.

Singer/Songwriters

The term *singer/songwriter* is a vague description of artists like Paul Simon, Carol King, Joni Mitchell, James Taylor, and Carly Simon, who write and record their own introspective and confessional songs. In the sixties, such singer/songwriters fit neatly into the folksinger category. However, once the term "folksinger" became a negative descriptor, a new label was applied. Additionally, the instrumental accompaniment of these songs is generally thin and sparse, probably because of the folk roots of the style. The nature of the accompaniment helped prevent these songs from crossing over other rock genres, because there were many artists who wrote and performed their own material. Chuck Berry, Buddy Holly, Hank Williams, and the Beatles wrote and performed their own songs, but they fit neatly into other categories, and their songs are not thought to be personal enough to be included as part of the singer/songwriter category.

Folk duo Simon and Garfunkel split after their *Bridge Over Troubled Water* album (1970), and Simon, except for a few reunions, recorded on his own with musicians from different stylistic and cultural backgrounds. He recorded with musicians such as Stephane Grapelli, the Dixie Hummingbirds, Ladysmith Black Mambazo, and assorted South American musicians. Simon has been fairly successful on the charts over a long period of time. His hits include "Me and Julio Down by the Schoolyard" (1972), "Kodachrome" (1973), "Loves Me Like a Rock" (1973), "50 Ways to Leave Your Lover" (1975), "Still Crazy After All These Years" (1976), "Slip Slidin' Away" (1977), "One Trick Pony" (1980), and "Graceland" (1986).

James Taylor and Carly Simon were the quintessential singer/songwriter couple during their marriage that lasted most of the decade. Both singers came from wealthy families and had musical siblings. Taylor's father was the dean of a medical school, and his brother Livingston and his sister Kate were both musicians. Carly Simon was from the Simon and Schuster publishing family; her sister Joanna was an opera singer and her sister Lucy was a folksinger. Carly and Lucy performer together as the Simon Sisters and recorded an album of children's songs for Kapp Records. When Lucy got married, Carly continued as a single act. Taylor's songs and singing style were soft and introspective, and his knack for reinterpreting the songs of others in his soft personal style was popular with his radio audience. Taylor's hit recordings include "Fire and Rain" (1970), "You've Got a Friend" (1971), "Don't Let Me Be Lonely Tonight" (1972), "How Sweet It Is" (1975), and "Handy Man" (1977). Simon and Taylor had a joint hit with "Mockingbird" (1974), originally recorded by Charles and Inez Foxx, although the lyrics are found in early African-American folk music. Simon, like Taylor, had a series of hits through the seventies, such as "Anticipation" (1971), "You're So Vain" (1972), "The Right Thing to Do" (1973), "Haven't Got Time for the Pain" (1974), and "Nobody Does It Better" (1977). Two of her recordings, "Anticipation" and "Nobody Does It Better," went on to "greater fame" when they were used in television commercials, which etched them in the minds of America's television public.

John Denver (Deutschendorf), former member of the Back Porch Majority, New Christy Minstrels, and Chad Mitchell Trio, wrote Peter, Paul, and Mary's last hit "Leaving on a Jet Plane." Denver had such great success in making hit recordings and sculpting a good, clean country-boy image that he had a hard time being seen as anything else. Songs like "Take Me Home Country Roads" (1971) and "Thank God I'm a Country Boy" (1975) sang the praises of country life in general. "Rocky Mountain High" was specifically about the good life in Colorado. The Colorado establishment loved him so much that the governor proclaimed him the state's poet laureate. However, Colorado's mountain hippies hated him for popularizing their mountain hideaway and blamed him for the state's population increase. Denver's other hits include "Sweet Surrender" (1972), "Sunshine on My Shoulders" (1974), "Annie's Song" (1974), "Back Home Again" (1974), and "I'm Sorry" (1975). In the second half of the seventies, Denver added acting to his skills and appeared in roles on television and in the movie *Oh, God!* with George Burns.

Denver continued performing, but his popularity faded during the eighties and nineties, possibly due to his clean "saccharine" image. He was killed in 1999 when the experimental aircraft he was piloting ran out of fuel and crashed into Monterey Bay off the coast of California.

Joni Mitchell is another good example of the crossover between folksinger and singer/songwriter. Born and educated in Canada, Mitchell moved to Detroit in 1966 with her folksinger husband, Chuck Mitchell. Within a year she was performing on the folk circuit, and her songs were being recorded by others: Judy Collins recorded "Both Sides Now" and "Michael From Mountains"; Fairport Convention recorded "Eastern Rain"; Tom Rush recorded "The Circle Game"; and Crosby, Stills, and Nash had a huge hit with "Woodstock."

Mitchell recorded several hit singles, such as "Big Yellow Taxi" (1970), "You Turn Me On (I'm a Radio)" (1971), and "Help Me" (1974), but she earned her reputation with her albums. During the mid-seventies, she began to blend her sound with that of jazz artists. In 1974, she recorded Annie Ross's "Twisted" and an album with the L.A. Express. In 1978, Mitchell collaborated with jazz bassist Charles Mingus on what was his final recorded performance. And in 1980, she recorded with a band that included Jaco Pastorius and Pat Metheny.

Other Singer/Songwriter Hits

Alice's Restaurant (1967)	Arlo Guthrie
If You Could Read My Mind (1970)	Gordon Lightfoot
Wide World (1971)	Cat Stevens
American Pie (1971)	Don McLean
Brand New Key (1971)	Melanie
City of New Orleans (1972)	Arlo Guthrie
Good Time Charlie's Got the Blues (1972)	Danny O'Keefe
Time in a Bottle (1973)	Jim Croce
Cat's in the Cradle (1974)	Harry Chapin
At Seventeen (1975)	Janis Ian
Longer (1979)	Dan Fogelberg

Southern Rock

Southern rock is hard to define as a separate style because it is similar, if not identical, to other hard rock blues and boogie music. Southern rock bands are known for blues-based rock and roll with extended improvisations, often with dueling lead guitars and two drummers. What is most Southern about these bands is the pride in being Southern, which is manifested through the display of Southern icons such as the Confederate flag and guns. The Allman Brothers Band was the first of this style, and after their success, a number of similar bands appeared using the same Southern identity. Remember, the record business is geographically minded. That is, when a band or style of music achieves success, other record companies begin to look for other bands from the same location, be it New Orleans, Austin, Chapel Hill, or Seattle.

The Allman Brothers Band established the instrumental format that others followed: twin lead guitars (Duane Allman and Dickey Betts) and dual drummers (Butch Trucks and Jaimoe Johanson). Duane and Gregg started playing in bands around 1960 in Florida and ended up in Los Angeles signed to Liberty Records in 1967 as the Hourglass. After experiencing no success, they returned to Florida by way of Muscle Shoals, Alabama, where they recorded in Rick Hall's FAME studio. As a result of those recordings, Duane was asked to play a session with Wilson Pickett, which brought him to the attention of Atlantic's Jerry Wexler. Hall and Wexler used Duane to accompany a variety of artists, including Aretha Franklin, Percy Sledge, Arthur Conley, and Delany and Bonnie. The most famous of his recording sessions was Eric Clapton's "Layla," on which he played the dual leads with Clapton.[5]

During this time, the Allman Brothers Band signed with the newly formed Capricorn Records, recorded two albums, toured, and developed a solid reputation as a great live act. In 1971, they released *At Fillmore East,* which reached the top ten. However, Duane was killed in a motorcycle accident shortly afterward. Less than a year later, their bass player, Berry Oakley was killed in a similar accident only three blocks away. As tragic as these deaths were, they enhanced the "fast-living, wild-eyed Southern boy" image of the band.

The band continued, with Dickey Betts writing, singing and playing lead guitar alone. Their biggest hit came in 1973 with "Ramblin' Man," written and performed by Betts, but growing trouble between him and Gregg eventually caused a breakup. Gregg Allman remained visible in the media because of his marriage to Cher and because of his testimony against the band's road manager at a drug trial. Betts formed a group called Great Southern, Chuck Leavell formed Sea Level, and Gregg led his own Gregg Allman Band. Each of these subsequent groups had very little commercial success. In 1978, much of the original band reformed into a new Allman Brothers Band and reached the charts with "Straight From the Heart." The Allman Brothers Band remains respected, but it is difficult to determine whether their reputation rests on their recorded output, nostalgia, or on a promise never fully realized.

The next important Southern band was Lynyrd Skynyrd, originally formed in Jacksonville, Florida, around 1966. Although they formed in the mid-sixties, they remained unsigned until record labels began looking for Southern bands to compete with the Allman Brothers. The original members met in high school and performed under various names, such as the Noble Five, the Wildcats, and the One Percent, until dropping out of school and changing their name to Lynyrd Skynyrd. They all lived together in a rural farm house and played local engagements until they worked their way out of the area and were discovered in Atlanta by Al Kooper, who was looking for Southern bands for MCA Records.

Kooper produced their first album *Pronounced Leh-Nerd Skin-Nerd* (1973), which contained "Free Bird" and earned them substantial FM airplay but no AM single. Peter Townsend liked the album and booked them to open for the Who's *Quadrophenia* Tour, where they were popular with audiences—rare for an opening act. Their second album (1974) launched "Sweet Home Alabama" as a hit single, which set their reputation as a Southern rock band. That reputation was further enhanced by MCA when it added a Confederate flag to their stage set. The following year, they reached the charts with "Saturday Night Special" (slang for a cheap handgun), and their follow-up album was called *Gimme Back My Bullets* (1976), which further enhanced their Southern image. In 1977, leader Ronnie Van Zant, guitarist Steven Gaines, and Gaines's sister Cassie were killed in the crash of their chartered 1947 Convair 240, which also seriously injured the rest of the band. The survivors of the crash regrouped in 1979 as the Rossington Collins Band and the Artimus Pyle Band. In 1987, they joined in a Lynyrd Skynyrd Tribute Tour that renewed enough interest in the band to lead to a recording contract with Atlantic Records (1990).

Other Southern rock bands like .38 Special, led by Ronnie Van Zant's brother Donnie Van Zant, and Molly Hatchet traded on the same hard-core Southern-boy image. However, there were a few other important Southern bands during the seventies with a different musical mix. The Marshall Tucker Band had a distinct country sound because of their vocal twang and the steel guitar, but tempered by a sax and flute that gave it a country jazz sound. The Charlie Daniels Band, although originally formed on the Allman model with dual lead guitars and two drummers, became known by the more countrified sound of their 1979 hit, "Devil Went Down to Georgia." The Amazing Rhythm Aces also leaned toward a country-harmony sound with their hit "Third Rate Romance" (1975), after which they began appearing on the country charts. A band of studio musicians, appropriately called Atlanta Rhythm Section, was on the pop side of Southern rock with hits like "So Into You" (1977) and "Imaginary

Lover" (1978). The Dixie Dregs leaned more toward a progressive rock/improvisational approach and at times was reminiscent of the jazz fusion group Mahavishnu Orchestra. Subsequently, they were popular among musicians who were not normally drawn to rock bands. ZZ Top, from Texas, could be included in this category, although they are often described as a Texas boogie band. The term *boogie*, as it is used here, has changed very little since the beginning of the century and still means "to dance" or "to party," and describes a style of music that suggests the boogie-woogie rhythmic feel. Since Texas is sometimes included as part of the South, and since they specialize in the blues, ZZ Top might qualify for the Southern rock category. Nevertheless, they are only a trio, and they exploit the Texan image rather than a "good-ole boy" image.

The entire Southern rock category may rest on the Allman Brothers' success and legend and the attempt by each record company to market its own version of them. It is possible that the Southern rock category lived in the minds of the audience and corporate boardrooms rather than in the intent of the musicians to forge a distinct regional variation to rock, because these bands usually described themselves as "playing good ole American rock and roll."

Disco

One of rock and roll's earliest and most important functions was as dance music; however, as rock grew more serious, it lost sight of its original role in teen culture. Disco returned rock to its role as music with a good beat, sufficient to lose yourself in a wild pagan dance-fever. African-American music seldom lost sight of its dance roots, and logically, R&B hits of the early seventies laid the musical foundation for the disco aesthetic. But its social origins can be found in the gay subculture of New York City.

Discotheques were not new but their place in American culture radically changed during the period. Discotheques, later called discos, were clubs that featured music played by a disc jockey rather than a live band. A DJ could play a wider variety of music than any single band and was cheaper than live music. In one sense, gay dance clubs were part of the gay liberation movement, because they encouraged gays to "come out" and publicly celebrate a love for dancing. Discotheques gradually became a theatrical fantasy environment filled with smoke-machine fog, flashing lights, and a mirrored-disco ball (a symbol of the glamorous 1940s ballroom era). Soon, dancing at discos became very fashionable, and some began to admit patrons based on their physical appearance or social status. In March 1977, a disco called Studio 54 opened its doors and molded itself as the "in" place for the rich and famous. The cover change was large, and a doorman enforced a strict dress code. Average people were not allowed in; one had to fit the image of the club to gain entrance.

The clothing one wore became an important statement. Men wore stylish trousers with loud open-collared polyester shirts and hung gold chains around their necks. Disco fashions were kinder to women, who got to wear the types of sexy gowns that had disappeared in the sixties. Drugs were a part of the culture, and cocaine was the drug of choice, because it gave the user the energy needed to dance all night, then get up early to go to work. Cocaine use was openly tolerated in discos, and a gold coke-spoon necklace was fashionable neckwear.

Disco music had an infectious beat, around 125 beats per minute, and its incessant beat is still with us today under names like *dance, techno,* and *rave.* The basic drum rhythm was simple, repetitive, and designed to help even the most rhythmically -challenged members of our culture find the beat of the music. The sound of the bass drum thumping out a quarter-note pulse was very important and was the predominant element of the drum set sound. The other important drum set elements were the sound of the hi-hat (foot-operated cymbals) opening while being struck with the drumstick between each bass drum note, and a big-sounding snare drum stroke on the second and fourth beat of each measure.

Disco Drum Beat

Tap:		tap		tap		tap		tap
Beats:	1	+	2	+	3	+	4	+
Sound:	Boom	- thess	- Wack	- thess	- Boom	- thess	- Wack	- thess

The other stylistic elements of the disco sound were diverse and included James Brown horn funk, complex orchestrations involving violins (like Barry White's Love Unlimited Orchestra), remakes of swing-era classics like "Chattanooga Choo Choo," refitted versions of classical compositions like Beethoven's *Symphony No. 5,* synthesizer creations like Kraftwerk's *Autobahn,* and hot Latin rhythms. As varied as these styles were, they had the disco drum beat in common.

Although the disco scene developed over several years, it seemed to be an overnight sensation for those Americans living outside major cities, especially after the release of the movie *Saturday Night Fever* (1977), starring John Travolta and Karen Lynn Gorney. By 1975, there were over 250 discos in New York City and a growing number across the country. They were a large market for dance music and became one of the test markets used by top-forty radio. The dance market was so important to the record industry that, in 1975, it spurred the creation of the twelve-inch single format. The larger twelve-inch recording made it possible to issue the song in a longer version than appeared on radio and to include several different "mixes." A "mix" was a version of the original song with changes in the supporting background instrumentation that rendered it suitable for several different styles of discotheques.

As popular as disco was, it was also greatly despised. Its highly stylized sound was viewed by many fans of earlier rock as an evil product of corporate-minded hit factories, mass-produced with the intent of destroying rock and roll. It is possible to shine a kinder light on disco by viewing its relationship to a particular time in American culture when, like the post–World War II pop music in the late 1940s and early 1950s, Americans tried to forget their troubles by having a good time after many years of a deadly war.

Disco died quickly and suddenly, so suddenly that the record companies were caught with their warehouses packed to the rafters with disco recordings. During the period, disco was so popular that the soundtrack to *Saturday Night Fever* was the largest selling album of all time. The record labels thought disco would never die, or at least would live longer than it did. The disco crash at the end of the sixties forced record labels into a serious financial situation because of their business practices; in order to insure a steady flow of new product, record merchants had the right to return unsold recordings to the record label for credit. So when those unsold disco recordings came back, they caused an incredible financial drain.

Rap

Rap developed as an underground urban music during the last part of the seventies, parallel to disco. By the end of the eighties, it was the dominant music of African-Americans. Rap involves rhythmic street speech/poetry delivered over a sparse instrumental accompaniment, sometimes including only drums. The word "rap" was commonly used during the sixties to mean a conversation, usually a personal one-on-one communication—as in, "Let's rap for a while." The first rappers were creative disc jockeys who added a touch of their own personality to the dance by talking to the dancers in a unique manner to let them know who was spinning records, much in the tradition of the R&B radio DJ. The rap DJs began to use instrumental recordings, or instrumental sections of popular records, as an accompaniment for their rap.

Rhythmic speech has a long tradition in the African-American community, especially in oration—as in a religious sermon—and is heard often in speeches by such figures as Reverend Jesse Jackson. Rhythmic speech and jazz united in early jazz recordings, such as Louis Armstrong's "Heebie Jeebies" or Cab Calloway's "Minnie the Moocher," in which the singer improvised vocally (*scat* singing) using nonsense syllables called *vocables*. In the 1940s, bebop jazz singers like Eddie Jefferson and King Pleasure took pre-existing recorded instrumental improvisations and wrote lyrics to fit (vocalize); this often involved rapid rap-like pronunciation. One of the most famous such bebop recordings used the melody from James Moody's solo on "I'm in the Mood for Love." The vocal result was then called "Moody's Mood for Love." It was important enough to the African-American musical culture to be included on Quincy Jones's *Q's Jook Joint* (1996).

Rap also has roots in the tradition of the Caribbean DJ, who was more entertainer than merely a player of recordings. Because records and phonographs were too expensive for the poorer classes and their radio stations were controlled by the tastes of the upper class, mobile DJs were used at social gatherings to supply the music people wanted to hear. These DJs often delivered "toasts" over recorded accompaniments. However, their toasts were more involved than those Americans would normally experience around a banquet table. These Caribbean toasts have been compared to the West African griot tradition. Griots were the oral historians who sang the history of a tribe or praises about a prominent family or ruler. The toast grew out of this tradition and during the slavery years was used as a vehicle for political and social comment. Jamaican DJs also remixed certain recordings to extend the length of a favorite instrumental section or to remove the vocal and make more room for the toast. New York City has a large Caribbean population, so it should be no surprise that early rappers like DJ Herc and Grandmaster Flash have roots in the Islands.

In more recent history, artists like Gil Scott-Heron and James Brown delivered rhythmic street-poetry conversations (raps) to their audiences over a sparse accompaniment. In fact, some of the early instrumental sections used by rappers were from Brown's recordings like "The Payback," "Get on the Good Foot," and "Sex Machine." Gil Scott-Heron, a novelist/poet who decided he could reach the people more easily with his message through music, issued a unique series of recordings that do not fit neatly into any musical genre. His songs (street poetry or rap) called attention to serious societal issues using humor and sarcasm. His most famous recording is "This Revolution Will Not Be Televised" (1973). Although rap seemed to develop suddenly and without precedent, it is a logical combination of the R&B DJ, Caribbean DJ, scat singing, James Brown, and Gil Scott-Heron.

Rappers began at small New York clubs like the Club 371, Charles Gallery, and Small's Paradise, and at dances in ballrooms like at the Hotel Diplomat and the Bronx River Community Center. They gradually branched out to other African-American neighborhoods. Although determining the first rapper is impossible, most accounts first mention DJ Kool Herc, who worked at a club called Helvado (1975), where he added raps over instrumental breaks on recordings. Herc often used sections of "Apache" by the Incredible Bongo Band, Bob James's "Mardi Gras," and the soundtrack of *Shaft in Africa* as an accompaniment to his raps.

The next major figure was Grandmaster Flash (Joseph Sadler), who developed record-scratching to a high art. Scratching was a unique phenomenon whereby a DJ used the sound of the record's grooves sliding back and forth under the turntable's stylus (needle) as a percussion instrument. Earlier, jug bands used a washboard to create rhythm in much the same way. In 1978, Flash formed a group with Cowboy, Kid Creole, and Melle Mel called Grandmaster Flash and the Three MCs. The group later expanded to the Furious Five with the addition of Kurtis Blow and Duke Bootee. Flash signed with Sugar Hill Records and recorded "Freedom" (1980) and "The Adventures of Grandmaster Flash on Wheels of Steel" (1981), which documented Flash's turntable mastery for the first time.

Later, rappers like Flash and Afrika Bambaataa used an electronic drum machine to fill in the background with a steady drum beat. The proliferation of personal computers made "sampling" possible, which meant that rappers could call up any recorded section (sample) with the touch of a finger rather than having to place a recording on the turntable and find the section while rapping and manipulating the other turntable. In sampling, a computer takes a "picture" of the sound or section, and from there it can be altered in the same way as any other cut-copy-paste function with computer data.

By the time rap appeared on recordings, it was already in a highly developed state because of the early work of rappers like DJ Cool Herc, Eddie Cheeba, Grandmaster Flash, Kurtis Blow, DJ Hollywood, Lovebug Starski, and Afrika Bambaataa. The Fatback Band's "King Tim III" (1979) is considered rap's first recording,[6] but it was not very successful. Although it was inspired by DJ Hollywood's performances at the Apollo Theater, the Fatback Band used an older-style R&B DJ who was not part of the new rap culture. In the same year, Sylvia Robinson attended a rap show at the Harlem International Disco and was impressed enough by the crowd's reaction to begin issuing rap recordings. Robinson started Sugar Hill Records and assembled a group called the Sugar Hill Gang to record "Rapper's Delight" (1979), which sold over two million copies. The members of the group were not considered by insiders to be real rappers, but they were the first to successfully transmit classic rap rhymes to a radio audience. The same year Kurtis Blow (Curtis Walker), who had left the Furious Five and signed with Mercury Records, released his first hit, "Christmas Rappin'." In the following year, he released "The Breaks," with Davy D.

One of the first displays of rap's growing popularity was the 1984 twenty-seven-city tour of the New York Fresh Fest, which included Run-DMC, Kurtis Blow, Whodini, and the Fat Boys. The tour grossed $3.5 million and caught the attention of the record industry, which then began to purchase smaller rap labels. Other important early rap recordings were "The Message" (1982) by

Grandmaster Flash, and "Looking for the Perfect Beat" (1982) and "Planet Rock" (1982) by Afrika Bambaataa. The next major highlight in rap history was the 1986 crossover recording of "Walk This Way" by Run-DMC and Aerosmith; the addition of heavy metal sounds and established rock group personalities helped the genre find broader acceptance. To further pursue the crossover potential of the music, DefJam Records (Run-DMC's label), signed a European-American ex-hardcore rap-oriented group called the Beastie Boys, who released their first album *Licensed to Ill* in 1987.

Punk Rock

During the second half of the 1970s, *punk rock* shocked the music world and reclaimed rock from the disco factories, overly regimented art rock bands, and instrumentally flashy heavy metal bands. There were two versions of the punk rock revolution: the British version that developed amid serious social and economic conditions in England, and the American version that grew out of New York's avant-garde art scene. English punk, above all, was a reaction to the pretenses of hippie music and heavy metal. Hippie music, preaching to love everyone, had no resonance in a generation that had grown up in hopeless poverty brought about by an unemployment rate nearing twenty-four percent. Heavy metal, with its pyrotechnic displays of instrumental prowess that elevated guitarists to superstar status, moved rock beyond the bounds of a simple music playable by average kids. This reaction to the professional music business caused English punks to hold amateurism up as an emblem and turn musical performance and production values upside down to the point where it became good to have poor instrumental skills. English punk bands often claimed to want no part of the professional record business and took great pains to insult those who were part of it, especially journalists. New York punk on the other hand, developed in the fertile avant-garde music and art scene in that city and, although they were rebellious, their ire was driven by the mainstream art culture rather than the fiscal condition of the nation.

Fashion, rather anti-fashion, became part of the punk aesthetic and generally embraced a deviant appearance designed to repulse mainstream society. Over time though, these "deviant" fashions were embraced by the mainstream consumer culture. The core punk costume was derived from sado-masochist clothing (leather, studded dog collars) and razor-slashed clothing. After these styles were absorbed by mainstream society, it was not unusual to find expensive slashed designer jeans in malls throughout America. Body art (piercing and tattoos) was another part of the punk look, and it was not uncommon for English punks to have body tattoos of the Nazi insignia, the swastika. Body piercing, first with safety pins then evolving to gold rings and studs, while not mainstream, is common enough among the 1990s college population that everyone likely knows someone with a pierced nose, lip, navel, eyebrow, or tongue. Punk hairstyles began with spiked hair, which progressed from a "just-got-out-of-bed" look to meticulously sculpted spikes that were up to seven inches long, and vividly colored (purple, pink, and green). Punk hair colors have so permeated American society that today, innocently colored hair is even found among members of high school orchestras.

Identifying the first punk band is problematic because some writers trace the roots of punk back to garage bands of the sixties, like the Kingsmen ("Louie, Louie"), the Mysterians ("96 Tears"), the Count Five ("Psychotic Reaction"), Cannibal and the Headhunters ("Land of a Thousand Dances"), and the Premiers ("Farmer John"). Most writers trace the roots of punk, or at least the punk aesthetic, as far back as the MC5 and Iggy and the Stooges, and most generally agree that New York punk begins with the Velvet Underground.

The Michigan Sound

The MC5 (Motor City Five) formed in Detroit in 1967 and earned a punkish reputation because of the politics of their manager, the lyric content of their debut album, and the way they handled the ensuing market censorship. John Sinclair, their manager, was a poet and jazz critic whose political views included legalization of marijuana and LSD, an end to private property, and free music. During their first performance at the Filmore East, they pressured Bill Graham into turning his club over to community action groups for free shows on Wednesdays. Eventually, a fight broke out and Graham was hit in the face with a chain.

Their 1969 album's title song contained the lyrics "Kick out the jams, motherfuckers", but Electra Records convinced them to release a clean version to get more radio play. The band refused to let it issue the clean version, and was livid when the company defied its position. When Hudson's, Detroit's biggest department store, refused to stock the album, the MC5 put an ad in an underground paper that said, "Kick out the jams, motherfucker . . . and kick in the door if the store won't sell you the album . . . fuck Hudson's." The ad included Electra's logo. Hudson's responded by refusing to stock any Electra recordings.[7]

Electra dropped MC5, and the band signed with Atlantic Records and released *Back in the USA* (1970), which was critically acclaimed but did not sell well. The opening cut was a very fast version (210 beats per minute) of Little Richard's "Tutti Frutti" that lasted for one minute and twenty-seven seconds. Their rapid-tempo short-song format was developed further by the Ramones a decade later. The rest of the MC5 album was filled with hard-core anti-social songs like "Call Me Animal," "Teenage Lust," "High School," and "Human Being Lawn Mower." The band self-destructed in 1971, but their albums were reissued in England in 1977 to meet the demand of the punk movement.

Iggy Pop (James Osterberg) was also a Michigan resident, but he came from the ultra-hip college town of Ann Arbor, home of the University of Michigan. While MC5 had a working-class rage, Iggy's version was less blue collar and had a touch of performance art. Iggy unveiled his bizarre stage personae in 1967—appropriately on Halloween—in Ann Arbor. His performances were marked by such nascent punk theatrics as self-mutilation (often cutting himself with a broken bottle or smearing raw meat over his shirtless torso), audience diving, and other self-destructive behavior. In 1968, Iggy signed with Electra, and in 1969 released his first album, *The Stooges*. The recording was not successful and the group disbanded after the next album (*Fun House*, 1970). In 1976, David Bowie took Iggy along on a European tour, thus introducing his stage antics to a larger international audience and jump-starting his career. Bowie helped Iggy further by producing two albums for him, *The Idiot* (1976) and *Lust for Life* (1977). Although Iggy's career was not monetarily successful, his stage persona was a major influence on English punk rockers.

The New York Sound

The New York punk sound was a natural outgrowth of the sixties avant-garde art scene and is best represented by the Velvet Underground (Lou Reed, John Cale, Sterling Morrison, Maureen Tucker, and Nico). The Velvet Underground was more successful in death than they were in real life; their performances were not well attended and their recordings did not sell well until the late seventies, when they were hailed by punks as the most important band of the era. Their lyrics were about the hard-core, seamy side of life (drugs, prostitution, masochism) and were laid over a sonic landscape of noise and distortion.

Although unique, their approach was the natural outcome of their combined education. Lou Reed, with classical piano training, studied English and poetry at Syracuse University and occasionally jammed with Sterling Morrison, who lived in his dorm. At Syracuse, Reed fell under the influence of resident poet Delmore Schwartz, who instilled in Reed the "sacred" nature of writing. Reed's education brought him into contact with the writings of authors like James Joyce, William Burroughs, Raymond Chandler, and Hubert Selby Jr., who likely influenced his choice of topics and writing style. Interestingly, Reed's first job was as a staff songwriter for Pickwick Records, where he was to write songs to capitalize on current trends, like his take on the "The Twist" called "The Ostrich," which also coincided with a short-lived fashion trend involving ostrich feathers. Writing in a song-factory environment helped Reed adapt his literary skills to the popular-song format and probably helped him avoid commercialized pop in his serious writing.

John Cale, born in Garnant, Wales, attended the Goldsmith College of Art in London and won a Leonard Bernstein scholarship to Tanglewood in 1963. From Tanglewood, Cale moved to New York and began working with the Dream Syndicate, composer LaMonte Young's experimental ensemble. Young's minimalist concepts of sound influenced Cale, which in turn directly affected the Velvet Underground's sonic "wall of sound" approach to music. Cale said that the Dream Syndicate would tune up their instruments to the amplifier's electronic hum and that the experience helped him "realize" that "once you amplified the instrument, you created this wide open landscape, this tapestry against which things could happen." He said that the Velvets tried to "to do Phil Spector as a four-piece" band, meaning they used their amplifiers to fill up the background in the same way Phil Spector used the recording process.

In December 1965, the Velvet Underground began performing at Greenwich Village's Cafe Bizarre and consequently met Andy Warhol, New York's most influential artist. Warhol was the founding father of the pop art movement and was famous for his Campbell's Soup can paintings and "comic book" painting of Marilyn Monroe. Warhol used the Velvet Underground as a musical element for his traveling show, or "happening," called the Exploding Plastic Inevitable. During this period, Warhol assumed management of the group, arranged for a contract with Verve Records, and recorded them with Nico, an icy European singer. Their first album, *The Velvet Underground and Nico,* was recorded in 1966 but was not released until March 1967, possibly because the lyric content of some of the songs, which included "Heroin" and "Venus in Furs," intimidated the label's executives. Their next album, *White Light/White Heat* (1968), was recorded without Nico and Warhol. Without Warhol's presence, it failed to sell as well as their first. In retrospect, it was an important recording and greatly influenced rock's future lyric and sonic content.

By 1970, Cale and Reed had left the group to continue solo but, in 1989, they reunited to record a tribute to Andy Warhol, *Songs for Drella.* Reed's biggest pop success was "Walk on the Wild Side" (1972), a cross-dressing tale produced by *glitter-rocker* David Bowie that helped set the tone for glitter and androgynous rockers. In the nineties, both Reed and Cale retained their solid reputations as the spiritual fathers of American punk.

The New York Dolls, formed in 1971, combined the sonic spirit of the Velvet Underground and MC5 with the stage presence of the Rolling Stones, and added to it a touch of glitter. They wore bizarre clothing and women's makeup. After being together only a short while, they toured England with Small Faces, an important mod band, and from that platform were able to influence future English musicians.

In 1974, Malcolm McLaren took over as their manager and served as the link between the New York avant-garde music scene and the British punk movement. McLaren had attended art colleges and was equipped to interpret the New York avant-garde music scene in which the Dolls and the Velvets flourished. To the Dolls' confrontational stance he added Communist artifacts like Russian and Chinese flags and red leather outfits. The new image did nothing to revive their career, so McLaren returned to England and later managed the Sex Pistols. The New York Dolls finally disbanded in 1977. Although their popularity never spread much beyond New York, the Dolls had a significant influence on Kiss, an extremely successful band that also wore heavy makeup and outlandish costumes.

The Ramones formed in 1974 and influenced the British punk movement more than any other band. Their music was simple and fast, their lyrics were comically punk—delivered in a cheerleader style—and they dressed like movie punks in black leather jackets and torn T-shirts. Titles like "Blitzkrieg Bop," "Beat on the Brat," "Judy Is a Punk," and "Now I Wanna Sniff Some Glue," were truly funny, and it is interesting that English punks took them so literally. The lyrics of "Now I Wanna Sniff Some Glue" consisted only of the phrase "now I wanna sniff some glue," sung in the fast-paced, power-chord, communal-chant style. Social conditions in England were such that these lyrics resonated and expressed the rage of the underclass, whereas in the New York music scene they were judged to be more campy than socially significant.

The Plasmatics, with lead singer Wendy O. Williams, were not an influential band in the course of rock history, but their stage routine was so unusual that they should not be overlooked. The band was created in 1978 by Rod Swenson (who had a masters degree in fine art), and was the ultimate sex-and-violence stage act. Williams had been a topless dancer, so being sexually provocative came naturally to her. In 1981, her performance led to obscenity charges in Milwaukee and Cleveland. Appearing on stage and on television, she smashed television sets with a sledgehammer, blew up Cadillac Coup de Villes, and cut guitars in half with a chainsaw. Although critics never used the label "performance art" in describing the group, they were as much a performance art band as anything Andy Warhol or Laurie Anderson ever exhibited.

British Punk

In England, the punk movement began with the Sex Pistols (Johnny Rotten, Glen Matlock [later replaced by Sid Vicious], Steve Jones, and Paul Cook) at the end of 1975, when the band was assembled by former New York Dolls manager, Malcolm McLaren. McLaren owned a counterculture clothing shop called Sex that specialized in rubber, leather, and other bondage fashions. The general assumption is that he formed the band as an extension of the political statement made by his clothing shop; however, there are two versions of their formation. The first is that McLaren formed the group as a calculated art statement designed to offend public sensibilities and to create a music that would return rock to its roots as a rebellious, aggressive, loud music. The second is that one of his part-time employees, Steve Jones, already had a band and asked McLaren to manage it. In both versions, McLaren decided that Jones was not lead-singer material and asked John Lydon (Johnny Rotten), one of the anti-social characters hanging around the store, to audition for the band. Lydon had never sung with a band, but he had the right attitude.

The Sex Pistols reveled in an anti-social stance that was more than a stage act. They took their image too seriously and let it affect their dealings with the record industry, causing them to self-destruct within a short period. The band began performing in clubs like the Marquee, 100 Club, and the Nashville. In an interview with *Sounds* magazine, Johnny Rotten summed up their attitude saying, "I hate shit. I hate hippies and what they stand for. I hate long hair. I hate pub bands. . . . I want people to see us and start something, or else I'm just wasting my time."[8] The punk aesthetic began to attract a larger audience, and by April 1976 the first punk rock fanzine, *Sniffin' Glue. . . And Other Rock 'n' Roll Habits,* appeared. In October 1976, the Pistols signed with EMI, and, within ten days, recorded their first single, "Anarchy in the U.K.," which entered the charts at number forty-five and was picked as *Sounds'* single of the week.

On December 1, 1976, their behavior caused trouble with their label when they appeared on NBC's *Today Show.* Guitarist Steve Jones replied to something host Bill Grundy asked with, "You dirty bastard . . . You dirty fucker . . . What a fuckin' rotter!" EMI braved that episode, but their January 4, 1977, airport scene was the final straw. EMI canceled their contract after the press reported that the band "spat, vomited and swore" in the terminal building. In March 1977, they signed with A&M Records in America, but another confrontation, this time a fight with Bob Harris at London's Speakeasy Club, caused their contract to be dropped. Bob Harris's management company represented one of A&M's top acts, and he demanded that A&M respond to this outrage. Four days later, the Pistol's contract was canceled. CBS passed on signing the band, but in May they were finally signed by Virgin Records who released their second single "God Save the Queen." The BBC banned the single, and the Independent Broadcasting Authority issued warnings to stations that the recording might be in breach of the Broadcasting Act. Despite the lack of airplay, the recording rose to the number-one position on the charts.

The Sex Pistols toured the United States in late 1977, but after a particularly disastrous concert in San Francisco, they disbanded on January 14, 1978. Sid Vicious, managed by his girlfriend, Nancy Spurgen, remained in America and continued performing. Unfortunately, Sid's punk stage image became his real identity, and Sid was arrested for murdering Nancy. Sid did not last long enough to stand trial. In true punk fashion, he died of a heroin overdose in 1979. Johnny Rotten began performing under his real name, John Lydon, and formed a new band, Public Image Ltd. In 1996, the Sex Pistols re-formed for a tour of the United States, which was not as successful as they had hoped.

The Clash (Mick Jones, Paul Simonon, Tory Crimes, Joe Strummer) took a different approach to punk. While the Sex Pistols approached their act with a drunken street-brawler attitude, The Clash were more a protest band in the folk rock tradition, although their sound had nothing to do with folk. Individually, they had performed with other bands and did not take pride in an "I don't know how to play my instrument" image. The Clash formed under the influence of punk music, and their first performances were as an opening band for the Sex Pistols. The Clash were one of the early bands to mix *reggae* with rock, which in itself was a political statement. In England, Jamaican immigrants were a dark-skinned class and were the target of racist sentiments.

In 1977, CBS signed the Clash, and their first album entered the British charts at number twelve, with "White Riot" as the single. "White Riot" spoke of the propensity of the staid British to silently endure their station in life while feeling that "all the power's in the hands of people rich enough to buy it," and that "everybody's doing just what they're told to." Their "Washington Bullets" is a blunt protest song about America's military involvement around the world. They mention Chile and Allende, the Bay of Pigs invasion, as well as Nicaragua, Afghanistan, and the Dalai Lama in the "hills of Tibet." Although it is never noted, the Clash is the most likely connection between the protest music of the late sixties and the punk and alternative scene of the late eighties.

New Wave

At some point after the Sex Pistols faded, the term *new wave* began to be applied to the next wave of punk bands, although the term had originally been applied to bands like Pere Ubu, Devo, the Talking Heads, the Cars, and the B-52s. The musical direction of these first new wave groups was entirely different from the kind of music played by the Sex Pistols and the Ramones. The new sound eventually veered away from rock's emotional sound and moved toward a computer-age style, which evolved into a style now called *techno*. Musically, these groups used a metronomic drumbeat with little variation, much like an early drum machine. They used repetitive computer-like riffs that were more minimalist than they were jump blues. Their type of singing is often described as "disaffected," or emotionless and detached.

Pere Ubu and Devo, both Ohio bands, took a conceptualist, modernist, "it's-an-industrialized-society" approach to their music. Pere Ubu, formed in

1975, was named after the central character in the first futurist play *Ubu Roi* (1896) by Alfred Jarry. They used synthesizers to create sounds of an industrial factory and breaking glass, very much in the futurist tradition. Devo, first recorded in 1976, organized to produce a video called *The Truth About De-Evolution*, which won a 1975 film festival award. Their songs were quick, perky, and bouncy, based on computer-like riffs, and delivered in a somewhat humorous disaffected manner. Their stage costumes supported the throwaway consumerism image—matching plastic suits with inverted plastic flower pots as hats. Their 1980 recording "Whip It" sold a million copies and reached high on the charts. Devo's approach to tempos and synthesizers brought the new wave closer toward the later techno sound.

The B-52s formed in Athens, Georgia, in 1976, and are generally referred to as a party band. They had the same quick-tempo, perky delivery over repetitive computer-like riffs as Devo. It was perfect dance music. The band reinterpreted the early-sixties aesthetic, and its two female members, Cindy Wilson and Kate Pierson, wore beehive hairstyles, go-go boots, and miniskirts and added a unique vocal element to the sound, something akin to Peruvian singer Yma Sumac's exotic musical approach. At the suggestion of a friend who worked in New York clubs, the B-52s traveled to New York to perform at an audition night at Max's Kansas City and consequently were invited for a return engagement. Soon they were commuting between Athens and New York to perform at clubs like Max's, CBGB's, and Club 57, and by the winter of 1978, they were the hottest club band in New York. Their self-recorded first single, "Rock Lobster," became a cult hit that attracted a recording contract from Warner Brothers in 1979. Their first album sold well, and their second album, *Wild Planet*, reached number eighteen. While in New York, they befriended members of the Talking Heads, and that band's lead singer David Byrne collaborated with them on other recordings.

Although the seventies are several decades removed, the meaning and influence of its music remains elusive. It is hard to describe the decade whose music began with love and ended with hate.

LISTENING TO THE MUSIC

𝄞♪♪ "Purple Haze"—performed by the Jimi Hendrix Experience

Hendrix wrote "Purple Haze" the afternoon of December 26, 1966, in the dressing room at the Upper Cut Club in London. What started as a lengthy poem inspired by a purple pill of LSD quickly became a vehicle for Hendrix's innovative guitar techniques. With "Purple Haze," Hendrix believed he was able to musically recreate his drug trip in sonic terms, over the powerful groove of his blues-rock trio.

Analysis of "Purple Haze"—2:46 in length, released by Reprise as his second single in March 1967

The song reached number sixty-five in the United States in May and was included on *Are You Experienced*, their 1967 debut album. The Experience: Jimi Hendrix, vocals and electric guitar; Noel Redding, electric bass; Mitch Mitchell, drums.

0:00 Introduction (8 measures): Begins with the hypnotic, distorted two-note lick that became the signature riff for this song. After two measures of bass and guitar, the drums enter and Hendrix adds standard blues figures that, with the added fuzztone, seem new and different.

0:22 Introduction continues (4 measures): Hendrix now plays sustained fuzz notes on his lower strings and sharp, edgy chords on the top to establish the accompaniment pattern for the first verse.

0:31 A Section, first verse (8 measures): The verse begins "Purple Haze" and continues for six measures over his masterfully distorted blues riff. There follows two bars of 6/4, the first filled by the solo voice, "'scuse me while I kiss the sky" followed by a six-beat lead-in to the next verse.

0:51 A Section second verse (8 measures): Again begins "Purple Haze" and follows the same pattern as the first verse.

1:11 B Section (11 measures): This is a very "trippy" guitar solo that begins with Hendrix exclaiming, "Help me, help me." Here Jimi proves himself the master of psychedelic, pyrotechnical, distorted guitar by creating a unique collage of bent notes and electronically altered blues figures. During the solo, there is moaning and speaking in the background to simulate the effects of tripping on acid.

1:36 C Section (8 measures): This is a reprise of the second part of the introduction with standard blues figures and with bassist Redding adlibbing "oohs" and "aahs" throughout.

1:54 A Section, third verse (8 measures): Again begins "Purple haze" and continues in the same form as the other verses.

2:13 B Section (4 measures): Using the same chords from the earlier B-section, Hendrix improvises in the upper register of the guitar as the rhythm section gains momentum and the drummer emphasizes his cymbals.

2:21 B Section continued (12 measures): Jimi discovers a high, distorted, piercing pitch that rides the texture like a wave over background voices as the song fades.

For Musicians

"Purple Haze" is a dichotomy of simple and complex musical elements, all directed at achieving a "psychedelic" texture. The opening two-note pattern of E to Bb indicates an E #9 chord will be the harmonic base for most of the song, and roots it in basic blues. Jimi's opening guitar line is basically pentatonic, with great uses of pitch bend and distortion for coloration. The harmonic progression of E to G to A is also the harmonic basis for the verses. The guitar/bass riff that occurs after the effective vocal breaks is doubled in octaves, a typical Experience technique. The bridge section starts with three bars of A to B to D before settling on a repeating phrase of E to F# to D for Jimi's experimental guitar solo.

Hendrix incorporates non-rhythmic melodic patterns with pitch bend and distortion effects to achieve a texture recreating his psychedelic experience in aural terms. The equipment Jimi used may have included Fender Stratocaster electric guitar, wah-wah pedal, reverb, echo, phase, tremolo, fuzz, and feedback through a large Marshall amp. The last section of "Purple Haze" relies heavily on this technology as Hendrix builds toward the final high distorted guitar line amidst musically controlled chaos.

Final Comments

"Purple Haze" became a concert showcase for Hendrix, giving him the perfect vehicle for both lengthy guitar improvisations and stage antics. Hendrix's performance of this song at the 1967 Monterey Pop Festival has become famous for both his onstage guitar burning and his pointing to Otis Redding while singing, "'scuse me while I kiss this guy."

♪♪♪ "Sweet Home Alabama" performed by Lynyrd Skynyrd

Written in response to Neil Young's 1971 song "Southern Man," Lynyrd Skynyrd's "Sweet Home Alabama" expresses true Southern pride through clever lyrics within a simple three-chord song. The South here is personified as a "she" with patriotic and personal affection, lyrically glorified. Guitars do the main work here, with a combination of blues, country, and rock elements, and political lyrics are accompanied by honky-tonk style piano.

Analysis of "Sweet Home Alabama"—4:38 in length, released on MCA 40258

This song was on the charts for eleven weeks in 1974 and was included on the gold album *Second Helping,* which charted at number twelve in 1975. The form is a simple verse-chorus structure with several instrumental interludes. The meter is in four foot-taps per measure. Personnel: Ronnie Van Zant, lead vocal and composer; Garry Rossington, guitar; Allen

Collins, guitar; Ed King, guitar; Leon Wilkeson, bass; Billy Powell, keyboards; Bob Burns, drums.Produced by Al Kooper. Also includes female backup singers.

0:00   Introduction (8 measures): Starting with a "one, two, three (pause)" count-off, "Sweet Home Alabama" establishes the three-chord pattern that is its trademark sound. A solo guitar plays the song's basic riff as "turn it up" is uttered. A second guitar line enters over a simple drumbeat, followed by another guitar part and the bass. Piano joins the background as the verse approaches.

0:22   First Verse (8 measures): Begins "Big wheels," possibly a reference to CCR's "Proud Mary" and continues with each line filling 1.5 measures. The last half of the measure is filled by a piano and guitar answer.

0:41   Instrumental interlude (4 measures): This well-rehearsed section features guitar and bass lines played in unison.

0:51   Second Verse (8 measures): Gospel-sounding female backup vocals are added, singing chordal harmony as Van Zant comments on Neil Young.

1:10   Chorus (8 measures): The chorus section of "Sweet Home Alabama" occurs with syncopated guitar and drum kicks adding some rhythmic drive. As with the A section, each line fills 1.5 measures with the last half-measures filled with an instrumental answer. The last bar of this phrase is quite clever, as they slip in one new chord emphasized by the guitar and vocals.

1:29   Instrumental interlude (4 measures): A brief guitar solo over the three-chord progression.

1:39   Third Verse (8 measures): Van Zant mentions Governor Wallace, a foe of the 1960s civil rights movement, which is answered by the female vocalists singing "Boo boo boo." The next lines about Nixon's Watergate scandal are punctuated by instrumental answers.

1:59   Chorus (8 measures): The chorus of "Sweet Home Alabama" with the rhythmic kicks returns.

2:18   Instrumental Solo (16 measures): The guitar solo over the three chords is composed of blues figures. Measures 5 to 7 employ a common rock and blues solo device, a short, repeated riff floating over the rhythm section. The female background singers enter in measure 9, and the drums are heavier here as well.

2:57   Instrumental Interlude (4 measures): The first interlude returns.

3:06   Fourth Verse (8 measures): This verse mentions Muscle Shoals, a recording center famous for the Allman Brothers, and is accompanied by the vocal group.

3:26   Chorus (8 measures): The chorus repeats.

3:44   Chorus (8 measures): The chorus repeats.

3:45   Coda (14 measures plus fade): Billy Powell wrings real emotion from the piano as he begins his solo with riffs previously used by the guitars, and continues while the song fades (4:38).

For Musicians

Don't scoff at this simple, three-major-chord tune! Lynyrd Skynyrd uses a huge bag of musical tricks to maintain both musical interest and rhythmic momentum. His verbal counting off the tune invites the listener to participate more intimately. The additive two-bar textures during the intro build thickness and anticipation, while the simple chord structure hooks the listener. Billy Powell's control of blues materials at the piano is worth study, as he both supports the other musicians and seems to play fills at just the right moment. His energy never flags during this song, and his improvised work on the song's fade-out set a standard for Southern rock players. By having D, C, and G dominate most of the song's harmonic motion, the occasional surprise F chord is even more effective. The cymbal and guitar kicks in on the "and" of four during the "Sweet Home Alabama" chorus, and the interwoven guitar parts throughout this song have made it a Southern rock classic.

Final Comments

The rich, three-guitar texture, bluesy harmonies, and honky-tonk piano fills lend this tune a unique musical personality and live quality that hasn't diminished even after extensive airplay.

---

[1] Jim Marshall, Baron Wolman, and Jerry Hopkins, *Festival: The Book of American Celebrations* (New York: Macmillan, 1970) 41.

[2] Irwin Stambier, *Encyclopedia of Pop, Rock and Soul* (New York: St. Martin's Press, 1974) 57.

[3] Elizabeth A. Schick, ed., *Current Biography* (Bronx, NY: H.W. Wilson, 1998) 441-42.

[4] David Wally, *No Commercial Potential* (New York: Dutton, 1972) 27.

[5] Jerry Wexler and David Ritz, *Rhythm and the Blues: A Life in American Music* (New York: Knopf, 1993) 225-26.

[6] Nelson George, *Buppies, B-Boys, Baps & Bohos: Notes on Post-Soul Black Culture* (New York: HarperCollins, 1992) 43.

[7] Fred Goodman, *The Mansion on the Hill: Dylan, Young, Geffen, Springsteen, and the Head-on Collision of Rock and Commerce* (New York: Random House, 1997) 169-72.

[8] John Ingham, "The Sex Pistols," *Sounds*, April 24, 1976.

Chapter Thirteen

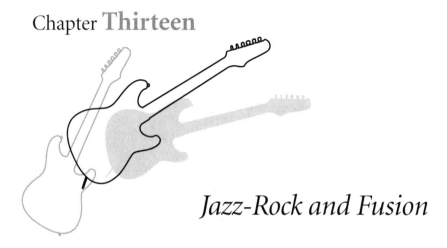

Jazz-Rock and Fusion

In the second half of the 1960s, a style called *jazz-rock* evolved that blended elements of jazz with rock. At almost the same time, there was a movement in jazz known as *fusion* that blended the features of rock with jazz, and there was a pre-existing blend of jazz, blues, and gospel now known as *soul jazz*. These developments should have been easy to predict: Young musicians educated in the public school system were exposed to jazz through participation in jazz ensembles, or dance/stage bands, as they were then known. Having grown up listening to rock in the fifties, it was perfectly natural for these young musicians to try some sort of blend between these styles. The same phenomenon occurred on the jazz side—that is, musicians destined for the jazz world who grew up listening to rock/soul also wanted to blend the styles.

Was such a blend possible? Yes and no. Both styles have the same roots, namely the blues. The most important element of jazz is the use of improvisation and the swing rhythm. Jazz is primarily an instrumental music, although there are plenty of jazz singers who improvise by *scat* singing. Rock is generally a vocal music that contains some improvisation; it moved to non-swing straight eighth-notes in the late 1950s. Early Elvis recordings had guitar solos by Scottie Moore, and doo-wop recordings often had jazz sax solos, often by King Curtis and Sam "The Man" Taylor.

By the 1960s, rock and jazz had parted ways in terms of swing rhythm, improvisation, and instrumentation. In rock, the guitar was the primary instrument, and improvised solos were very short, except in the music of early jam bands like the Grateful Dead and the Yardbirds. Jazz instruments, such as the saxophone, trumpet, and trombone, were relegated to background instruments in the studio orchestra. During this time, however, R&B bands continued to use a horn section as part of their overall sound. Such horn sections played an important role in the sound of James Brown and many of the

Memphis-style soul recordings of artists such as Wilson Pickett, Otis Redding, and Sam and Dave.

The line of distinction between jazz-rock and R&B bands is very vague, and it is probably not possible to separate the two. In fact, many of the early jazz-rock bands were influenced by R&B bands. Soul music was beginning to cross over to the pop charts in such a big way that, in 1964, *Billboard* eliminated its rhythm and blues charts thinking that the Hot 100 could accurately reflect the state of music. However, pressure from the R&B world caused it to reinstate the chart in the following year. Even though James Brown had been around since 1956, many European-Americans were not aware of him until 1965 when his recordings of "Papa's Got a Brand New Bag" and "I Got You (I Feel Good)" crossed over onto pop radio.

The fact that American teens were hearing jazz on pop radio during the first half of the 1960s also had an influence on young music-makers. Bobby Darin made the switch from teen idol to jazzy swinger à la Frank Sinatra with "Mack the Knife" in 1959 and "Beyond the Sea" in 1960. Veteran jazz musicians Dave Brubeck, Vince Guaraldi, and Stan Getz made it to pop radio with "Take Five" in 1961, "Cast Your Fate to the Wind" in 1963, and "Girl From Ipanema" in 1964. The most direct evidence that teens were hearing the message of jazz was that Cannonball Adderley's 1966 recording of "Mercy, Mercy, Mercy!" was covered by a vocal version the following year by the Buckinghams.

JAZZ-ROCK BANDS

The two most famous jazz-rock bands were Blood, Sweat & Tears and Chicago, and some writers have credited the Buckinghams with first adding a horn section to its recordings and inspiring future groups. The one element that united all three bands was producer James Guercio, a Chicago native who grew up playing with some of the musicians who later formed the group Chicago. He left town and began a career in Los Angeles performing and songwriting. (He even played in early versions of Frank Zappa's Mothers of Invention.) Guercio developed a relationship with Columbia Records, and after that company bought the Buckinghams' hit recording "Kind of a Drag," its executives asked Guercio to produce the band's next recordings.

The Buckinghams formed in 1965 and recorded a few singles with a small Chicago label. None of their singles attracted any chart attention until "Kind of a Drag" reached number one in 1967. The group did not contain a horn section but used studio horn players on their recordings. Guercio produced their follow-up hits, which included "You Don't Care," "Mercy, Mercy, Mercy!" "Hey Baby (They're Playing Our Song)," and "Susan." The Buckinghams' style was a precursor to the jazz-rock style because it helped inspire some rockers to add horn sections to their bands.

Blood, Sweat & Tears

Blood, Sweat & Tears (BS&T) had its beginnings with an earlier band called the Blues Project, which formed in 1965. The Blues Project was made up of former acoustic blues, bluegrass, and folk musicians, most notably Danny Kalb and Steve Katz, and, most importantly, Al Kooper. Kooper had found success in the music business as a session musician and songwriter ("This Diamond Ring"). Just prior to joining the Blues Project, he had recorded the famous organ part on Bob Dylan's "Like a Rolling Stone." The Blues Project has been described as an early underground jam band, and that style can be heard on their first album, *Live at the Café Au Go Go.* Their second album, *Projections,* contained successful two songs, "I Can't Keep From Crying Sometimes" and "Flute Thing," that received healthy airplay on the new FM radio format. "Flute Thing," a jazzy flute solo, possibly hinted at a new direction for Al Kooper.

After the Blues Project disbanded in 1967, Al Kooper joined with Steve Katz and drummer Bobby Colomby to form a group that further explored the combination of jazz and rock. The result was the eight-piece Blood, Sweat & Tears, which featured a four-piece horn section, including the future jazz star Randy Brecker on trumpet, and vocals by Kooper and Katz. Al Kooper served as the musical director and chief songwriter. The resulting album, *Child Is Father to the Man,* released in February 1968, was hailed by the critics and reached number forty-seven on the *Billboard* album charts but did not have any top forty singles.

The album, often compared to the Beatles' *Sgt. Peppers Lonely Hearts Club Band* and the Beach Boys' *Pet Sounds,* opens with an orchestral overture and concludes with an underture outlining some of the musical themes. There are a few folky songs reminiscent of the Blues Project, but most songs integrate the horns beyond the standard R&B uses. There are jazz sax solos by Fred Lupsius and funky Motown-esque bass lines by Jim Fielder. "My Days Are Numbered" is probably closest to the future BS&T sound of the second album. The recording was a clear break from the past and opened the door to further jazz-rock explorations.

While preparing for a second album, a dispute arose over the musical direction of the band, which resulted in Al Kooper's departure. Canadian soul-singer David Clayton-Thomas joined the band, and Columbia brought in James Guercio as producer. Al Kooper went on to record the influential *Supper Session* album with former Electric Flag blues guitarist Mike Bloomfield and Steven Stills. In 1972, Kooper moved to Atlanta where he discovered and signed Lynyrd Skynyrd to his own record label.

During the summer of 1968, Guercio moved the band Chicago from Chicago to Los Angeles to try to groom them for a recording contract. While he was doing this, Columbia asked him if he would produce the second BS&T album. He was probably called in because of his producer relationship with the Buckinghams, also from Chicago. By some reports, Guercio disliked some of the members of BS&T and did not stay around during the whole recording process. According to Columbia recording engineer, Roy Halee in a 2001 interview in *Mix* magazine, one of his early production credits was with BS&T, so it is possible he finished producing the album after Guercio left.

The second album, released in December 1968, simply titled *Blood, Sweat and Tears,* produced several top forty hits, including "Spinning Wheel," "You've Made Me So Very Happy," and "And When I Die." The album won five Grammys and earned them a headliner spot at Woodstock, although they did not appear in the film because they felt the $7,500 fee wasn't enough. The album again opened and closed with an atypical choice: a flute version of a restful piano composition by French composer Eric Satie.

The third album did well, with the hits "Hi-De-Ho" and "Lucretia MacEvil," and the fourth album managed to place "Go Down Gamblin' " on the charts. In 1971, David Clayton-Thomas decided to pursue a solo career, and Fred Lipsius, the chief arranger left. Thomas returned to the band in 1975, but it was too late to recapture the magic and Columbia finally dropped BS&T from the label in 1976. All in all, the band survived in an interesting time in popular music history when the public was tolerant of unusual musical blends. Interesting music could usually find a home on the new FM radio format. However, in the end, BS&T was just too jazzy for the mainstream record buying public.

Chicago

The band Chicago developed at about the same time as BS&T and was probably helped along by their success. Ultimately, Chicago had a much longer career than did BS&T, which can be attributed to their being more of a rock band with a horn section as opposed to a rock band playing jazz.

Chicago began life in the city of Chicago as a group called The Big Thing. Several of the musicians were students at DePaul University and, in addition to their classical studies, had fun playing in rock bands using an R&B horn section. The band started with saxophonist Walt Parazaider, Terry Kath on bass, Danny Seraphine on drums, and Lee Loughnane on trumpet. Later, trombonist James Pankow, transferred to DePaul, and they found keyboardist, Robert Lamm, playing in a band on the South Side of Chicago.

The Big Thing played their first gig as a rock band with horns in March 1967 and traveled extensively throughout the Midwest. Later that year, they arranged a meeting with James Guercio, who was by then a producer with Columbia Records. Guercio had been friends with Parazaider and Kath since their teen years, and the three had played together in bands. After meeting with Guercio, the band began to develop their songwriting skills and, before meeting Guercio a second time, added Peter Cetera on bass, completing the Chicago lineup.

In June 1968, Guercio moved the band to Los Angeles, changed their name to Chicago Transit Authority, and began to groom them for a record contract. The bandEarlier, Guercio had moved another band, Illinois Speed Press, to Los Angles and recorded two albums with them. While Guercio was working with the bands he was asked by Columbia to produce the second Blood, Sweat & Tears album.

Chicago went to New York to record their first album, which was released in April 1969. The album got good airplay on FM stations, but AM stations, then the format of mainstream rock radio, did not play any cuts. The album did well, reaching number seventeen on the charts without the help of a hit single.

Chicago II was released in January 1970, and two of the songs, "Make Me Smile" and "25 or 6 to 4," became hit singles. "Make Me Smile" featured powerful brass punches during the vocals and a unison horn line in the center. "25 or 6 to 4" opened with a strong brass introduction over a repeated descending bass line and heavy guitar solo in the center. These songs caught the public's attention, and Columbia then went back to the first album and edited down "Does Anybody Really Know What Time It Is" and "Beginnings" to make them suitable for airplay. The lovely ballad "Colour My World," the flip side of "Beginnings," got a lot of airplay and became a standard for wedding bands.

The group continued to have success, most notably with "Saturday in the Park" in 1972, but in 1978 singer, Terry Kath, died of an accidentally self-inflicted gunshot wound, and afterwards the band's popularity began to cool down. They were dropped by Columbia in 1981. Replacing Kath as lead singer was Bill Champlin, who had been the leader of a band in San Francisco called the Sons of Champlin. Chicago signed with Warner Brothers and, in 1982, began to have even greater success on the charts than before. As of this writing, Chicago has released thirty albums.

The Electric Flag

The Electric Flag grew out of the European-American blues movement that fermented in the hip underground of the mid-sixties. Mike Bloomfield and Nick Gravenites left the Paul Butterfield Blues Band (which had backed Bob Dylan at his infamous 1965 Newport Folk Festival performance) in 1967 and joined with drummer Buddy Miles and pianist Barry Goldberg. Goldberg, along with Steve Miller, had been the Goldberg-Miller Blues Band. The Electric Flag's debut performance was at the 1967 Monterey Pop Festival. Columbia signed them, along with several other bands that appeared at the festival, and their first album made it to the top forty. Internal strife caused a breakup after only eighteen months, rendering the band less influential than they should have been. Buddy Miles continued on with his own band, eventually teaming up with Jimi Hendrix, and Mike Bloomfield recorded the influential *Super Session* album with Al Kooper.

Other Jazz-Rock Bands

There were many other jazz-rock bands, although not many had sustained success on the charts. Bands often broke up after failing to have follow-up hits, but many of the bands reunited and continued to play for their original fan base.

The Ides of March did not have a hit recording until 1970 with "Vehicle," but they had been together since 1964. The band had a few minor hits, but fame eluded them until "Vehicle," written by lead singer Jim Peterik, reached number two on the charts. The band was criticized for sounding like BS&T, but they actually predated the successful jazz-rock band. They were unable to reach the charts again, and Peterik left to follow a solo career, finally co-founding Survivor and co-writing their hit "Eye of the Tiger."

Chase, led by Bill Chase, formed in 1970 and had a hit called "Get It On" in 1971. Bill Chase, who had performed with jazz greats Woody Herman, Maynard Ferguson, and Stan Kenton, based his sound on the dazzling trumpet section of Maynard Ferguson, and featured four trumpets instead of the trumpet/trombone/sax horn section favored by other jazz-rock groups. "Get It On" made it to number twenty-four, and jazz fans loved the album. The group failed to have any substantial follow-up hits. Bill Chase and three of the band's members were killed in a small plane crash in 1974.

Cold Blood, with singer Lydia Pense, was a nine-piece soul/R&B band also sporting a horn section. They formed in San Francisco in 1968 and recorded five albums for Bill Graham's San Francisco label. Their single "You've Got Me Hummin'" only made it to number fifty-two, and they lived in the shadow of Janis Joplin and Tower of Power. They disbanded in the late 1970s, but regrouped a decade later and are popular on the California festival and fair circuit.

Ten Wheel Drive was a ten-piece rock band with a five-man horn section that featured Genya Ravan as lead singer. Ravan was the former lead singer of Goldie and the Gingerbreads (1963-1968), the first all-female rock band signed to a major label. Goldie and the Gingerbreads reached number twenty-five on the British charts and shared the stage with the Rolling Stones, the Kinks, and the Yardbirds. After the breakup of the Gingerbreads, Ravan joined with songwriters Aram Schefrin and Mike Zager to form Ten Wheel Drive. The band recorded four albums—three with Ravan—got airplay on FM radio, and reached number seventy-four on the pop charts with "Morning Much Better." As they did with Lydia Pense, people compared Ravan to Janis Joplin and, as if there was only room for one European-American female soul singer, she never reached the level of popularity her voice deserved. Genya Ravan left in 1971 and formed her own band called Baby and, in 1975, she became the first woman hired as a producer by a major record label, RCA.

Lighthouse was a thirteen-piece Canadian jazz-rock-classical band formed by Skip Prokop, Paul Hoffert, and Ralph Cole in 1986. They reached the American top ten in September 1971 with "One Fine Morning," although they have five top-thirty hits in Toronto. The band performed at the major rock festivals and venues, including Monterey, Newport, Isle of Wright, Fillmore East, and Fillmore West. Lighthouse is still performing for their Canadian fans.

Tower of Power is one of the most successful horn-driven bands that developed out of the San Francisco R&B movement. Although they are not generally considered under the jazz-rock heading, their sound has always been dominated by a strong, tight horn section. Their sound was so well known that the horn section recorded with many different acts, including Santana, Elton John, Lyle Lovett, Rod Stewart, Jefferson Starship, and Heart. They had chart success with "So Very Hard to Go" (1972), "Don't Change Horses (in the Middle of a Stream)" (1974), "You're Still a Young Man" (1974), and "What Is Hip," (1974). The band still has a loyal following of fans, and the horn section often sits in with Paul Shaffer's band on *The David Letterman Show.*

SOUL JAZZ

In the 1950s, *soul jazz,* called *funky jazz* by some, was an offshoot of the *hard bop jazz* style focused on the blues, and gospel roots of jazz. The style is typified by uncluttered, bluesy improvisations, often over a straight-eighth-note rhythmic foundation. Jazz used, and approved of, the straight-eighth-note rhythm when playing Latin-based music—i.e., mambo and bossa nova—but other uses that hinted at rock and roll were considered by serious jazz fans to be "selling out." In fact, in the 1960s any jazz recording that appeared on the pop charts was viewed as suspect by jazz fans. Having a hit record on the pop charts was detrimental to one's credibility in the jazz world.

In the 1960s, jazz musicians found they were losing audience members, and jazz venues were being replaced by pop music. This financial reality and the desire to be current with a young African-American audience led many jazz musicians to the style. Soul jazz occupied an unusual place in history, often looked down upon by jazz fans and undiscovered by European-American teens until the acid-jazz movement of the 1990s.

At the beginning of the soul-jazz movement was the Horace Silver Quintet that grew out of the Jazz Messengers. Horace Silver began by simplifying his piano style and grafting on bits of blues and gospel piano. To further simplify the music, he often doubled the line of the bass player with his left hand.

Horace Silver frequently recorded songs, such as "Song for My Father" and "The Jody Grind," that, because of their Latinesque rhythm, could be thought of as rock tunes. Other pianists followed his lead, and there grew an entire soul jazz piano school with pianists like Ramsey Lewis, Bobby Timmons, Herbie Hancock, and Les McCann and organists like Jimmy Smith, Brother Jack McDuff, and Groove Holmes. The organists often fall into a category called *organ trios*.

One of the earliest jazz artists to appear on the pop charts was saxophonist Eddie Harris, whose 1961 version of "Exodus" eventually sold over two million records. Later, he introduced the Varitone, by the Selmer Company, that electronically altered the amplified sound of an instrument, sometimes doubling it an octave up or down and adding distortion. In 1965, Harris released an album containing a song called "Freedom Jazz Dance" that was later made famous by Miles Davis. As originally recorded, the drummer used a jazz rhythm, but it moved at twice the speed (doubletime) of the perceived melody, creating a bouncy funk groove. Today, musicians use straight eighth-notes and play it in a funk style.

There are several other examples of soul jazz that made appearances on the pop charts. Herbie Mann started his career as a saxophonist but found more work, and recognition, on the flute. At the time, flute was used extensively in Latin music, so he organized an Afro-Cuban sextet in 1958. In 1962, Herbie Mann recorded *Live at the Village Gate*— from the famous Greenwich Village jazz club—which included a bouncy tune called "Comin' Home Baby." The drummer plays quarter notes on the cymbal, and the other instruments use a bouncy swing rhythm: Consequentially the recording lives somewhere between the jazz and rock worlds of 1962. On later recordings, drummers usually use a "rock beat." The recording got noticed by radio and made it to number thirty on the pop charts. Mann had great success reaching the public, and, from 1962 to 1979, twenty-five of his recordings made it to the Top 200 album charts.

In 1962, pianist Herbie Hancock recorded his composition "Watermelon Man" using a rock beat, and the following year a version by Latin-jazz artist Mongo Santamaria made it into the Top 30 on the pop charts. In 1964, Hancock recorded "Cantaloupe Island" in a similar style, which was sampled by the band Us3 for their 1993 recording "Cantaloop." Hancock later gained jazz fame by performing with Miles Davis. After leaving Davis in 1969, he recorded the soundtrack for Bill Cosby's *Fat Albert and the Cosby Kids*. In 1973, Hancock broke new ground with the synthesizer funk classic "Chameleon" reaching number forty-two, and in 1983 he reached number seventy-one on the pop charts with "Rockit," one of the first African-American recordings to receive airplay on MTV.

Vince Guaraldi's piano style is familiar to most Americans as the music in the *Charlie Brown* cartoon series. Before starting his own trio in 1955, he worked with Latin-tinged vibraphonist Cal Tjader. In 1962, Guaraldi recorded an album called *Jazz Impression of Black Orpheus,* and on the flip side of a single from the album was a song called "Cast Your Fate to the Wind." DJs began playing that side, and the song did well on the pop charts, eventually earning a gold record and the 1963 Grammy for Best Instrumental Jazz Composition. That song brought him to the attention of producer/director Lee Mendelson who was working on the television special "A Charlie Brown Christmas." Guaraldi's airy West Coast style fit the cartoon perfectly, and such compositions as "Linus and Lucy," "The Great Pumpkin Waltz," and "Christmas Time Is Here" have become piano standards.

Chicago pianist Ramsey Lewis first recorded with his group, the Ramsey Lewis Trio, in 1956 and finally reached the pop charts in 1965 with two recordings—"The In Crowd" (#5) and "Hang On Sloopy" (#11)—and in 1966 with "Wade in the Water" (#19). In 1965, his bass player and drummer left to form the Young-Holt Unlimited and, in 1969, they were successful with "Soulful Strut (#3). The soul jazz piano style continued to resonate with the American public, and Lewis again had success with "Sun Goddess," which reached number twelve in 1975. Lewis even recorded two albums of Christmas standards in a soul jazz style.

In 1967, **Cannonball Adderley's** soul jazz instrumental "Mercy, Mercy, Mercy" reached into the top ten on the pop charts and won a Grammy for Best Instrumental Jazz Performance. Later that year, The Buckinghams recorded a vocal version of the song and reached number five in June. Adderley, an alto saxophonist descendent of Charlie Parker, had his feet in both the bop and soul jazz world and included both styles on his albums. Other recordings in the style are "Work Song," "Jive Samba," "Dat, Dere," and "Why (Am I Treated So Bad)."

Texas natives Joe Sample, Wilton Felder, Wayne Henderson, and Stix Hooper moved to Los Angeles and formed the Jazz Crusaders. Their sound was a soulful blend of tenor sax and trombone that resembled the Memphis style of rhythm and blues. Throughout the 1960s, they were successful with a wide jazz audience, but they did not have any success crossing over to the pop charts until 1971 when they dropped "Jazz" from their name and became the Crusaders. It did not take long for them to be noticed by record audiences. They began to place on the charts in 1972 with "Put It Where You Want It" (#39, 1972), "Don't Let It Get You Down" (#31, 1973), "Keep That Same Old Feeling" (#21, 1976), and "Street Life" (#17, 1979). If they had changed their name earlier, they might have found chart success with the same audience that appreciated Ramsey Lewis, Mongo Santamaria, and Cannonball Adderley.

Organ Trios

In the 1950s and 1960s, small groups using the Hammond B3 organ proliferated in the urban centers of the East and Midwest. The Hammond B3 was the standard for jazz, R&B, and rock bands throughout the period, and no other organ was considered acceptable. The B3 is usually combined with a Leslie speaker cabinet with rotating horns to give it a real acoustic vibrato. The B3, and its church cousin the C3, had a double manual and bass pedals; both the lower manual or the pedals could be used to play the bass line, thus eliminating the need for a live bass player. Typically, the other members would be a drummer plus a guitarist or saxophonist. The sound of the organ was so famous that it was one of the first sounds to be duplicated by synthesizers in the 1970s.

The best known organist was Jimmy Smith, who recorded from 1956 until his death in 2005. Smith worked in a variety of settings, from trio to big band, and played soul jazz, blues, and rock songs from the charts. He even recorded did an album of Christmas songs. Other important organists of the period were "Brother" Jack McDuff, Richard "Groove" Holmes, and Jimmy McGriff. Today, it is not unusual to hear bits of soul jazz organ sampled in hip hop recordings. Even jam bands like Medeski, Martin, and Wood have incorporated the organ trio into their sound.

JAZZ FUSION

Jazz Fusion is the name given to the fusion of jazz, rock, and other styles that occurred as a result of the Miles Davis recording *Bitches Brew*. Davis's jazz credentials were so unsoiled by any implication of selling out that when he began to record songs with a rock-style rhythm, it became acceptable for others to follow. Once musicians performed with Miles Davis, they had enough credibility to lead their own bands and negotiate deals with record labels.

Miles Davis holds an important place in jazz history: He was an ever-changing musician who was responsible for creating, or at least co-creating, several different styles of jazz. Davis came to New York in 1944 to study at the Juilliard School of Music, but he spent much of his time hanging around with Dizzy Gillespie, Charlie Parker, and the rest of the boppers. In 1945, he replaced Gillespie in Parker's band and recorded many times.

In 1949 and 1950, Miles recorded a series of arrangements in a new style using a nine-piece band that included tuba and French horn. The style became known as *cool*, and the music produced at the sessions was called *The Birth of the Cool*. The new style tried to unite the organizational level of swing-era bands with the improvisational style of bebop. The music was softer and more organized than bop and became very influential for the next generation of musicians. This sense of organization helped the general listener to keep track of the musical form and was therefore easier to understand. Cool was a big hit with the public. Musicians from that band went on to have successful careers: Gerry Mulligan was one of the most important names in the West Coast jazz style, John Lewis became the musical director of the Modern Jazz Quartet, Gil

Evans became known as an important arranger and later collaborated with Miles, Lee Konitz became an important performer in the cool style, and Gunther Schuller became an important classical composer and founding member of the *third-stream jazz* style. From this point forward it seemed that anyone who was associated with Miles Davis had a successful jazz career.

Although the sound of Miles Davis's trumpet was the model for the cool sound of the 1950s, many of his recordings are considered quintessential hardbop recordings, especially those from 1955 through 1958. During this period, Miles led what has come to be called The Classic Miles Davis Quintet. Among the saxophonists he used were Cannonball Adderley, Sonny Rollins, and John Coltrane. During this period, Miles also recorded a series of collaborations with arranger Gil Evans that included a large ensemble using a tone pallet of subtle shadings, which reminded listeners of the *Birth of the Cool* sessions.

In 1959, Miles changed the face of jazz again with a style called *modal jazz*. For the *Kind of Blue* recording session, Miles brought in loose sketches of what he had in mind and gave the musicians great freedom and enough space to create. According to the liner notes by pianist Bill Evans, the musicians had never seen or played the compositions before and what appears on the album are the first recorded takes of each song[1]. Spontaneity was the most important element Miles wanted to capture. Music theorists are quick to point out that the music is not really modal and does not use modal harmony. What Miles really did is to change the past practice of improvising to a series of rapidly changing chords to a style in which there were very few chords, sometimes only two chords per song. This meant that musicians could create melodies using one or two scales, or modes, per song. The concept changed jazz forever.

During the years 1963 to 1968, Miles Davis formed his Second Classic Quintet, which continued the exploration of slower harmonic movement and greater creative freedom. The group featured Tony Williams on drums, Herbie Hancock on piano, Wayne Shorter on tenor sax, and Ron Carter on bass. Tony Williams was seventeen and had been playing professionally since he was thirteen. In his autobiography, Miles said that he built the group around Williams. Williams had studied with Alan Dawson at the Berklee College of Music and was well versed in traditional drumming, but with Davis he created his own style. Williams played around with the beat, often implying other tempos based on triplets, and he seldom functioned as a time-keeper. Bassist Ron Carter was the solid time-keeper of the band, and even Miles said of Williams, "You had to pay attention to everything he did, or he'd lose you in a second."[2] Wayne Shorter grew into the role of composer with Miles and honed his skills for his own band, Weather Report.

Miles began a new direction in 1968 that involved the assimilation of elements of rock and funk. During the period, he was listening to James

Brown, Sly and the Family Stone, and Jimi Hendrix. His younger sidemen had been coaxing him toward the sound of avant-garde free jazz and rock, and Miles was always willing to lead the way to new styles of expression. The first change he made was the addition of electric bass so the bass line could be heard more prominently. His bass player Ron Carter left and was replaced by Miroslav Vitous and Dave Holland. Miles also wanted to use the sound of the Fender Rhodes piano, and he started using Joe Zawinul, composer of "Mercy, Mercy, Mercy!" and Chick Corea in addition to his usual player, Herbie Hancock.

The first appearance of the new sound was the 1968 album *Filles de Kilimanjaro*, which included a combination of the new and old players. The first track, "Frelon Brun," opens using rock-inspired rhythms on the drums and a repeating bass line, but the general feeling is avant-garde rather than repetitious rock. The fourth track, "Filles De Kilimanjaro," also used the straight-eighth-note rhythmic feel over a repeating bass line. This was the beginning of the change.

In 1969, Miles recorded *In a Silent Way*, which signaled a new method of recording for him. He took guitarist John McLaughlin and three keyboardists (Herbie Hancock, Joe Zawinul, and Chick Corea) into the studio and recorded their improvisations, getting . . . he recorded everything including John McLaughlin tuning up. Longtime Miles producer Teo Macero took, edited, and shaped the recording into a cohesive musical whole. Miles essentially went into the studio with the musicians, let nature take its course, and edited the resulting tape into various tracks. Most reviewers and researchers refer to *In a Silent Way* as the first fusion album.

At this point, interesting pressures began to influence Miles. In his autobiography, *Miles*, he notes that for the first time he was playing to half-filled clubs in America while still playing to packed houses in Europe. Then, Clive Davis, the new president of Columbia, balked at giving Miles an advance on his next recording. Miles typically sold about 60,000 records, so his usual advance was based on that number. Clive had recently signed BS&T and Chicago, and they were selling a lot of albums. Clive suggested to Miles that he record something for the new young audience.[3] It is interesting to note that the rock bands trying to blend elements of jazz were now forcing one of jazz's most influential musicians to come to terms with the rock audience and their expectations.

Miles's most important recording from this era was *Bitches Brew*. Miles went into the studio for three days in August 1969 with his regular saxophonist, Wayne Shorter, and Bennie Maupin on bass clarinet, three drummers (Lenny White, Jack DeJohnette, and Charles Alias), three keyboardists (Chick Corea, Joe Zawinul, and Larry Young), two bass players (Dave Holland and Harvey Brooks), and John McLaughlin. As he had done for *Kind of Blue* and

In a Silent Way, he brought musical sketches that contained a few chords aligned with a rhythmic idea and told the musicians they could play whatever they wanted. Miles told Teo Macero to record everything and not to interrupt the recording for any reason.[4] Once the band started playing, Miles conducted the direction of the music by writing down an idea for someone to play or giving verbal instructions. The ensuing recordings were edited into a cohesive two-record set released in 1970. The editing process had become part of the creative process, and the resulting tracks were sometimes nonlinear—i.e., the recordings were cut up and reassembled. Later that year, Miles went into the studio to record similar material, which was released in 2004 by Sony Records as a four-disc boxed set titled *The Complete Bitches Brew Sessions.* The original six *Bitches Brew* tracks released on the two-record set were recorded during the August 1969 sessions. The editing process also blurred the distinction between albums because material recorded for one album often appeared on another album.

After the session, rock impresario Bill Graham booked Miles into the Fillmore West in San Francisco to open for the Grateful Dead, and the audience loved him. *Bitches Brew* opened Miles to a whole new audience, and he was once again playing to packed houses. The recording went gold and won a Grammy for Best Jazz Performance. The real result of Miles's recording was that it was now acceptable for jazz musicians to record rock-inspired material, and many of those associated with Miles during this period left and ventured into different fusions of jazz with other music. Herbie Hancock eventually had a jazz funk crossover hit with his Headhunters; Chick Corea fused jazz and samba with his Return to Forever; Wayne Shorter and Joe Zawinul formed Weather Report; John McLaughlin combined jazz and Indian music with his Mahavishnu Orchestra; and Tony Williams formed a trio called the Tony Williams Lifetime.

Miles Davis–Inspired Fusion

The first group to result from the Miles Davis sessions was the Mahavishnu Orchestra. John McLaughlin, who had been brought over from England by Tony Williams to play in his band Lifetime, formed the group in 1970 with Billy Cobham on drums, Jan Hammer on keyboards, Jerry Goodman on violin, and Rick Laird on bass. The music was a fusion of jazz, Indian classical music, and progressive rock. Part of the fusion of Indian music involved the complex rhythmic cycles, so many of the Mahavishnu songs were in odd meters. Their first album, *Inner Mounting Flame* (1971), was immediately successful among young jazz and progressive rock fans. Billy Cobham, whom McLaughlin had met in the Miles sessions following *Bitches Brew,* created a very tight, complex funk style that changed the way jazz drummers thought of jazz. When Miles's drummers played rock rhythms, they still played with a loose, flowing jazz approach, but Cobham's approach was very precise and military. The original Mahavishnu Orchestra lasted until 1973, and McLaughlin continued to perform with various combinations, both acoustic and electric.

Chick Corea was developing a successful career by the time he performed with Miles on *Filles De Kilimanjaro, In a Silent Way,* and *Bitches Brew.* He had played with Latin greats Mongo Santamaria and Willie Bobo, Blue Mitchell, Herbie Mann, and Stan Getz before recording with his own group in 1966. In 1970, Corea and bassist, Dave Holland, left Miles's band to explore avant-garde collaborative jazz with a group called Circle. Toward the end of 1971, he formed Return to Forever with Stanley Clarke on bass, Joe Ferrell on sax, Airto Moreira on drums, and vocalist, Flora Purim. Airto and Flora were from Brazil, and the ensuing musical fusion was a blend of jazz and samba. Their first album, *Return to Forever,* was released in 1972 and was embraced by the jazz community. The album contained "La Fiesta," which became an instant jazz radio favorite. The following album, *Light As a Feather,"* contained what became Corea's most famous composition, "Spain." Return to Forever was as original in scope as the Mahavishnu Orchestra and sounded nothing like Miles-inspired fusion. If anything, it resembled an updated version of the bossa nova style popular in the mid-1960s.

In 1973, Chick Corea changed the direction of Return to Forever toward a type of progressive rock. The band added an electric guitarist, first Bill Connors and then Al Di Meola, and brought in Lenny White on drums. Gone were the light Brazilian rhythms. The music is tightly composed progressive rock. Chick Corea continues to be an innovative musician performing in a variety of different styles.

Herbie Hancock left Miles Davis in 1968, although he continued to appear on some recording dates, to form his own band. Hancock explored an R&B-jazz fusion and began incorporating the electronic sounds of the newly developing synthesizer. The music from his first post-Miles period, referred to as the Mwandishi albums, are rhythmically dense with layered rhythms common in African music and make use of the synthesizer for atmospheric background sounds. The recordings had the loose, improvisational feel of the Miles Davis fusion recordings and were not financially successful.

Around 1973, Hancock retooled his sound to align it with the funky bass and drum lines of Sly and the Family Stone. The new band, Headhunters, and the new sound were immediately successful, and the resulting album, *Head Hunters,* was the first jazz album to go platinum. "Chameleon," a simple, tight, repetitive, and funky song, was the biggest hit on the album, and over thirty years later, there are still jazz and marching band arrangements of it available from music publishers.

Herbie Hancock continued to record in a variety of styles. He did not abandon mainstream and assembled the group VSOP to make music in the style of Miles's second great quintet as well as trio and quartet albums. He realized the importance of producing recordings that sounded "current" and spoke to young audiences. In 1978, he recorded the album *Sunlight* to respond to the disco craze. On "I Thought It Was You" Hancock sang through a vocoder that electronically altered the sound of his voice. The song reached the charts in England. In 1983, his recording "Rockit" was extremely successful on the dance and R&B charts, eventually winning a Grammy for best R&B instrumental. The music video for "Rockit" featured dancing robotic limbs and was one of the first by an African-American musician to appear on MTV. He won another Grammy the following year for "Sound System."

Wayne Shorter and Joe Zawinul left Miles Davis and formed Weather Report in 1970. The band had a long career and some extensive changes in style. It began as an avant-garde improvisational group with a Miles approach—i.e., soaring, expansive melodies laid over a churning rhythm section of bass, drums, and percussion. Shorter and Zawinul had a shifting cast of sidemen with as many as ten drummers during the first eight years. The bass chair was a bit more stable, starting with Miroslav Vitous, Alphonso Johnson, and then Jaco Pastorius, who left in early 1982. The band made an immediate impact on the jazz audience, and the first album, *Weather Report*, won *Downbeat* magazine's Album of the Year award. The band began to evolve with their second album, *I Sing the Body Electric*, with Zawinul adding the ARP 2600 synthesizer to his set-up, and the music took a step forward into a more electric sound.

In 1973, Weather Report changed direction toward a funkier, more commercial sound, i.e., the melodies were less expansive, the bass and drum parts were tighter and more repetitious, and the improvisation sections were more structured. The band continued to win awards. In 1977, they recorded *Black Market*, containing the song "Birdland"—named for the famous jazz nightclub on 52nd Street in New York—which became their best-known recording. As with Hancock's "Chameleon," the song is still available for jazz, concert, and marching bands. In 1979, the band won their only Grammy for best jazz fusion performance for their live album, *8:30*. The following year, the vocal jazz group Manhattan Transfer recorded a vocalese version of "Birdland," and won a Grammy for Best Jazz Fusion Performance. Vocalese is a type of jazz vocal where hip jazz lyrics, akin to beat poetry, are set to a well-known lyric-less song or a famous improvised solo. Weather Report finally disbanded in 1986.

These four post-Miles jazz fusion groups were the most commercially and artistically successful groups to emerge at the beginning of the 1970s. Although soul jazz had previously existed, it took an artist of Miles Davis's stature to give the style artistic credibility. The motives of soul jazz were similar to those of fusion jazz—to remain relevant to the African-American culture. Once Miles Davis accepted the premise, that gave carte blanche to the rest of the jazz world, including the critics, to accept the new model.

Fusion Beyond Miles Davis

While it was the fusion groups the grew out of the Miles Davis association that were the most influential of the period, there were also other notable artists exploring fusion territory. Creed Taylor formed CTI Records in 1968 and released albums that were an extension of the soul jazz idiom. Taylor had been responsible for producing the bossa nova recordings by Charlie Byrd and later Stan Getz, as well as John Coltrane's *A Love Supreme* and Oliver Nelson's *Blues and the Abstract Truth*. With CTI he recorded Hubert Laws, Stanley Turrentine, Wes Montgomery, Milt Jackson, George Benson, and Freddie Hubbard. These recordings had high production values, had a groove-oriented rhythm section, were packaged beautifully, and were mainstays on jazz radio of the 1970s.

The sound of CTI records was cohesive because Taylor tended to use the same stable of players on all the albums he produced, which gave them a similar feel and groove. Taylor surrounded hard-bop guitarist Wes Montgomery with an orchestra and recorded elaborate versions of the Beatles' "A Day in the Life" and other pop hits. Stanley Turrentine was one of the early radio jazz hits with "Sugar" in 1971 and so was Grover Washington, Jr., with "Mister Magic" in 1974. Also in 1974, Brazilian pianist Eumir Deodato crossed over to the pop charts with a fusion version of "Thus Spoke Zaratustra," the theme from the movie *2001 Space Odyssey*. Flautist Hubert Laws recorded jazz versions of "Amazing Grace," "The Rite of Spring," Bach's "Brandenburg Concerto No. 3," and James Taylor's "Fire and Rain." CTI Records had updated the sound of soul jazz for the 1970s, and its stylistic elements are alive today in the smooth jazz format.

LISTENING TO THE MUSIC

𝄞♪♪ "Spinning Wheel"—performed by Blood, Sweat & Tears

Analysis of "Spinning Wheel" (album track)—4:07 in length, released by Columbia CS 9720. Columbia released the single version in June 1969 backed with "More and More." The song reached number two on the charts and went gold. The album won a Grammy for Best Album of the Year, and Fred Lipsius won the Grammy for Best Arrangement Accompanying Vocalist(s) in 1969. The meter is "in 4" and the form is AABA with eight-bar sections. Personnel: David

Clayton-Thomas, vocals; Steve Katz, guitar; Bobby Colomby, drums; Jim Fielder, bass; Fred Lipsius, alto sax; Lew Soloff, trumpet solo; Alan Rubin, trumpet, Jerry Hyman, trombone; Dick Halligan, organ, piano, flute.

0:00   Intro: The track opens with a brass chord crescendo ending with the song's signature rhythm.

0:08   AA Section (8 measures): Begins "What goes up must come down" accompanied for two bars by the bass and piano. Tap your foot and count 1-2-3-4-2-2-3-4-. The cowbell enters in the third bar 3 followed by the drums in bar 5five. There is a stop-time in measures 7seven and 8eight.

0:28   A Section (8 measures): Begins "Ya got no money . . . " accompanied by brass punches.

0:47   B Section (8 measures + 4 measure extension): Begins "Did you find . . ." The texture and rhythm changes for the chorus. The drums emphasize all four beats instead of only 2 and 4. The chorus does a psychedelic-type dissolve beginning in measure 10 on "colors that are real."

1:16   Interlude (6 measures): This extends the word "real," which dissolves into a muted trumpet trill, followed by the signature brass rhythm from the introduction ending in a one-bar drum fill.

1:31   A Section (8 measures): Begins "Someone is waiting . . ."

1:51   Interlude (4 measures): A vamp using the rhythm of the A section.

2:00   A Section jazz trumpet solo (approx 15 measures): The rhythm goes into doubletime, meaning the bass and drums are playing twice as fast as they were. The bass plays a walking bass line, while the drums play traditional jazz rhythm. The solo ends quoting part of the typical racetrack trumpet call and the drums lead the band into the next section.

2:38   A Section (8 measures): Begins "Someone's waiting . . ." Accompaniment is the same as in the previous A section.

2:57   Coda: The meter changes to 3/4 time, and the tempo doubles with a section that alternates between brass punches and spacey flutes.

♪♪ "Make Me Smile"—performed by Chicago

Analysis of "Make Me Smile" (3:00). From the album *Chicago II*, "Make Me Smile" was Chicago's first single to be picked up by AM radio. The meter is "in 4," and the form is ABAB; the A section is 12 measures. Personnel: Walt Parazaider, saxophone; Terry Kath, bass; Danny Seraphine, drums; Lee Loughnane, trumpet; James Pankow, trombone; Robert Lamm, keyboard; Peter Cetera, bass

0:00   Introduction (2 measures): Begins with one brass chord followed by a drum fill, then two brass chords followed by drums.

0:05   A Section (12 measures): Begins "Children play . . . " accompanied by bass, drums, and guitar.

0:28   B Section (12 measures): Begins "I'm so happy . . . " the brass accompanies with punches.

0:51   A Section (12 measures): Begins "Living life . . . " This time the brass section accompanies the section.

1:14   B Section (12 measures): Begins "Oh my darling . . . "

1:37   C Section (20 measures): Brass section plays a complex unison line, a written-out solo for the section called a "soli." Added to the rhythm section is a tambourine and, eight bars later, a guiro (Latin American gourd "scratcher")

2:16   B Section (12 measures): Begins "Now I need you . . . "

2:37   Coda: The song closes with a four-bar drum solo beginning and ending with two brass chords.

---

[1] Miles Davis, *Kind of Blue,* Miles Davis, Columbia CS8163.

[2] Miles Davis and Quincy Troupe, *Miles, the Autobiography* (New York: Simon and Schuster, 1989), 264.

[3] Ibid., 297-98.

[4] Ibid., 299.

Bibliography

Barnard, Stephen. *Rock, An Illustrated History.* New York: Schirmer Books, 1986.

Basie, Count. *Good Morning Blues.* New York: Donald Fine Inc., 1985.

Bayles, Martha. *Hole In Our Soul: The Loss of Beauty and Meaning in American Popular Music.* New York: Free Press, 1994.

Berry, Chuck. *Chuck Berry: The Autobiography.* New York: Fireside Books, 1988.

Betrock, Alan. *Girl Groups: The Story of a Sound.* New York: Delilah Books, 1982.

Billboard Chart Research. *Top Pop Singles of the Year: 1946-1990.* Report prepared for the authors by the Billboard Chart Research Department, New York, 1990.

Billboard Chart Research. *Top Rhythm and Blues Singles of the Year: 1946-1990.* Report prepared for the authors by the Billboard Chart Research Department, New York, 1990.

Blake, John. *All You Needed Was Love.* New York: G. P. Putnam's Sons, 1981.

Booth, Stanley. *Rhythm Oil.* London: Jonathan Cape, 1991.

Brewer-Giorgro, Gail. *Is Elvis Alive?* New York: Tudor Publishing Co., 1988.

Brongson, Fred. *Billboard's Hottest Hot 100 Hits.* New York: Billboard Books, 1991.

Bronson, Fred. *The Billboard Book of Number One Hits.* New York: Billboard Publications, 1988.

Carr, Roy and Tony Tyler. *The Beatles: An Illustrated Record.* New York: Harmony Books, 1981.

Castleman, Harry and Walter Podrazik. *All Together Now.* New York: Ballantine Books, 1975.

Charles, Ray and David Ritz. *Brother Ray.* New York: Dial Press, 1978.

Clark, Dick and Richard Robinson. *Rock, Roll & Remember.* New York: Thomas Y. Crowell, 1976.

Clarke, Donald, ed. *The Penguin Encyclopedia of Popular Music.* London: Penguin Books, 1989.

Clifford, Mike, ed. *The Harmony Illustrated Encyclopedia of Rock and Roll.* New York: Harmony Books, 1988.

Dachs, David. *Encyclopedia of Pop/Rock.* New York: Scholastic Book Services, 1972.

Dance, Helen Oakley. *Stormy Monday: The T-Bone Walker Story.* New York: Da Capo Press, 1987.

Dannen, Frederic. *Hit Men.* New York: Random House, 1990.

Davies, Hunter. *The Beatles.* New York: McGraw-Hill Book Co., 1968.

Davis, Miles with Quincy Troupe. Miles, the Autobiography. New York: Simon and Schuster, 1989.

Davis, Stephen. *Hammer of the Gods: The Led Zeppelin Saga.* New York: William Morrow & Co., Inc., 1985.

DeCurtis, Anthony and James Henke with Holly George-Warren, eds. *The Rolling Stone Illustrated History of Rock and Roll.* New York: Random House, 1992.

DeCurtis, Anthony and James Henke, ed. *The Rolling Stone Illustrated History Of Rock and Roll.* New York: Random House, 1992.

DeCurtis, Anthony and James Henke, eds. *The Rolling Stone Album Guide.* New York: Random House, 1992.

Delano, Julia. *The Beatles Album.* New York: Smithmark Publishers, 1991.

Densmore, John. *Riders on the Storm: My Life with Jim Morrison and the Doors.* New York: Delacorte Press, 1990.

Dowlding, William J. *Beatlesongs.* New York: Simon & Schuster, Inc., 1989.

Escott, Colin with Martin Hawkins. *Good Rockin' Tonight: Sun Records and the Birth of Rock 'n' Roll.* New York: St. Martin's Press, 1991.

Evans, Mike. *The Art of the Beatles.* New York: Beech Tree Books, 1984.

Friede, Goldie, Robin Titone, and Sue Weiner. *The Beatles A to Z.* New York: Metheucn, Inc., 1980.

Gaar, Gillian G. *She's a Rebel: The History of Women in Rock & Roll.* Seattle: Seal Press, 1992.

Garland, Phyl. *The Sound of Soul.* Chicago: Henry Regnery, 1969.

George, Nelson. *The Death of Rhythm and Blues.* New York: Penguin, 1988.

George, Nelson. *Where Did Our Love Go?: The Rise and Fall of the Motown Sound.* New York: St. Martin's Press, 1985.

Gillett, Charlie. *The Sound of the City: The Rise of Rock and Roll.* Revised ed. London: Souvenir Press, 1983.

Goldman, Albert. *The Lives of John Lennon.* New York: William Morrow and Co., 1988.

Golson, G. Barry, ed. *The Playboy Interviews with John Lennon & Yoko Ono.* New York: Playboy Press, 1981.

Gregory, Huge. *Soul Music A-Z.* London: Blandford, 1991.

Gross, Michael. *Bob Dylan: An Illustrated History.* New York: Grosset & Dunlap, 1978.

Guralnick, Peter. *Searching for Robert Johnson.* New York: Dutton Obelisk, 1989.

Hammond, John. *John Hammond on Record.* New York: Penguin, 1977.

Handy, W. C. *Father of the Blues: An Autobiography.* New York: Da Capo Press, 1969.

Harbison, W. A. *The Illustrated Elvis.* New York: Grosset and Dunlap, Inc., 1975.

Hardy, Phil and Dave Laing. *The Faber Companion to 20th Century Popular Music.* London: Faber and Faber, 1990.

Herzhaft, Gerhard. *Encyclopedia of the Blues.* Fayetteville, Arkansas: University of Arkansas, 1992.

Hirshey, Gerri. *Nowhere to Run, the Story of Soul Music*. New York: Penguin Books, 1984.

Hoare, Ian, ed. *The Soul Book*. New York: Delta, 1976.

Hopkins, Jerry and Danny Sugarman. *No One Here Gets Out Alive*. New York: Warner Books, 1980.

Hopkins, Jerry. *The Rock Story*. New York: Signet Books, 1970.

Joyner, David Lee. *American Popular Music*. Dubuque, Iowa: Brown & Benchmark, 1993.

Kooper, Al with Ben Edmonds. *Backstage Passes: Rock 'n' Roll Life in the Sixties*. New York: Stein and Day, 1977.

Larkin, Colin, ed. *The Guiness Who's Who of Sixties Music*. London: Square One Books, Ltd., 1992.

Larkin, Colin, ed. *The Guiness Who's Who of Seventies Music*. London: Square One Books, Ltd., 1993.

Lewisohn, Mark. *The Beatles Recording Sessions*. New York: Harmony Books, 1988.

Lichtenstein and Laura Dankner. *Musical Gumbo: The Music of New Orleans*. New York: Norton, 1993.

Malone, Bill. *Country Music U.S.A.* Publication of the American Folklore Society, ed. John Greenway, vol. 54. Austin, Texas: University of Texas Press, 1968.

Marchbank, Miles and Pearce, eds. *Beatles in Their Own Words*. New York: Omnibus Press, 1978.

Marcus, Greil. *Mystery Train: Images of America in Rock 'n' Roll Music*. 3rd revised ed. New York: Plume Books, 1990.

Marsh, Dave and Kevin Stein. *The Book of Rock Lists*. New York: Dell Publishing Co., Inc., 1981.

Marsh, Dave. *The Heart of Rock and Soul*. New York: New American Library, 1989.

Martin, George. *All You Need is Ears*. New York: St. Martin's Press, 1979.

McCabe, Peter and Robert D. Schonfeld. *John Lennon: For the Record*. New York: Bantam Books, 1984.

Mellers, Wilfrid. *The Music of the Beatles: Twilight of the Gods*. New York: Macmillan Publishing Co., 1973.

Nite, Norm. *Rock on Almanac*. New York: Harper & Row, 1989.

Nite, Norm. Rock On: *The Illustrated Encyclopedia of Rock and Roll*. New York: Thomas Y. Crowell, 1974.

Norman, Philip. Shout: *The Beatles in Their Generation*. New York: Simon & Schuster, 1981.

Ochs, Michael. *Rock Archives*. New York: Doubleday, 1984.

Oliver, Paul, Max Harrison, and William Bolcom. *The New Grove Gospel, Blues and Jazz*. New York: W. W. Norton & Co., 1986.

Palmer, Robert. *A Tale of Two Cities: Memphis Rock and New Orleans Roll.* Brooklyn, NY: Institute for Studies in American Music, Department of Music, School of Performing Arts, Brooklyn College of the City University of New York, 1979.

Palmer, Robert. *Deep Blues.* New York: Penguin Books, 1982.

Pareles, Jon and Patricia Romanowski, eds. *The Rolling Stone Encyclopedia of Rock and Roll.* New York: Summit Books, 1983.

Pascall, Jeremy, ed. *The Beatles.* London: Octopus Books, Ltd., 1973.

Rees, Dafydd and Luke Crampton, eds. *Rock Movers and Shakers.* New York: Billboard Books, 1991.

Ribowsky, Mark. *He's A Rebel: The Truth About Phil Spector—Rock and Roll's Legendary Madman.* New York: E. P. Dutton, 1989.

Riley, Tim. *Tell Me Why.* New York: Random House, 1988.

Rinzler, Alan. *Bob Dylan: The Illustrated Record.* New York: Harmony Books, 1978.

Rolling Stone, ed. *The Rolling Stone Interviews.* New York: Straight Arrow, 1971.

Sanchez, Tony. *Up and Down with the Rolling Stones.* New York: Signet, 1980.

Sanjek, Russell. *American Popular Music and Its Business. Vol. 2, From 1790 to 1909.* New York: Oxford, 1988.

Sanjek, Russell. *American Popular Music and Its Business. Vol. 3, From 1900 to 1984.* New York: Oxford, 1988.

Scaduto, Anthony. *Bob Dylan.* New York: Grosset and Dunlap, 1971.

Schaefer, George. Drumset Performance Practices on Pop and Rhythm and Blues Hit Recordings, 1960-69. DMA diss., Arizona State University, 1994.

Schaffner, Nicholas. *The Beatles Forever.* New York: McGraw-Hill, 1977.

Shaw, Arnold. *Honkers and Shouters.* New York: Collier Books, 1978.

Shotton, Pete and Nicholes Schaffner. *The Beatles, Lennon and Me.* New York: Stein & Day, 1983.

Small, Christopher. *Music of the Common Tongue: Survival and Celebration in Afro-American Music.* New York: Riverrun Press, 1987.

Smith, Was. *The Pied Pipers of Rock 'n' Roll: Radio Deejays of the 50s and 60s.* Marietta, Georgia: Longstreet Press, 1989.

Southern, Eileen. *The Music of Black Americans: A History.* New York: Norton, 1971.

Spector, Ronnie with Vince Waldron. *Be My Baby.* New York: Harper Perennial, 1991.

Spence, Helen. *The Beatles Forever.* New York: Crescent Books, 1981.

Spitz, Bob. *Dylan: A Biography.* New York: McGraw-Hill, 1989.

St. Michael, Mick. *Heavy Metal.* Conn.: Longmeadow Press, 1990.

Stambler, Irwin. *Encyclopedia of Pop, Rock & Soul*. New York: St. Martin's Press, 1974.

Swenson, John. *The Beatles: Yesterday and Today*. New York: Kensington Publishing Corporation, 1977.

Taraborrelli, J. Randy. *Call Her Miss Ross: The Unauthorized Biography of Diana Ross*. New York: Birch Lane Press, 1989.

Taylor, Derek. *It Was Twenty Years Ago Today*. New York: Simon & Schuster, 1987.

Tobler, John, ed. *Who's Who in Rock and Roll*. New York: Crescent Books, 1991.

Tosches, Nick. *Unsung Heroes of Rock 'n' Roll*. New York: Harmony, 1991.

Vellenga, Dirk with Mick Farren. *Elvis and the Colonel*. New York: Delacorte Press, 1988.

Wade, Dorothy and Justine Picardie. *Music Man: Ahmet Ertegun, Atlantic Records, and the Triumph of Rock 'n' Roll*. New York: W. W. Norton & Co., 1990.

Wallgren, Mark. *The Beatles on Record*. New York: Simon and Schuster, 1982.

Ward, Ed, Geoffrey Stokes, and Ken Tucker. *Rock of Ages: The Rolling Stone History of Rock & Roll*. New York: Summit Books, 1986.

Watson, Jack M. and Corrine. *A Concise Dictionary of Music*. New York: Dodd, Mead & Co., 1965.

Wenner, Jann. *Lennon Remembers: The Rolling Stone Interviews*. New York: Popular Library, 1971.

Wexler, Jerry and David Ritz. *Rhythm and the Blues: A Life in American Music*. New York: Knopf, 1993.

Whitcomb, Ian. *After The Ball: Pop Music From Rag to Rock*. New York: Simon and Schuster, 1972.

Whitcomb, Ian. *Irving Berlin and Ragtime America*. New York: Limelight, 1988.

Wilson, Brian with Todd Gold. *Wouldn't It Be Nice: My Own Story*. New York: Harper Collins, 1991.

Wolfe, Charles and Kip Lornell. *The Life and Legend of Leadbelly*. New York: Harper Collins Publishers, 1992.

Wyman, Bill with Ray Coleman. *Stone Alone: The Story of a Rock 'n' Roll Band*. New York: Signet Books, 1991.

Zappa, Frank and Peter Occhiogrosso. *The Real Frank Zappa Book*. New York: Poseidon Press, 1989.

Index